PHILOSOPHICAL SELECTIONS

MALEBRANCHE

Philosophical Selections

from
The Search after Truth

Translated by
Thomas M. Lennon and Paul J. Olscamp

from
*Elucidations of
The Search after Truth*

Translated by
Thomas M. Lennon

from
Dialogues on Metaphysics

Translated by
Willis Doney

and from
Treatise on Nature and Grace

Translated by
Thomas Taylor
Revised by
Steven Nadler

Edited by
STEVEN NADLER

Hackett Publishing Company. Inc.
Indianapolis/Cambridge

12 11 10 09 08   3 4 5 6 7 8

Cover design by Listenberger Design & Associates

For further information, please address:
  Hackett Publishing Company, Inc.
  P.O. Box 44937
  Indianapolis, Indiana 46244-0937

  www.hackettpublishing.com

Library of Congress Cataloging-in-Publication Data

Malebranche, Nicolas, 1638–1715.
      [Selections. English. 1992]
      Philosophical selections: from The search after truth, Dialogues
  on metaphysics, Treatise on nature and grace/Malebranche; edited
  by Steven Nadler.
      p.   cm.
      Includes bibliographical references.
      ISBN 0-87220-153-8
      ISBN 0-87220-152-X (pbk.)
      1. Knowledge, Theory of. 2. Metaphysics. 3. Grace (Theology)
  I. Nadler, Steven M., 1958–   . II. Title.
  B1892.E5N33   1992
  194 — dc20
                                              92-19801
                                                  CIP

ISBN-13: 978-0-87220-153-8 (cloth)
ISBN-13: 978-0-87220-152-1 (pbk.)

Contents

All footnotes in *The Search after Truth* are Malebranche's own. Numbered footnotes in the *Dialogues on Metaphysics* are those of Malebranche; lettered footnotes are the translator's. Note that the translator in the *Dialogues on Metaphysics* refers to the *Oeuvre Complètes* by 'M.'

INTRODUCTION

Life and Works

Nicolas Malebranche was born in Paris on August 6, 1638, one of the many children of Nicolas Malebranche, a royal secretary, and his wife, Catherine de Lauzon. Because of a malformation of the spine that would affect him for the rest of his life, he was kept at home for his education, under the direction of his intelligent and pious mother, until the age of sixteen. In 1654, he entered the Collège de la Marche, from which he graduated two years later as Maître ès Arts. The education he received there, heavily laden with Aristotelianism, left Malebranche highly dissatisfied. After studying theology for three years at the Sorbonne—a Scholastic curriculum with which he was equally discontent—and rejecting the offer of a canonry at Notre-Dame de Paris, Malebranche entered the Oratory in 1660. He was ordained on September 14, 1664.

His four years in the Oratory proved to be of great intellectual consequence for Malebranche, particularly with respect to his philosophical and theological development. The order had been founded in 1611 by Cardinal Bérulle, who had a deep veneration for St. Augustine and who was also a good friend of Descartes (although the Oratory was, on the whole, firmly anti-Cartesian in its sentiments). While studying Biblical criticism, ecclesiastical history, and Hebrew, Malebranche, like other Oratorians, immersed himself in the writings of Augustine. He also certainly knew of the doctrines of Descartes through those professors of the order who considered themselves adherents of this new philosophy. He did not actually read any of Descartes's works until 1664, however, when, strolling down the rue St. Jacques, he happened upon a copy of Descartes's *Treatise on Man* (*L'homme*) in a bookstall. The event was life-changing: Malebranche's early biographer, Father André, tells us that the joy of becoming acquainted with so many discoveries "caused him such palpitations of the heart that he had to stop reading in order to recover his breath." Malebranche devoted the next ten years of his life to studying mathematics and philosophy, especially of the Cartesian variety. He was particularly taken by Descartes's critique of the Aristotelian philosophy that he had earlier found so stultifying and sterile.

Those years of study culminated in the publication in 1674–75 of *The Search after Truth* (*De la recherche de la vérité*), Malebranche's most important work. The *Search* represents a grand synthesis of the systems of Malebranche's two intellectual mentors, Descartes and Augustine. It is a wide-ranging treatise that deals with questions of knowledge, metaphysics, physics, sense physiology, methodology, and philosophical theology. Malebranche's stated goal in the *Search* is to investigate the sources of human error and to direct us toward the clear and distinct perception of truth—truth about ourselves, about the world around us, and about God. He is ultimately concerned to demonstrate the essential and fundamentally active role of God in every aspect—material, cognitive, and moral—of the world He has created. This becomes particularly clear when one considers Malebranche's three most famous doctrines: occasionalism, the vision in God, and his theodicy.

Occasionalism is the doctrine that all finite created entities are absolutely devoid of causal efficacy and that God is the only true causal agent. Bodies do not cause effects in other bodies or in minds, and minds do not cause effects in bodies or even within themselves. God is directly, immediately, and solely responsible for bringing about all phenomena. When a needle pricks the skin, the physical event is merely an occasion for God to cause the relevant mental state (pain); a volition in the soul to raise an arm or to think of something is only an occasion for God to cause the arm to rise or the idea to be present to the mind; and the impact of one billiard ball upon another is an occasion for God to move the second ball. In all three contexts—mind-body, body-body, and mind alone—God's ubiquitous causal activity proceeds in accordance with certain general laws, and (except in the case of miracles) He acts only when the requisite material or psychic conditions obtain. This theory, far from being an ad hoc solution to a Cartesian mind-body problem, as it is often portrayed, is argued for from general philosophical considerations regarding the nature of causal relations, from an analysis of the Cartesian concept of matter and of the necessary impotence of finite substances, and, perhaps most important, from theological premises about the essential ontological relationship between an omnipotent God and the created world that He sustains in existence. Occasionalism can also be regarded as a way of providing a metaphysical foundation for explanations in mechanistic natural philosophy. Malebranche and other occasionalists, such as Géraud de Cordemoy and Louis de la Forge, are arguing that motion must ultimately have its source in something higher than the passive, inert extension of Cartesian bodies, emptied of the substantial forms of the Scholastics; it needs a causal ground in an active power. But if a body consists in extension alone, motive force cannot be an inherent property of bodies. Occasionalists thus identify force with the ever-active will of God.

The doctrine of the vision in God demonstrates how we as knowers are as cognitively dependent upon the divine understanding, as bodies in motion are ontologically dependent upon the divine will. Malebranche agrees with Descartes and other philosophers that ideas, or immaterial representations present to the mind, play an essential role in knowledge and perception. But whereas

Descartes's ideas are mental entities, or modifications of the soul, Malebranche argues that the ideas that function in human cognition are in God—they just are the essences and ideal archetypes that exist in the divine understanding. As such, they are eternal and independent of finite minds, and our access to them makes possible the clear and distinct apprehension of objective, necessary truth. Malebranche presents the vision in God as the correct Augustinian view, albeit modified in the light of Descartes's epistemological distinction between understanding (via clear and distinct concepts) and sensation. The theory explains both our knowledge of universals and of mathematical and moral principles, as well as the conceptual element that, he argues, necessarily informs our perceptual acquaintance with the world. And like Descartes's theory of ideas—in which God guarantees our rational faculties—Malebranche's doctrine is at least partly motivated by an antiskepticism, since divine ideas cannot fail to reveal either eternal truths or the essences of things in the world created by God.

Finally, Malebranche, in his theodicy, or explanation of how God's wisdom, goodness, and power are to be reconciled with the apparent imperfections and evils in the world, claims that God could have created a more perfect world, free from all the defects which plague this one, but that this would have involved greater complexity in the divine ways. God must act in the manner most in accord with His nature. Thus, God always acts in the simplest way possible and only by means of lawlike general volitions; God never acts by "particular" or ad hoc volitions. But this means that, while on any particular occasion God could intervene and forestall an apparent evil that is about to occur by the ordinary course of the laws of nature (e.g. a drought), He will not do so, for this would compromise the simplicity of His means. The perfection or goodness of the world per se is thus relativized to the simplicity of the laws of that world (or, which is the same thing, to the generality of the divine volitions which, on the occasionalist view, govern it). Taken together, the laws and the phenomena of the world form a whole which is most worthy of God's nature—in fact, the best combination possible. This account explains God's manner of operation, not just in the natural world of body and of mind-body union, but also in the moral world of beings endowed with freedom who depend upon grace for their everlasting happiness.

While the Abbé Simon Foucher (1644–97), canon of Sainte Chappelle of Dijon, was the first in a long line of critics of Malebranche's doctrines, the Jansenist theologian and Cartesian philosopher Antoine Arnauld (1612–94) was undoubtedly the harshest and most acute. Arnauld approved of the *Search* upon first reading it. But when he later learned of Malebranche's views on grace and divine providence—only sketchily presented in the *Search* but more fully expounded in the *Treatise on Nature and Grace* (*Traité de la Nature et de la Grace*) in 1680—he embarked on a detailed critique of the major elements of the *Search*. Arnauld's *Des vraies et des fausses idées*, published in 1683, and Malebranche's reply, *Réponse du Père Malebranche au livre des vraies et des fausses idées* (1684), were only the opening salvos of what would come to be a long and often bitter public battle on both philosophical and (more important, at least to the participants) theological matters. Although Arnauld succeeded in having the *Treatise* put on the Index in 1690 (the *Search* was added in 1709), their exchanges—public and private—continued until Arnauld's death. The Malebranche-Arnauld debate is one of the great intellectual events of the seventeenth century, and it attracted the attention of many, including Leibniz, Spinoza, Locke, and Newton.

After the publication of the *Search*, Malebranche turned to a "justification" of the Catholic religion and morality, presented in suitably Malebranchian terms, published as the *Conversations Chrétiennes* in 1677. This was followed in 1683 by the *Méditations Chrétiennes et Métaphysiques*, which consists of dialogues in which "the Word" explains and defends Malebranche's system. That same year, Malebranche also published his *Traité de Morale*, in which he undertakes a rigorous demonstration of a true Christian ethic.

By the mid 1680s, Malebranche was widely regarded as the most important, if highly unorthodox, representative of the Cartesian philosophy. He was corresponding with thinkers such as Leibniz, who criticized the Cartesian account of the laws of motion (as well as Malebranche's occasionalism), and the physicist Pierre-Sylvain Régis, who defended a more orthodox brand of Cartesianism and engaged Malebranche in debate over some points in natural philosophy and over the nature of ideas.

Having been forced in his polemics with Arnauld, Régis and others to clarify, develop, and even modify his doctrines, Malebranche decided, at the urging of friends, to compose a treatise that both presented an up-to-date and concise picture of his theories and defended them as a proper Augustinian (and Catholic) system. The *Dialogues on Metaphysics* (*Entretiens sur la métaphysique*) were published in 1688 and were supplemented in 1696 by the *Entretiens sur la mort*, which Malebranche wrote after an illness from which he did not expect to recover. In 1699, he was elected to the Académie Royale des Sciences for his *Traité des lois de la communication du mouvement* (1682).

During the last decade and a half of his life, Malebranche remained actively engaged in philosophical, theological, and scientific matters, publishing the *Entretien d'un philosophe chrétien avec un philosophe chinois, sur l'existence et la nature de Dieu* in 1708 and his *Réflexions sur la prémotion physique* in 1715. He also continued to work on the *Search*, producing the sixth edition, the last to appear in his lifetime, in 1712.

On June 20, 1715, Malebranche became ill while visiting a friend in Villeneuve St. Georges. A few days later, he was taken back to the Oratory in Paris, where he died on October 13.

The Selections

Malebranche's recent renown rests mainly on the two doctrines of the vision in God and occasionalism—and for good reason: These, along with his theodicy, represent his most significant philosophical contributions. They are also those aspects of Malebranche's system that most influenced later thinkers. Berkeley's theory of ideas, for example, clearly owes much to Malebranche's doctrine of "seeing all things in God" and to the modifications he introduced into the philosophy of ideas. Hume's conclusions regarding causation and induction are foreshadowed in Malebranche's arguments for occasionalism, which Hume knew well. And Leibniz, in his *Theodicy* and other writings, is certainly indebted to Malebranche's views on reconciling God's wisdom and beneficience with the existence of evil in the world.

Accordingly, I have selected writings from Malebranche that present the best and clearest picture of these three doctrines, taking the selections from Malebranche's major philosophical works: *The Search after Truth*, the *Dialogues on Metaphysics*, and the *Treatise on Nature and Grace*. I have tried to provide readings that convey a sense not just of each doctrine in itself—its theses and distinguishing features—but also of the arguments behind it, which Malebranche often furnishes in great length and detail. This will, I hope, show Malebranche at his best, rigorously arguing for extreme claims that, on the face of it, are highly counterintuitive and contrary to all sensible experience, as Malebranche himself recognizes.

In the case of the *Search*, a long work covering many topics, I have had to do quite a bit of excerpting, occasionally taking only a crucial passage or two from a chapter. As the table of contents shows, I have organized this material thematically, much as Malebranche presents it. The *Dialogues*, on the other hand, are a more coherent, unified, and (I believe) better written work. I have thus included Dialogues 1–7 complete, so that the reader, in addition to seeing the full presentations of the doctrines and the uninterrupted flow of the arguments, can also appreciate Malebranche's literary achievement in composing the dialogues. (Although he was no Plato, Malebranche did have a considerable skill in the dialogue form.) Dialogues 1–6 are mostly but not exclusively epistemological; they cover Malebranche's theory of ideas and the vision in God. Dialogue 7 and the excerpt from Dialogue 8 present his occasionalism, and the excerpts from Dialogues 9 and 12 present his philosophical theology, also expanding on both the vision in God and occasionalism. The selections from the *Treatise* concentrate mainly on Malebranche's theodicy, as it regards divine providence and the problem of evil and imperfection in the realm of nature, and exclude much important material on his doctrine of grace. I have, however, also included Malebranche's discussion of the will and human freedom, as a sample of his moral philosophy.

Given space limitations, certain interesting and important aspects of Malebranche's thought could not be included in this volume. His mathematics and physics, for example, are not represented in the selections, although I have included excerpts from the chapter in the *Search* in which Malebranche criticizes Descartes's account of rest and solidity and his laws of motion, since Malebranche believes these corrections constitute an important consequence of his discoveries regarding God's role in causal relations. And I have not made any selections from Malebranche's philosophically rich correspondence, crucial as it is for seeing the development of his thought. Nonetheless, the major writings presented here will provide the reader with a good foundation for understanding the doctrines of this highly important, influential, and fascinating philosopher, one whose significance for the history of early modern thought is only recently again coming to be fully appreciated.

Translations

The selections from the *Search after Truth* and the *Elucidations* to the *Search* are from the translation by Thomas M. Lennon and Paul J. Olscamp (Columbus, Ohio: Ohio State University Press, 1980). The selections from the *Dialogues on Metaphysics* are from the translation by Willis Doney (New York: Abaris Books, 1980). I am extremely grateful to Professors Lennon and Doney and to the Ohio State University Press for their permission to reprint this material. The selections from the *Treatise on Nature and Grace* are, in substance, from Thomas Taylor's seventeenth-century translation (I use the second [1700] edition). I have, however, in addition to updating spelling, syntax, and punctuation, made quite a few corrections and modifications in Taylor's translation—not just for ease in reading, but also for accuracy.

Selected Bibliography

A. Malebranche's Works

The standard edition of Malebranche's writings are the *Oeuvres complètes de Malebranche*, André Robinet, dir., 20 volumes (Paris: J. Vrin, 1958–1967). The volumes of this collection are as follows:

I–III	*De la recherche de la vérité* (sixth edition, 1712); volume III contains the *Éclaircissements*
IV	*Conversations chrétiennes* (1675)
V	*Traité de la nature et de la grâce* (1680)
VI–IX	*Recueil de toutes les réponses à M. Arnauld*
X	*Méditations chrétiennes et métaphysiques* (1683)
XI	*Traité de morale* (1683)
XII	*Entretiens sur la métaphysique et sur la religion* (1688)
XIII	*Entretiens sur la mort* (1696)
XIV	*Traité de l'amour de Dieu (1697) et lettres au P. Lamy*
XV	*Entretien d'un philosophe chrétien et d'un philosophe chinois* (1708)
XVI	*Réflexions sur la prémotion physique* (1715)
XVII–1	*Pièces jointes et Écrits divers*
XVII–2	*Mathematica*
XVIII	*Correspondances et actes (1638–1689)*
XIX	*Correspondances et actes (1690–1715)*
XX	*Documents biographiques et bibliographiques*
*	*Index des citations, bibliques, patristiques, philosophiques, et scientifiques*

English translations of *De la recherche de la vérité*:

Father Malebranche's Treatise Concerning the Search after Truth, translated by Thomas Taylor, 2 vols. (Oxford, 1694; second edition, London, 1700).

Malebranche's Search after Truth, or a Treatise of the Nature of the Humane Mind and of its Management, R. Sault, trans. 2 vols. (London, 1694–95).

The Search after Truth/Elucidations of the Search after Truth, Thomas M. Lennon and Paul J. Olscamp, trans. (Columbus, Ohio: Ohio State University Press, 1980).

English translations of *Entretiens sur la métaphysique*:

Dialogues on Metaphysics, Willis Doney, trans. (New York: Abaris Books, 1980).

Dialogues on Metaphysics and Religion, Morris Ginsberg, trans. (New York: Macmillan, 1923).

English translations of *Traité de la Nature et de la Grâce*:

Treatise of Nature and Grace, Thomas Taylor, trans., appended to his translation of the *Recherche* (Oxford, 1694; second edition, London, 1700).

Treatise on Nature and Grace, Patrick Riley, trans. (Oxford: Oxford University Press, 1992).

B. Other Seventeenth-Century Sources

Arnauld, Antoine, *Des vraies et des fausses idées* (Paris: Fayard, 1986).

Cordemoy, Géraud de, *Oeuvres philosophiques*, P. Clair and F. Girbal, eds. (Paris: Presses Universitaires de France, 1968).

Fontenelle, Bernard le Bovier de, "Doutes sur le système physique des causes occasionelles", in *Oeuvres complètes*, vol. 1 (Paris: Fayard, 1990).

Foucher, Simon, *Critique de la Recherche de la vérité* (Paris: Martin Coustelier, 1675; New York: Johnson Reprint Corp., 1969).

La Forge, Louis de, *Oeuvres philosophiques*, P. Clair, ed. (Paris: Presses Universitaires de France, 1974).

Leibniz, Gottfried Wilhelm, *Philosophical Essays*, D. Garber and R. Ariew, trans. (Indianapolis: Hackett, 1989).

Locke, John, "An Examination of P. Malebranche's Opinion of Seeing All Things in God", in *The Works of John Locke*, 10 vols. (London: Tegg, 1823), vol. 9.

Régis, Pierre Sylvain, *Cours entier de Philosophie, ou Système Générale selon les principes de M. Descartes*, 3 vols. (Amsterdam: Huguetan, 1691; New York: Johnson Reprint Corp., 1970).

C. Secondary Works

Alquié, Ferdinand, *Le Cartésianisme de Malebranche* (Paris: J. Vrin, 1974).

André, P., *La vie du R. P. Malebranche, prêtre de l'Oratoire, avec l'histoire de ses ouvrages* (Paris, 1886; Geneva: Slatkine Reprints, 1970).

Bouillier, Francisque, *Histoire de la philosophie Cartésienne*, 2 vols. (Paris: Durand, 1854).

Brown, Stuart, ed., *Malebranche: His Philosophical Critics and Successors* (Assen: Van Gorcum, 1991).

Church, Ralph W., *A Study in the Philosophy of Malebranche* (London: George Allen and Unwin, 1931).

Connell, Desmond, *The Vision in God: Malebranche's Scholastic Sources* (Paris and Louvain: Nauwelaerts, 1967).

Dreyfus, Ginette, *La volonté selon Malebranche* (Paris: J. Vrin, 1958).

Gaonach, J.-M., *La théorie des idées dans la philosophie de Malebranche* (Brest, 1908; Geneva: Slatkine Reprints, 1970).

Gouhier, Henri, *La philosophie de Malebranche et son expérience religieuse* (Paris: J. Vrin, 1948).

_____, *La vocation de Malebranche* (Paris: J. Vrin, 1926).

Gueroult, Martial, *Malebranche*, 3 vols. (Paris: Aubier, 1955).

Jolley, Nicholas, *The Light of the Soul: Theories of Ideas in Leibniz, Malebranche, and Descartes* (Oxford: Clarendon Press, 1990).

Luce, A. A., *Berkeley and Malebranche* (Oxford: Oxford University Press, 1934).

McCracken, Charles, *Malebranche and British Philosophy* (Oxford: Clarendon Press, 1983).

Nadler, Steven, *Malebranche and Ideas* (Oxford: Oxford University Press, 1992).

Radner, Daisie, *Malebranche: A Study of a Cartesian System* (Assen: Van Gorcum, 1978).

Riley, Patrick, *The General Will before Rousseau* (Princeton: Princeton University Press, 1986).

Robinet, André, *Système et existence dans l'oeuvre de Malebranche* (Paris: J. Vrin, 1965).

Rodis-Lewis, Geneviève, *Nicolas Malebranche* (Paris: Presses Universitaires de France, 1963).

Rome, Beatrice, *The Philosophy of Malebranche* (Chicago: Henry Regnery, 1963).

Watson, Richard A., *The Breakdown of Cartesian Metaphysics* (Atlantic Highlands, New Jersey: Humanities Press, 1987).

D. Further Bibliography

Easton, Patricia, Thomas M. Lennon, and Gregor Sebba, *Bibliographia Malebranchiana (1638–1988)* (Edwardsville: Southern Illinois University Press, 1991).

Sebba, Gregor, *Bibliographia Cartesiana* (The Hague: Martinus Nijhoff, 1964).

THE SEARCH AFTER TRUTH

✤

Wherein Are Treated the Nature of
Man's Mind and the Use He Must Make of It to
Avoid Error in the Sciences

1. Theory of Knowledge

a. The Search after Truth

From the
Preface

✣

The mind of man is by its nature situated, as it were, between its Creator and corporeal creatures, for, according to Saint Augustine,[a] there is nothing but God above it and nothing but bodies below it. But as the mind's position above all material things does not prevent it from being joined to them, and even depending in a way on a part of matter, so the infinite distance between the sovereign Being and the mind of man does not prevent it from being immediately joined to it in a very intimate way. The latter union raises the mind above all things. Through it, the mind receives its life, its light, and its entire felicity, and at many points in his works Saint Augustine speaks of this union as the one most natural and essential to the mind. The mind's union with the body, on the contrary, infinitely debases man and is today the main cause of all his errors and miseries.

I am not surprised that ordinary men or pagan philosophers consider only the soul's relation and union with the body, without recognizing the relation and union it has with God; but I am surprised that Christian philosophers, who ought to prefer the mind of God to the mind of man, Moses to Aristotle, and Saint Augustine to some worthless commentator on a pagan philosopher, should regard the soul more as the *form* of the body than as being made in the image and for the image of God, i.e., according to Saint Augustine,[b] for the Truth to which alone it is immediately joined. It is true that the soul is joined to the body and is naturally its *form*; but it is also true that it is united to God in a much closer and more essential way. The relation it has to its body may cease; but the relation it has to God is so essential that God could not conceivably create a mind without it.

[a]"Nihil est potentius illa creatura, quae mens dicitur rationalis, nihil est sublimius."

"Quidquid supra illam est, jam creator est." *Tract.* 23 on St. John.

"Quod rationali anima melius est, omnibus consentientibus Deus est." Aug. [*De immortalitate animae,* ch. 13.]

[b]"Ad ipsam similitudinem non omnia facta sunt, sed sola substantia rationalis; quare omnia per ipsam, sed ad ipsam non nisi anima rationalis. Itaque substantia rationalis & per ipsam facta est, & ad ipsam; non enim est ulla natura interposita." *Lib. imp. de Gen. ad litt.* [Ch. 60.]

"Rectissime dicitur factus ad imaginem & similitudinem Dei, non enim aliter incommutabilem veritatem posset mente conspicere." *De vera rel.* [Ch. 44.]

It is evident that God can act only for Himself, that He can create minds only to know and love Him, and that He can endow them with no knowledge or love that is not for Him or that does not tend toward Him; but He need not have joined to bodies the minds now joined to them. Hence, the relation that minds have to God is natural, necessary, and absolutely indispensable; but our mind's relation to our body, although natural to our mind, is neither absolutely necessary nor indispensable.

This is not the place to adduce all the arguments and appeals to authority that might lead one to believe that it is more of the nature of the mind to be joined to God than to be joined to the body; these matters would lead us too far afield. To present this truth properly, it would be necessary to overthrow the fundamental principles of pagan philosophy, to explicate the disorders of sin, to combat what is falsely called experience, and to argue against the prejudices and illusions of the senses. Hence it is too difficult an undertaking in a preface to make this truth perfectly comprehensible to ordinary men.

But it is not so difficult to prove this to attentive minds who have been instructed in the true Philosophy. For it suffices to have them recall that as the will of God orders the nature of each thing, it is more of the nature of the soul to be joined to God through its knowledge of the truth and its love of good than to be joined to the body, since it is certain, as we have just said, that God made minds to know and love Him rather than for *informing* bodies. . . .

Yet men are not altogether unaware that they have a soul and that the soul is the most important part of their being.[a] They have also been convinced a thousand times over by both reason and experience that it is no great advantage to have fame, riches, and health for a few years, and, in general, that all bodily goods and those we possess only through or because of the body are passing, imaginary goods. Men know that it is better to be just than to be rich, to be reasonable than to be learned, to have a lively and penetrating mind than to have a swift and agile body. These truths cannot be erased from their mind, and they infallibly discover them when it pleases them to think about them. For example, Homer, who praises the swiftness of his hero, could have seen, had he wished to, that this is the praise one should give to hunting dogs and horses. Alexander, so celebrated in history for his plundering exploits, sometimes heard in the most secret recesses of his reason the same reproaches that murderers and thieves hear, in spite of the tumultuous din made by the crowd of flatterers surrounding him. And Caesar crossing the Rubicon could not conceal the reproaches that terrified him when he finally resolved to sacrifice his country's freedom to his own ambition.

Although closely joined to the body, the soul is still joined to God, and even while it receives these lively and confused sensations through the body and is moved by its passions, it is informed of its duty and its disorders by the eternal Truth that presides over its mind.[b] When its body misleads it, God sets it right;

---

[a] "Non exigua hominis portio, sed totius humanae, universitatis substantia est." Amb. 6. hexa. 7.

[b] "Ubique veritas praesides omnibus consulentibus te, simulque respondes omnibus etiam diversa consulentibus. Liquide tu respondes, sed non liquide omnes audiunt. Omnes unde volunt consulunt, sed non semper quod volunt audiunt." Aug. *Confess*. bk. 10. ch. 26.

when the body flatters it, God castigates it; when the body praises and acclaims it, God afflicts it internally with bitter reproaches and condemns it by the manifestations of a law that is purer and more holy than the law of the flesh it has followed.

Alexander did not need the Scythians to come and teach him his duty in a foreign tongue;[a] he knew the rules of justice he should have followed from the same one who instructs the Scythians and the most barbaric nations. The light of truth that illumines everyone illumined him as well; and the voice of nature,[b] which speaks neither Greek nor Scythian nor any barbarian tongue, spoke to him, as it does to the rest of men, a very clear and very intelligible language. The Scythians reproached him in vain for his conduct; they spoke only to his ears. Since God did not speak to his heart or, rather, since God did speak to his heart, but while he was listening only to the Scythians, who succeeded but in arousing his passions and in directing his attention away from himself, he failed to hear the voice of truth (though it had struck him), and to see its light (though it had penetrated him).

It is true that our union with God is diminished and weakened to the extent that our union with sensible things is increased and strengthened; but it is impossible that this union should be entirely broken without the destruction of our being, for while those plunged in vice and intoxicated with pleasures might be insensible to the truth, they are yet joined to it.[c] The truth does not abandon them, it is they who abandon the truth. Its light shines in the darkness but does not always dispel it, just as the sun's light surrounds those who are blind or who shut their eyes, although it enlightens neither of them.[d]

The same is true of our mind's union with our body.[e] This union diminishes as our union with God increases, but it is entirely broken only by our death. For even if we were as enlightened and as detached from all sensible things as were the Apostles, there is still the necessity stemming from Original Sin that our mind should depend on our body, and that we should feel the law of our flesh resisting and constantly opposing the law of our mind.

The mind becomes purer, more luminous, stronger, and of greater scope as its union with God increases, because this union constitutes its entire perfection. It becomes corrupted, blind, weakened, and restricted as its union with its body is increased and strengthened, because this union constitutes all its imperfection.

---

[a]Vid. *Quint. Curc.* bk. 7. ch. 8.

[b]"Intus in domicilio cogitationis, nec Hebraea, nec Graeca, nec Latina, nec Barbara VERITAS, sine oris & linguae organis, sine strepitu syllabarum." Aug. *Confess.* bk. 11. ch. 3.

[c]"Videtur quasi ipse a te occidere cum tu ab ipso occidas." Aug. on Ps. 25 [*Ennar.* 2:3].

[d]"Nam etiam sol iste, & videntis faciem illustrat & caeci; ambobus sol praesens est, sed praesente sole unus absens est. Sic & Sapientia Dei Dominus Jesus Christus ubique praesens est, quia ubique est veritas, ubique Sapientia." Aug. on St. John, *Tract.* 35.

[e]What I say here about the mind's two unions with God and the body should be understood according to the ordinary way of conceiving things. For it is true that the mind can be immediately joined only to God, i.e., it depends only on Him. And it is joined to, or depends on the body, only because the will of God is efficacious in establishing this union, which since the Fall has had its order of dependence reversed, but all this will be made clearer in what follows.

Thus, a man who judges all things by his senses, who follows the impulses of his passions in all things, who perceives only what he senses and loves only what flatters him, is in the most wretched state of mind possible. In this state he is infinitely removed from the truth and from his good. But when a man[a] judges things only according to the mind's pure ideas, when he carefully avoids the noisy confusion of creatures, and, when entering into himself, he listens to his sovereign Master with his senses and passions silent, it is impossible for him to fall into error.

God never deceives those who consult Him with serious purpose and with their mind turned fully toward Him, although He does not always make them hear His responses; but when the mind turns from God and expends itself externally, when it consults only its body to be instructed in the truth, when it listens only to its senses, imagination, and passions, which speak to it constantly, then it must of necessity be deceived. Wisdom and perfection and felicity are not goods to be hoped for from the body; He who alone is above us, and from whom we have received our being, is the only one who can perfect it.

This is what Saint Augustine teaches us with these elegant words.[b] "Eternal wisdom," he says, "is the source [*principe*] of all creatures capable of understanding, and this immutable wisdom never ceases speaking to His creatures in the most secret recesses of their reason so that they might be inclined toward Him, their source, because only the vision of eternal wisdom gives minds being, only eternal wisdom can complete them, so to speak, and give them the ultimate perfection of which they are capable." "When we see God as He is in Himself, we will be like unto Him," says the apostle Saint John.[c] Through this contemplation of eternal truth, we shall be exalted to the heights toward which all spiritual creatures tend by the necessity of their nature. But while we are on earth, the body "weighs down the mind,"[d] constantly withdraws it from the presence of God or the inner light that illumines it; it strives constantly to strengthen its union with sensible objects, and it forces it to represent things not as they are in themselves, but according to the relation they have to the preservation of life.

The body, according to the Book of Wisdom,[e] fills the mind with so many sensations that it becomes incapable of knowing things that are at all hidden. Corporeal vision dazzles and distracts the mind's vision so that there is great difficulty in clearly seeing a given truth with the soul's eyes while we are using

---

[a]"Quis enim bene se inspiciens non expertus est, tanto se aliquid intellixisse sincerius, quanto removere atque subducere intentionem mentis a corporis sensibus potuit." Aug. *De immortalitate animae* ch. 10.

[b]"Principium creaturae intellectualis est aeterna sapienta, quod principium manens in se incommutabliter, nullo modo cessat occulta inspiratione vocationis loqui ei creaturae, cui principium est, ut convertatur ad id ex quo est; quod aliter formata ac perfecta esse non possit." *Lib. imp. de Gen. ad litt.* ch. 50 [ch. 5].

[c]"Scimus quoniam cum apparuerit similes ei erimus, quoniam videbimus eum sicuti est." *Tract.* on St. John's Epistle One, ch. 3, v. 2.

[d]"Corpus quod corrumpitur aggravat animam." Wisd. 9:10 [9:15].

[e]Terrena inhabitatio deprimit sensum multa cogitantem, & difficile aestimamus quae in terra sunt, & quae in prospectu sunt invenimus cum labore." Wisd. 9:15.

the body's eyes to know it. This shows that it is only by the mind's attention that any truths are discovered or any sciences acquired, because the mind's attention is in fact only its conversion and return to God, who is our sole Master,[a] who alone teaches us all truth through the manifestation of His substance, as Saint Augustine says,[b] and without the intervention of any creature.

From all this it is clear that we must constantly resist the body's influence on the mind, and that because we should not pause over, or occupy ourselves with, anything that belongs to the sensible order, we must gradually become accustomed to disbelieving the reports our senses make about all the bodies surrounding us, which they always portray as worthy of our application and respect. . . .

It is absolutely necessary for those who wish to become happy and wise to be convinced to the core of what I have just said. It is not enough that they should take my word, or that they should be persuaded by the luster of some fleeting light; they must be convinced of it by a thousand unquestionable proofs and experiences. These truths must be indelible in their mind and must always be present to them while they pursue their studies and all the other activities of their life.

Those who take the trouble to read carefully the work that I am now publishing will, unless I am mistaken, enter into this frame of mind; for in it I demonstrate in several ways that our senses, our imagination, and our passions are altogether useless for discovering the truth and our good, that, on the contrary, they dazzle us and seduce us in every instance, and generally that all the knowledge the mind receives through the body, or on account of some motion occuring in the body, is false and confused in relation to the objects it represents (although this knowledge is quite useful to the preservation of the body and of goods related to the body).

In this work I combat several errors and especially those most universally received or those that cause a greater disorder of the mind, and I show that these errors are almost all consequences of the mind's union with the body. In several places I try to make the mind realize its servitude and dependence relative to all sensible things so that it might be awakened from its somnolence and make an effort to free itself.

---

[a]"Aug. *De magistro* [11–12].

[b]"Deus intelligibilis lux, in quo, & a quo, & per quem intelligibiliter lucent, quae intelligibiliter lucent omnia." 1 *Sol.* [1:3].

"Insinuavit nobis [Christus] animam humanam & mentem rationalem non vegetari, non illuminari, non beatificari, nisi ab ipsa SUBSTANTIA Dei." Aug. *Tract.* 23 on St. John. "Nulla natura interposita." Quest. 83, q. 51.

b. Understanding and Will

From
BOOK ONE: THE SENSES
Chapter One

⚜

Being neither material nor extended, the mind of man is undoubtedly a simple, indivisible substance without composition of parts; but nonetheless, it is customary to distinguish two faculties in it, to wit, the *understanding* and the *will*, which first need to be explained so that we can attach a precise notion to these two words, for it seems that our notions or ideas of these two faculties are neither clear nor distinct enough.

But because these ideas are quite abstract and do not fall within the scope of the imagination, it seems appropriate to express them by comparison with the properties that belong to matter. These properties, being more easily imagined, will make the notions properly attached to the two words *understanding* and *will* more distinct and even more familiar. It should be noted only that these comparisons between mind and matter are not entirely appropriate, and that I compare them only in order to make the mind more attentive, and, as it were, to illustrate my meaning to others.

Matter or extension contains two properties or faculties. The first faculty is that of receiving different figures, the second, the capacity for being moved. The mind of man likewise contains two faculties; the first, which is the *understanding,* is that of receiving various *ideas,* that is, of perceiving various things; the second, which is the *will,* is that of receiving *inclinations,* or of willing different things. We shall first of all explain the analogies found between the first of the two faculties belonging to matter, and the first of those that belong to the mind.

Extension can receive two kinds of figure. Some are external only, like the roundness of a piece of wax; others are internal, and characterize all the particles of which the wax is composed, for all the particles that make up a piece of wax undoubtedly have figures quite different from those that make up a piece of iron. Figure that is external, then, I call simply *figure,* and I call *configuration* that figure which is internal and which is necessary to all the parts of the wax in order for it to be what it is.

We can likewise say that the soul's perceptions of ideas are of two kinds. The first, which are called pure perceptions, are, as it were, accidental to the soul: they do not make an impression on it and do not sensibly modify it. The second, which are called sensible, make a more or less vivid impression on it. Such are

8

pleasure and pain, light and colors, tastes, odors, and so on. For it will be seen later on that sensations are nothing but modes of the mind [*manieres d'être de l'esprit*], and it is for this reason that I call them *modifications* of the mind.

Inclinations of the soul might also be called *modifications* of the soul. For since it is certain that the inclination of the will is a mode of the soul [*maniere d'être de l'ame*], it can be called a *modification* of the soul, just as motion in bodies being a mode of those bodies, we might say that motion is a *modification* of matter. Nevertheless, I do not call inclinations of the will or motion in matter modifications, because these inclinations and instances of motion are ordinarily related to something external, for inclinations are related to the good, and motion is related to some foreign body. But the figures and configurations of bodies and the sensations of the soul have no necessary relation to anything external. For just as a figure is round when all the exterior parts of a body are equally distant from one of its parts called its center, independently of any external body, so all the sensations of which we are capable could subsist without there being any object outside us. Their being contains no necessary relation to the bodies that seem to cause them (as will be proved elsewhere), and they are nothing but the soul modified in this or that fashion; consequently, they are indeed *modifications* of the soul. Let me therefore so name them in order to clarify matters.

The first and principal agreement found between the faculty that matter has of receiving different figures and configurations and that which the soul has of receiving different *ideas* and *modifications* is that just as the faculty of receiving different figures and configurations in bodies is entirely passive and contains no action, so the faculty of receiving different ideas and modifications in the mind is entirely passive and contains no action; and I call that faculty, or that capacity which the soul has of receiving all these things, UNDERSTANDING.

From this it must be concluded that it is the understanding that perceives or that knows, since only it receives ideas of objects; for it is the same thing for the soul to perceive an object as to receive the idea that represents the object. Also, it is the understanding that perceives modifications of the soul, or that senses them, since I understand by this word *understanding* that passive faculty of the soul by means of which it receives all the modifications of which it is capable. For it is the same thing for the soul to receive the mode called pain as to perceive or sense pain, since it cannot receive pain in any other way than by perceiving it. From this it can be concluded that it is the understanding that imagines absent objects and senses those that are present, and that the *senses* and the *imagination* are nothing but the understanding perceiving objects through the organs of the body, as we shall explain later on.

But because when we sense pain, or anything else, we ordinarily perceive it through the mediation of the *sense* organs, men ordinarily say that the senses do the perceiving, without knowing distinctly what they mean by the word *sense*. They think there is some faculty distinct from the soul that enables it or the body to sense, for they believe that the sense organs really take part in our perceptions. They imagine that the body so aids the mind in sensing that if the mind were separated from the body, it could never sense anything. But they believe all these things only through prejudice, and because in our present state we never sense anything without the use of the sense organs, as we shall explain elsewhere at greater length.

In order to conform to the ordinary way of speaking, we shall say in what follows that the senses do sense; but by the word *sense* we mean nothing other than that passive faculty of the soul we have just spoken about, that is, the understanding perceiving something upon occasion of the appropriate natural events taking place in the organs of its body, as will be explained elsewhere.

The other agreement between the passive faculty of the soul and that of matter is that as matter is not really altered by any change in its figure—I mean, for example, that as wax receives no considerable change for being round or square—so the mind receives no significant change through the diversity of ideas that it has, i.e., though in perceiving a square or a circle it receives the idea of a square or a circle, the mind is not thereby significantly changed.

Furthermore, as matter can be said to receive significant change when a piece of wax changes into fire and smoke by losing the configuration appropriate to the parts of wax in order to receive the configuration appropriate to fire and smoke, so the soul might be said to receive quite significant change when it alters its modifications and suffers pain after having sensed pleasure. From this it must be concluded that pure perceptions are to the soul roughly what figures are to matter, and that configurations are to matter roughly what sensations are to the soul. But it must not be imagined that the analogy is exact; I propose it only in order to make the notion of this word *understanding* perceptible to the senses. . . .

The other faculty of matter is that it is capable of receiving various *instances of motion*, whereas the other faculty of the soul is that it is capable of receiving various *inclinations*. Let us compare these *faculties*.

Just as the Author of nature is the universal cause of all *motion* found in matter, so is He also the general cause of all natural *inclinations* found in minds; and just as all motion proceeds in a straight line [*en ligne droite*] unless it encounters particular external causes that influence its course and that by their opposition alter it so that it proceeds in a curved path, so all the inclinations that we have from God are right [*droites*] and could have no other end but the possession of good and of truth were there not some external cause that directed the impression of nature toward evil ends. Now it is this external cause that is the cause of all our evils, and that corrupts all our inclinations.

For a proper understanding of this, it must be realized that there is a very significant difference between the impression or motion that the Author of nature produces in matter, and the impression or impulse [*mouvement*] toward the good in general that the same Author of nature continuously impresses in the mind. For matter is altogether without action; it has no force to arrest its motion or to direct it and turn it in one direction rather than another. Its motion, as has just been said, always proceeds in a straight line; and when it is impeded from continuing in this way, it describes the greatest possible circular path and consequently most approximates a straight line, because God impresses its motion on it and controls its direction. But such is not the case with the will,[a] which in a sense can be said

---

[a]See the *Elucidations* [1].

to be active, because our soul can direct in various ways the inclination or impression that God gives it. For although it cannot arrest this impression, it can in a sense turn it in the direction that pleases it, and thus cause all the disorder found in its inclinations, and all the miseries that are the certain and necessary results of sin.

Consequently, I propose to designate by the word WILL, or capacity the soul has of loving different goods, *the impression or natural impulse that carries us toward general and indeterminate good;* and by FREEDOM, I mean nothing else but *the power that the mind has of turning this impression toward objects that please us so that our natural inclinations are made to settle upon some particular object,* which inclinations were hitherto vaguely and indeterminately directed toward universal or general good, that is, toward God, who alone is the general good because He alone contains in Himself all goods.

From this it is easy to see that although natural inclinations are voluntary, they are still not free with the freedom of indifference of which I speak, which contains the potential of willing or not willing, or even of willing the contrary of what our natural inclinations carry us toward. For although it is voluntarily and freely, or without constraint, that we love good in general (since we can love only by the will, and since it is a contradiction that the will should ever be constrained), we nonetheless do not love it freely in the sense I have just explained, since it is not in the power of our will not to wish to be happy.

But it must be carefully noted that insofar as a mind is thrust toward good in general, it cannot direct its impulse toward a particular good unless that same mind, insofar as it is capable of ideas, has knowledge of that particular good. In plain language, I mean that the will is a blind power, which can proceed only toward things the understanding represents to it. As a result, the will can direct both the impression it has for good, and all its natural inclinations in various ways, only by ordering the understanding to represent to it some particular object.[a] The power our soul has of directing its inclinations therefore necessarily contains the power of being able to convey the understanding toward the objects that please it.

I shall clarify by an example what I have just said about the will and freedom. A person represents some honor to himself as a good that he might hope for; the will immediately wills this good; that is, the *impression* toward indeterminate and universal good that the mind is continuously receiving conveys it toward this honor. But as this honor is not the universal good, and is not considered as the universal good by a clear and distinct perception of the mind, for the mind never sees clearly what is not universal, the *impression* that we have toward the universal good is not entirely brought to rest by this particular good. The mind tends to proceed still further; it does not necessarily and indomitably love this honor, and it is free with regard to it. Now its *freedom* consists in the fact that not being fully convinced that this honor contains all the good it is capable of loving, it can suspend its judgment and love, and then, as we shall explain in the third book, by its union with the universal being, or the being that contains all good, it

[a]See the *Elucidations* [2].

can think about other things and consequently love other goods. Finally, it can compare all goods, love them according to order to the extent to which they ought to be loved, and relate them all to that which contains all goods and which, being alone capable of fulfilling our total capacity of loving, is alone worthy of limiting our love.

It is roughly the same thing with the knowledge of truth as with love of good. We love knowledge of truth, like enjoyment of good, by a natural impression; and this impression, like the one that conveys us toward the good, is not indomitable —only through clarity or through complete and perfect knowledge of the object is it indomitable; and we are as free in our false judgments as in our inordinate loves, as will be shown in the next chapter.

From
BOOK ONE: THE SENSES
Chapter Two

⚜

I. Judgments and inferences. II. That they depend on the will. III. The use that should be made of freedom with regard to them. IV. Two general rules for avoiding error and sin. V. Requisite comments on these rules.

I. Judgments and inferences.

It might fairly be concluded from what we have said in the preceding chapter that the understanding never judges since it does nothing but perceive (or that judgments and inferences on the part of the understanding are but pure perceptions), that it is the will alone that really judges by assenting to, and voluntarily remaining with, what the understanding represents to it, and that thus it alone plunges us into error. But these matters must be explained at greater length.

I say, then, that there is no difference on the part of the understanding between a simple perception, a judgment, and an inference, other than that the understanding by a simple perception perceives a simple thing without any relation to anything else whatsoever, that in judgments it perceives the relations between two or more things, and that in inferences it perceives the relations among the relations of things. Consequently, all the *operations*[a] of the understanding are nothing but *pure perceptions*.

It is only a *simple perception* when, for example, one perceives twice two or four. When one judges that twice two is four, or that twice two is not five, the understanding still does nothing but perceive the relation of equality found between twice two and four, or the relation of inequality found between twice two and five. Thus *judgment* on the part of the understanding is only *the perception of the relation found between two or more things*. But *inference* is the perception of the relation found, not between two or more things, for this would be a judgment, but *the perception of the relation found between two or more relations of two or more things*. Thus, when I conclude that, four being less than six, twice two,

---

[a] Here I am obliged to speak in ordinary language. It will be seen at the appropriate time that these operations of the understanding are nothing but modifications produced in the soul through the efficacy of the divine ideas as a result of the laws concerning the union of the soul with Sovereign Reason and with its own body.

being equal to four, is consequently less than six, I perceive not only the relation of inequality between twice two and six, for this would be only a judgment, but also the relation of inequality between the relation of twice two and four, and the relation between four and six, which is an inference.

The understanding, therefore, does nothing but perceive the relations between ideas, which relations, when they are clear, are expressed by clear ideas; for the relation of six to three, for example, is equal to two, and is expressed by two. And only the will judges and reasons, by voluntarily remaining with what the understanding represents to it, as has just been said.

II. That judgments and inferences depend on the will.

But nevertheless, when the things we consider are altogether evident, it seems to us that we no longer consent to them voluntarily. As a result, we are led to believe that it is not our will but our understanding that judges them.

In order to recognize our error, it must be realized that the things we consider appear entirely evident to us only when the understanding has examined them from all sides and has examined all the relations necessary to judge them. Whence it happens that the will, being unable to function without knowledge, can no longer act on the understanding, that is, the will cannot further desire that the understanding represent something new in its object because it has already considered all aspects related to the question to be decided. It is therefore obliged to rest with what the understanding has already represented, and to cease activating it and applying it to useless considerations. This repose is what is properly called judgment and inference. Thus, this repose or judgment, not being free when things are completely evident, also seems to us not to be voluntary.

But to the extent that there is something obscure in the subject we are considering, or that we are not entirely certain that we have discovered everything needed to resolve the question, as almost always happens with those that are difficult and contain many relations, we are free not to consent, and the will can still order the understanding to apply itself to something new. This inclines us to believe that the judgments we form on these subjects are voluntary.

Nonetheless, most philosophers maintain that these very judgments we form on obscure things are not voluntary, and they would generally have it that consent to truth is an action of the understanding, which they call assent, *assensus,* as opposed to consent to good, which they attribute to the will and call consent, *consensus.* But here is the source of their distinction and their mistake.

In our present state, we often clearly perceive truths with no reason to doubt them, and hence the will is not at all indifferent in the consent it gives to these evident truths, as we have just explained. But it is not the same with goods, of which we know none without some reason to doubt that we ought to love it. Our passions and the inclinations we naturally have for sensible pleasures are confused but very strong reasons due to the corruption of our nature. These passions and inclinations make us cold and indifferent in our love even of God; and thus we clearly sense our indifference, and are inwardly convinced that we make use of our freedom when we love God.

But we do not likewise perceive that we make use of our freedom in consenting to truth, especially when it appears altogether evident to us; and this makes us believe that consent to truth is not voluntary. As if it were necessary that our actions be indifferent to be voluntary, and as if the blessed did not love God quite voluntarily, without being diverted by anything whatever, just as we consent to this evident proposition, that twice two is four, without being diverted from believing it by anything indicating otherwise.

But in order to clearly distinguish the will's consent to truth from its consent to goodness, it is necessary to know the difference between truth and goodness taken in the ordinary sense and with reference to us. That difference consists in the fact that goodness concerns and affects us, whereas truth does not; for truth consists only in the relation between two or more things, whereas goodness consists in the relation of agreement things have with us.[a] As a result, there is but one action of the will with regard to truth, which is its assent [*acquiescement*] or consent to the representation of the relation between things; but there are two with regard to goodness, its assent or consent to the relation of agreement between the thing and us, and its love or impulse toward that thing, which actions are quite different, however they might ordinarily be confused. For there is quite a difference between simply assenting and being conveyed by love to what the mind represents, since one often assents to things that one avoids and wishes were nonexistent.

Now if we consider these things closely, we will clearly recognize that it is always the will that assents, not only to things agreeable to it, but to the representation of things; and the reason why the will always assents to the representations of things that are completely evident is, as we have already said, that there is in these things no further relation to be considered that the understanding has not already perceived. Consequently, it is necessary, as it were, for the will to cease its agitation and useless self-exhaustion, and for it to assent with full assurance that, since there is nothing further toward which it can direct its understanding, it is not mistaken.

As it is agreed on all hands that rash judgments are sinful, and that all sin is voluntary, it must also be agreed that it is therefore the will that judges by assenting to the confused, compound perceptions of the understanding. But the question as to whether the understanding alone judges and reasons at bottom seems rather useless and merely a verbal question. I say the understanding alone, for it does have the role in our judgments that I have assigned it, since it is necessary to know or to sense before judging and consenting. Furthermore, as the understanding and the will are but the soul itself, it actually perceives. judges, reasons, wills, and so on. For reasons that will be seen in what follows, I have assigned to the word *understanding* the notion of a passive faculty or a capacity for receiving ideas.

It must especially be noted that in our present state we know things only imperfectly, and that consequently it is absolutely necessary that we have this freedom of indifference by which we can refrain from consenting.

---

[a]Geometers do not love the truth, but knowledge of the truth, whatever might otherwise be said.

To see the necessity for this, it must be considered that we are led by our natural inclinations toward truth and goodness, as a result of which, the will, being led only to things that the mind has some knowledge of, must be led to what has the appearance of truth and goodness. But because what has the appearance of truth and goodness is not always what it seems, it is obvious that if the will were not free and if it were infallibly and necessarily led to everything having the appearance of truth and goodness, it would almost always be deceived. From this we could conclude that the Author of its being was the Author of its disorders and errors as well.

III. The use we ought to make of our freedom in order never to err.

Freedom is therefore given by God in order that we may refrain from falling into error, and into all the evils that follow from our errors, by never fully resting with probabilities, but only with truth, i.e., by constantly applying the mind and ordering it to continue investigating until everything to be investigated is unraveled and brought to light. For truth is almost never found except with evidence, and evidence consists only in the clear and distinct perception of all the constituents and relations of the object necessary to support a well-founded judgment.

The use, therefore, that we should make of our freedom is TO MAKE AS MUCH USE OF IT AS WE CAN, that is, never to consent to anything until we are forced to do so, as it were, by the inward reproaches of our reason.

To submit to the false appearances of truth is to enslave oneself against the will of God; but to submit in good faith to these secret reproaches of our reason that accompany the refusal to yield to evidence is to obey the voice of eternal truth that speaks to us inwardly. Here, then, are two rules based on what I have just said, which of all rules are the most necessary for the speculative sciences and for morals, and which can be regarded as the foundation of all the sciences of man.

IV. General rules for avoiding error.

Here is the first, which concerns the sciences. *We should never give complete consent except to propositions which seem so evidently true that we cannot refuse it of them without feeling an inward pain and the secret reproaches of reason;* that is, unless we clearly knew that ill use would be made of our freedom if consent were not willed, or if we willed to extend its power over things no longer in its power.

The second, which concerns morals, is this. *We should never absolutely love some good if we can without remorse refuse to love it.* From this it follows that God alone ought to be loved absolutely and intrinsically, for Him alone can we not abstain from loving without remorse; i.e., provided that He is known through reason or faith, we cannot abstain from loving Him without clearly knowing that we are doing wrong.

V. Requisite comments on these two rules.

But it must be noted here that when the things we perceive appear to us quite probable, we are strongly led to believe them; we even feel pain when we do not let ourselves be persuaded by them. Consequently, if we are not wary, we run the risk of consenting to them and consequently of being mistaken; for it is unlikely that truth should conform completely to probable opinion. For this reason I have expressly made it a point in these two rules that nothing should be consented to until it is clearly seen that we would make ill use of our freedom if we were not to consent.

Now, while we might feel strongly inclined to consent to probability, yet if we are careful to note whether we clearly see that we are obliged to consent to it, we shall undoubtedly find that the answer is no. For if probability is based on our sense-impressions—probability or verisimilitude [*vrai-semblance*] is really a misnomer—we shall then be very much inclined to yield to it; but no other cause of this inclination will be discovered than some passion or general affection we have for what affects the senses, as will be seen in what follows.

If on the other hand probability is due to some conformity with truth, as our probabilistic knowledge, in a certain sense, is ordinarily true, then if one reflects inwardly, one will feel led to do two things: to believe, and to go on investigating. But one will never find himself so persuaded that he clearly believes he is doing something wrong when he does not give complete consent.

Now, these two inclinations we have with regard to probabilities are very sound. For consent can and ought to be given to probabilities insofar as they indicate truth; but complete consent should not yet be given, as we have set out in our rule. The unknown aspects must be examined in order to enter fully into the nature of the thing, to distinguish the true from the false, and then to consent fully if the evidence obliges us to do so.

It is therefore necessary to become well accustomed to distinguishing truth from probability by inward self-examination, as I have just explained, because it is for lack of having attended to self-examination of this sort that we feel affected in almost the same way by two things so different. In short, it is of the greatest importance to make good use of our freedom by always refraining from consenting to things and loving them until forced to do so by the powerful voice of the Author of Nature, which till now I have called the reproaches of our reason and the remorse of our conscience.

All the duties of spiritual beings, as much for angels as for men, consist chiefly in this proper usage; and it can be said without fear that if they use their freedom with care, without becoming slaves of lies and vanity, they are on the road to the greatest perfection of which they are naturally capable, provided, however, that their understanding does not remain idle, that they continually take care to urge it toward new knowledge, and that they make it capable of greater truths by continual meditations on subjects worthy of its attention.

To perfect the mind, it is not enough to make use of freedom by never consenting to anything, like those people who glorify knowing nothing and doubting everything. Nor is it necessary to consent to everything, like certain others, who fear nothing so much as not knowing something, and pretend to know everything. Rather, we must make such good use of our understanding by continual meditations that we can often consent to what it represents to us with no fear of being mistaken.

From
BOOK ONE: THE SENSES
Chapter Four

❦

We have just seen that we fall into error only because we do not use our freedom as we should, that we err for failure to regulate the eagerness and ardor of the will for the mere appearances of truth, and that error consists only in consent of the will when extended beyond the perception of the understanding, because we would not err at all were we to judge only about what we perceive.

The occasional causes of error; that there are five principal ones.

Although, properly speaking, only the misuse of freedom is the cause of error, it can nevertheless be said that we have many faculties that are causes of our errors—not real causes, but causes that might be called *occasional*. All our ways of perceiving are to us so many occasions of error, for since our false judgments include two things, the consent of the will and the perception of the understanding, it is quite clear that each of the ways in which we perceive can provide us with an occasion for error, since they can lead us to precipitous consent.

But because the mind must first be made aware of its weaknesses and aberrations in order to acquire the proper desire to deliver itself from them and more easily discard its prejudices, we shall try to give a precise division of the ways it perceives, which will be the headings under which the different errors to which we are subject will be grouped in what follows.

The soul can perceive things in three ways, by the *pure understanding*, by the *imagination*, and by the *senses*.

By the *pure understanding* it perceives spiritual things, universals, common notions, the ideas of perfection and of an infinitely perfect being, and generally all its thoughts when it knows them through self-reflection. By the pure understanding it even perceives material things, extension with its properties; for only pure understanding can perceive a perfect circle, a perfect square, a figure of a thousand sides, and similar things. These sorts of perceptions are called *pure intellections*, or *pure perceptions*, because the mind need not form corporeal images in the brain to represent all these things.

Through the *imagination* the soul perceives only material beings, making them present when in fact they are absent, by forming images of them, as it were, in the brain. It is in this way that we imagine all sorts of figures: a circle, a triangle, a face, a horse, cities, and the countryside, whether we have already seen them or not. These sorts of perceptions might be called *imaginations*, because the soul represents these objects to itself by forming images of them in the brain; and, since images of spiritual things cannot be formed, it follows that the soul cannot imagine them (and this should be noted well).

Finally the soul perceives by the *senses* only sensible and gross objects, either when, being present, they make an impression on the external organs of its body and this impression is communicated to the brain or, when in their absence, the flow of animal spirits makes a similar impression in the brain. In this way the soul sees plains and rocks before its eyes, knows the hardness of iron, the point of a sword, and similar things; and these sorts of perceptions are called *feelings* [*sentimens*] or *sensations* [*sensations*].

The soul, then, perceives only in these three ways, which can easily be seen if it be considered that the things we perceive are either spiritual or material. If they are spiritual, only the pure understanding can know them. But if they are material, they will be either present or absent. If they are absent, the soul ordinarily represents them to itself only through the imagination; but if they are present, the soul can perceive them through the impressions they make on its senses. Thus our souls perceive things in only three ways, by the *pure understanding*, by the *imagination*, and by the *senses*.

These three faculties, then, can be considered as reliable headings under which men's errors and the causes of these errors might be grouped, and thus we can avoid the confusion into which their great number would inevitably plunge us were we to speak of them without ordering them.

But our *inclinations* and *passions* also act very strongly on us; they dazzle our mind with false lights, cover it, and fill it with shadows. Our inclinations and passions involve us in an infinite number of errors when we follow this false and deceptive light they produce in us. They must be considered, then, along with the three faculties of the mind, as sources of our aberrations and errors; and the errors attributable to the passions and inclinations must be added to those of the senses, the imagination, and the pure understanding. . . .

c. Mind and Body

From
BOOK ONE: THE SENSES
Chapter Ten

✤

I assume at the outset that the soul can be distinguished from the body by the positive attributes and properties these two substances will admit. The body is only extension in height, breadth, and depth, and all its properties consist only in (a) motion and rest, and (b) an infinity of different figures.[a] For it is clear: (1) that the idea of extension represents a substance, since one can think of extension without thinking of anything else; (2) this idea can represent only successive or permanent relations of distance, i.e., instances of motion and figure, for one can perceive in extension only what it contains. If it be assumed that extension is divided into such parts as may be imagined, at rest or in motion near each other, the relations among these parts will be clearly conceived; but one will never conceive them to be relations of joy, pleasure, pain, heat, taste, color, or any of the other sensible qualities, although these qualities are sensed when a certain change occurs in the body. I feel pain, for example, when a thorn pricks my finger; but the hole it makes is not the pain. The hole is in the finger—it is clearly conceived—and the pain is in the soul, for the soul senses it keenly and is disagreeably modified by it. Only the properties I have just spoken of, then, should be attributed to the body. The soul, on the other hand, is that in me which thinks, which senses, which wills—it is the substance in which are found all the modifications of which I have an inner sensation [*sentiment intérieur*], and which subsist only in the soul that perceives them. Thus, no property other than its diverse thoughts should be attributed to the soul. I assume, then, that the soul can be distinguished from the body. If what I have just said is not enough to illustrate the difference between these two substances, one can read and meditate on some passages of Saint Augustine, such as chapter 10 of the tenth book of *The Trinity*, chapters 4 and 14 of the *Quantity of the Soul*, or Descartes's *Meditations*, particularly the part concerned with the distinction between the soul and body, or finally, the sixth discourse from Cordemoy's *Discernement de l'ame & du corps.*

[a]*Dialogues on Metaphysics,* Dialogue 1, no. 1.2.

From
BOOK THREE
[Part One:] The Understanding, or Pure Mind
Chapter One

✤

I. Thought alone is essential to the mind. Sensing and imagining are only modifications of it.

I do not think that, after some serious thought on the matter, it can be doubted that the mind's essence[a] consists only in thought, just as the essence of matter consists only in extension. Nor can it be doubted that, depending on the various modifications of thought, the mind now wills, now imagines, and has many other particular forms, just as matter, depending on the various modifications of extension, is now water, now fire, now wood, and has an infinity of other particular forms.

I warn only that by the word *thought*, I do not mean the soul's particular modifications, i.e., this or that thought, but rather substantial thought, thought capable of all sorts of modifications or thoughts, just as extension does not mean this or that extension, such as a circle or a square, but extension capable of all sorts of modifications or figures. This comparison will be uncomfortable only because we have no clear idea of thought as we do of extension, for thought is known only through inner sensation or *consciousness*, as I shall explain below.

I think, further, that no mind can be conceived of that does not think, though it is quite easy to conceive of one that does not sense or imagine, and that does not even will, just as unextended matter cannot be conceived of, though it is possible to conceive of matter that is neither earth nor metal, neither square nor round, and that even has no motion. From this it must be concluded that as there can be matter that is neither earth nor metal, neither square nor round, nor even in motion, there can also be a mind that perceives neither hot nor cold, neither joy nor sadness, imagines nothing and even wills nothing; consequently, such modifications are not essential to it. Thought alone, then, is the essence of mind, just as extension alone is the essence of matter.

But as matter or extension without motion would be useless and could not assume the forms for which it was created, and as an intelligent being could not conceivably have willed to produce such a thing, so a mind or thought without volition would clearly be altogether useless, since the mind would never be led toward the objects of its perceptions and would not love the good for which it was

[a]By the essence of a thing, I mean what is first conceived in the thing, on which all the modifications noticed in it depend.

created. Consequently, an intelligent being could not conceivably have willed to produce the mind in this state. Nonetheless, as motion is not the essence of matter since it presupposes extension, so willing is not the essence of mind since willing presupposes perception.

Thought alone, then, is what properly constitutes the essence of mind, and the different modes of thinking, such as sensing and imagining, are but the modifications of which it is capable and by which it need not always be modified. But willing is a property that always accompanies it, whether joined to, or separated from, the body, but that is not essential to it, since volition presupposes thought and since like a body without motion, a mind without volition is conceivable.

Nevertheless, the power of volition, though it is not essential to it, is inseparable from mind—as mobility, though not essential to it, is inseparable from matter. For just as immovable matter is inconceivable, so a mind incapable of willing or of some natural inclination is inconceivable. But again, as matter can conceivably exist without any motion, likewise can the mind conceivably be without any impression of the Author of nature, leading it toward the good; and consequently it can be without any volition, for the will is nothing but the impression of the Author of nature that leads us toward the good in general, as has been explained at length in the first chapter of this work.

II. We do not know all the modifications of which our soul is capable.

What we have said in this treatise concerning the senses, as well as what we have just said about the nature of the mind, does not presuppose that we know all the modifications of which it is capable. We make no such assumption. On the contrary, we believe the mind has a capacity for receiving, one after another, an infinity of different modifications previously unknown to it.

The least part of matter can receive a figure of three, six, ten, or ten thousand sides, or finally a circular or eliptical shape that may be viewed as a figure of an infinite number of sides and angles. There is an infinite number of different kinds of each of its figures—an infinite number of different kinds of triangles, and even more different figures of four, six, ten, and ten thousand sides, or of infinite polygons, for the circle, the ellipse, and generally every figure (regularly or irregularly curvilinear) can be considered as an infinite polygon. The ellipse, for example, can be considered as an infinite polygon whose angles forming its sides are unequal, being greater toward the small diameter than toward the large, and so on for other more complex and more irregular infinite polygons.

A simple piece of wax is therefore capable of an infinite number, or rather, of an infinitely infinite number of modifications that no mind can comprehend— why believe, then, that the soul, which is much nobler than the body, is capable only of the modifications it has already received?

If we had never felt pleasure or pain, if we had never seen color or light, in a word, if we were with regard to everything as the blind and the deaf are to colors and sounds, we would be right to conclude that we were incapable of all the sensations we have of objects. Yet these are but modifications of our soul, as we have proved in our treatment of the senses.

It must be agreed, then, that the soul's capacity for receiving different modifications is as great as its capacity for conceiving, i.e., as the mind cannot exhaust or comprehend all the figures of which matter is capable, so it cannot comprehend all the various modifications the mighty hand of God can produce in the soul, even if it were true (as it is not, for the reasons I shall give in chapter seven of the second part of this book) that the mind knew the soul's capacity as distinctly as it knows matter's.

If our soul in its present state receives but few modifications, it is because the soul is joined to a body and depends on it. All its sensations are related to its body, and as it is not possessed of God, it has none of the modifications that possession must produce. The matter of which our body is composed is capable of but few modifications during our lifetime. This matter cannot be broken down into earth and moisture until after our death. Right now it cannot become air, fire, diamond, or metal, it cannot become round, square, or triangular; it has to be flesh, brain, nerves, and the rest of a man's body so that the soul may be joined to it. The same is true of our soul; it must have sensations of heat, cold, color, light, sounds, odors, tastes, and several other modifications in order to remain joined to its body. All its sensations direct the soul to the preservation of its machine. They agitate the soul and frighten it as soon as the least spring is unwound or broken, and as a result the soul must be subject to the body as long as the body is subject to corruption. But it is reasonable to believe that when the body is clothed with immortality, and we no longer fear the dissolution of its parts, our soul will no longer be affected by the unpleasant sensations we feel against our wishes. Instead, it will be affected by an infinity of completely different sensations of which we now have no idea, and which will be beyond all sensation and will be worthy of the goodness and grandeur of the God we shall possess. . . .

From
BOOK ONE: THE SENSES
Chapter Ten

⚜

III. The soul is immediately joined to that part of the brain where the filaments of the sense organs are.

It might be noted here in passing that it is known through experience that we can feel pain in parts of our bodies that have been amputated, because if the corresponding filaments of the brain are disturbed in the same way as if these parts had been injured, the soul senses a very real pain in these imaginary parts. All these things clearly show that the soul immediately resides in that part of the brain to which all the sense organs lead. When I say that it *resides* there, I mean only that it is aware of all the changes taking place there in relation to the objects that cause them, or customarily cause them, and that it perceives what happens outside this part only through the agency of the fibers ending there, or if you wish, through the agency of the different reactions of the spirits contained in these fibers. For I am convinced that the soul can immediately *reside* only in ideas, which alone can affect and stir the soul, and make it happy or unhappy, as I shall explain elsewhere. With this laid out and well understood, it will not be very difficult to see how sensation occurs, which must be explained with an example.

IV. An example of the effect objects have on the body.

When the point of a needle is pressed against the hand, the point separates and stimulates the fibers of the flesh. These fibers extend from this point to the brain, and when one is awake, they are taut enough to be disturbed only if those of the brain are disturbed. It follows then, that the extremities of these fibers in the brain are also stimulated. If the movement in the hand's fibers is moderate, so also will be the movement of the brain's fibers, and if the movement is violent enough to cause rupture in the hand, it will likewise be stronger and more violent in the brain.

Likewise, if the hand is brought near fire, the particles of wood, which are continually emitted in great number and with great violence (as reason, upon the default of vision, demonstrates), strike these fibers and communicate to them part of their agitation. If this action is moderate, then that of the extremities of the fibers in the brain, which correspond to the hand, will be moderate; and if this motion is violent enough to sever its parts, as happens when it is burned, the movement of the interior fibers of the brain will be proportionately stronger and more violent. This is what can be understood of what happens to our body when objects strike us; we must now see what happens to our soul.

V. The effect of objects on the soul and the reasons why the soul is unaware of the motion of the body's fibers.

It resides primarily, if I may so express it, in the part of the brain to which the filaments of our nerves lead. It is located there for the maintenance and preservation of all the parts of our body, and, consequently, it must be advised of all its changes and must be able to distinguish those that are agreeable to our body's constitution from those that are not, because it would be of no use to know them absolutely and without this relation to its body. Thus, although all these changes in our fibers really consist only in motion, which generally varies only in degree, the soul of necessity regards them as essential changes. For though they vary in themselves very little, changes in motion must always be taken as essential changes in relation to the preservation of the body.

The motion that causes pain, for example, often enough differs but little from that which causes a tickling sensation. There need not be any essential difference between these two motions, but there must be an essential difference between the tickling sensation and the pain that these motions cause in the soul. For the disturbance of the fibers accompanying the tickling sensation[a] is evidence to the soul of the well-being of its body, that it has sufficient strength to resist the object's impression, and that it need not fear being hurt by it. But the motion accompanying pain, being rather more violent, can rupture the body's fibers, and the soul must be warned of this by some unpleasant sensation so that it may guard against it. Thus, although the motions occurring in the body differ in themselves only in degree, nonetheless, if considered in relation to the preservation of our life, they can be said to differ essentially.

This is why our soul is unaware of the disturbances that objects excite in the fibers of our flesh. It would be of no use for the soul to know them, and it would not be thereby enlightened in order to judge whether the things surrounding us were capable of destroying or maintaining the body's equilibrium. But it feels affected by impressions that differ essentially and that, showing the qualities of objects in relation to the body, make it immediately and acutely aware of whether these objects are capable of doing it harm.

It should be considered, further, that if the soul perceived only what takes place in the hand when it is being burned, if it saw in it only the movement and rupture of fibers, it would hardly take any notice; it might even derive from it some whimsical satisfaction, like those simpletons who amuse themselves by breaking everything in furious orgies of destruction.

Or just as a prisoner would hardly be upset at seeing the walls enclosing him being demolished, and would even rejoice in the hope of soon being freed, so too if we perceived only the separation of the parts of our body when we were being burned, or were receiving some wound, we would soon be convinced that our

[a]This confused inference or natural judgment which applies to the body what the soul senses, is but what might be called a compound sensation. See what I have already said about natural judgments, and the first chapter of the third book, 3.

happiness was not contained in a body that prevents us from enjoying the things that ought to make us happy. Thus, we would be very content to see it destroyed.

Hence, it was with great wisdom that the Author of the union of our soul and body ordained that we should feel pain when a change capable of destroying it occurs in the body (as when a needle enters the flesh or fire separates some of its parts), and that we should feel a tickling sensation or a pleasant warmth when this movement is moderate, without perceiving what really happens in our bodies, or the movement of the fibers we have just spoken about. [There are three reasons for this:]

First, because while feeling pleasure and pain, which are things differing more than in degree, we more easily distinguish the objects that occasion them. Second, because if we must either embrace or flee the bodies surrounding us, this way of informing us is the quickest, and further, it less exhausts the capacity of a mind made only for God. Finally, because pleasure and pain are modifications of the soul that it feels in relation to the body, and that affect it more than the awareness of movement in the body's fibers—all of which forces the soul to take careful note of them and results in a very close union between the two parts of man. It is clear from all this that the senses were given us only for the preservation of our bodies and not for the acquisition of truth. . . .

In almost all sensations there are four different things that we confuse because they all occur instantaneously and together. This confusion is the basis for all other errors of our senses.

VI. Four things we confuse in each sensation.

The first is the *action* of the object, i.e., in heat, for example, the motion and *impact* of the particles of wood against the fibers of the hand.

The second is the *passion* of the sense organ, i.e., the agitation of the fibers of the hand caused by the agitation of the tiny particles of fire, which agitation is communicated to the brain, because otherwise the soul would sense nothing.

The third is the *passion*, sensation, or perception of the soul, i.e., what each of us feels when near fire.

The fourth is the *judgment* the soul makes that what it perceives is in the hand and in the fire. Now this natural judgment is only a sensation, but the sensation or natural judgment is almost always followed by another, free judgment that the soul makes so habitually that it is almost unable to avoid it.

Obviously, these are four different things that are not difficult to distinguish but that one is likely to confuse because of the close union between soul and body, which union prevents us from precisely distinguishing the properties of matter from those of mind.

Nonetheless, it is easy to see that, of the four things taking place in us when we perceive some object, the first two pertain to the body but the latter can pertain only to the soul—provided that, as I have assumed, some thought be given to the nature of the soul and of the body. . . .

BOOK THREE
PART TWO: THE PURE UNDERSTANDING.
THE NATURE OF IDEAS
Chapter One

❖

I. What is meant by ideas. That they really exist and are necessary in order to perceive any material object. II. A classification of all the ways external objects can be seen.

<I. What is meant by ideas.>

I think everyone agrees that we do not perceive objects external to us by themselves. We see the sun, the stars, and an infinity of objects external to us; and it is not likely that the soul should leave the body to stroll about the heavens, as it were, in order to behold all these objects. Thus, it does not see them by themselves, and our mind's immediate object when it sees the sun, for example, is not the sun, but something that is intimately joined to our soul, and this is what I call an *idea*. Thus, by the word *idea*, I mean here nothing other than the immediate object, or the object closest to the mind, when it perceives something, i.e., that which affects and modifies the mind with the perception it has of an object.

It should be carefully noted that for the mind to perceive an object, it is absolutely necessary for the idea of that object to be actually present to it—and about this there can be no doubt; but there need not be any external thing like that idea. For it often happens that we perceive things that do not exist, and that even have never existed—thus our mind often has real ideas of things that have never existed. When, for example, a man imagines a golden mountain, it is absolutely necessary that the idea of this mountain really be present to his mind. When a madman or someone asleep or in a high fever sees some animal before his eyes, it is certain that what he sees is not nothing, and that therefore the idea of this animal really does exist, though the golden mountain and the animal have never existed.

Yet given that men are naturally led, as it were, to believe that only corporeal objects exist, they judge of the reality and existence of things other than as they should. For as soon as they perceive an object, they would have it as quite certain that it exists, although it often happens that there is nothing external. In addition, they would have the object be exactly as they see it, which never happens. But as for the idea that necessarily exists, and that cannot be other than as it is seen, they ordinarily judge unreflectingly that it is nothing—as if ideas did not have a great number of properties, as if the idea of a square, for example, were not different from that of a circle or a number, and did not represent completely different things, which can never be the case for nonbeing, since nonbeing has no properties. It is therefore indubitable that ideas have a very real existence. But now let us examine their nature and essence, and let us see what there can be in the soul that might represent all things to it.

Everything the soul perceives belongs to either one of two sorts: either it is in the soul, or outside the soul. The things that are in the soul are its own thoughts, i.e., all its various modifications—for by the words *thought, mode of thinking,* or *modification of the soul,* I generally understand all those things that cannot be in the soul without the soul being aware of them through the inner sensation it has of itself—such as its sensations, imaginings, pure intellections, or simply conceptions, as well as its passions and natural inclinations. Now, our soul has no need of ideas in order to perceive these things in the way it does, because these things are in the soul, or rather because they are but the soul itself existing in this or that way—just as the actual roundness and motion of a body are but that body shaped and moved in this or that way.

But as for things outside the soul, we can perceive them only by means of ideas, given that these things cannot be intimately joined to the soul. Of these, there are two sorts: spiritual and material. As for the spiritual, there is reason to believe they can be revealed to the soul by themselves and without ideas. For although experience teaches us that we cannot communicate our thoughts to one another immediately and by ourselves, but only through speech or some other sensible sign to which we have attached our ideas, still it might be said that God has established this state of affairs only for the duration of this life in order to prevent the disorder that would now prevail if men could communicate as they pleased. But when order and justice reign, and we are delivered from the captivity of our body, we shall perhaps be able to communicate through the intimate union among ourselves, as the angels seem to be able to do in heaven. Accordingly, it does not seem to be absolutely necessary to have ideas in order to represent spiritual things to the soul, because they might be seen through themselves, though in imperfect fashion.

I shall not inquire[a] *here how two minds can be united, or whether they can in this way reveal their thoughts to each other. I believe, however, that the only purely intelligible substance is God's, that nothing can be revealed with clarity except in the light of this substance, and that a union of minds cannot make them visible to each other. For although we may be closely joined together, we are and shall be unintelligible to each other until we see each other in God, and until He presents us with the perfectly intelligible idea He has of our being contained in His being. Thus, although I may seem to allow that angels can by themselves show to each other both what they are and what they are thinking (which I really do not believe), I warn that it is only because I have no desire to dispute the*

---

[a]This paragraph is italicized because you may omit it as being too difficult to understand unless you know my views about the soul and the nature of ideas.

point—provided that you grant me what cannot be disputed, to wit, that you cannot see material things by themselves and without ideas.

In the seventh chapter I shall explain my view on how we know minds, and I shall show that for the moment we cannot know them entirely by themselves, although they might be capable of union with us. But here I am speaking mainly about material things, which certainly cannot be joined to our soul in the way necessary for it to perceive them, because with them extended and the soul unextended, there is no relation between them. Besides which, our souls do not leave the body to measure the heavens, and as a result, they can see bodies outside only through the ideas representing them. In this everyone must agree.

II. *A classification of all the ways external objects can be seen.*

We assert the absolute necessity, then, of the following: either (a) the ideas we have of bodies and of all other objects we do not perceive by themselves come from these bodies or objects; or (b) our soul has the power of producing these ideas; or (c) God has produced them in us while creating the soul or produces them every time we think about a given object; or (d) the soul has in itself all the perfections it sees in bodies; or else (e) the soul is joined to a completely perfect being that contains all intelligible perfections, or all the ideas of created beings.

We can know objects in only one of these ways. Let us examine, without prejudice, and without fear of the difficulty of the question, which is the likeliest way. Perhaps we can resolve the question with some clarity though we do not pretend to give demonstrations that will seem incontrovertible to everyone; rather, we merely give proofs that will seem very persuasive to those who consider them carefully, for one would appear presumptuous were one to speak otherwise.

BOOK THREE: PART TWO
Chapter Two

❧

That material objects do not transmit species resembling them.

The·most commonly held opinion is that of the Peripatetics, who hold that external objects transmit species that resemble them, and that these species are carried to the common sense by the external senses. They call these species *impressed*, because objects impress them on the external senses. These impressed species, being material and sensible, are made intelligible by the *agent*, or *active intellect*, and can then be received in the *passive intellect*. These species, thus spiritualized, are called *expressed* species, because they are expressed from the impressed species, and through them the *passive intellect* knows material things.

We shall not pause here to further investigate these lovely things and the different ways different philosophers conceive of them. For although they disagree about the number of faculties they attribute to the interior sense and to the understanding, and although there are many of them who doubt whether an *agent intellect* is needed in order to know sensible objects, still they practically all agree that external objects transmit species or images that resemble them, and with only this as their basis, they multiply their faculties and defend their *agent intellect*. As this basis has no solidity, as will be shown, it is not necessary to pause further in order to overthrow everything that has been built upon it.

We assert, then, that it is unlikely that objects transmit images, or species, that resemble them, and here are some reasons why. The first is drawn from the impenetrability of bodies. All objects (such as the sun, the stars, as well as those closer to our eyes) are unable to transmit species of a nature other than their own. This is why philosophers commonly say that these species are gross and material as opposed to the expressed species, which are spiritualized. These impressed species are therefore little bodies. They therefore cannot penetrate each other or the whole of the space between the earth and the heavens, which must be full of them. From this it is easy to conclude that they must run against and batter each other from all directions, and that hence they cannot make objects visible.

Furthermore, a great number of objects located in the sky and on earth can be seen from the same place or the same point; the species of all these objects would then have to be capable of being reduced to a point. Now since they are extended they are impenetrable; therefore, . . . and so on.

But not only can a great number of very large objects be seen from the same point; there is no point in the universe's vast stretches from which an almost infinite number of objects cannot be discovered, and even objects as large as the sun, moon, and heavens. In the entire world there is no point[a] where the species of all these things ought not meet—which is contrary to all indications of the truth.

The second reason is based on the change that occurs in the species. It is certain that the closer an object is, the larger its species must be, since we see the object as larger. Now, I do not see what can make this species diminish or what can become of the parts composing it when it was larger. But what is even harder to understand on their view is how, if we look at this object with magnifying glasses or a microscope, the species suddenly becomes five or six hundred times larger than it was before, for still less do we see with what parts it can so greatly increase its size in an instant.

The third reason is that when we look at a perfect cube, all the species of its sides are unequal, and yet we see all its sides as equally square. And likewise when we look at a picture of ovals and parallelograms, which can transmit only species of the same shape, we see in it only circles and squares. This clearly shows that the object we are looking at need not produce species that resemble it in order for us to see it.

Finally, it is inconceivable how a body that does not sensibly diminish could continually emit species in all directions, or how it could continually fill the vast spaces around it with them—and all this with inconceivable speed. For a hidden object can be seen at the very moment of its discovery from several million leagues away and from every direction. And, what seems stranger still, very active bodies, such as air and a few others, lack the force to emit images resembling them—as coarser and less active bodies, such as earth, stones, and almost all hard bodies do.

But I do not wish to linger to adduce all the reasons opposed to this view, since it would be an endless task and the least mental effort will yield an inexhaustible number of them. Those we have just given are enough, and even they are not necessary after what was said about this subject in the first book, where the errors of the senses were explained. But so many philosophers hold this view that I thought it necessary to say something about it in order to provoke them to reflect on their thoughts.

---

[a]To see how the impressions of visible objects, however opposed, can be communicated without being diminished, read the last two Eludications found at the end of this work.

BOOK THREE: PART TWO
Chapter Three

✤

That the soul does not have the power to produce ideas. The cause of our error in this matter.

The second view belongs to those who believe that our souls have the power of producing the ideas of the things they wish to think about, and that our souls are moved to produce them by the impressions that objects make on the body, though these impressions are not images resembling the objects causing them. According to them, it is in this that man is made after the image of God and shares in His power. Further, just as God created all things from nothing, and can annihilate them and create new things in their place, so man can create and annihilate ideas of anything he pleases. But there is good reason to distrust all these views that elevate man. These are generally thoughts that come from his pride and vanity, and not from the Father of lights.

This share in God's power that men boast of for representing objects to themselves and for several other particular actions is a share that seems to involve a certain independence (as it is generally explained). But it is also an illusory share, which men's ignorance and vanity makes them imagine. Their dependence upon the power and goodness of God is much greater than they think, but this is not the place to explain the matter. Let us try only to show that men do not have the power to form ideas of the things they perceive.

Since ideas have real properties, no one can doubt that they are real beings, or that they differ from one another, and that they represent altogether different things. Nor can it be reasonably doubted that they are spiritual and are very different from the bodies they represent. This seems to raise a doubt whether the ideas by means of which bodies are seen are not more noble than the bodies themselves. Indeed, the intelligible world must be more perfect than the material, terrestrial world, as we shall see in what follows. Thus, when it is claimed that men have the power to form such ideas as please them, one runs the risk of claiming that men have the power of creating beings worthier and more perfect than the world God has created. Yet this is never thought about, because an idea is fancied to be nothing since it cannot be sensed—or if it is considered as a being, it is only as a meager and insignificant being, because it is thought to be annihilated as soon as it is no longer present to the mind.

But even if it were true that ideas were only lesser and insignificant beings, still they are beings, and spiritual beings at that, and given that men do not have the power of creation, it follows that they are unable to produce them. For the production of ideas in the way they explain it is a true creation, and although they may try to palliate the temerity and soften the harshness of this view by saying that the production of ideas presupposes something whereas creation presupposes nothing, still they have not resolved the fundamental difficulty.

For it ought to be carefully noted that it is no more difficult to produce something from nothing than to produce it by positing another thing from which it cannot be made and which can contribute nothing to its production. For example, it is no more difficult to create an angel than to produce it from a stone, because given that a stone is of a totally contrary kind of being, it can contribute nothing to the production of an angel. But it can contribute to the production of bread, of gold, and such, because stone, gold, and bread are but the same extension differently configured, and they are all material things.

It is even more difficult to produce an angel from a stone than to produce it from nothing, because to make an angel from a stone (insofar as it can be done), the stone must first be annihilated and then the angel must be created, whereas simply creating an angel does not require anything to be annihilated. If, then, the mind produces its own ideas from the material impressions the brain receives from objects, it continuously does the same thing, or something as difficult, or even more difficult, as if it created them. Since ideas are spiritual, they cannot be produced from material images in the brain, with which they are incommensurable.

But if it be said that an idea is not a substance, I would agree—but it is still a spiritual thing, and as it is impossible to make a square out of a mind, though a square is not a substance, so a spiritual idea cannot be formed from a material substance, even though an idea is not a substance.

But even if the mind of man were granted a sovereign power of annihilating and creating the ideas of things, still it would never use it to produce them. For just as a painter, no matter how good he is at his art, cannot represent an animal he has never seen and of which he has no idea—so that the painting he would be required to produce could not be like this unknown animal—so a man could not form the idea of an object unless he knew it beforehand, i.e., unless he already had the idea of it, which idea does not depend on his will. But if he already has an idea of it, he knows the object, and it is useless for him to form another idea of it. It is therefore useless to attribute to the mind of man the power of producing its ideas.

It might be said that the mind has general and confused ideas that it does not produce, and that those of its own making are clearer, more distinct, particular ideas. But this amounts to the same thing. For just as an artist cannot draw the portrait of an individual in such fashion that he could be certain of having done a proper job unless he had a distinct idea of the individual, and indeed unless the subject were to sit for it—so a mind that, for example, has only the idea of being or of animal in general cannot represent a horse to itself, or form a very distinct idea of it, or be sure that the idea exactly resembles a horse, unless it already has an initial idea against which it compares the second. Now if it already has one idea, it is useless to form a second, and therefore the question about the first idea, . . . , and so on.

It is true that when we conceive of a square through pure intellection, we can still imagine it, i.e., perceive it by tracing an image of it for ourselves in the brain. But it should be noted, first, that we are neither the true nor the principal cause of the image (but this is too long a matter to be explained here), and second, that far from being more distinct and more accurate than the first idea, the second idea accompanying the image is accurate only because it resembles the first, which serves as a model [*regle*] for the second. For ultimately, the imagination and the senses themselves should not be taken as representing objects to us more distinctly than does the pure understanding, but only as affecting and moving the mind more. For the ideas of the senses and of the imagination are distinct only to the extent that they conform to the ideas of pure intellection.[a] The image of a square that the imagination traces in the brain, for example, is accurate and well formed only to the extent that it conforms to the idea of a square we conceive through pure intellection. It is this idea that governs the image. It is the mind that conducts the imagination and requires it, as it were, to consider occasionally whether the image it depicts is a figure composed of four straight and equal lines, and exactly right-angled—in a word, whether what one is imagining is like what one conceives.

After what has been said, I do not think anyone can doubt that those who claim the mind can form its own ideas of objects are mistaken, since they attribute to the mind the power of creating, and even of creating wisely and with order, although it has no knowledge of what it does—which is inconceivable. But the cause of their error is that men never fail to judge that a thing is the cause of a given effect when the two are conjoined, given that the true cause of the effect is unknown to them. This is why everyone concludes that a moving ball which strikes another is the true and principal cause of the motion it communicates to the other, and that the soul's will is the true and principal cause of movement in the arms, and other such prejudices—because it always happens that a ball moves when struck by another, that our arms move almost every time we want them to, and that we do not sensibly perceive what else could be the cause of these movements.

But when an effect does not so frequently follow something not its cause, there are still people who believe it to be caused by that thing, though not everyone falls into this error. For example, a comet appears and a prince dies, stones are

---

[a] "Tanto meliora esse judico quae oculis cerno, quanto pro sui natura viciniora sunt iis quae animo intelligo." Aug. *Vera religione*, ch. 3. "Quis bene se inspiciens non expertus est, tanto se aliquid intellexisse sincerius, quanto removere atque subducere intentionem mentis a corporis sensibus potuit." Aug. *De immortalite animae*, ch. 10.

exposed to the moon and are eaten by worms, the sun is in conjunction with Mars at the birth of a child and something extraordinary happens to the child. This is enough to convince many people that the comet, the moon, and the conjunction of the sun and Mars are the causes of the effects just noted and others like them; and the reason why not everyone is of the same belief is that these effects are not always observed to follow these things.

But given that all men generally have ideas of things present to the mind as soon as they want them, and that this occurs many times daily, practically everyone concludes that the will attending the production, or rather, the presence of ideas is their true cause, because at the time they see nothing they can assign as their cause, and because they believe that ideas cease to exist as soon as the mind ceases to perceive them and begin to exist again when they are represented to the mind. This is also why some people judge that external objects transmit images resembling them, as we have just pointed out in the preceeding chapter. Unable to see objects by themselves, but only through their ideas, they judge that the object produces the idea—because as soon as it is present, they see it; as soon as it is absent, they no longer see it; and because the presence of the object almost always attends the idea representing it to us.

Yet if men were not so rash in their judgments, they would conclude from the fact that the ideas of things are present to their mind as soon as they wish, only this, that in the order of nature their will is generally necessary for them to have these ideas, but not that the will is the true and principal cause that presents ideas to their mind, and still less that the will produces them from nothing or in the way they explain it. They should conclude not that objects transmit species resembling them because the soul ordinarily perceives them only when they are present, but only that the object is ordinarily necessary for the idea to be present to the mind. Finally, because a ball does not have the power to move itself, they should not judge that a ball in motion is the true and principal cause of the movement of the ball it finds in its path. They can judge only that the collision of the two balls is the occasion for the Author of all motion in matter to carry out the decree of His will, which is the universal cause of all things. He does so by communicating to the second ball part of the motion of the first, i.e., to speak more clearly, by willing that the latter ball should acquire as much motion in the same direction as the former loses, for[a] the motor force of bodies can only be the will of Him who preserves them, as we shall show elsewhere.

---

[a]See chapter 3 of the second part on Method, and the Elucidation of this chapter [15].

BOOK THREE: PART TWO
Chapter Four

❧

That we do not perceive objects by means of ideas created with us. That God does not produce ideas in us each time we need them.

The third view is held by those who would have it that all ideas are innate or created with us.

To see the implausibility of this view, it should be considered that there are in the world many totally different things of which we have ideas. But to mention only simple figures, it is certain that their number is infinite, and even if we fix upon only one, such as the ellipse, the mind undoubtedly conceives of an infinite number of different kinds of them when it conceives that one of its diameters may be infinitely lengthened while the other remains constant.

Likewise, an infinite number of different kinds of triangles can be conceived, given that the altitude can be infinitely increased or decreased while the base remains the same; moreover, and this is what I ask be noted here, the mind to some extent perceives this infinite number of triangles, although we can imagine very few of them and cannot simultaneously have particular and distinct ideas of many triangles of different kinds. But it should be especially noted that the mind's general idea of this infinite number of different kinds of triangles suffices to prove that if we do not conceive of all these different triangles by means of particular ideas, in short, if we do not comprehend the infinite, the fault does not lie with our ideas, and that our failure to grasp the infinite is only for lack of capacity and scope of mind. If a man were to apply himself to an investigation of the properties of all the different kinds of triangles, and even if he should continue his investigation forever, he would never want for further particular ideas. But his mind would exhaust itself for no purpose.

What I have just said about triangles is applicable to figures of five, six, a hundred, a thousand, of ten thousand sides, and so on to infinity. And if the sides of a triangle can have infinite relations with each other, making an infinity of different kinds of triangles, it is easy to see that figures of four, five, or a million sides can have even greater differences, since they can have a greater number of relations and combinations of their sides than can simple triangles.

The mind, then, perceives all these things; it has ideas of them; it is certain that it will never want for ideas should it spend countless centuries investigating even a single figure, and that if it does not perceive these figures in an instant, or if it does not comprehend the infinite, this is only because of its very limited scope. It has, then, an infinite number of ideas—what am I saying?—it has as many infinite numbers of ideas as there are different figures; consequently, since there is an infinite number of different figures, the mind must have an infinity of infinite numbers of ideas just to know the figures.

Now, I ask whether it is likely that God created so many things along with the mind of man. My own view is that such is not the case, especially since all this could be done in another, much simpler and easier way, as we shall see shortly. For as God always acts in the simplest ways, it does not seem reasonable to explain how we know objects by assuming the creation of an infinity of beings, since the difficulty can be resolved in an easier and more straightforward fashion.

But even if the mind had a store of all the ideas necessary for it to perceive objects, yet it would be impossible to explain how the soul could choose them to represent them to itself, how, for example, the soul could make itself instantly perceive all the different objects whose size, figure, distance and motion it discovers when it opens its eyes in the countryside. Through this means it could not even perceive a single object such as the sun when it is before the body's eyes. For, since the image the sun imprints in the brain does not resemble the idea we have of it (as we have proved elsewhere), and as the soul does not perceive the motion the sun produces in the brain and in the fundus of the eyes, it is inconceivable that it should be able to determine precisely which among the infinite number of its ideas it would have to represent to itself in order to imagine or see the sun and to see it as having a given size. It cannot be said, then, that ideas of things are created with us, or that this suffices for us to see the objects surrounding us.

Nor can it be said that God constantly produces as many new ideas as there are different things we perceive. This view is refuted well enough by what has just been said in this chapter. Furthermore, we must at all times actually have in us the ideas of all things, since we can at all times will to think about anything—which we could not do unless we had already perceived them confusedly, i.e., unless an infinite number of ideas were present to the mind; for after all, one cannot will to think about objects of which one has no idea. Furthermore, it is clear that the idea, or immediate object of our mind, when we think about limitless space, or a circle in general, or indeterminate being, is nothing created. For no created reality can be either infinite or even general, as is what we perceive in these cases. But all this will be seen more clearly in what follows.

BOOK THREE: PART TWO
Chapter Five

✤

That the mind sees neither the essence nor the existence of objects by considering its own perfections. That only God sees them in this way.

The fourth view is that the mind needs only itself in order to see objects, and that by considering itself and its own perfections, it can discover all external things.

It is certain that the soul sees in itself, and without ideas, all the sensations and passions that affect it at the moment—pleasure, pain, cold, heat, colors, sounds, odors, tastes, its love and hatred, its joy and sadness, and all the rest—because none of the soul's sensations and passions represent anything resembling them outside the soul, and are but modifications of which a mind is capable.[a] But the difficulty lies in knowing whether the ideas representing something outside the soul and resembling them to some extent (such as the ideas of the sun, of a house, a horse, a river, etc.) are merely modifications of the soul, as a result of which the mind would need only itself to represent external things to itself.

There are some people who do not hesitate to affirm that with the soul made for thinking, it has within itself all that it needs to perceive objects, i.e., by considering its own perfections, because given that the soul is indeed more noble than anything it distinctly conceives of, it can to some extent be said to contain them *eminently*, as the School would put it, i.e., in a way more noble and sublime than they are in themselves. They would have it that higher things contain the perfections of lower things in this way. Thus, given that they are the noblest creature they know of, these people claim to have within themselves in a spiritual way all that exists in the visible world, and to be able to modify themselves in such fashion as to perceive all that the human mind is capable of knowing. In a word, they would have the soul be like an intelligible world, which contains in itself all that the material and sensible world contains, and indeed, infinitely more.

But it seems to me rash to wish to maintain this view. Unless I am mistaken, it is natural vanity, love of independence, and the desire to be like Him who contains in Himself all beings that confound the mind and lead us to fancy that

---

[a]See Arnauld's *Dex vrayes et des fausses idées* [ch. 27].

we possess what in fact we do not. "Say not that you are a light unto yourself," says Saint Augustine,[a] for only God is a light unto Himself and can see all that He has produced and might produce by considering Himself.

It cannot be doubted that only God existed before the world was created and that He could not have produced it without knowledge or ideas; consequently, the ideas He had of the world are not different from Himself, so that all creatures, even the most material and terrestrial, are in God, though in a completely spiritual way that is incomprehensible to us.[b] God therefore sees within Himself all beings by considering His own perfections, which represent them to Him. He also knows their existence perfectly, because given that they depend for their existence on His will, and given that He cannot be ignorant of his own volitions, it follows that He cannot be ignorant of their existence, and consequently, God sees in Himself not only the essence of things but also their existence.

But such is not the case with created minds, which can see in themselves neither the essence nor the existence of things. They cannot see the essence of things within themselves since, given their own limitations, created minds cannot contain all beings as does God, who might be termed universal being, or simply, *He Who is*,[c] as He calls Himself. Therefore, since the human mind can know all beings, including infinite beings, and since it does not contain them, we have a sure proof that it does not see their essence in itself. For the mind not only sees things one after another in temporal succession, but it also perceives the infinite, though it does not comprehend it, as we have said in the preceding chapter. Consequently, being neither actually infinite nor capable of infinite modifications simultaneously, it is absolutely impossible for the mind to see in itself what is not there. It does not see the essence of things, therefore, by considering its own perfections or by modifying itself in different ways.

Nor does it see their existence in itself, because they do not depend for their existence upon its will, and because the ideas of things can be present to the mind though the things themselves might not exist. For everyone can have the idea of a golden mountain without there being a golden mountain in nature, and although one may rely on the reports of the senses to judge the existence of objects, nevertheless reason does not assure us that we should always believe our senses, since we clearly detect that they deceive us. When a man's blood is heated, for example, or simply when he is asleep, he sometimes sees country scenes, battles, and other such things before his eyes that are not present nor perhaps ever were. Undoubtedly, then, it is not in itself or through itself that the mind sees the existence of things, but rather it depends on something else for this.

[a]See the *Réponse aux vrayes & aux fausses idées*, & the *Réponse à une 3e Lettre de M. Arnauld*, in the fourth volume of my *Replies*. "Dic quia tu tibi lumen non es." Serm. 8, *De verbis Domini*.

[b]"Cum essentia Dei habeat in se quidquid perfectionis habet essentia cujusque rei alterius, & adhuc amplius, Deus in se ipso potest omnia propria cognitione cognoscere. Propria enim natura cujusque consistit, secundum quod per aliquem modum naturam Dei participat." St. Thomas, I. P. q. 14. art. 6.

[c]Exod. 3:14.

BOOK THREE: PART TWO
Chapter Six

❧

That we see all things in God.

In the preceding chapters we have examined four different ways in which the soul might see external objects, all of which seem to us very unlikely. There remains only the fifth, which alone seems to conform to reason and to be most appropriate for exhibiting the dependence that minds have on God in all their thoughts.

To understand this fifth way, we must remember what was just said in the preceding chapter—that God must have within Himself the ideas of all the beings He has created (since otherwise He could not have created them), and thus He sees all these beings by considering the perfections He contains to which they are related. We should know, furthermore, that through His presence God is in close union with our minds, such that He might be said to be the place of minds as space is, in a sense, the place of bodies. Given these two things, the mind surely can see what in God represents created beings, since what in God represents created beings is very spiritual, intelligible, and present to the mind. Thus, the mind can see God's works in Him, provided that God wills to reveal to it what in Him represents them. The following are the reasons that seem to prove that He wills this rather than the creation of an infinite number of ideas in each mind.

Not only does it strictly conform to reason, but it is also apparent from the economy found throughout nature that God never does in very complicated fashion what can be done in a very simple and straightforward way. For God never does anything uselessly and without reason. His power and wisdom are not shown by doing lesser things with greater means—this is contrary to reason and indicates a limited intelligence. Rather, they are shown by doing greater things with very simple and straightforward means. Thus, it was with extension alone that He produced everything admirable we see in nature and even what gives life and movement to animals. For those who absolutely insist on substantial forms, faculties, and souls in animals (different from their blood and bodily organs) to perform their functions, at the same time would have it that God lacks intelligence, or that He cannot make all these remarkable things with extension alone. They measure the power and sovereign wisdom of God by the pettiness of their own mind. Thus, since God can reveal everything to minds simply by willing that they see what is in their midst, i.e., what in Him is related to and represents these things, there is no likelihood that He does otherwise, or that He does so by producing as many infinities of infinite numbers of ideas as there are created minds.

But it should be carefully noted that we cannot conclude from their seeing all things in God in this way that our minds see the essence of God. God's essence is His own absolute being, and minds do not see the divine substance taken absolutely but only as relative to creatures and to the degree that they can participate in it. What they see in God is very imperfect, whereas God is most perfect. They see matter that is shaped, divisible, and so on, but there is nothing divisible or shaped in God, for God is all being, since He is infinite and comprehends everything; but He is no being in particular. Yet what we see is but one or more particular beings, and we do not understand this perfect simplicity of God, which includes all beings. In addition, it might be said that we do not so much see the ideas of things as the things themselves that are represented by ideas, for when we see a square, for example, we do not say that we see the idea of the square, which is joined to the mind, but only the square that is external to it.

The second reason for thinking that we see beings because God wills that what in Him representing them should be revealed to us (and not because there are as many ideas created with us as there are things we can perceive) is that this view places created minds in a position of complete dependence on God—the most complete there can be. For on this view, not only could we see nothing but what He wills that we see, but we could see nothing but what He makes us see. ''Non sumus sufficientes cogitare aliquid a nobis, tamquam ex nobis, sed sufficientia nostra ex Deo est.''[a] It is God Himself who enlightens philosophers in the knowledge that ungrateful men call natural though they receive it only from heaven. ''Deus enim illis manifestavit.''[b] He is truly the mind's light and the father of lights. ''Pater luminum''[c]—it is He who teaches men knowledge—''Qui docet hominem scientiam.''[d] In a word, He is the true light that illumines everyone who comes into the world: ''Lux vera quae illuminat omnem hominem venientem in hunc mundum.''[e]

For after all, it is difficult enough to understand distinctly the dependence our minds have on God in all their particular actions, given that they have everything we distinctly know to be necessary for them to act, or all the ideas of things present to their mind. And that general and confused term *concourse*, by means of which we would explain creatures' dependence on God, rouses not a single distinct idea in an attentive mind; and yet it is good that men should distinctly know that they are capable of nothing without God.

[a]2 Cor. 3:5.
[b]Rom. 1:19.
[c]James 1:17.
[d]Ps. 93:10.
[e]John 1:9.

But the strongest argument of all is the mind's way of perceiving anything. It is certain, and everyone knows this from experience, that when we want to think about some particular thing, we first glance over all beings and then apply ourselves to the consideration of the object we wish to think about. Now, it is indubitable that we could desire to see a particular object only if we had already seen it, though in a general and confused fashion. As a result of this, given that we can desire to see all beings, now one, now another, it is certain that all beings are present to our mind; and it seems that all beings can be present to our mind only because God, i.e., He who includes all things in the simplicity of His being, is present to it.

It even seems that the mind would be incapable of representing universal ideas of genus, species, and so on, to itself had it not seen all beings contained in one. For, given that every creature is a particular being, we cannot say that we see a created thing when, for example, we see a triangle in general. Finally, I think that sense can be made of the way the mind knows certain abstract and general truths only through the presence of Him who can enlighten the mind in an infinity of different ways.

Finally, of the proofs of God's existence, the loftiest and most beautiful, the primary and most solid (or the one that assumes the least)[a] is the idea we have of the infinite. For it is certain that (a) the mind perceives the infinite, though it does not comprehend it, and (b) it has a very distinct idea of God, which it can have only by means of its union with Him, since it is inconceivable that the idea of an infinitely perfect being (which is what we have of God) should be something created.

But not only does the mind have the idea of the infinite, it even has it before that of the finite. For we conceive of infinite being simply because we conceive of being, without thinking whether it is finite or infinite. In order for us to conceive of a finite being, something must necessarily be eliminated from this general notion of being, which consequently must come first. Thus, the mind perceives nothing except in the idea it has of the infinite, and far from this idea being formed from the confused collection of all our ideas of particular beings (as philosphers think), all these particular ideas are in fact but participations in the general idea of the infinite; just as God does not draw His being from creatures, while every creature is but an imperfect participation in the divine being.

Here is an argument that may prove demonstrative for those accustomed to abstract reasoning. It is certain that ideas are efficacious, since they act upon the mind and enlighten it, and since they make it happy or unhappy through the pleasant or unpleasant perceptions by which they affect it. Now nothing can act immediately upon the mind unless it is superior to it—nothing but God alone; for only the Author of our being can change its modifications. All our ideas, therefore, must be located in the efficacious substance of the Divinity, which alone is intelligible or capable of enlightening us, because it alone can affect intelligences. "Insinuavit nobis Christus," says Saint Augustine,[b] "animam

[a]This proof will be found treated at greater length in chapter 11 of the following book.
[b]*Tract.* 23 on St. John.

humanam & mentem rationalem non vegetari, non beatificari, NON ILLUMINARI NISI AB IPSA SUBSTANTIA DEI.''

Finally, God can have no other special end for His actions than Himself. This is a notion common to all men capable of a little reflection, and Sacred Scripture allows no doubt that God made all things for Himself. Therefore, not only must our natural love, i.e., the impulse He produces in our mind, tend toward Him but also the knowledge and light He gives it must reveal to us something in Him, for everything coming from God can be only for God. If God had made a mind and had given the sun to it as an idea, or immediate object of knowledge, it seems to me God would have made this mind and its idea for the sun and not for Himself.

God can make a mind in order for it to know His works, then, only if that mind to some extent sees God in seeing His works. As a result, it might be said that if we do not to some extent see God, we see nothing, just as if we do not love God, i.e., if God were not continuously impressing upon us the love of good in general, we would love nothing.[a] For, given that this love is our will, we could neither love nor will anything without it, since we can love particular goods only by directing toward these goods the impulse of love that God gives us for Himself. Thus, as we love something only through our necessary love for God, we see something only through our natural knowledge of God; and all our particular ideas of creatures are but limitations of the idea of the Creator, as all the impulses of the will toward creatures are only determinations of its impulse toward the Creator.

I do not think there are any theologians who will disagree that the impious love God with this natural love I am speaking about, and Saint Augustine and several other Fathers maintain as indubitable that the impious see eternal truths and moral rules in God. Accordingly, the view I am expounding should upset no one.[b] Here is how Saint Augustine expresses it:

> Ab illa incommutabilis luce veritatis etiam impius, dam ab ea avertitur, quodammodo tangitur. Hinc est quod etiam impii cogitant aeternitatem, & multa recte reprehendunt, recteque laudant in hominum moribus. Quibus ea tandem regulis judicant, nisi in quibus vident, quemadmodum quisque vivere debeat, etiam si nec ipsi eodem modo vivant? Ubi autem eas vident? Neque enim in sua natura. Nam cum procul dubio mente ista videantur, eorumque mentes constet esse mutabiles, has vero regulas immutabiles videat, quisquis in eis & hoc videre potuerit. . . ubinam ergo sunt istae regulae scriptae, nisi in libro lucis illius, quae veritas dicitur, unde lex omnis justa describitur. . . in qua videt quid operandum sit, etiam qui operatur injustitiam, & ipse est qui ab illa luce avertitur a qua tamen tangitur.[c]

Saint Augustine has an infinity of such passages by which he proves that we already see God in this life through the knowledge we have of eternal truths. The truth is uncreated, immutable, immense, eternal, and above all things. It is true by itself. It draws its perfection from no other thing. It renders creatures more

---

[a]Bk. 1, ch. 1.

[b]See the preface to the *Dialogues on Metaphysics,* and the *Réponse aux vrayes & fausses idées* chs. 7 & 21.

[c]Book 14, *De Trin.* ch. 15.

perfect, and all minds naturally seek to know it. Only God can have all these perfections. Therefore, truth is God. We see some of these immutable, eternal truths. Therefore, we see God. These are the arguments of Saint Augustine— ours are somewhat different, and we have no wish to make improper use of the authority of so great a man in order to support our own view.

We are of the opinion, then, that truths (and even those that are eternal, such as that twice two is four) are not absolute beings, much less that they are God Himself. For clearly, this truth consists only in the relation of equality between twice two and four. Thus, we do not claim, as does Saint Augustine, that we see God in seeing truths, but in seeing the *ideas* of these truths—for the ideas are real, whereas the equality between the ideas, which is the truth, is nothing real. When we say, for example, that the cloth we are measuring is three ells long, the cloth and the ells are real. But the equality between them is not a real being—it is only a relation found between the three ells and the cloth. When we say that twice two is four, the ideas of the numbers are real, but the equality between them is only a relation. Thus, our view is that we see God when we see eternal truths, and not that these truths are God, because the ideas on which these truths depend are in God—it might even be that this was Saint Augustine's meaning. We further believe that changeable and corruptible things are known in God, though Saint Augustine speaks only of immutable and incorruptible things, because for this to be so, no imperfection need be placed in God, since, as we have already said, it is enough that God should reveal to us what in Him is related to these things.

But although I may say that we see material and sensible things in God, it must be carefully noted that I am not saying we have sensations of them in God, but only that it is God who acts in us; for God surely knows sensible things, but He does not sense them. When we perceive something sensible, two things are found in our perception: *sensation* and pure *idea*. The sensation is a modification of our soul, and it is God who causes it in us. He can cause this modification even though He does not have it Himself, because He sees in the idea He has of our soul that it is capable of it. As for the idea found in conjunction with the sensation, it is in God, and we see it because it pleases God to reveal it to us. God joins the sensation to the idea when objects are present so that we may believe them to be present and that we may have all the feelings and passions that we should have in relation to them.

We believe, finally, that all minds see eternal laws, as well as other things, in God, but with a certain difference. They know order and eternal truths, and even the beings that God has made according to these truths or according to order, through the union these minds necessarily have with the Word, or the wisdom of God, which enlightens them, as has just been explained. But it is through the impression they constantly receive from the will of God, who leads them toward Him and who tries, as it were, to make their will entirely like His own, that they realize that the immutable order is their own indispensable law, an order which thus includes all eternal laws, such as that we ought to love good and avoid evil, that justice should be prized more than all riches, that it is better to obey God than to command men, and an infinity of other natural laws. For the knowledge of all these laws, or of the obligation minds are under to conform to the immutable order, is not different from the knowledge of this impression, which they always feel in themselves, though they do not always follow it through the free choice of their will, and which they know to be common to all minds, though it is not equally strong in all minds.

It is through this dependence, this relation, this union of our mind with the Word of God, and of our will with His love, that we are made in the image and likeness of God. And though this image may be greatly effaced through sin, yet it must subsist as long as we do. But if we bear the image of the Word humiliated upon earth, and if we follow the impulses of the Holy Ghost, this union of our mind with the Word of the Father, and with the love of the Father and the Son, will be reestablished and made indelible. We shall be like God if we are like the God-man. Finally, God will be entirely in us, and we in Him in a way much more perfect than that by which we must be in Him and He in us that we might subsist.

These are some of the reasons that might lead one to believe that minds perceive everything through the intimate presence of Him who comprehends all in the simplicity of His being. Each of us will judge[a] the matter according to the inner conviction he receives after seriously considering it. But I do not think there is any plausibility in any of the other ways of explaining these things, and this last way seems more than plausible. Thus, our souls depend on God in all ways. For just as it is He who makes them feel pain, pleasure, and all the other sensations, through the natural union He has established between them and our bodies, which is but His decree and general will, so it is He who makes them know all that they know through the natural union He has also established between the will of man and the representation of ideas contained in the immensity of the Divine being, which union is also but His general will. As a result of this, only He can enlighten us, by representing everything to us—just as only He can make us happy by making us enjoy all sorts of pleasures.

Let us hold this view, then, that God is the intelligible world or the place of minds, as the material world is the place of bodies; that from His power minds receive their modifications; that in His wisdom they find all their ideas; that through His love they receive their orderly impulses, and because His power and love are but Himself, let us believe with Saint Paul, that He is not far from any of us, and that in Him we live and move and have our being. "Non longe est ab unoquoque nostrum, in ipso enim vivimus, movemus, & sumus."[b]

---

[a]See the *Elucidations* [4]. The *Réponse au livre des vrayes & fausses Idées*. The *1ère Lettre contre la Défense* against this *Réponse:* the first two *Dialogues on Metaphysics*. The *Réponse à M. Régis*, and especially my *Réponse à une 3e Lettre de M. Arnauld*. There perhaps my view will be found more clearly demonstrated.

[b]Acts 17:28.

BOOK THREE: PART TWO
Chapter Seven

✤

I. The four different ways of perceiving things. II. How we know God. III. How we know bodies. IV. How we know our own souls. V. How we know pure spirits and the souls of other men.

In order to clarify and simplify the view I have just laid out concerning the way in which the mind perceives all the various objects of its knowledge, I must distinguish its four ways of knowing.

I. The four ways of perceiving things.

The first is to know things by themselves.

The second is to know them through their ideas, i.e., as I mean it here, through something different from themselves.

The third is to know them through *consciousness*, or inner sensation.

The fourth is to know them through conjecture.

We know things by themselves and without ideas when they are intelligible by themselves, i.e., when they can act on the mind and thereby reveal themselves to it. For the understanding is a purely passive faculty of the soul, whereas activity is found only in the will. Even its desires are not the true causes of ideas—they are but the occasional or natural causes of their presence as a result of the natural laws concerning the union of our soul with universal Reason, as I have explained elsewhere. We know things through their ideas when they are not intelligible by themselves, whether because they are corporeal or because they cannot affect the mind or reveal themselves to it. Through consciousness we know everything that is not distinct from ourselves. Finally, through conjecture we know those things that are different both from ourselves and from what we know either in itself or through ideas, such as when we believe that certain things are like certain others we know.

II. How we know God.

Only God do we know through Himself, for though there are other spiritual beings besides Him, which seem intelligible by their nature, only He can act on our mind and reveal Himself to it. Only God do we perceive by a direct and immediate perception. Only He can enlighten our mind with His own substance. Finally, only through the union we have with Him are we capable in this life of knowing what we know, as we have explained in the preceding chapter; for He is the only master, according to Saint Augustine,[a] ruling our mind without the mediation of any creature.

I cannot conceive how a created thing can represent the infinite, how being that is without restriction, immense and universal, can be perceived through an idea, i.e., through a particular being different from universal and infinite being. But as far as particular beings are concerned, there is no difficulty in conceiving how they can be represented by the infinite being that contains them in His most efficacious and, consequently, most intelligible substance. Thus, it must be said that (a) we know God through Himself, though our knowledge of Him in this life is very imperfect, and (b) we know corporeal things through their ideas, i.e., in God, since only God contains the intelligible world, where the ideas of all things are located.

But while we can see all things in God, it does not follow that we in fact do so—we see in God only the things of which we have ideas, and there are things we perceive without ideas, or know only through sensation.

III. How we know bodies.

Everything in this world of which we have some knowledge is either a mind or a body, a property of a mind or a property of a body. Undoubtedly, we know bodies with their properties through their ideas, because given that they are not intelligible by themselves, we can perceive them only in that being which contains them in an intelligible way. Thus, it is in God and through their ideas that we perceive bodies and their properties, and for this reason, the knowledge we have of them is quite perfect—i.e., our idea of extension suffices to inform us of all the properties of which extension is capable, and we could not wish for an idea of extension, figure, or motion more distinct or more fruitful than the one God gives us.

As the ideas of things in God include all their properties, whoever sees their ideas can also see all their properties successively; for when we see things as they are in God, we always see them in perfect fashion, and the way we see them would be infinitely perfect if the mind seeing them were infinite. What is lacking to our knowledge of extension, figures, and motion is the shortcoming not of the idea representing it but of our mind considering it.

IV. How we know our own soul.

Such is not the case with the soul, [which] we do not know through its idea—we do not see it in God; we know it only through *consciousness*, and because of this, our knowledge of it is imperfect. Our knowledge of our soul is limited to what we sense taking place in us. If we had never sensed pain, heat, light, and such, we would be unable to know whether the soul was capable of sensing these things, because we do not know it through its idea. But if we saw in

[a]Humanis mentibus nulla interposita natura praesidet.'' Aug. *De vera relig.* ch. 55.

God the idea corresponding to our soul, we would at the same time know, or at least could know all the properties of which it is capable—as we know, or at least can know, all the properties of which extension is capable, because we know extension through its idea.

It is true that we know well enough through our consciousness, or the inner sensation we have of ourselves, that our soul is something of importance. But what we know of it might be almost nothing compared to what it is in itself. If all we knew about matter were some twenty or thirty figures it had been modified by, we certainly would know almost nothing about it in comparison with what we can know about it through the idea representing it. To know the soul perfectly, then, it is not enough to know only what we know through inner sensation—since the consciousness we have of ourselves perhaps shows us only the least part of our being.

From what we have just said it might be concluded that although we know the existence of our soul more distinctly than the existence of both our own body and those surrounding us, still our knowledge of the soul's nature is not as perfect as our knowledge of the nature of bodies, and this might serve to reconcile the differing views[a] of those who say that nothing is known better than the soul, and those who claim to know nothing less.

This might also serve to prove that the ideas which represent to us things outside us are not modifications of our soul. For if the soul saw all things by considering its own modifications, it would have to know its own nature or essence more clearly than that of bodies, and all the sensations or modifications of which it is capable more clearly than the figures or modifications of which bodies are capable. However, it knows itself capable of a given sensation not through the perception it has of itself in consulting its idea but only through experience, whereas it knows that extension is capable of an infinite number of figures through the idea it has of extension. There are even certain sensations like colors and sounds which are such that most people cannot tell whether or not they are modifications of the soul, but there is no figure that everyone, through the idea he has of extension, does not recognize as the modification of a body.

What I have just said also shows why the modifications of the soul cannot be made known through definition; for since we know neither the soul nor its modifications through ideas but only through sensation, and since such sensations as, for example, pleasure, pain, heat, and so on, are not attached to any words, it is clear that if someone had never seen color or felt heat, he could not be made to know these sensations through any definition of them that might be given him. Now, given that men have their sensations only on account of their body, and given that their bodies are not all disposed in the same way, it often happens that words are equivocal, that the words we use to express the modifications of our soul mean just the opposite of what we intend, and that we often make people think of bitterness, for example, when we believe we are making them think of sweetness.

---

[a]See the Elucidations [11].

Although our knowledge of our soul is not complete, what we do know of it through consciousness or inner sensation is enough to demonstrate its immortality, spirituality, freedom, and several other attributes we need to know. And this seems to be why God does not cause us to know the soul, as He causes us to know bodies, through its idea. The knowledge that we have of our soul through consciousness is imperfect, granted; but it is not false. On the other hand, that knowledge we have of bodies through sensation or consciousness, if the confused sensation we have of what takes place in our body can be called consciousness, is not only imperfect, but also false. We therefore needed an idea of the body to correct our sensations of it—but we need no idea of our soul, since our consciousness of it does not involve us in error, and since to avoid being mistaken in our knowledge of it, it is enough not to confuse it with the body—and reason enables us to do this since our idea of the body reveals to us that the modalities of which it is capable are quite different from those we sense. Finally, if we had an idea of the soul as clear as that which we have of the body, that idea would have inclined us too much to view the soul as separated from the body. It would have thus diminished the union between our soul and body by preventing us from regarding it as dispersed through all our members, though I shall not further explain the matter here.

V. How we know other men's souls.

Of all the objects of our knowledge, only the souls of other men and pure intelligences remain; and clearly we know them only through conjecture. At present we do not know them either in themselves or through their ideas, and as they are different from ourselves, we cannot know them through consciousness. We conjecture that the souls of other men are of the same sort as our own. We suppose them to feel what we feel in ourselves, and even when these sensations have no relation to the body, we are certain we are not mistaken because we see in God certain ideas and immutable laws from which we know with certainty that God acts uniformly in all minds.

I know that twice two is four, that it is better to be just than rich, and I am not mistaken in believing that others know these truths as well as I do. I love pleasure and good, I abhor pain and evil, I want to be happy, and I am not mistaken in believing that all men, the angels, and even demons have these same inclinations. I even know that God will never make a mind that does not desire to be happy, or that can desire to be unhappy. But I know this with evidence and certainty because it is God who teaches it to me—for who else but God could reveal to me His designs and volitions? But when the body plays a part in what happens in me, I am almost always mistaken in judging others by myself. I feel heat, I see something of a certain size, a certain color, I taste such and such a flavor upon the approach of certain bodies—but I am mistaken if I judge others by myself. I am subject to certain passions, I have a liking or an aversion for such and such things, and I judge that others are like me—but my conjecture is often false. Thus, the knowledge we have of other men is very liable to error if we judge them only by the sensations we have of ourselves.

If there are beings different from God and ourselves, as well as from bodies and pure spirits, they are unknown to us. I can hardly persuade myself of their existence, and after examining the arguments of certain philosophers holding that there are these things, I have found them unsound. This reinforces our view that since all men have the same nature, we all have the same ideas, because we all need to know the same things.

From
BOOK FOUR
Chapter Eleven

✤

. . . [S]o that we shall be able to understand Descartes's proof for the existence of God still more distinctly, and to reply more clearly to any criticisms one could make of it, here is what it seems to me must be added to it. One must remember that when we see a creature, we see it neither in itself nor of itself, for we see it (as we proved in the third book) only through the perception of certain perfections in God that represent it. Thus, we can see the essence of this creature without seeing its existence, i.e., we can see its idea without seeing it; we can see in God that which represents it without its existing. It is uniquely because of this that necessary existence is not included in the idea that represents it, since it is not necessary for it actually to exist in order for us to see it, unless we claim that created objects are immediately visible, intelligible in themselves, and capable of illuminating, affecting, and modifying intelligences. But it is not the same with infinitely perfect being; one can see it only in itself, for nothing finite can represent the infinite. Therefore, one cannot see God without His existing; one cannot see the essence of an infinitely perfect being without seeing its existence; one cannot conceive it simply as a possible being; nothing limits it; nothing can represent it. Therefore, if one thinks of it, it must exist.

This reasoning appears conclusive to me. Yet there are people who support the proposition that the finite can represent the infinite; and that the modes of our soul, although finite, are essentially representative of infinitely perfect being, and generally, of all that we perceive, a gross error, which by its consequences destroys the certitude of all the sciences, as is easy to prove. But it is so false that the modes of the soul are representative of all beings that they cannot be representative of any, not even the being of which they are modes: for although we have an inner sensation of our existence and of our actual modes, we do not know them at all.

Certainly the soul has no clear idea of its substance, according to what I mean[a] by *clear idea*. It cannot discover by examining itself whether it is capable of this or that modification it has never had. It truly experiences its pain, but it does not know it; it does not know how its substance must be modified in order to suffer pain, and to suffer one pain rather than another. There is a great difference

[a]See ch. 7, pt. 2, bk. 3, and the Elucidation relating to it [10].

51

between sensing and knowing itself. God, who continually acts in the soul, knows it perfectly; He sees clearly, without suffering pain, how the soul must be modified to suffer pain, whereas the soul, on the other hand, suffers pain and does not know it. God knows it without feeling it, and the soul feels it without

God knows the nature of the soul clearly because He finds in Himself a clear and representative idea of it. God, as Saint Thomas says,[a] knows His substance or His essence perfectly, and as a result He discovers all the ways in which created things can participate in His substance. Hence His substance is truly representative of the soul, because it contains its eternal model or archetype. For God can only draw His knowledge from Himself. He sees in His essence the ideas or essences of all possible beings, and in His volitions (He sees) their existence and all its circumstances. But the soul is only darkness to itself; its light comes to it from elsewhere. Of all the beings that it knows and can know, none is a resemblance of its substance, and none participates in it. It does not contain their perfections eminently. The modes of the soul therefore cannot be, as in God, representative of the essence or the idea of possible beings. It is therefore necessary to distinguish the ideas that enlighten us, that affect us, and that represent these beings, from the modes of our soul, i.e., from our perceptions of them. And as the existence of created things does not depend upon our wills but upon that of the Creator, it is again clear that we cannot be assured of their existence except by some kind of revelation, either natural or supernatural.

But in addition, if all beings were resemblances of our soul, how could it see them in its supposedly representative modes, the soul that does not know its substance perfectly, "secundum omnem modum quo cognoscibilis est," that does not know how it is modified through its perception of objects—what am I saying?—that confuses itself with the body, and often does not know which modes belong to it; the soul that when moved, or affected by the efficacy of ideas, experiences its modes or perceptions within itself (for where else would it experience them?) but that will never discover clearly what it is, its nature, its properties, all the modes of which it is capable, until the luminous and always efficacious substance of the divinity reveals to the soul the idea that represents it, the intelligible mind, the eternal model upon which it has been formed? But let us try to clarify this matter further, to force the attentive mind to yield to this proposition, which has seemed clear to me in and of itself: that nothing finite can represent the infinite, and that therefore God exists, since we think of Him.

It is certain that nothingness or the false is not perceptible or intelligible. To see nothing is not to see; to think of nothing is not to think. It is impossible to perceive a falsehood, a relation of equality, for example, between two and two, and five; for this or any like relation that does not exist can be believed but

---

[a]"Deus essentiam suam perfecte cognoscit. Unde cognoscit eam secundum omnem modum quo cognoscibilis est. Potest autem cognosci non solum secundum quod in se est, sed secundum quod est participabilis, secundum aliquem modum similitudinis a creaturis. Una quaeque autem creatura habet propriam speciem secundum quod aliquo modo participat divinae essentiae similitudinem. Sic igitur in quantum Deus cognoscit suam essentiam ut sic imitabilem a tali creatura cognoscit eam ut propiam rationem & ideam hujus creaturae; & similiter de aliis," I. p. q. 15. art. 2. V quaest. 14. art. 6.

certainly cannot be perceived because nothingness is not perceptible. Properly speaking, this is the first principle of all our knowledge; it is also the one with which I began the *Dialogues on Metaphysics,* whose first two dialoques might be read with profit here. For the principle generally accepted by the Cartesians, that whatever is clearly conceived to be contained in the idea representing a thing can be asserted of that thing, depends on it; and this principle is true only if we assume that ideas are immutable, necessary, and divine. For if our ideas were only our perceptions, if our modes were representative, how would we know that things correspond to our ideas, since God does not think, and consequently does not act, according to our perceptions but according to His own; and therefore He did not create the world according to our perceptions but in accordance with His ideas, on its eternal model that He finds in His essence. Now it follows from this that nothingness is not perceptible, and that everything we see clearly, directly, immediately, necessarily exists. I say what we immediately see, attest to, or conceive; for to speak strictly, the objects we immediately see are very different from those we see externally, or rather from those we think we see or look at; for in one sense it is true that we do not see these latter, since we can see, or rather believe we see, external objects that are not there, notwithstanding the fact that nothingness is not perceptible. But there is a contradiction in saying that we can immediately see what does not exist, for this is to say that at the same time we see and do not see, since to see nothing is not to see.

But although something must be in order to be perceived, everything that is, is not thereby perceptible in itself; for in order to be so, it must be able to act immediately upon the soul, it must be able of itself to enlighten, affect, or modify minds. Otherwise, our soul, which is purely passive so far as being able to perceive, will never perceive it. For even if the soul is imagined to be in the object and to penetrate it, as it is normally assumed to be in the brain and to penetrate it, the soul could not perceive it, since it cannot even discover the particles composing its brain, where it is said to make its principal residence. This is because there is nothing perceptible and intelligible in itself except what can act upon minds.

Nevertheless, let us assume these two false propositions: (1) that all reality can be perceived by the supposed action of the mind, and (2) that the soul does not have merely an inner sensation of its being and modes but that it knows them perfectly. Provided only that you agree with me that nothingness is not perceptible, as I have just demonstrated, it is very easy to conclude from this that the modes of the soul cannot represent the infinite. For we cannot see three realities where there are only two, since we would see a nothingness, a reality that would not be. We cannot see a hundred real things where there are only forty, for we would see sixty real things that would not be at all. Therefore, we cannot see the infinite in the soul or in its finite modes, for we would see an infinite that would not exist. Now, nothingness is neither perceptible nor intelligible; therefore, the soul cannot see in its substance or in its modes an infinite reality, for example, that intelligible extension which one sees so clearly to be infinite that one is certain the soul could never exhaust it. But to be able to represent the infinite is not <merely> to be able to perceive it, or to be able to have a very slight or infinitely limited perception of it, such as we have; it is to be able to perceive it in itself, and consequently to contain it, so to speak (since nothingness cannot be perceived) and to contain it in such a way that it is intelligible or efficacious in itself, and capable of affecting the intelligent substance of the soul.

It is clear, then, that the soul, its modes, or anything finite, cannot represent the infinite, that we cannot see the infinite except in itself and in virtue of the efficacy of its substance, that the infinite does not and cannot have an archetype, or an idea distinct from it, that represents it, and that therefore if we think of the infinite, it must exist. But certainly we do think of it; we have of it, I do not say an *understanding* or a perception that describes and embraces it, but some perception of it, i.e., an infinitely limited perception, by contrast to a perfect understanding.

It should be noted carefully that it takes neither more thought nor a greater capacity for thinking to have an infinitely limited perception of the infinite than to have a perfect perception of something finite, since all finite magnitude, compared to or divided by the infinite, is to this finite magnitude as this same magnitude is to the infinite. This is evident by the same argument that proves that $1/1000$ is to 1 as 1 is to 1,000; that two, three, or four millionths is to two, three, or four as two, three, or four is to two, three, or four million. For even if the zeros are infinitely increased, it is clear that the proportion always remains the same. This is because a finite magnitude or reality is equivalent to an infinitely small reality of the infinite, or in relation to the infinite; I say in relation to the infinite, because the large and the small are so only relatively speaking. Hence, it is certain a mode or finite perception can in itself be the perception of the infinite, provided that the perception of the infinite is infinitely small in relation to an infinite perception, or to the perfect understanding of the infinite.

To try to understand more distinctly how a finite mind can perceive the infinite, let us imagine that the soul's capacity for perceiving it is, for example, of four degrees, and that the idea of its hand or of a foot of extension affects it so vividly with pain that the soul's entire capacity for thought is filled by it. It is clear that if the idea of two feet of extension affects it with half this, its capacity for thought will suffice to perceive this extension. In the same way, if the immediate object affecting it is a million times greater, but only affects it with a force one-millionth of the former, its capacity for thought will suffice to perceive it; and the product, so to speak, of the infinity of the object and the infinitely small perception will always equal the soul's capacity for thought. For the product of the infinite and the infinitely small is a finite and constant magnitude, as is the soul's thinking capacity. This is evident, and it is the foundation of the property of hyperbolas between asymptotes, the product of whose abscissae increasing to infinity and the ordinates infinitely decreasing, is always equal to the same magnitude. Now, the product of infinity and zero is certainly zero, and our capacity for thinking is not zero; it is not null. It is therefore clear that our mind, although finite, can perceive the infinite, but by virtue of a perception that, though infinitely weak, is certainly quite real.

It must be noted above all that one should not judge the magnitude of objects or the reality of ideas according to their strength and vivacity, or, to speak with the schools, according to the degree of *intention* of the modes or perceptions by which ideas affect our soul. The point of a thorn that pricks me, a glowing coal that burns me, does not have as much reality as the countryside I see. Nonetheless, my capacity for thinking is filled more by the pain of the prick or by the burn than by the sight of the countryside. In the same way, when my eyes are open in the middle of a countryside, I have a sensible perception of a limited extension that is much more vivid and that occupies my soul more than the perception I have when I think of the extension with my eyes closed. But the idea of extension that affects me through the sensation of various colors does not have more reality than the one that affects me only by pure intellection even when my eyes are closed; for through pure intellection I see extension infinitely beyond that which I see with open eyes. It is therefore not necessary to judge, I do not say the efficacy, but the reality of ideas according to the strength with which they affect us; but it is necessary to judge the extent of their reality by what we discover in them, however weak be the mode by which they affect us, however feeble the perception we have of them. It is necessary to judge of their reality because we perceive it, and because nothingness cannot be perceived. I say this so it will be understood there is no contradiction in saying the infinite can be perceived by a finite perceptual capacity, and to disabuse those who, deceived by this supposed contradiction, maintain that we have no idea of the infinite, notwithstanding the inner sensation that teaches us that we actually think about the infinite, or, to speak as others, that we naturally have the idea of God or of the infinitely perfect being.

I could have proved that the soul's modes are not representative of the infinite or of anything else, or that ideas are very different from our perceptions of them, by proofs other than the ones I have just drawn from this common notion, that nothingness is not perceptible. For it is clear that the soul's modes are changeable but ideas are immutable; that its modes are particular, but ideas are universal and general to all intelligences; that its modes are contingent, but ideas are eternal and necessary; that its modes are obscure and shadowy, but ideas are very clear and luminous (i.e., its modes are only obscurely, though vividly, felt, but ideas are clearly known as the foundation of all the sciences); that these ideas are indeed efficacious because they act in the mind, they enlighten it and make it happy or unhappy, which is evident by the pain that the idea of the hand causes in those who have had an arm cut off. But I have already written so much about the nature of ideas in this and many other works that I think I have some right to direct the reader to those places.

It is as evident, then, that there is a God as it is to me that I am. I conclude that I am because I experience myself, and because nothing cannot be experienced. I conclude in the same way that God exists, that the infinitely perfect being exists, because I perceive it, and because nothing cannot be perceived, nor consequently can the infinite be perceived in the finite. . . .

From
BOOK FIVE
Chapter Five

✦

That the mind's perfection consists in its union with God through its knowledge of truth and love of virtue, whereas its imperfection springs only from its dependence on the body because of the disorder of its senses and passions.

The least reflection suffices to see that the good of the mind is necessarily something spiritual. Bodies are inferior to the mind, they cannot act on it through their own powers, they cannot even be immediately related to it, and finally they are not intelligible by themselves. They therefore cannot be its good. Spiritual things, on the other hand, are by their nature intelligible, they can be immediately related to the mind; they therefore can be its good, given that they are superior to the mind. For in order for something to be the mind's good it is not enough for it to be spiritual like the mind, it must also be superior to it. It must be able to act on the mind, enlighten it, reward it; otherwise, it can make the mind neither happier nor more perfect, and as a result, it cannot be its good. Of all intelligible or spiritual things, only God is in this way superior to the mind; it therefore follows that only God is, or can be, our true good. Therefore, we can become happier and more perfect only through the possession of God.

Everyone is convinced that knowledge of truth and love of virtue make the mind more perfect, that mental blindness and disorders of the heart make it more imperfect. Knowledge of truth and love of virtue, therefore, cannot be anything other than the mind's union with God and a kind of possession of God, whereas mental blindness and disorders of the heart cannot be anything other than the mind's separation from God and its union with something below it, i.e., with the body, since only this union can make it unhappy and imperfect. Thus, to know God is to know the truth or to know things according to the truth, and to love God is to love virtue or to love things to the extent to which they are worthy of love, or according to the rules of virtue.

The mind is, as it were, between God and body, between good and evil, between that which enlightens it and that which blinds it, that which sets it in order and that which disrupts it, between that which can make it perfect and happy and that which can make it unhappy and imperfect. When it discovers some truth or sees things as they are in themselves, it sees things in God's ideas, i.e., with a clear and distinct perception of what represents them. For, as I have already said, man's mind does not contain in itself the perfections or ideas of all the beings that it can perceive; it is not universal being. Thus, it does not see in itself things that are different from itself. It is not instructed or enlightened through its own resources, for its own perfection and enlightenment do not depend on it—it needs the immense light of eternal truth to be enlightened. Thus, when the mind knows the truth, it is united to God, and, to a certain extent, knows and possesses God.

But not only might we say that the mind that knows the truth to a certain extent also knows God who contains the truth, we might even say that to a certain extent it knows things as God knows them. Indeed, this mind knows their true relations, which God also knows. This mind knows them in the perception of God's perfections that represent them, and God, too, knows them in this way. For God neither senses nor imagines, but sees in Himself, in the intelligible world He contains, the material and sensible world He has created. The same is true of a mind that knows the truth; it neither senses nor imagines—sensations and phantasms represent only false relations to the mind, and whoever discovers the truth perceives it only in the intelligible world to which the mind is joined and in which God Himself sees it, for the material and sensible world is not intelligible by itself. Everything the mind clearly sees, then, it sees in the light of God even as does God Himself, although it sees them only in a way that is very imperfect and therefore different from the way in which God sees them. Thus, when the mind perceives the truth, not only is it joined to God, not only does it possess God and to a certain extent see God, but it also in a sense perceives the truth as God perceives it.

Likewise, when we love according to the rules of virtue, we love God. For when we love according to these rules, the impression of love that God continuously produces in our heart in order to incline us toward Him is neither diverted by free will nor converted into self-love. All the mind then does is to freely follow this impression that God gives it. Now, since God never gives it an impression that does not lead toward Him, since He acts only for Himself, to love according to the rules of virtue is clearly to love God.

But not only is this to love God, it is also to love as God loves. God loves only Himself—He loves His creations only because they are related to His perfections, and He loves them to the extent to which they have this relation—in the final analysis God loves Himself and the things He has created with the same love. To love according to the rules of virtue is to love God alone and to love Him in all things; it is to love things to the extent to which they participate in the goodness and the perfections of God, since this is to love them to the extent to which they are worthy of love; finally, it is to love with the impression of the same love by which God loves Himself, for it is God's self-love and everything related to it that animates us when we love as we should love. We love, therefore, as God loves.

It is clear, therefore, that knowledge of truth and love of virtue together constitute our entire perfection, since they are the ordinary consequences of our union with God and give us possession of Him to the extent to which we are capable of it in this life. Mental blindness and derangement of heart, on the other hand, together constitute our entire imperfection. They too are the consequences of a union of our mind with our body, as I have proved in several places while showing that we never know truth or love true good when we follow the impressions of our senses, imagination, or passions.

These things are clear. Yet men, all of whom fervently desire the perfection of their being, hardly bother about strengthening the union they have with God and work constantly to strengthen and extend the one they have with sensible things. The cause of such an extreme disorder cannot be explained at too great a length.

The possession of good must naturally produce two effects in its possessor. It should make him more perfect and at the same time happier; but this does not always happen. I grant the mind cannot actually possess some good and at the same time not be more perfect; but it can actually possess some good without being happier. Those who best know the truth and most love the goods worthiest of love are always more perfect than those in a state of blindness and disorder, but they are not always happier. The same is true of evil—it should make us imperfect and unhappy; but although it always makes men more imperfect, it does not always make them unhappier, or it does not make them unhappy to the extent to which it makes them imperfect. Virtue is often hard and distasteful and vice easy and pleasant, and it is mainly through faith and hope that the righteous are truly happy while the wicked revel in their pleasures. This should not be the case, but it is. Sin has caused this disorder, as I have just explained in the preceding chapter, and it is this disorder that is the main cause not only of all our heart's derangements but also of our mind's blindness and ignorance.

This disorder convinces our imagination that the body can be the mind's good because, as I have already said several times, pleasure is the sensible mark or sign of good. Now of all the pleasures that we enjoy here below, the most sensible are those that we imagine we receive through the body. Without much thought we therefore judge that the body can be, and in fact is, our good. For it is very difficult to fight natural instinct and to resist the persuasion of sensation— indeed, we do not even think about them. We do not think about the disorder of sin. We do not consider that bodies can act on the mind only as occasional causes, that the mind cannot immediately or by itself possess anything corporeal and cannot unite itself to an object except through its knowledge and love, that only God is above it and can reward or punish it though sensations of pleasure or pain, or can enlighten or move it—in a word, only He can act on it. These truths, though very clear to attentive minds, are not as convincing as the deceptive experience of sense impressions.

When we consider something as part of ourselves or ourselves as part of something else, we judge that our good consists in being joined to it, we have a love for it, and our love increases as the thing in question seems to be a greater part of the whole that we make up together with it. Now there are two kinds of proofs that convince us that something is part of ourselves: the instinct of sensation and the evidence of reason.

Through the instinct of sensation, I am persuaded that my soul is joined to my body, or that my body is part of my being; I have no evidence for this. I do not know it through the light of reason, but only through the pain or pleasure I sense when objects strike me. Our hand is pricked, and we feel pain in it; therefore, our hand is part of ourselves. Our clothing gets torn, and we do not feel anything; therefore, our clothing is not part of ourselves. Our hair can be cut but not torn out without pain. This bothers philosophers; they do not know what to say, but their dilemma proves that even the wisest of men judge by means of the instinct of sensation rather than by the light of reason as to whether something is part of themselves. For were they to judge the matter by the light of reason and its evidence, they would soon realize that the mind and the body are two entirely contrary kinds of beings, that the mind cannot by itself join itself to the body, and that only through the union it has with God is the soul hurt when the body is struck—as I have explained elsewhere. Only through the instinct of sensation, therefore, do we regard our body and all sensible things to which we are joined as part of ourselves, i.e., as parts of what thinks and senses in us, for what is not cannot be known with the evidence of reason, which never reveals anything but the truth.

But with intelligible things just the opposite is the case, for by the light of reason we recognize the relation that we have with them. Through the mind's clear vision we discover that we are united to God in a closer and more essential way than we are to our bodies, that without God we are nothing, that without Him we can know nothing, do nothing, will nothing, and sense nothing, that He is our all, or that with Him we make a whole—if it may be so expressed—of which we are an infinitely small part. The light of reason reveals to us a thousand reasons for loving only God and scorning bodies as unworthy of our love. Not through the instinct of sensation are we persuaded that God is our all—unless it is through the grace of Jesus Christ, which in certain people causes this sensation in order to help them overcome the opposite sensation by which they are joined to the body. For God as the Author of nature leads minds to His love through enlightened knowledge and not by instinctive knowledge. From what we can tell, only since the Fall has God as the Author of grace added instinct and prevenient delight to illumination because our light is now greatly diminished and is incapable of leading us to God, and because the strain of pleasure or of the contrary instinct continuously weakens it and makes it ineffective.

Thus, we discover through the light of the mind that we are united to God and to the intelligible world He contains, and through sensation we come to believe that we are joined to our body, and through our body to the sensible world that God has created. But as our sensations are more lively and more frequent, affect us more, and are even stronger than our illuminations, we should not be surprised that our sensations excite us and awaken our love for all sensible things, while our illuminations dissipate and vanish without arousing any desire in us for the truth. . . .

From
ELUCIDATION TEN

✤

On the nature of ideas, in which I explain how all things, eternal laws, and truths, are seen in God.

I hoped that what I said about the nature of ideas would have been enough to show that it is God who enlightens us, but experience has taught me that there are many people who are incapable of sufficiently close attention to understand the arguments that I have given for this principle. What is abstract is incomprehensible to most men. Only what is sensible awakens them, and fixes and sustains their mind's perception. They cannot consider and hence cannot understand what does not come under the senses or the imagination. This is something that I have said often, but that bears repetition.

It is evident that bodies are not visible by themselves and that they cannot act on our mind or represent themselves to it. This needs no proof—it can be seen through simple perception with no need of reasoning, for the slightest attention of the mind to the clear idea of matter suffices to show it. This is infinitely more certain than that bodies communicate their motion when they collide; but it is certain only to those who silence their senses in order to listen to their reason. Thus, everyone believes, though utterly without foundation, that bodies can move one another, because the senses say so; but no one believes that bodies are by themselves entirely invisible and incapable of acting on the mind, because the senses do not say so and seem to say the contrary.

Nonetheless, there are some people whose firm and steadfast reason rises to the most abstract of truths; they meditate attentively and they courageously resist the impression of their senses and imagination. But the body gradually weighs down the mind, and they fall back. These ideas vanish, and as the imagination stirs up livelier and more sensible ideas, the ideas of abstract truths then seem to be only wraiths exciting fear and mistrust.

We are easily led to mistrust people or things with which we are unfamiliar, or which do not afford us some sensible pleasure, for it is pleasure that wins the heart and familiarity that calms the uncertain mind. Thus, those who are unaccustomed to abstract or metaphysical truths are easily persuaded that we are trying only to lead them astray when we would enlighten them. With mistrust and with a kind of loathing do they look at non-pleasant, non-sensible ideas, and the love they have for repose and felicity soon delivers them from this troubling perception that seems incapable of satisfying them.

If the question before us were not of the greatest importance, the reasons I have just given (as well as certain others I need not relate) would preclude further discussion—for I can see that whatever I might say on this topic will never penetrate the minds of certain people. But it seems to me that the principle that only God enlightens us, and that He enlightens us only through the manifestation of an immutable and necessary wisdom or reason so conforms to religion, and furthermore, that this principle is so absolutely necessary if a sound and unshakable foundation is to be given to any truth whatsoever, that I feel myself under an indispensible obligation to explain and defend it as much as I possibly can. I prefer to be called a visionary, or one of the Illuminati, or any of the lovely things with which the imagination (always sarcastic in insignificant minds) usually answers arguments it does not understand and against which it is defenseless, than to agree that bodies can enlighten me, that I am my own master, reason, and light, and that in order to be well-versed in anything I need only consult myself or other men who can perhaps fill my ears with noise, but who certainly cannot fill my mind with light. Here, then, are several more arguments for the view I proposed in the chapters on which I am now writing.

No one disagrees that all men can know the truth, and even the least enlightened of philosophers agree that man participates in a certain *Reason* that they do not determine. This is why they define man as *animal* RATIONIS *particeps*; for everyone knows, at least in confused fashion, that man's essential difference consists in the necessary union he has with universal Reason (although it is not generally known who it is who contains this Reason, and little effort is made to find out).[a] I see, for example, that twice two is four, and that my friend is to be valued more than my dog; and I am certain that no one in the world does not see this as well as I. Now, I do not see these truths in the mind of other people, just as other people do not see them in mine. There must, therefore, be a universal Reason that enlightens me and all other intelligences. For if the reason I consult were not the same that answers the Chinese, it is clear that I could not be as certain as I am that the Chinese see the same truths as I do. Thus, the Reason we consult when we withdraw into ourselves is a universal Reason. I say, when we withdraw into ourselves, because I am not here talking about the reason followed by a man in passion. When a man values the life of his horse more than the life of his coachman, he has his reasons for doing so; but they are particular reasons that every reasonable man abhors. They are reasons that at bottom are unreasonable, because they do not conform with Sovereign Reason, or the Universal Reason that all men consult.

I am certain that the ideas of things are immutable,[b] and that eternal laws and

---

[a] "Si ambo videmus verum esse quod dicis, & ambo videmus verum esse quod dico, ubi quaeso id videmus? Nec ego utique in te, nec tu in me, sed ambo in ipsa quae supra mentes nostras est incommutabili veritate." *Conf.* of St. Aug. bk. 12. ch. 25.

[b] See Aug. *De libero arbitrio.* bk. 2. ch. 8 ff.

truths are necessary—it is impossible that they should not be as they are. Now, I see nothing in me of a necessary or immutable nature—I am able not to be, or not to be such as I am; there might be minds unlike me, yet I am certain that there can be no mind that sees truths and laws different from those I see—for every mind necessarily sees that twice two is four, and that one's friend is to be valued more than one's dog. It must be concluded, then, that the reason consulted by all minds is an immutable and necessary Reason.

Furthermore, it is evident that this Reason is infinite. The mind of man clearly conceives that there are, or can be, infinite numbers of intelligible triangles, tetragons, pentagons, and other such figures. Not only does it conceive that it will never lack for ideas of figures, and that it will always discover new ones, even if it were to attend only to these kinds of ideas for all eternity; it even perceives infinity in extension, for the mind cannot doubt that its idea of space is inexhaustible. The mind clearly sees that the number which when multiplied by itself produces 5, or any of the numbers between 4 and 9, 9 and 16, 16 and 25, and so on, is a magnitude, a proportion, a fraction whose terms have more numbers than could stretch from one of the earth's poles to the other. The mind sees clearly that this proportion is such that only God could comprehend it, and that it cannot be expressed exactly, because to do so, a fraction both of whose terms were infinite would be required. I could relate many such examples demonstrating not only that the mind of man is limited but also that the Reason he consults is infinite. For, in short, the mind clearly sees the infinite in this Sovereign Reason, although he does not comprehend it. In a word, the Reason man consults must be infinite because it cannot be exhausted, and because it always has an answer for whatever is asked of it.

But if it is true that the Reason in which all men participate is universal, that it is infinite, that it is necessary and immutable, then it is certainly not different from God's own reason, for only the infinite and universal being contains in itself an infinite and universal reason. All creatures are particular beings; universal reason, therefore, is not created. No creature is infinite; infinite reason, therefore, is not a creature. But the reason we consult is not only infinite and universal, it is also independent and necessary, and in one sense, we conceive it as more independent than God Himself. For God can act only according to this reason—He has to consult and follow it. Now, God consults only Himself and depends on nothing. This reason, therefore, is not different from Himself.; it is, therefore, coeternal and consubstantial with Him. We see clearly that God cannot punish innocence, that He cannot subject minds to bodies, that He is constrained to observe order. We see, then, the rule, the order, the reason of God—for what wisdom other than God's could we see when we dare to say that God is constrained to follow it?

But, after all, is any wisdom other than God's conceiveable? Does Solomon, who describes it so well, distinguish two kinds of wisdom? Does he not teach us that the wisdom that is coeternal with God Himself and by which He established the order we see in His works is the same wisdom that presides over all minds and is consulted in the legislation of just and reasonable laws. One need only read the eighth chapter of Proverbs to be convinced of this truth. I know that Sacred Scripture speaks of a certain wisdom it calls the wisdom of the age, the wisdom of men. But this is because it speaks of things according to appearance, or in a popular vein, for elsewhere it teaches us that this wisdom is but folly and abomination, not only before God, but before all men who consult Reason.

Surely, if eternal laws and truths depended on God, if they had been established by a free volition of the Creator, in short, if the Reason we consult were not necessary and independent, it seems evident to me that there would no longer be any true science and that we might be mistaken in claiming that the arithmetic or geometry of the Chinese is like our own. For in the final analysis, if it were not absolutely necessary that twice four be eight, or that the three angles of a triangle be equal to two right angles, what assurance would we have that these kinds of truths are not like those that are found only in certain universities, or that last only for a certain time? Do we clearly conceive that God cannot stop willing what He has willed with an entirely free and indifferent will? Or rather, do we clearly see that God could not have willed certain things, for a certain time, for a certain place, for certain people, or for certain kinds of beings—given, as some would have it, that He was entirely free and indifferent in His willing? As for me, I can conceive no necessity in indifference, nor can I reconcile two things that are so opposite.

Yet I will suppose that we clearly see that God through an entirely indifferent will has established eternal laws and truths for all times and for all places, and that they are now immutable because of His decree. But where do men see this decree? Has God created some being representative of this decree? Will they say that this decree is a modification of their soul? They clearly see this decree, for they have learned from it that immutability attaches to eternal laws and truths; but where do they see it? Certainly, unless they see it in God, they do not see it; for this decree can be only in God, and it can be seen only where it is. Philosophers can be certain of nothing, then, unless they consult God and He answers them. Their protests here are in vain—they must either submit or remain silent.

But at bottom, this decree is an unfounded product of the imagination. When we think about order and eternal truths and laws, we do not naturally seek their cause, for they have none. We do not clearly see the necessity of this decree, nor do we immediately think about it—rather, we see with evidence through simple perception that the nature of numbers and of intelligible ideas is immutable, necessary, and independent. We clearly see that it is absolutely necessary that twice four be eight and that the square of the diagonal of a square be double that square. If anyone doubts the absolute necessity of these truths, it is because he looks away from their light, reasons on some false premiss, and seeks their nature, immutability, and independence elsewhere than in the truths themselves. Thus, the decree of immutability for these truths is a fiction of the mind, which, supposing that it does not see what it perceives in God's wisdom, and knowing that God is the cause of all things, feels itself constrained to imagine a decree in order to ascribe immutability to certain truths it cannot fail to recognize as immutable. But the supposition is false and must be guarded against. Only in the wisdom of God do we see eternal, immutable, and necessary truths. Nowhere else but in this wisdom do we see the order that God Himself is constrained to follow, as I have just indicated. The mind is created only for this wisdom, and in a certain sense the mind can see only it; for if the mind can see creatures, it does so only because He whom it sees (though in a very imperfect way during this life) comprehends all creatures in the immensity of His being in an intelligible fashion suited to the mind, as I have indicated elsewhere.

It seems clear to me that if we did not have within us the idea of the infinite, and if we did not see everything through the natural union of our soul with infinite and universal Reason, we would not be free to think about all things. For the mind can will to apply itself only to the things of which it has some idea, and it now has the power to think about only those things to which it can will to apply itself. Thus, man is stripped of his freedom to think about all things if his mind is severed from Him who contains all things. Furthermore, given that we can love only what we see, it is clear that if God gave us only particular ideas He would determine all the impulses of our will in such a way that we could love only particular beings. For in the final analysis, if we did not have an idea of the infinite, we could not love it; and if those who assert that they have no idea of God spoke the truth, I would not hesitate in saying that they never have loved God, for it appears to me quite certain that one can love only what one sees.

Finally, if order and eternal laws were not immutable by the necessity of their nature, the foundation of the clearest and strongest arguments of religion would seemingly be destroyed, as well as freedom and the most certain of the sciences. For it is certain that the Christian religion, which offers us the mediation and reparation of Jesus Christ, assumes the corruption of nature by Original Sin. Now, what proof can we have of this corruption? The flesh struggles against the mind, you will say, the flesh subjugates and dominates the mind. I agree. But this, a libertine will answer, is no disorder. It pleases God, He has ordained it thus, He is the master of His decrees, He establishes whatever order pleases Him amongst His creatures. How will you prove to him that it is a disorder for minds to be subordinated to bodies unless you have a clear idea of order and its necessity, unless you know that God Himself is constrained to follow this order by the necessary love He bears for Himself? Besides, if this order depends on God's free decree, it will always be necessary to call upon God to learn of His decree; God will always have to be consulted (in spite of the disliking certain learned people have for appealing to Him); we shall have to yield to this truth, that our instruction depends upon God. But this free decree that caused order is, for the reasons I have already given, a fiction of the mind.

If it is not a necessary order according to which man be made for his Author and that our will conform to the order that is the essential and necessary rule of God's will, if it is not true that actions are good or evil as they conform or not with an immutable and necessary order and that this same order requires that the former be rewarded and the latter punished, finally, if all men do not naturally have a clear idea of order, but an order that is such that God Himself cannot will otherwise than as this order prescribes (because God cannot will disorder), then surely I can see nothing but universal confusion. For how could we criticize the most infamous and most immoral actions of pagans to whom God has not given any laws? What reason will dare to judge them if there is no sovereign reason that condemns them, if there is no immutable order or indispensable law according to which they should be judged?

There was a poet[a] who said that it is impossible to distinguish what is moral from what is immoral. There was a philosopher[b] who said that it is a weakness to be ashamed of infamous actions. Similar paradoxes are often proposed as a result of a heated imagination or in a fit of passion. But why will you condemn these opinions unless there is an order, a rule, a universal and necessary reason, that is always present to those who know how to retreat within themselves. In many instances we have no hesitation in judging ourselves and others, but by what authority do we act unless the Reason that judges in us when it seems to us that we pronounce judgments against ourselves and others is sovereign over us and all other men?

But if this Reason were not present to those who retreat within themselves, and if pagans too were not naturally united to some extent with the immutable order I am speaking of, what sin or what disobedience would they have been guilty of, and according to what justice would God punish them? I say this because there is a prophet[c] who tells me that God Himself wills men to be His arbiter between Him and His people provided that they judge them according to the immutable and necessary order of justice. Nero killed his mother, granted. But in what did his evil consist? He followed the natural impulse of his hatred. In no way did God forbid him in this. The law of the Jews was not given to him. Perhaps you will say that the natural law prohibits such actions and that this law was known to him. But what proof have you of this? For my part, I agree, because this indeed is an irresistible proof that there is a necessary and immutable order and that every mind knows this order more clearly as it is more closely joined to the universal reason and as it is less sensible to the impressions of its senses and passions—in short, as it is more reasonable. But I must now explain as clearly as I can the view I have of order and the divine or natural law, for the difficulty in agreeing with what I say perhaps springs from failing to perceive distinctly my thought.

It is certain that God contains within Himself in an intelligible fashion the perfection of all the beings He has created or can create, and that through these intelligible perfections He knows the essence of all things, as through His volitions He knows their existence. Now, these perfections are also the human mind's immediate object (for the reasons I have already given). Therefore, the intelligible ideas or perfections that are in God and that represent to us what is external to God are absolutely immutable and necessary. Now, truths are but relations of equality or inequality between these intelligible beings (since it is true that twice two is four or that twice two is not five only because there is a

[a]"Nec natura potest justo secernere iniquum." Lucretius.

[b]Diogenes.

[c]"Nunc ergo habitatores Jerusalem & viri Juda judicate inter me & vineam meam." Isa. 53 [5:3].

relation of equality between twice two and four, and one of inequality between twice two and five). Truths, therefore, as well as ideas, are necessary and immutable. It has always been true that twice two is four and this cannot become false. This is clear, without it being necessary *that God as sovereign legislator has established these truths,* [a] as Descartes has asserted in his reply to the sixth objections against his metaphysical meditations.

We understand easily enough what truth is, but we have some difficulty in conceiving what the necessary and immutable order is, or what the natural and divine law is that God necessarily wills and that the righteous likewise will. For what makes a man moral is that he loves order and conforms his will to it in all things —just as the sinner is such only because he does not find order pleasing in all things and because he would have order conform to his own wishes. Yet it seems to me that these things are not as mysterious as might be imagined, and I think the reason why they are found so troublesome comes from the mind's difficulty in raising itself up to abstract and metaphysical thoughts. Here, then, are some of my thoughts on order.

It is evident that the perfections in God that represent created or possible beings are not all equal insofar as they represent these beings, and that those, for example, that represent bodies are not as noble as those that represent minds, and furthermore, that even among those that represent only bodies or only minds, there are infinite degrees of perfection. All this is easily and clearly conceived, although there is a great deal of difficulty in reconciling the Divine Being's simplicity with this variety of intelligible ideas that He contains in His wisdom. For it is clear that if all God's ideas were in every sense equal, He could not distinguish among His works, since He sees His creatures only in what in Him represents them, and if the idea of a watch that shows, besides the hour, all the different motions of the planets were not more perfect than the idea of a watch that shows only the hour, or than the idea of a circle or of a square, then a watch would not be more perfect than a circle. For one can judge the perfection of works only through the perfection of the ideas one has of them; and if there were no more intelligence or mark of wisdom in a watch than in a circle, there would be no greater difficulty in conceiving the most complex machines than in conceiving a square or a circle.

If it is true, then, that God, who is the universal Being, contains all beings within Himself in an intelligible fashion, and that all these intelligible beings that have a necessary existence in God are not in every sense equally perfect, it is clear that there will be a necessary and immutable order among them, and that just as there are necessary and eternal truths because there are relations of magnitude among intelligible beings, there must also be a necessary and immutable order because of the relations of perfection among these same beings. An immutable order has it, then, that minds are more noble than bodies, as it is a necessary truth that twice two is four, or that twice two is not five.

So far, order seems to be more of a speculative truth than a necessary law. For

[a] Art. 6 and 8.

if we consider order as we have just done, we clearly see, for example, that it is a truth that minds are more noble than bodies, but we do not see that this truth is at the same time an order that has the force of law and that we are obliged to prefer minds to bodies. It must be considered, then, that God loves Himself with a necessary love, and that thus He loves what in Him represents or contains greater perfection more than what contains less—so much so that if we wish to suppose an intelligible mind to be a thousand times more perfect than an intelligible body, the love by which God loves Himself would necessarily be a thousand times greater for the intelligible mind than for the intelligible body; for God's love is necessarily proportionate to the order among the intelligible beings He contains, since He necessarily loves His own perfections. As a result of this, the order that is purely speculative has the force of law with regard to God Himself, given, as is certainly the case, that God necessarily loves Himself and that He cannot contradict Himself. Furthermore, God cannot love intelligible bodies more than intelligible minds, although He can love created bodies more than minds, as I shall soon show.

Now, this immutable order that has the force of law with regard to God Himself clearly has the same force with regard to us. For, since God has created us in His image and likeness, He cannot will that we love more what deserves to be loved less—He wills that our will conform with His and that here below we freely and hence meritoriously render things the justice that He necessarily renders them. His law, the immutable order of His perfections, is therefore also ours; and this order is not unknown to us, and even our natural love excites us to follow it when we retreat within ourselves and our senses and passions leave us free—in short, when our self-love does not corrupt our natural love. Given that we are made for God and cannot be entirely separated from Him, we see this order in Him and we are naturally led to love it, for it is His light that illumines us and His love that animates us (although our senses and passions obscure this light and turn the impression we have for loving Him according to this order against order itself). However, in spite of concupiscence, which conceals order from us and prevents us from following it, order is always a law that is essential and without exception with regard to us, and not only with regard to us but to all created intelligences and even the damned—for I do not think that they are so removed from God that they do not yet have some faint idea of order in which they find some beauty and that they are not perhaps even ready to conform themselves to it in certain particular cases where their self-love is not at stake.

Corruption of the heart consists in opposition to order. Therefore, given that the evil or the corruption of will is not equal even among the damned, it is clear that they are not equally opposed to order, and that they do not detest it in everything, unless they do so as a result of their hatred of God. For just as one cannot detest the good considered simply as such, one can detest order only when it seems to be contrary to our inclinations. But even if it should appear contrary to our inclinations, it still remains for us a law that condemns and even punishes us by a worm that never dies [Mark 9:44].

Perhaps, then, we can now see the nature of the immutable order of justice and how this order has the force of law through the necessary love that God has for Himself. We can conceive how this law is universal for all minds as well as for God Himself, why it is necessary and absolutely without exception. We can see clearly (provided that what I have just said is seriously considered) that to maintain that ideas that are eternal, immutable, and common to all intelligences, are only perceptions or momentary particular modifications of the mind, is to establish Pyrrhonism and to make room for the belief that what is moral or immoral is not necessarily so, which is the most dangerous error of all. Finally, we can easily conceive in general that this law, the immutable order, is the principle of all human and divine laws, and that it is according to this law that all intelligences are judged and all creatures given the rank they deserve.

I admit that it is not easy to explain all this in detail, and I shall not risk the undertaking. For if my intention were to show the connection between certain particular laws and the general law, or between certain ways of behaving and order, I would necessarily become involved in difficulties that I could not perhaps resolve, and that would lead me far from my topic.

Nonetheless, if you consider that God has not and cannot have any law other than His wisdom and the necessary love He has for it, you will easily judge that all the divine laws must depend on it. And if you take note that He created the world only in relation to this wisdom and love (since He acts only for Himself), you will have no doubt that all natural laws must tend to the preservation and perfection of this world according to indispensable order and depending upon necessary love—for the wisdom and will of God rule all things.

I need not explain this principle at greater length. What I have said is enough for the following conclusion, that as nature was first instituted, minds could not have been subordinated to bodies. For since God cannot act in ignorance and in spite of Himself, He created the world according to wisdom and through the impulse of His love—He made all things through His Son and in the Holy Spirit as Scripture teaches us. Now, in the wisdom of God, minds are more perfect than bodies; and as a result of the necessary love that God has for Himself, He prefers the more perfect to the less perfect. Thus, minds could not have been subordinated to bodies as nature was first instituted. Otherwise we would have to say that in creating the world God did not follow the direction of His eternal wisdom, nor the impulses of His natural and necessary love, which is inconceiveable and which even contains a manifest contradiction.

It is true that the created mind is now subordinated to the body, but this is because order considered as a necessary law would have it so. This is because God, whose self-love is a necessary love and is always His inviolable law, cannot love minds that are opposed to Him; consequently, He cannot prefer them to bodies in which there is nothing that is evil or that He hates. For God does not love sinners in themselves; they subsist in the universe only through Jesus Christ. God preserves and loves them only so that they might cease being sinners through the grace of Jesus Christ, or, if they remain sinners eternally, so that they might be eternally condemned by the immutable and necessary order and by the judgment of Jesus Christ (through whose power they subsist for the glory of divine justice, for without Jesus Christ they would be annihilated). I mention this in passing to remove certain difficulties that might remain from what I said elsewhere about Original Sin or the general corruption of nature.

It seems to me worthwhile to point out that the mind knows objects in only two ways: through illumination [*par lumiere*] and through sensation. It sees things through *illumination* when it has a *clear idea* of them, and when by consulting this idea it can discover all the properties of which these things are capable. It sees things through *sensation* when it finds no clear idea of these things in itself to be consulted, when it is thus unable to discover their properties clearly, and when it knows them only through a confused sensation, without illumination and without evidence. Through illumination and through a clear idea, the mind sees numbers, extension, and the essences of things. Through a confused idea or through sensation, it judges about the existence of creatures and knows its own existence.

The things the mind preceives through illumination or through a clear idea it perceives in very perfect fashion, and it even sees clearly that whatever obscurity or imperfection there is in its knowledge is due to its own weakness and limitation or some lack of attentiveness on its part, and not to the imperfection of the idea it perceives. But what the mind perceives through sensation is never clearly known to it, not because of some lack of attentiveness on its part (for we always attend closely to what we sense), but because of the inadequacy of the idea, which is extremely obscure and confused.

From this we can judge that it is in God or in an immutable nature that we see all that we know by means of illumination or clear idea—not only because through illumination we see only numbers, extension, and the essences of things, which do not depend on a free act of God, as I have already pointed out, but also because we know these things in very perfect fashion, and because we would even know them in an infinitely perfect fashion if our capacity for thought were infinite, since nothing is lacking to the idea representing them. We must also conclude that everything we know through sensation is seen in itself. However, this is not to say that we can produce in ourselves any new modification, or that our soul's sensations or modifications can represent objects upon whose occasion God excites them in us, but only that our sensations (which are in no way different from us, and which as a result can never represent anything different from ourselves) can, nonetheless, represent the existence of beings or, rather, make us judge that they exist. For as God, upon the presence of objects, excites our sensations in us through an insensible action that we do not perceive, we imagine that we receive from the object not only the idea that represents its essence but also the sensation that makes us judge that it exists—for there is always a *pure idea* and a *confused sensation* in the knowledge we have of the existence of beings, the knowledge of God and of our soul excepted. I exclude the existence of God, which we know through a pure idea and without sensation, because His existence depends on no cause and is contained in the idea of an infinite and necessary being, for as I have proved elsewhere,[a] if He is thought of,

---

[a]Bk. 4, ch. 11.

He must exist. I also exclude the existence of our soul, because we know through inner sensation that we think, will, and perceive, and because we have no clear idea of our soul, as I have sufficiently explained in the seventh chapter of the second part of the third book and elsewhere.

Here are some of the arguments that can be added to those I have already given to prove that only God enlightens us and that the immediate and direct object of our clear and evident knowledge is an immutable and necessary nature. Several objections are commonly raised against this view; I shall now try to answer them.

Objections

Against what has been said: that only God enlightens us and that we see all things in Him.

First Objection

Our soul thinks because of its *nature*. In creating it, God gave it the *faculty* of thinking and it needs nothing more; but if it does need something, let us stick to what experience teaches us about our senses, i.e., that they are the cause of our ideas. To argue against experience is a bad way of philosophizing.

Reply

I am amazed that the Cartesian gentlemen who so rightly reject the general terms *nature* and *faculty* should so willingly employ them on this occasion. They criticize those who say that fire burns by its *nature* or that it changes certain bodies into glass by a natural *faculty*, and yet some of them do not hesitate to say that the human mind produces in itself the ideas of all things by its *nature*, because it has the *faculty* of thinking. But, with all due respect, these terms are no more meaningful in their mouth than in the mouth of the Peripatetics. True, our soul is what it is by its nature and necessarily perceives what affects it, but God alone can act on it; He alone can illuminate it, affect it, or modify it through the efficacy of His ideas.

I realize that the soul can think, but I also know that extension can have figures; the soul is capable of volition as matter is of motion. But just as it is false that matter, although capable of figure and motion, has in itself a *power*, a *faculty*, a *nature* by which it can move itself or give itself a figure that is now round, now square, so it is false that the soul, although naturally and essentially capable of knowledge and volition, has any *faculties* by which it can produce in itself its own ideas or its own impulse toward the good,[a] for it necessarily wishes to be happy. There is a big difference between being mobile and moving oneself. Matter is by its nature mobile and capable of figure; it cannot even subsist without figure. But it cannot move itself, it cannot shape itself, and lacks a faculty to do so. The mind is by its nature capable of impulses and ideas, I agree.

[a]As opposed to particular goods; see the first Elucidation.

But it cannot move itself, it cannot enlighten itself—it is God who works everything of a material nature in minds as well as in bodies. Can it be said that God works the changes that take place in matter but not those that take place in the mind? Is it to render to God His due to leave these latter beings to their own devices? Is He not equally the master of all things? Is He not the creator, preserver, and true mover of minds as well as of bodies?

But if you would have it that creatures have the faculties they are ordinarily conceived to have,[a] or that natural bodies be said to have a *nature* that is the principle of their motion and rest (as Aristotle and his followers would have it), all my ideas would be overthrown. But I would rather agree to this than to say that the mind enlightens itself, or that the soul has the power to move the members of its body in various ways and to communicate to them feeling and life, or that it is the soul that gives heat to the blood, motion to the spirits, and its size, disposition, and figure to the rest of the body—I would rather all this than to say that the mind gives itself its own impulse and light. If God does not do all things, let Him do at least what is greatest and most perfect in the universe. And if creatures do something, let them move bodies and order them as they will, but let them not act on minds.

Let us say that bodies move each other after being moved themselves, or, rather, let us ignore the cause of these different dispositions of matter, which does not concern us. But let our minds not be ignorant of Him from whom their enlightenment comes, the *Reason* to which they are essentially related, the Reason that is spoken about so much and understood so little. Let our minds know Him from whom they receive everything capable of making them happier and more perfect, and let them realize the full extent of their dependence on God, who continually gives them all that they now have, for as a great saint says in another context,[b] *it is culpable pride to use the things that God gives us as if they were natural to us.* Above all, let us not imagine that the senses instruct reason, or that the body enlightens the mind, or that the soul receives from the body what it itself lacks. It is better to believe that one is self-dependent than truly dependent on bodies; it is better to believe oneself one's own master than to seek one's master among creatures that have no value to us. But it is best to accede to the eternal truth, which assures us in the gospel that only it is our teacher,[c] than to rely on the reports of our senses or of men who dare to speak to us as our teachers. Experience, whatever is to be said of it, does not encourage prejudice, for our senses are but the occasional causes of God's action on us. Our teachers are only prompters—they too are but the occasional causes of the instruction that eternal wisdom gives us in the most secret recesses of our reason. But because this wisdom enlightens us in a completely non-sensible way, we fancy that our eyes, or the words of those who reverberate the air against our ears, produce this

---

[a]See the last Elucidation concerning the efficacy of secondary causes [15].

[b]"Est quippe superbia & peccatum maximum uti datis tanquam innatis." St. Bern. *De diligendo Deo.*

[c]Matt. 23 [vv. 8–10]. See St. Augustine's *De magistro.*

illumination, or express the intelligible voice that instructs us inwardly. It is for this reason, as I have pointed out elsewhere, that Jesus Christ was not satisfied with instructing us through His divinity in an intelligible way; He wished further to instruct us in sensible fashion by His humanity; He wished to teach us that He is our master in every way. And because we are unable without difficulty to retreat within ourselves in order to consult Him as the eternal truth, the immutable order, the intelligible light, He made the truth sensible through His words, order worthy of love through His example, and light visible through a body that adapts it to our weakness. And yet we remain ungrateful, immoral, stupid, and insensible enough to consider (against His express prohibition) as our teachers or the cause of our knowledge, not merely other men, but perhaps even the vilest and most despicable of bodies.

Second Objection

Given that the soul is more perfect than bodies, why can it not contain what represents them? Why could the idea of extension not be one of its modifications? Only God acts on it and modifies it—granted, but why should it see bodies in God if it can see them in its own substance? The soul is not material, admitted. But God, though He is a pure spirit, sees bodies in Himself; why could not the soul, then, see them by considering itself, even though it itself is spiritual?

Replies

Do you not see that there is this difference between God and the human soul, that God is a being without restriction, a universal and infinite being, whereas the soul is a kind of particular being? It is a property of an infinite being to be simultaneously one and all things, compounded, as it were, of an infinity of perfections, and to be so simple that each perfection it possesses contains all other perfections without any real distinction; for since each divine perfection is infinite, it constitutes the entire divine being. But as the soul is a particular being, a limited being, it cannot have extension in it without becoming material, without being composed of two substances. God, then, contains bodies within Him in an intelligible way. He sees their essences or ideas in His wisdom, and their existence in His love or volitions. We must speak this way because God made bodies, and because He knew what He made even before anything was made. But the soul cannot see in itself what it does not contain; it cannot even see clearly what it does contain, which it can only sense in a confused way. Let me explain this point.

The soul does not contain intelligible extension as one of its modes because this extension is not perceived as a mode of the soul's being, but simply as a being. This extension is conceived by itself and without thinking of anything else; but modes cannot be conceived without perceiving the subject or being of which they are modes. We perceive this extension without thinking about our mind; we cannot even conceive that this extension could be a modification of our mind. A figure is disclosed in it when this extension is conceived as limited; but the mind's limits do not serve to give it figure. Since this extension has parts, it can be divided in the same sense that it is extended, i.e., into intelligible parts; but we see nothing in the soul that is divisible. The extension we see, then, is not a mode of the soul, and therefore it cannot be seen in it.

But, you will say, for these same reasons God would not be able to see His creatures in Himself. This would be true if ideas of creatures were modifications of His substance, but the Infinite Being is incapable of modifications.[a] God's ideas of creatures are, as Saint Thomas says, only His essence, insofar as it is participable or imperfectly imitable, for God contains every creaturely perfection, though in a divine and infinite way; He is one and He is all. Thus, He can see them in Himself and only in Himself, for His knowledge is drawn only from Himself. But the soul, however it might sense itself, does not know either itself or its modifications, the soul which is a particular being, a very limited and imperfect being. Certainly it cannot see in itself what is not there in any way at all. How could we see in one species of being all species of being, or in a finite and particular being a triangle in general and infinite triangles? For the soul indeed perceives a triangle or circle in general, while it is a contradiction that the soul should be able to have a modification in general. The sensations of color that the soul ascribes to figures makes them particular, because no modification of a particular being can be general.

To be sure, we can assert what we clearly conceive. Now, we clearly conceive that the extension we see is something distinct from ourselves. We can say, then, that this extension is not a modification of our being, and that it is indeed something distinct from ourselves. For it should be noted that the sun that we see, for example, is not the one we look at. The sun, and everything else in the material world, is not visible by itself. This I have proved elsewhere. The soul can see only the sun to which it is immediately joined, only that sun that like it occupies no place. Now, we see clearly and perceive distinctly that this sun is something distinct from us. Thus, we speak contrary to our light and consciousness when we say that the soul sees in its own modifications all the objects it perceives.

Pleasure, pain, taste, heat, color, all our sensations and all our passions, are modifications of our soul. But be that as it may, do we clearly know them? Can we compare heat with taste or smell with color? Do we know the relation between red and green, or even between two shades of green? Such is not the case with different figures, which we can compare with each other; we know their relations exactly, we know precisely that the square of the diagonal of a square is double that square. What relation is there between these intelligible figures, which are very clear ideas, and our soul's modifications, which are but confused sensations? Why suppose, then, that these intelligible figures cannot be perceived by the soul unless they are its modifications, since the soul knows nothing of what happens to it through a clear idea, but only through consciousness or inner sensation, as I have proved elsewhere and as I shall again prove in the following Elucidation. If we could see the figures of bodies only in ourselves,

---

[a] See my *Réponse* to the third posthumous letter of Arnauld.

they would be, on the contrary, *unintelligible*, for we do not know ourselves. We are but shadows to ourselves; to see ourselves, we must look beyond ourselves, and we shall never know what we are until we view ourselves in Him who is our light and in whom all things become light. For only in God are the most material beings perfectly intelligible; but outside of Him the most spiritual of substances become utterly invisible. For only what is intelligible can affect intelligences. Surely, only God, only His always efficacious substance, can affect, enlighten and nourish our minds, as Saint Augustine says. It is not possible that we should, I do not say, sense, for we can sense ourselves only in ourselves, but clearly know ourselves, i.e., discover the nature and properties of our soul, elsewhere than in our divine and eternal model, that is, elsewhere than in the always luminous substance of the divinity, insofar as it can be participated in by a spiritual creature, or insofar as it is representative of such a creature. We know clearly the nature and properties of matter, for the idea of extension that we have in God is very clear. But as we do not see in God the idea of our soul, we sense both what we are and whatever actually takes place in us. But it is impossible for us to discover clearly what we are, or any of the modifications of which we are capable.

Third Objection

Nothing in God can be moved, nothing in Him can have figure. If there is a sun in the intelligible world, this sun is always equal to itself. The visible sun appears greater when it is near the horizon than when it is at a great distance from the horizon. Therefore, it is not this intelligible sun that we see. The same holds true for other creatures. Therefore, we do not see God's works in Him.

Reply

A sufficient reply to this would be that nothing in God is really figured and thereby capable of motion, but that there are in God figures that are intelligible and, consequently, intelligibly mobile. For it cannot be doubted that God has the idea of the bodies He has created and constantly moves, that He can find this idea only in His substance, and that He is at least able to inform us of it. But to clarify this matter, it must be realized that God contains in Himself an ideal or intelligible infinite extension; for since He has created it, God knows extension, and He can know it only in Himself. Thus, since the mind can perceive a part of this intelligible extension that God contains, it surely can perceive in God all figures; for all finite intelligible extension is necessarily an intelligible figure, since figure is nothing but the boundary of extension. Furthermore, we see or sense a given body when its idea, i.e., when some figure composed of intelligible and general extension, becomes sensible and particular through color or some other sensible perception by which its idea affects the soul and that the soul ascribes to it, for the soul almost always projects its sensation on an idea that strikes it in lively fashion. Therefore, there need be in God no sensible bodies or real figures in intelligible extension in order for us to see them in God or in order for God to see them in Himself. It is enough that His substance, insofar as it can be participated in by the corporeal creature, should be able to be perceived in different ways.

Likewise, if, as it were, a figure of intelligible extension made sensible by color should be taken successively from different parts of this infinite extension, or if a figure of intelligible extension could be perceived as turning on its center or as gradually approaching another, we would perceive motion in an intelligible or sensible figure without there being any actual motion in intelligible extension. For God does not see the actual motion of body in His substance, or in the idea He has of them in Himself, but only in the knowledge He has of His volitions with regard to them. Even their existence He sees only in this way, because only His will gives being to all things. God's volitions change nothing in His substance, they do not move it. In this sense, intelligible extension cannot be moved even intelligibly. But although we might suppose that the intelligible parts of the idea of extension always maintain the same relation of intelligible distance between them and that this idea therefore cannot be moved even intelligibly, nonetheless, if we conceive of a given created extension to which there corresponds a given part of intelligible extension as its idea, we shall be able through this same idea of space (though intelligibly immobile) to see that the parts of the created extension are mobile, because the idea of space, although assumed intelligibly immobile, necessarily represents all sorts of relations of distance and shows that the parts of a body can fail to maintain the same situation relative to each other. Furthermore, although we do not see bodies in themselves, but only through intelligible extension (let this extension be assumed intelligibly immobile or not), we can through it actually see or imagine bodies in motion because it appears mobile to us due to the sensation of color, or the confused image remaining after the sensation that we successively attach to different parts of the intelligible extension that furnishes us with an idea when we see or imagine the motion of some body. It is easier to understand all this than to give an unambiguous explanation of it.

From what I have just said, you can understand why you see the intelligible sun now greater, now smaller, although it is always the same with regard to God. All that is needed for this is that we sometimes see a greater part of intelligible extension and sometimes a smaller. Since the parts of intelligible extension are all of the same nature, they may all represent any body whatsoever.

It should not be imagined that the intelligible world is related to the sensible, material world in such a way that there is an intelligible sun, for example, or an intelligible horse or tree intended to represent to us the sun or a horse or a tree, or that everyone who sees the sun necessarily sees this hypothetical intelligible sun. Given that all intelligible extension can be conceived of as circular, or as having the intelligible figure of a horse or a tree, all of intelligible extension can serve to represent the sun, or a horse or a tree, and consequently can be the sun or a horse or a tree of the intelligible world and can even become a visible and sensible sun, horse, or tree if the soul has some sensation upon the occasion of bodies to attach to these ideas, i.e., if these ideas affect the soul with sensible perceptions.

Thus, when I said that we see different bodies through the knowledge we have of God's perfections that represent them, I did not exactly mean that there are in God certain particular ideas that represent each body individually, and that we see such an idea when we see the body; for we certainly could not see this body as sometimes great, sometimes small, sometimes round, sometimes square, if we saw it through a particular idea that would always be the same. But I do say that we see all things in God through the efficacy of His substance, and particularly sensible things, through God's applying intelligible extension to our mind in a thousand different ways, and that thus intelligible extension contains all the perfections, or rather, all the differences of bodies due to the different sensations that the soul projects on the ideas affecting it upon the occasion of these same bodies. I have spoken in a different way, but you should realize that I did so only to make certain of my arguments stronger and more intuitive, and you must not think on the basis of what I have just said that these arguments no longer obtain. If it were necessary, I could give the reasons for the different ways in which I have explained myself.

I shall not venture to treat this subject in depth[a] for fear of saying things either too abstract or out of the ordinary, or, if you will, in order not to risk saying things I do not know and cannot discover. Here instead are several passages from Scripture that seem contrary to what I have just asserted. I shall try to explain them.

Fourth Objection

In his gospel and the first of his epistles, Saint John says *That no one has ever seen God,* "DEUM nemo vidit unquam,[b] unigenitus qui est in sinu patris ipse enarravit.[c]

Reply

I answer that seeing His creatures in Him is not really seeing God. Seeing the essences of creatures in His substance is not seeing His essence, just as merely seeing the objects it represents is not seeing a mirror. Seeing the essence of God, not in its absolute being, but in relation to creatures or insofar as it is representative of them, is not seeing the essence of God.

---

[a]See my *Réponse aux vrayes & fausses idées,* my first *Lettre touchant la defense* & especially my *Réponse à une 3 lettre posthume de M. Arnauld,* as well as certain other passages that can perhaps eliminate all the difficulties the most attentive and most careful reader might form.

[b]Ch. 1. 18 [Ep. (1), 4, 12].

[c]Ch. 4. 12 [Ev. 1. 18].

ELUCIDATION SIX

✤

On what I said at the beginning of the tenth chapter of the first book and in the sixth chapter of the second book on method: That it is very difficult to prove that there are bodies. What ought to be thought of the proofs given of their existence.

It is quite common for men to be perfectly ignorant of what they think they know best and to know certain other things well enough of which they imagine they do not even have ideas. When their senses play a role in their perceptions they yield to what they do not understand, or understand only in very imperfect fashion; and when their ideas are purely intelligible, or contain nothing sensible affecting them, they accept incontestable demonstrations only with difficulty.

What does the ordinary man think, for example, when most metaphysical truths are proved to him, when we demonstrate for him the existence of God, the efficacy of His will, the immutability of His decrees, that there is but one God or one true cause that does everything in all things, that there is but one sovereign Reason in which all intelligences participate, that there is but one necessary love that is the principle of all created wills? He thinks we are speaking with words devoid of sense, that we have no ideas of the things we are proposing and that we would do better to keep quiet. Since metaphysical truths and arguments contain nothing sensible, men are not affected by them, and as a result they do not remain convinced by them. Nonetheless, it is certain that abstract ideas are the most distinct and metaphysical truths the clearest and most evident.

Men sometimes say that they have no idea of God nor any knowledge of His will, and often they even think this as they say it; but this is because they think they do not know what they perhaps know best. For where is the man who hesitates to answer when asked whether God is wise, just, and powerful, whether or not He is triangular, divisible, mobile, or subject to any possible change? Yet one cannot answer without fear of error as to whether certain qualities belong or do not belong to some subject if one does not have any idea of the subject. Similarly, where is the man who would dare say that God does not act in the simplest ways, that His intentions are disordered, that He creates monsters by a positive, direct, and particular will and not by a kind of necessity in order not to upset the simplicity and generality of His ways, in short, that His will could be contrary to the order of which all men have some knowledge? But if we had no idea of God's will, we might at least doubt whether He acts according to certain laws we very clearly conceive that He must follow, given that He wills to act.

Men have ideas, then, of purely intelligible things, and these ideas are much clearer than those of sensible objects. Men are more certain of the existence of God than of bodies, and when they withdraw into themselves they find the will of God, according to which He produces and conserves all beings, more clearly than the will of their best friends or of those they have spent their whole life studying. For their mind's union with God and of their will with His, i.e., with eternal law or the immutable order, is an immediate, direct, and necessary union, whereas the union they have with sensible objects, which is established only for the preservation of their health and life, gives them knowledge of these objects only in relation to this design.

This direct and immediate union, which according to Saint Augustine is known only by those whose mind is purified, enlightens us in the most secret recesses of our reason, and exhorts and moves us in the most intimate part of our heart. Through it we learn what God thinks and even what He wills, eternal truths and laws, for it cannot be doubted that we know at least some of them with evidence. But the union we have with our best friends teaches us with evidence neither what they think nor what they will. We believe we know, but we are almost always mistaken when we know only because of what they say.

Nor can the union we have through our senses with surrounding bodies enlighten us; for what the senses report is never entirely true, and often it is entirely false, as I have explained in this book. For this reason I say here that it is more difficult than one would have thought to prove definitely that there are bodies, even though our senses might assure us of it, because reason does not so readily assure us as we might think and because reason must be consulted very attentively if we are to be enlightened.

But since men are more sensible than reasonable, and since they listen more readily to the testimony of their senses than to that of inner truth, they have always relied on their eyes to assure themselves of the existence of matter without bothering to consult their reason. This is why they are surprised when told that it is difficult to prove the existence of matter. They think that they have but to open their eyes in order to assure themselves that there are bodies, and if there is some reason to suspect an illusion, they think it suffices to approach the bodies and touch them—after which they have difficulty conceiving that one might yet have reasons for doubting their existence.

But our eyes represent colors to us on the surface of bodies and light in the air and in the sun; our ears make us hear sounds as if spread out through the air and in the resounding bodies; and if we believe what the other senses report, heat will be in fire, sweetness will be in sugar, musk will have an odor, and all the sensible qualities will be in the bodies that seem to exude or diffuse them. Yet it is certain (for the reasons that I have given in the first book of *The Search After Truth*) that all these qualities do not exist outside the soul that perceives them—at least it is not evident that they are in the bodies that surround us. Why should we conclude then, merely on the testimony of the senses that deceive us on all sides, that there really are external bodies, and even that these bodies are like those we see, i.e., like those that are the soul's immediate object, when we look at them with the eyes of the body. Whatever is to be said of this view, it certainly is not without difficulties.

Furthermore, if on the basis of what the senses report we can assure ourselves of the existence of a given body, that body is the one to which the soul is immediately joined. The most lively sensation and the one that seems to have the most necessary relation to some actually existing body is pain. Yet it often happens that those who have lost an arm feel very severe pain in it even long after the loss of the arm. They know very well that they no longer have the arm when they consult their memory or look at their body; but the sensation of pain deceives them. And if, as often happens, we assume them to have entirely forgotten what they were and to have no other senses than that through which they feel the pain in their imaginary arm, surely they could not be persuaded that they do not have an arm in which they feel such tormenting pain.

There have been those who believed they had horns on their head and others who imagined they were made of butter or glass or that their body was not shaped like other men's, that it was like that of a cock, a wolf, or an ox. They were mad, you will say, and I agree; but their soul was able to be mistaken in these things, and hence all other men can fall into similar errors if they judge objects on the testimony of their senses. For it should be noted that these madmen really see themselves as they think they are—error is not strictly in the sensation they have but in the judgment they form. If they said only that they sensed themselves or perceived themselves to be like a cock, they would not in the least be mistaken. They err solely in the fact that they believe that their body is like the one they sense, i.e., like their mind's immediate object when they consider themselves. Thus, those who believe themselves to be such as they really are, are no more judicious in their judgments of themselves than the mad if they base their judgments solely on what their senses report. They fail to be deceived, not through reason, but through good fortune.

But in the final analysis, can we be certain that those we call mad really are so? Might it not be said that they only pass for mad because their sensations are peculiar? For it is clear that a man passes for mad not because he perceives what is not but precisely because he sees the opposite of what others see, whether they are deceived or not.

A peasant, for example, whose eyes are disposed in a way to see the moon as it is, or as we only see it or shall perhaps see it some day with glasses yet to be invented, looks at it with wonder and exclaims to his companions: I see high mountains and deep valleys and seas and lakes and gulfs and high rocks![a] Do you not see many seas on the eastern side and that there is hardly anything but land and mountains toward the west and the south? Do you not see in the same area a

---

[a]This is roughly what one sees when one looks at the moon with a telescope.

mountain higher than any we have ever seen, and are you not amazed at an entirely black sea or a terrifying gulf that appears in the center of this star? How will his companions answer such exclamations and what will they think of him? That he is mad and fallen under the evil influences of the planet he beholds and admires. He is alone in his view and that is enough. Thus, to be mad in the opinion of others, it is not necessary really to be so; it is enough to think or to see things differently than others; for if all men believed themselves to be like cocks, he who believed himself to be as he is would surely be considered insane.

You will say, but do men have a beak at the end of their nose or a comb on their head? I do not think so. But I know nothing of the matter when I judge only according to my senses and do not know how to make proper use of them. In vain do I touch my face or my head. I feel my body and those surrounding me only with hands whose length and figure I do not know. I do not even know for sure that I really have hands; I know so only because when it seems to me that I am moving them certain motions take place in a certain part of my brain, which according to current belief is the seat of the common sense. But perhaps I do not even have this part of the brain about which so much is said and so little known. At least I am not aware of it within me, whereas I am aware of my hands. Consequently, I ought to believe that I have hands rather than that I have this little gland that is constantly the object of controversey. But I know neither the figure nor the motion of this gland, yet I am assured that I can learn only by means of them the figure and motion of my body and those surrounding me.

What, then, is to be thought of all this? That reason is not instructed by the body, that even the part of the body to which the soul is immediately joined is neither perceptible nor intelligible by itself, that neither our body nor those surrounding it can be our mind's immediate object, that we cannot learn from our brain whether it actually exists, much less whether there are bodies surrounding us; that we must therefore recognize that there is some superior intelligence that alone is capable of acting on us, and that can act on us in such a way as to truly represent to us bodies outside us, without giving us the least idea of our brain, though the motion produced in our brain is an occasion for this intelligence to reveal these bodies to us. For in short, we see the figure of bodies surrounding us with eyes whose figure we do not know; and although the colors that appear on these objects are no more lively than those depicted on the optic nerve, we see none of these latter even while we admire the splendor of the former.

But after all, under what obligation is this intelligence to reveal bodies to us when certain kinds of motion take place in our brain? Furthermore, why need there be external bodies for this motion to be stirred up in our brain? Do not sleep, the passions, and madness produce this motion without the aid of external bodies? Is it evident that bodies that cannot move one another[a] should be able to communicate to bodies they meet a motor force that they themselves do not have? Nonetheless, I would have bodies move themselves and those they strike, and set the fibers of our brain in motion. Cannot He who gives being to all things

---

[a]See the third chapter of the second part of book six, and the Elucidation [15] on this chapter.

also by Himself excite the motion in our brain to which our mind's ideas are attached? Finally, how is it contradictory that our soul should have new ideas while our brain keeps the same motion, since it is certain that the brain's motion does not produce the soul's ideas, that we do not even have any awareness of this motion, that only God can represent our ideas to us—as I have proved elsewhere?[a] To be completely certain of the existence of external bodies, then, it is absolutely necessary to know God, who gives us the sensation of them, and to realize that, since He is infinitely perfect, He cannot deceive us. For if the intelligence that gives us the ideas of all things wanted to amuse itself, so to speak, by representing to us bodies as actually existing—even though there were no such objects—it is clear that doing so would not be very difficult for it.

For these reasons, or reasons like them, Descartes, who wanted to establish his philosophy on unshakable foundations, thought he could not assume that there are bodies, and that he should not prove that there are on the basis of sensible proofs, even though they would seem very persuasive to the ordinary man. Clearly he knew as well as we do that he had only to open his eyes to see bodies and that we can approach them and touch them to ascertain whether our eyes deceive us in what they report. He knew the mind of man well enough to judge that such proofs had not been rejected. But he sought neither sensible probabilities nor the vain applause of men. He preferred the truth, even though scorned, to the glory of an undeserved reputation, and he preferred to seem ridiculous to insignificant minds with his doubts that to them might seem extravagant than to accept things that he did not judge certain and undeniable.

But although Descartes has given the strongest proofs that reason alone can muster for the existence of bodies, and although it is evident that God is no deceiver and that He would be said really to deceive us if we deceived ourselves by making the use we must of our mind and of our other faculties of which He is the Author—still we can say that the existence of matter is not yet perfectly demonstrated, i.e., with geometric rigor. For in philosophical matters, we must not believe anything till evidence obliges us to do so. We must make as much use of our freedom as possible; our judgments should have no greater extent than our perceptions. Thus, when we perceive bodies, let us judge only that we perceive them and that these perceptible or intelligible bodies actually exist; but why should we judge positively that there is an external material world like the intelligible world we perceive?

Perhaps you will say that we perceive bodies external to us and even at some distance from the body we animate and that therefore we can judge that they are external to us without our judgments extending beyond our perceptions. But how? Do we not see light external to us and in the sun, even though it is not there? Nevertheless, I would have these bodies we see external to us really be external to us, for in the final analysis this is beyond question. But is it not clear that there are outnesses and distances, that there are intelligible spaces in the intelligible world that is our mind's immediate object? Let us be careful here: the

[a]See the sixth chapter of the second part of book three and the Elucidation [10] on this chapter.

material world we animate is not the one we see when we look at it, i.e., when we turn the body's eyes toward it. The body we see is an intelligible body and there are intelligible spaces between this intelligible body and the intelligible sun we see, just as there are material spaces between our body and the sun we look at. Certainly God sees that there are spaces between the bodies He has created; but He does not see these bodies or spaces by themselves. He can see them only through the ideas He has of them, only through intelligible bodies and spaces. God derives His light only from Himself; He sees the material world only in the intelligible world He contains and in the knowledge He has of His volitions, which actually give existence and motion to all things. Therefore, there are intelligible spaces between the intelligible bodies that we see, as there are material spaces between the bodies we look at.

Now it must be noted that since only God knows His volitions (which produce all beings) by Himself, we can know only from Him whether there really is a material world external to us like the one we perceive, because the material world is neither perceptible nor intelligible by itself. Thus, in order to be fully convinced that there are bodies, we must have demonstrated for us not only that there is a God and that He is no deceiver, but also that He has assured us that He has really created such a world, which proof I have not found in the works of Descartes.

God speaks to the mind and constrains its belief in only two ways: through evidence and through faith. I agree that faith obliges us to believe that there are bodies; but as for evidence, it seems to me that it is incomplete and that we are not invincibly led to believe there is something other than God and our own mind. It is true that we have a strong propensity to believe that there are bodies surrounding us; I agree here with Descartes.[a] But this propensity, as natural as it is, does not constrain our belief through evidence; it merely inclines us toward belief through impression. Now, our free judgments should follow only light and evidence; and if we let ourselves be led by sense impressions, we shall be mistaken almost always.

Why are we mistaken in the judgments we form concerning sense qualities, the size, figure, and motion of bodies, if not because we follow an impression like the one that leads us to believe there are bodies? Do we not perceive that fire is hot, that snow is white, and that the sun is brilliant with light; do we not perceive sense qualities as well as bodies external to us? Yet it is certain that these sense qualities we perceive external to us are not really external to us (or if you will, nothing is certain on this matter). What reason have we, then, that besides the intelligible bodies we perceive there are still others we look at? What evidence do you have that an impression that is deceptive not only with regard to sense qualities but also with regard to the size, figure, and motion of bodies, is not so with regard to the actual existence of these same bodies? I ask what evidence of this you have, for I agree that you have no lack of probabilities.

I realize there is this difference between sense qualities and bodies, that reason

[a]Meditation 6.

corrects the impression or natural judgments related to sense qualities much more easily than those related to the existence of bodies, and even that all of reason's corrections with regard to sense qualities agree with religion and Christian morality, and that the existence of matter cannot be denied according to the principles of religion.

It is easy to understand that pleasure and pain, heat, and even colors are not modes of bodies, that sense qualities in general are not contained in the idea we have of matter, in short, that our senses do not represent sensible objects to us as they are in themselves, but as they are in relation to the preservation of our life and health. This agrees not only with reason but even more so with religion and Christian morality, as is shown in several places in this work.

But it is not so easy to ascertain positively that there are no bodies external to us as we positively ascertain that pain and heat are not in the bodies that seem to cause them in us. Certainly it is at least possible that there are external bodies. We have nothing that proves to us there are not any, and on the contrary we have a strong inclination to believe there are bodies. We have, then, more reason to believe there are bodies than to believe there are not any. Thus, it seems that we should believe there are bodies; for we are naturally led to follow our natural judgment when we cannot positively correct it through light or evidence. For since all natural judgments come from God, we can make our voluntary judgments agree with them when we find no means of discovering them to be false; and if we are mistaken in these instances, the Author of our mind would seem to be to some extent the Author of our errors and faults.

This argument is perhaps sound enough. Nevertheless, it must be agreed that it should not be taken as a necessary demonstration of the existence of bodies, for God does not invincibly urge us to yield to it. If we consent to it, we do so freely—we are able not to consent to it. If the argument I have just given is sound, we must believe it entirely probable that there are bodies; but we must not rest fully convinced by this single argument. Otherwise, it is we who act and not God in us. It is by a free act, and consequently one liable to error, that we consent and not by an invincible impression; for we believe because we freely will to do so, and not because we perceive with an evidence necessitating us to believe, as in the case of mathematical demonstrations.

Surely only faith can persuade us that there really are bodies. We cannot have an exact demonstration of other than a necessary being's existence. And if you attend closely, you will see that it is not even possible to know with full evidence whether or not God is truly the creator of the material and sensible world. For such evidence is found only in necessary relations, and there is no necessary relation between God and such a world. He was able not to create it, and if He did create it, it is because He willed to do so and willed freely to do so.

The saints in heaven see by an evident light that the Father begets His Son and that the Father and the Son produce the Holy Spirit, for these emanations are necessary. But since the world is not a necessary emanation in God, those who most clearly see His being do not see with evidence that He produces anything external. Nonetheless, I believe the blessed are certain that there is a world; but this is because God assures them of it by revealing His will to them in a way unknown to us. We here below are certain of the existence of the world because faith teaches us that God has created it, and because faith agrees with our natural judgments or our compound sensations when they are confirmed by all our senses and when they are corrected by our memory and reason.

It is true that initially faith seems to assume the existence of bodies, *fides ex auditu*. It seems to assume prophets, apostles, Sacred Scripture, miracles; but if you attend closely you will see that although only the appearances of men, prophets, apostles, Sacred Scripture, miracles, and so on, are assumed, what we learn from these supposed appearances is absolutely undeniable because, as I have proved in several places in this work, only God can represent these appearances to the mind, and because God is no deceiver, for faith itself assumes all this. Now in the appearance of Sacred Scripture and from the appearance of miracles we learn that God has created a heaven and an earth, that the Word was made flesh, and other such truths that assume the existence of a created world. Hence it is certain through faith that there are bodies, and that through it all these appearances become realities. There would be no point to my pausing here to reply at greater length to an objection that seems too abstract to the ordinary man, and I believe that the above will satisfy anyone who is not overly demanding.

From all this, therefore, it must be concluded that we can and even must correct the natural judgments or the compound perceptions relating to the sensible qualities we attribute to bodies surrounding us or the one we animate. But as for the natural judgments relating to the actual existence of bodies, although in an absolute sense we can avoid forming voluntary judgments that agree with them, we should not do so, because these natural judgments are in perfect agreement with faith.

Furthermore, I have made this observation mainly to provoke some serious thought about the following truths: that bodies cannot act on, or reveal themselves to, minds, and that the bodies we look at when we open our eyes are quite different from the ideas that represent them and that affect us; that our soul finds its light, its life, and its sustenance only in God; that it can have an immediate and direct relation only with Him and that the relation it has with its body and those surrounding it necessarily depends on the relation it has with the efficacious and luminous substance of the Divinity—a substance that discloses creatures to us as possible or as existing or as belonging to us, depending on the different ways in which it affects us insofar as it represents them: (1) as possible when the perception of the idea affecting us is pure, (2) as existing when the perception is sensible, and (3) as belonging to us and forming a part of us when the perception is very absorbing and lively, as is pain. I realize that the ordinary man will not agree with this observation and that, depending on whether he has too few or too many animal spirits, he will either ridicule or be alarmed at the arguments I have just given, for the imagination cannot endure strange or abstract truths; it views them either as terrifying specters or as ridiculous shadows. But I prefer to be the object of the mockery of strong imaginations and the object of the fear of weak and fearful imaginations than to fail in my duty to the truth and to those who, in struggling valiantly against the body's influence on their mind, can distinguish the replies of the wisdom that enlightens us from what their senses tell them and from the confused din of the imagination, which disturbs and seduces us.

f. Knowledge of the Soul

ELUCIDATION ELEVEN

⚜

On the seventh chapter of the second part of the third book, where I prove that we have no clear idea either of our soul's nature or of its modifications.

I have said in a number of places, and I even think that I have sufficiently proved in the third book of the *Search after Truth*, that we have no *clear idea* of our soul, but only *consciousness* or inner sensation of it, and that thus we know it much less perfectly than we do extension. This seemed to me so evident that I did not think it necessary to argue so at further length. But the authority of Descartes,[a] who clearly says *that the nature of the mind is better known than the nature of any other thing*, has so prejudiced some of his disciples that what I wrote on the topic has served only to make me seem a person of weak character who cannot grasp and hold fast to abstract truths incapable of arousing and maintaining the attention of those who consider them.

I grant that I am extremely weak, sensuous, and coarse, and that my mind depends on my body in more ways than I can express. I know this and I feel it; and I work incessantly to increase this knowledge I have of myself. For if we cannot avoid being miserable, at least we must know and feel it. We must at least be humbled at the sight of our inner miseries and recognize the need we have of being delivered from this body of death that injects trouble and confusion into all the soul's faculties.

Yet the present question is so suited to the mind's capacity that I do not see the need for any great effort to resolve it (which is the reason I did not pause over it). For I think I can say that the ignorance of most men with regard to their own soul, of its distinction from the body, of its spirituality, immortality, and other properties, is enough to show clearly that they have no clear and distinct idea of it.

We are able to say that we have a clear idea of the body because in order to know the modifications it can have, it suffices to consult the idea representing it. We clearly see that it can be round or square, in motion or at rest. We have no difficulty conceiving that a square can be divided into two triangles, two parallelograms, two trapezia. When we are asked whether something does or does not

[a]Reply to the fifth objection against the second Meditation, toward the end.

86

belong to extension, we never hesitate in our response, because as the idea of extension is clear, we see without any difficulty through simple perception what it contains and what it excludes.

θ But surely we have no idea of our mind which is such that, by consulting it, we can discover the modifications of which the mind is capable. If we had never felt pleasure or pain we could not know whether or not the soul could feel them. If a man had never eaten a melon, or seen red or blue, he would consult this alleged idea of his soul in vain and would never discover distinctly whether or not it was capable of these sensations or modifications. I maintain, furthermore, that even if one is actually feeling pain or seeing color, one cannot discover through simple perception whether these qualities belong to the soul. One imagines that pain is in the body that occasions it, and that color is spread out on the surface of objects, although these objects are distinct from our soul.

In order to determine whether sensible qualities are modes of the mind, we do not consult the alleged idea of the soul—the Cartesians themselves consult, rather, the idea of extension, and they reason as follows. Heat, pain, and color cannot be modifications of extension, for extension can have only various figures and motion. Now there are only two kinds of beings, minds and bodies. Therefore, pain, heat, color, and all other sensible qualities belong to the mind.

Since we have to consult our idea of extension in order to discover whether sensible qualities are modes of our mind, is it not evident that we have no clear idea of the soul? Would we otherwise ever bother with such a roundabout way? When a philosopher wishes to learn whether roundness belongs to extension, does he consult the idea of the soul, or some idea other than that of extension? Does he not see clearly in the idea itself of extension that roundness is a modification of it? And would it not be strange if, in order to learn of it, he reasoned as follows. There are only two kinds of beings, minds and bodies. Roundness is not the mode of a mind. It is therefore the mode of a body.

We discover by simple perception, then, without any reasoning and merely by applying the mind to the idea of extension, that roundness and every other figure is a modification belonging to body, and that pleasure, pain, heat, and all other sensible qualities are not modifications of body. Every question about what does or does not belong to extension can be answered easily, immediately, and boldly, merely by considering the idea representing it. Everyone agrees on this subject, for those who say that matter can think do not believe that it has this faculty because it is extended; they agree that extension, taken precisely as such, cannot think.

But there is no agreement on what should be believed about the soul and its modifications. There are people who think that pain and heat, or at least color, do not belong to the soul. You even make a fool of yourself before certain Cartesians if you say that the soul actually becomes blue, red, or yellow, and that the soul is painted with the colors of the rainbow when looking at it. There are many people who have doubts, and even more who do not believe, that when we smell carrion the soul becomes formally rotten, and that the taste of sugar, or of pepper or salt, is something belonging to the soul. Where, then, is the clear idea of the soul so that the Cartesians might consult it, and so that they might all agree on the question as to where colors, tastes, and odors are to be found?

But even if the Cartesians should agree on these difficulties, we could not conclude from their agreement that they have a clear idea of the soul. For if they agree finally that it is the soul that is actually green or red when we see greenness or redness, they will do so only as a result of lengthy arguments. They will never see it through simple perception; they will never arrive at this by consulting the supposed idea of the soul, but rather, by consulting the idea of body. They will maintain that sensible qualities belong to the soul only because these qualities do not belong to extension, of which they have a clear idea. They will never convince anyone of this whose insufficiency of mind precludes complex perceptions or reasoning, or rather, anyone who does not stop to consider the clear idea of body and who confuses everything. There will always be peasants, women, children, and perhaps savants and doctors, who will have doubts about it. But women and children, the learned and the ignorant, the most enlightened and the most dense, have no difficulty in conceiving through the idea they have of extension that it can have all sorts of figures. They clearly understand that extension is incapable of pain, taste, odor, or of any sensation, when they faithfully and attentively consider the single idea that represents it. For there is no sensible quality contained in the idea that represents extension.

It is true that they might have doubts as to whether or not body is capable of sensation, or of receiving some sensible quality; but this is because they understand body as something other than extension, and because they have no idea of body taken in this sense. But when Descartes, or the Cartesians to whom I am speaking, assert that we know the soul better than body, they mean by body only extension. How, then, can they maintain that we know the nature of the soul more clearly than that of body, since the idea of body or extension is so clear that everyone agrees on what it contains and what it excludes, whereas the idea of the soul is so confused that the Cartesians themselves constantly dispute as to whether modifications of color belong to it.

"We know the nature of a substance more distinctly," say these philosophers following Descartes,[a] "as we know more of its attributes. Now there is nothing whose attributes we know more of than our mind, because as many attributes as we know in other things can be counted in the mind from the fact that it knows them. And thus its nature is better known than the nature of any other thing."

But who does not see that there is quite a difference between knowing through a clear idea and knowing through *consciousness*? When I know that twice two is four, I know this very clearly, but I do not know clearly what it is in me that knows it. I sense it, granted; I know it through consciousness or inner sensation. But I have no clear idea of it as I have of numbers, between which I can clearly discover relations. I can *count* that there are in my mind three properties: that of knowing that two times two is four, that of knowing that three times three is nine, and that of knowing that four times four is sixteen. If you wish, an infinity of

[a]In the passage just cited.

properties in me can thus be counted, since these three properties are different from each other. [But I deny that the nature of the things thus capable of being *counted* can be known *clearly*. To be counted, they need only be sensed.]

We can be said to have a clear idea of a being and to know its nature when we can compare it with others of which we also have a clear idea, or at least when we can compare the modifications of which the being is capable. We have clear ideas of numbers and of parts of extension because we can compare these things. We can compare two with four, four with sixteen and each number with every other. We can compare a square with a triangle, a circle with an ellipse, a square or a triangle with every other square or triangle, and we can thus clearly discover the relations between these figures and between these numbers. But we cannot compare our mind with other minds in order to discover clearly some relation between them. We cannot even compare the modes of our mind, its own perceptions. We cannot discover clearly the relation between pleasure and pain, heat and color, or to speak only of modes of the same kind, we cannot exactly determine the relation between green and red, yellow and violet, or even between violet and violet. We sense that the one is darker or more brilliant than the other, but we do not know clearly either by how much, or in what being darker or more brilliant consists. We therefore have no clear idea either of the soul or of its modifications, and although I see or sense colors, tastes, odors, I can say, as I have, that I do not know them through a clear idea, because I am unable to discover clearly their relations.

It is true that I can discover exact relations between sounds, that the octave, for example, is two to one, the fifth three to two, the fourth four to three. But I cannot know these relations through the sensation I have of them. If I know that the octave is two to one, it is because I have learned through experience that a given string sounds the octave when, having been plucked at full length, it is then plucked after having been divided into two equal parts. It is because I know that there are twice as many vibrations in an equal amount of time, or something like this. It is because the disturbances in the air, the vibrations of the string, and the string itself are things that can be compared through clear ideas, and because we know distinctly the relations that can obtain between the string and its parts as well as between the rates of different vibrations. But the sounds cannot be compared in themselves, or insofar as they are sensible qualities and modifications of the soul. We cannot know their relations in this way. And although musicians distinguish different consonances very well, this is not because they distinguish their relations through clear ideas. For them, the ear alone judges the difference in sounds; their reason knows nothing. But the ear cannot be said to judge through a clear idea or otherwise than through sensation. Even musicians, then, have no clear idea of sounds taken as sensations or modifications of the soul. Consequently, neither the soul nor its modifications is known through a clear idea, but only through consciousness or inner sensation.

Furthermore, we do not know what the soul's dispositions consist in which make it readier to act and represent objects to itself. We cannot even conceive what such dispositions could consist in. I say further that through reason we cannot ascertain whether the soul when separated from the body or taken in isolation from the body is capable of having any habits or memory. But how can we be ignorant of these things if the nature of the soul is better known than that of the body? We have no difficulty in seeing what constitutes the animal spirits' readiness to be distributed in the nerves in which they have already flowed many times. Or at least we have no difficulty in discovering that as the passages in the nerves become larger and their fibers relax in a certain way, the spirits can easily pass through them. But what could conceiveably increase the soul's readiness for action or thought? For my part, I admit that I understand nothing of this. In vain do I examine myself in order to discover these dispositions; I have no answer for myself. I cannot enlighten myself on the matter, even though I have a very lively sensation of the readiness with which certain thoughts are excited in me. And if I did not have good reasons that lead me to believe that I do in fact have such dispositions (although I am not aware of them in me), I would judge by consulting only inner sensation that my soul has neither habits nor a spiritual memory. But our hesitation in this is a sure sign that we are not as enlightened as we might say, for doubt does not agree with evidence and clear ideas.

It is certain that the most enlightened man does not know with evidence whether he is worthy of love or hatred, as the wise man says.[a] The inner sensation we have of ourselves cannot decide. Saint Paul says that his conscience gives him no reproach,[b] but he does not claim that because of this he is justified. He claims, on the contrary, that this does not justify him and that he dares not judge himself because it is the Lord who judges him. But given that we have a clear idea of order, if we also had a clear idea of the soul through our inner sensation of ourselves, we would know clearly whether the soul conformed to order; we would know whether we are righteous or not. We would even be able to know with precision all its inner dispositions toward good and evil when having a sensation of them. But if we could know ourselves as we are, we would not be so liable to presumption. And it is likely that Saint Peter would not have said to his Master, whom he was soon to deny,[c] "Why cannot I follow you now, I will give my life for you, Animam meam pro te ponam." For with an inner sensation of his own strength and good will, he would have been able to see clearly whether he had the strength or courage to conquer death, or rather the insults of a maid and a few servants.

If the nature of the soul is better known than the nature of any other things, if the idea we have of it is as clear as the idea we have of the body, then I ask only this: how is it that there are so many people who confuse the two? Is it possible to confuse two entirely different clear ideas? Let us do justice to everyone. Those who are not of our opinion are as reasonable as we, they have the same ideas of things, they participate in the same reason. Why, then, do they confuse what we

---

[a]Eccles. 9:1.

[b]"Sed neque meipsum judico. Nihil enim mihi conscius sum: sed non in hoc justificatus sum: qui autem judicat me Dominus est." 1 Cor. 4:4.

[c]John 12:37.

disinguish? Have they on any other occasion ever confused things of which they have clear ideas? Have they ever confused two different numbers? Have they ever taken a square for a circle? Yet the soul is more different from the body than a square is from a circle, for they are substances that agree in nothing, and yet these people confuse them. There is, then, some difficulty in recognizing their difference. Their difference is not found by simple perception, and reasoning is required to conclude that the one is not the other. The idea of extension must be carefully consulted, and it must be seen that extension is not a mode of bodies but body itself (since it is represented to us as a subsisting thing and as the principle of everything we clearly conceive in bodies); and thus, since the modes of which a body is capable are in no way related to sense qualities, the subject of these qualities, or rather, the being of which these qualities are modes, must be very different from body. Such arguments must be produced in order to avoid confusing the soul with the body. But if we had a clear idea of the soul, as we do of the body, we certainly would not have to take such a roundabout way to distinguish it from the body. We could do so at a single glance, as easily as we see that a square is not a circle.

I shall pause for no further proof that we do not know the soul or its modifications through clear ideas.[a] We come to realize this no matter how we look at ourselves, and I add this to what I have already said in the *Search after Truth* only because of the criticism it received from certain Cartesians. If this does not satisfy them, then let them show me this clear idea of the soul that, no matter how I try, I cannot find in myself.

---

[a]You might see the ninth of the *Meditations chrétiennes*.

BOOK SIX: PART TWO
Chapter Three

❧

The most dangerous error of the philosophy of the ancients.

Not only do philosophers say what they do not conceive when they explain natural effects through certain beings of which they have not one single particular idea, they even furnish a principle from which one can directly infer very false and very dangerous conclusions.

For if we assume, in accordance with their opinion, that bodies have certain entities distinct from matter in them, then, having no distinct idea of these entities, we can easily imagine that they are the true or major causes of the effects we see. That is even the general opinion of ordinary philosophers; for it is mainly to explain these effects that they think there are substantial forms, real qualities, and other similar entities. If we next consider attentively our idea of cause or of power to act, we cannot doubt that this idea represents something divine. For the idea of a sovereign power is the idea of sovereign divinity but a genuine one, at least according to the pagans, assuming that it is the idea of a genuine power or cause. We therefore admit something divine in all the bodies around us when we posit forms, faculties, qualities, virtues, or real beings capable of producing certain effects through the force of their nature; and thus we insensibly adopt the opinion of the pagans because of our respect for their philosophy. It is true that faith corrects us; but perhaps it can be said in this connection that if the heart is Christian, the mind is basically pagan. Perhaps it will be said that substantial forms, those *plastic* forms, for example, that produce animals and plants, do not know what they are doing and that, thus lacking intelligence, they have no relation to the divinities of the pagans. But who will be able to believe that what produces works that manifest a wisdom that surpasses all philosophers produces them without intelligence?

Furthermore, it is difficult to be persuaded that we should neither fear nor love true powers—beings that can act upon us, punish us with pain, or reward us with pleasure. And as love and fear are true adoration, it is also difficult to be persuaded that we should not adore these beings. Everything that can act upon us as a true and real cause is necessarily above us, according to Saint Augustine and according to reason; and according to the same saint and the same reason, it is an immutable law that inferior things serve superior ones. It is for these reasons that this great saint recognizes[a] that the body cannot act upon the soul,[b] and that nothing can be above the soul except God.

In the Sacred Scriptures, when God proves to the Israelites that they must adore Him, i.e., that they must fear and love Him, the main reasons He gives are drawn from His power to reward and punish them. He shows them the benefits they have received from Him, the evils for which He chastised them, and that He still has the same power. He forbids them to adore the gods of the pagans because they have no power over them and can do them neither good nor evil. He wants them to honor only Him because He alone is the true cause of good and evil, and because nothing happens in their city, according to one prophet,[c] that He himself does not cause: because natural causes are not the true causes of the ill they appear to cause us, and because, as it is God alone who acts in them, it is He alone who must be feared, and who must be loved in them; "Soli Deo honor et gloria" [1 Tim. 1:17].

Finally, this opinion that we should love and fear what can be the true cause of good and evil appears so natural and right that it is impossible to disbelieve it. Hence, if we assume this false opinion of the philosophers, which we are here trying to destroy, that the bodies that surround us are the true causes of the pleasures and ills we feel, reason seems to some degree to justify a religion similar to that of the pagans, and to approve the universal disorder of morals.

It is true that reason does not teach that it is necessary to adore onions and leeks, for example, as the sovereign divinity, because they cannot make us completely happy when we have them, nor entirely unhappy when we do not. Also the pagans never gave them as much honor as they gave to the great Jupiter, on whom all their divinities depended, or as they gave to the sun, which our senses represent to us as the universal cause that gives life and motion to all things, and that we cannot help regarding as a divinity if we assume with the pagan philosophers that it encompasses in its being the true causes of everything it seems to produce, not only in our bodies and minds, but also in all the beings that surround us.

But if one should not render sovereign honor to leeks and onions, one can always render them some particular adoration; I mean, one can think of them and love them to some extent, if it is true that they can to some extent make us happy. We should render them honor in proportion to the good they can do. And certainly, men who heed the reports of their senses think these vegetables are capable of doing them good. The Israelites, for example, would not have missed them so much in the desert, they would not have considered themselves unhappy for want of them, had they imagined themselves in some way happy because of their enjoyment of them. Perhaps drunkards would not love wine so much if they

---

[a]"Ego enim ab anima hoc corpus animari non puto, nisi intentione facientis; nec ab isto quicquam illam pati arbitror, sed facere de illo et in illo, tamquam subjecto divinitus dominationis suae." 1. 6. *Mus*.C. 5.

[b]See chapter 34 of St. Augustine *De quantitate animae*.

[c]Amos, chs. 3, 6.

were well aware of what it is, and that the pleasure they find in drinking it comes from the Almighty, who commands them to be temperate and whom they unjustly cause to serve their intemperance. Those are the disorders in which we involve reason itself when it is joined to the principles of pagan philosophy and when it follows the impressions of the senses.

In order that we shall no longer be able to doubt the falseness of this detestable philosophy and shall clearly recognize the soundness of the principles and the distinctness of the ideas being used, it is necessary clearly to establish the truths that are opposed to the errors of the ancient philosopher, and to prove in few words that there is only one true cause because there is only one true God; that the nature or power of each thing is nothing but the will of God; that all natural causes are not *true* causes but only *occasional* causes, and certain other truths that will follow from these.

It is clear that no body, large or small, has the power to move itself. A mountain, a house, a rock, a grain of sand, in short, the tiniest or largest body conceivable does not have the power to move itself. We have only two sorts of ideas, ideas of minds and ideas of bodies; and as we should speak only of what we conceive, we should only reason according to these two kinds of ideas. Thus, since the idea we have of all bodies makes us aware that they cannot move themselves, it must be concluded that it is minds which move them.[a] But when we examine our idea of all finite minds, we do not see any necessary connection between their will and the motion of any body whatsoever. On the contrary, we see that there is none and that there can be none. We must therefore also conclude, if we wish to reason according to our lights, that there is absolutely no mind created that can move a body as a true or principal cause, just as it has been said that no body could move itself.

But when one thinks about the idea of God, i.e., of an infinitely perfect and consequently all-powerful being, one knows there is such a connection between His will and the motion of all bodies, that it is impossible to conceive that He wills a body to be moved and that this body not be moved. We must therefore say that only His will can move bodies if we wish to state things as we conceive them and not as we sense them. The motor force of bodies is therefore not in the bodies that are moved, for this motor force is nothing other than the will of God. Thus, bodies have no action; and when a ball that is moved collides with and moves another, it communicates to it nothing of its own, for it does not itself have the force it communicates to it. Nevertheless, a ball is the natural cause of the motion it communicates. A natural cause is therefore not a real and true but only an occasional cause, which determines the Author of nature to act in such and such a manner in such and such a situation.

It is certain that all things are produced through the motion of either visible or invisible bodies, for experience teaches us that bodies whose parts have more motion are always those that act more and produce more change in the world. All

---

[a]See the seventh *Dialogue on Metaphysics* and the fifth of the *Christian Meditations* [3–9 and 14–18].

natural forces are therefore nothing but the will of God, which is always efficacious. God created the world because He willed it: "Dixit, & facta sunt" [Ps. 32:9]; and He moves all things, and thus produces all the effects that we see happening, because He also willed certain laws according to which motion is communicated upon the collison of bodies; and because these laws are efficacious, they act, whereas bodies cannot act. There are therefore no forces, powers, or true causes in the material, sensible world; and it is not necessary to admit the existence of forms, faculties, and real qualities for producing effects that bodies do not produce and for sharing with God the force and power essential to Him.

But not only are bodies incapable of being the true causes of whatever exists: the most noble minds are in a similar state of impotence. They can know nothing unless God enlightens them. They can sense nothing unless God modifies them. They are incapable of willing anything unless God moves them toward good in general, i.e., toward Himself. They can determine the impression God gives them toward Himself toward objects other than Himself, I admit; but I do not know if that can be called power. If the ability to sin is a power, it will be a power that the Almighty does not have, Saint Augustine says somewhere. If men held, of themselves, the power to love the good, we could say they had some power; but men can only love because God wills them to and because His will is efficacious. Men can only love because God incessantly pushes them toward the good in general, i.e., toward Himself; for God having created them only for Himself, He never preserves them without turning and pushing them toward Himself. It is not they who move themselves toward the good in general, it is God who moves them. They merely follow this impression through an entirely free choice according to the law of God, or they determine it toward false goods, according to the law of the flesh; but they can determine it only through the perception of good, for, being capable only of what God makes them do, they can love only the good.

But were one to assume what is in one sense true, that minds have in themselves the power to know truth and to love good, still, if their thoughts and wills produced nothing externally, one could always say that they are capable of nothing. Now it appears to me quite certain that the will of minds is incapable of moving the smallest body in the world; for it is clear that there is no necessary connection between our will to move our arms, for example, and the movement of our arms. It is true that they are moved when we will it, and that thus we are the natural cause of the movement of our arms. But *natural* causes are not true causes; they are only *occasional* causes that act only through the force and efficacy of the will of God, as I have just explained.

For how could we move our arms? To move them, it is necessary to have animal spirits, to send them through certain nerves toward certain muscles in order to inflate and contract them, for it is thus that the arm attached to them is moved; or according to the opinion of some others, it is still not known how that happens. And we see that men who do not know that they have spirits, nerves, and muscles move their arms, and even move them with more skill and ease than those who know anatomy best. Therefore, men will to move their arms, and only God is able and knows how to move them. If a man cannot turn a tower upside down, at least he knows what must be done to do so; but there is no man who knows what must be done to move one of his fingers by means of animal spirits. How, then, could men move their arms? These things seem obvious to me and, it seems to me, to all those willing to think, although they are perhaps incomprehensible to all those willing only to sense.

But not only are men not the true causes of the movements they produce in their bodies, there even seems to be some contradiction (in saying) that they could be. A true cause as I understand it is one such that the mind perceives a necessary connection between it and its effect. Now the mind perceives a necessary connection only between the will of an infinitely perfect being and its effects. Therefore, it is only God who is the true cause and who truly has the power to move bodies. I say further (a) that it is inconceivable that God could communicate His power to move bodies to men or angels, and (b) that those who claim that our power to move our arms is a true power should admit that God can also give to minds the power to create, annihilate, and to do all possible things; in short, that He can render them omnipotent, as I shall show.

God needs no instruments to act; it suffices that He wills[a] in order that a thing be, because it is a contradiction that He should will and that what He wills should not happen. Therefore, His power is His will, and to communicate His power is to communicate the efficacy of His will. But to communicate this efficacy to a man or an angel signifies nothing other than to will that when a man or an angel shall will this or that body to be moved it will actually be moved. Now in this case, I see two wills concurring when an angel moves a body; that of God and that of the angel; and in order to know which of the two is the true cause of the movement of this body, it is necessary to know which one is efficacious. There is a necessary connection between the will of God and the thing He wills. God wills in this case that, when an angel wills this or that body be moved, it will be moved. Therefore, there is a necessary connection between the will of God and the movement of the body; and consequently it is God who is the true cause of its movement, whereas the will of the angel is only the occasional cause.

But to show this still more clearly, let us suppose that God wills to produce the opposite of what some minds will, as might be thought in the case of demons or some other minds that deserve this punishment. One could not say in this case that God would communicate His power to them, since they could do nothing they willed to do. Nevertheless, the wills of these minds would be the natural causes of the effects produced. Such bodies would be moved to the right only because these minds willed them moved to the left; and the volitions of these minds would determine the will of God to act, as our willing to move the parts of our bodies determines the first cause to move them. Thus, all the volitions of minds are only occasional causes.

---

[a]It is clear that I am speaking here about practical volitions, or those God has when He wills to act.

But if after all these arguments someone still wishes to maintain that the will of an angel who moved a body would be a true and not an occasional cause, it is clear that this same angel could be the true cause of the creation and annihilation of all things. For God could communicate to him His power to create and annihilate bodies, as <He does> the power to move them, if He willed all things to be created and annihilated, in a word if He willed all things to happen as the angel would will, just as He willed bodies to be moved as the angel would will. Therefore, if someone claims that an angel and a man are true movers because God moves bodies when they will it, they must also say that a man and an angel can truly be creators, since God could create beings when they would will it. Perhaps one could even say that the most vile animals, or matter all by itself, would effectively cause the creation of some substance, if one assumed as do the philosophers[a] that God produced substantial forms when required by matter. Finally, because God resolved from all eternity to create certain things in a certain time, one could also say that these times would be the causes of the creation of these beings; just as one claims that a ball that collides with another is the true cause of the movement it communicates to it, because God willed through His general will, which causes the order of nature, that when two bodies collide, such a communication of motion occurs.

There is therefore only one single true God and one single cause that is truly a cause, and one should not imagine that what precedes an effect is its true cause. God cannot even communicate His power to creatures, if we follow the lights of reason; He cannot make true causes of them, He cannot make them gods. But even if He could, we cannot conceive why He would. Bodies, minds, pure intelligences, all these can do nothing. It is He who made minds, who enlightens and activates them. It is He who created the sky and the earth, and who regulates their motions. In short, it is the Author of our being who executes our wills: *semel jussit, semper paret*. He moves our arms even when we use them against His orders; for He complains through His prophet[b] that we make Him serve our unjust and criminal desires.

All these insignificant pagan divinities and all these particular causes of the philosophers are merely chimeras that the wicked mind tries to establish to undermine worship of the true God in order to occupy the minds and hearts that the Creator has made only for Himself. It is not the philosophy received from Adam that teaches these things; it is that received from the serpent; for since Original Sin, the mind of man is quite pagan. It is this philosophy that, together with the errors of the senses, made men adore the sun, and that today is still the universal cause of the disorder of men's minds and the corruption of men's hearts. Their actions and sometimes even their words ask why we should not love the body, since bodies are capable of gorging us with pleasure. And why do people mock the Israelites who longed for the cabbages and onions of Egypt, since they were actually unhappy being deprived of something that could make

---

[a]See the Elucidation on the efficacy of secondary causes [15], *Dialogues on Metaphysics,* seventh Dialogue.

[b]Isa. 43:24.

them to some extent happy. But the philosophy that is called new, which is represented as a specter to frighten feeble minds, which is scorned and condemned without being understood, the new philosophy, I say (since it is the fashion to call it thus), ruins all the arguments of the skeptics through the establishment of the greatest of its principles, which is in perfect harmony with the first[a] principle of the Christian religion: that we must love and fear only one God, since there is only one God who can make us happy.

For if religion teaches us that there is only one true God, this philosophy shows us that there is only one true cause. If religion teaches us that all the divinities of paganism are merely stones and metals without life or motion, this philosophy also reveals to us that all secondary causes, or all the divinities of philosophy, are merely matter and inefficacious wills. Finally, if religion teaches us that we must not genuflect before false gods, this philosophy also teaches us that our imaginations and minds must not bow before the imaginary greatness and power of causes that are not causes at all; that we must neither love nor fear them; that we must not be concerned with them; that we must think only of God alone, see God in all things, fear and love God in all things.

But that is not the inclination of some philosophers. They do not want to see God, they do not want to think about God; for since sin there is a secret opposition between man and God. They take pleasure in fabricating gods at their whim, and they willingly love and fear the figments of their imaginations, as the pagans do the works of their hands. They are like children who tremble before their companions after they have painted their faces. Or if one wishes a more noble comparison, although perhaps not as accurate, they resemble those famous Romans who had fear and respect for the figments of the imagination, and who foolishly worshiped their emperors after they had released the eagle at their apotheoses.

---

[a]Haec est religio Christiana, fratres mei, quae praedicatur per universum mundum horrentibus inimicis, et ubi vincuntur murmurantibus, ubi praevalent savientibus, haec est religio Christiana ut *COLTUR UNUS DEUS NON MULTI DII, QUIA NON FACIT ANIMAM BEATAM NISI UNUS DEUS.''* Aug. *Tract.* 23 on St. John [C. 5].

ELUCIDATION FIFTEEN

❧

On the third chapter of the second part of the sixth book. Concerning the efficacy attributed to secondary causes.

Since the sin of the first man, the mind constantly spreads itself externally; it forgets itself and Him who enlightens and penetrates it, and it lets itself be so seduced by its body and by those surrounding it that it imagines finding in them its perfection and happiness. God, who alone is capable of acting on us, is now hidden to our eyes; His operations contain nothing sensible, and although He produces and conserves all beings, the mind, which so arduously seeks the cause of all things, has difficulty in recognizing Him, although it encounters Him at every moment. Some philosophers prefer to imagine a *nature* and certain *faculties* as the cause of the effects we call natural, than to render to God all the honor that is due His power; and although they have neither a proof nor even a clear idea of this nature or these faculties, as I hope to show, they prefer to speak without knowing what they say and to respect a purely imaginary power, than to make any effort of mind to recognize the hand of Him who does everything in all things.

I cannot help believing that one of the most deplorable consequences of Original Sin is that we no longer have any taste or feeling for God, or that we experience and encounter Him only with a kind of horror or fear. We should see God in all things, sense His power and might in all natural effects, admire His wisdom in the marvelous order of creatures—in a word, we should adore only Him, fear and love only Him in all His works. But there is now a secret opposition between man and God. Feeling himself a sinner, man hides, flees the light, fears encountering God and prefers to imagine in the bodies surrounding him a blind nature or power that he can master and without remorse use toward his bizarre and disordered intentions, than to find in them the terrible power of a just and holy God who knows all and who does all.

I grant that there are many people who through a principle different from that of the pagan philosophers follow their opinion on *nature* and secondary causes. But I hope it will be seen from the following discourse that they yield to this opinion only through a prejudice from which it is almost impossible to deliver oneself without the aid that can be drawn from the principles of a philosophy that has not always been sufficiently known. For it is apparently this which has prevented them from declaring themselves in favor of the opinion I think ought to be held.

There are many reasons preventing me from attributing to *secondary* or *natural* causes a force, a power, an efficacy to produce anything. But the principal one is that this opinion does not even seem conceivable to me. Whatever effort I make in order to understand it, I cannot find in me any idea representing to me what might be the force or the power they attribute to creatures. And I do not even think it a temerarious judgment to assert that those who maintain that creatures have force and power in themselves advance what they do not clearly conceive. For in short, if philosophers clearly conceived that secondary causes have a true force to act and produce things like them, then being a man as much as they and participating like them in sovereign Reason, I should clearly be able to discover the idea that represents this force to them. But whatever effort of mind I make, I can find force, efficacy, or power only in the will of the infinitely perfect Being.

In addition, when I think about the different opinions of philosophers on this subject, I cannot doubt what I am proposing. For if they clearly saw what the power of creatures is, or what in them truly has this power, they would all agree in their opinion about it. When people who have no special interest preventing them from agreeing cannot agree, it is a sure sign that they have no clear idea of what they are saying and do not understand each other, especially if they are disputing about subjects that are not complex or difficult to discuss, such as the present question, for it would not be very difficult to resolve it if man had some clear idea of a created power or force. Here then are some of their views so that you might see how little they agree with each other.

There are some philosophers[a] who assert that secondary causes act through their matter, figure, and motion, and these philosophers are right in a sense; others assert that they do so through a *substantial form*; others through accidents or *qualities,* and some through *matter* and *form;* of these some through *form* and *accidents*, others through certain *virtues* or *faculties* different from the above. There are some who maintain that the substantial form produces forms and the accidental form accidents, others that forms produce other forms and accidents, and others, finally, that accidents alone are capable of producing accidents and even forms. But it should not be imagined that those who say, for example, that accidents can produce forms through the virtue they have received from the form to which they are joined understand this in the same way. Some would have it that these accidents are but the very power or virtue of the substantial form; others that these accidents incorporate the influence of the form and thus act only through its virtue; and others, finally, that they are only instrumental causes. But these last are not yet in total agreement among themselves about what should be understood by instrumental cause, nor what the virtue is that it receives from the

[a]For the most extraordinary of these views, see Suarez's *Metaph.* Disp. 18. sec. 2 & 3; Scotus, in 4 *Sent.* Dis. 12.1. D. 37.2. D. 17; LaPalud, in 4 *Sent.* D. 12. Q. 1. art. 1; Pereira, 8 Phy. ch. 3; *Conimbricenses* on Aristotle's physics, and several others cited by Suarez.

primary cause. Philosophers do not even agree about the action by which secondary causes produce their effects.[a] Some of them claim that *causality* must not be produced, for it is what produces. Others would have them truly act through their *action*; but they find such great difficulty in explaining precisely what this action is, and there are so many different views on the matter that I cannot bring myself to relate them.

There you have a great variety of views, although I have not related those of the ancient philosophers, or those who were born in very distant countries. But you can judge well enough that they no more entirely agree among themselves on the subject of secondary causes than those of whom I have just spoken. Avicenna, for example, does not believe that corporeal substances can produce anything but accidents. And here[b] is his system as related by Ruvio. He claims that God immediately produces a very perfect spiritual substance, that this substance produces another, less perfect substance, and this substance a third, and so on, till the last, which produces all corporeal substances, and the corporeal substances produce the accidents. But since he was unable to understand how corporeal substances,[c] which cannot penetrate each other, should be capable of altering each other, Avicebron claims that only minds are capable of acting on bodies because only they can penetrate them. For as these gentlemen did not accept the void or the atoms of Democritus, and as Descartes's subtle matter was not sufficiently known to them, they did not join the Gassendists and the Cartesians in the view that there are bodies small enough to enter the pores of those that appear hardest and most solid.

It seems to me that this diversity of views gives us the right to view men as often talking about things they do not know, and that since the power of creatures is a fiction of the mind of which we naturally have no idea, it is fancy that leads everyone to imagine it.

It is true that in all times this power has been recognized as real and true by most men, but this certainly has been without proof—I do not say without demonstrative proof, I say without proof capable of making any impression on an attentive mind. For the confused proofs that are based only on the deceiving testimony of the senses and imagination should not be accepted by those who make use of their reason.

Speaking of what is called *nature*, Aristotle[d] said that it is ridiculous to wish to prove that natural bodies have an inner principle of their motion and rest, because, he says, this is a thing known by itself. Nor does he doubt that a ball that collides with another has the force to set it in motion. This is the way it appears to the eyes, and that is enough for this philosopher; for he almost always follows the testimony of the senses and rarely that of reason, and he is indifferent as to whether that testimony be intelligible or not.

[a]See Fonseca's *Metaph*. q. 13. sec. 3; Soncinas's and Javelle's on the same question.

[b]Ruvio, book 2. ph. tract. 4. q. 2.

[c]See Suarez Disp. 18. sec. 1.

[d]Ch. 1. of bk. 2. of his *Physics*.

Those who contest the view of certain theologians who have written against secondary causes say, as did Aristotle, that the senses convince us of their efficacy; this is their first and chief proof. It is clear, they say,[a] that fire burns, that the sun illuminates, and that water cools; one must be a fool to doubt these things. The authors of the opposite view, says the great Averroes, are out of their minds. Almost all the Peripatetics say that those who deny this efficacy must be convinced through sensible proofs and must thus be obliged to admit that they are capable of being acted upon and hurt. This is a judgment that Aristotle[b] has already pronounced against them, and we should execute it.

But this alleged demonstration is pitiful. For it shows the weakness of the human mind, and it shows that even philosophers are infinitely more sensuous than they are rational. It shows that those who glory in seeking the truth do not even know what they must consult to learn of it, whether it is the sovereign Reason, who never deceives and who always discloses things as they are in themselves, or whether it is the body, which speaks only in self-interest and which discloses things only in relation to the preservation and convenience of life. For in the end, what prejudices shall we not justify if we take the senses as judges, to which practically all prejudices owe their origin, as I have shown in the *Search after Truth*.

When I see one ball strike another, my eyes tell me, or seem to tell me, that the one is truly the cause of the motion it impresses on the other, for the true cause that moves bodies does not appear to my eyes. But when I consult my reason I clearly see that since bodies cannot move themselves, and since their motor force is[c] but the will of God that conserves them successively in different places, they cannot communicate a power they do not have and could not communicate even if it were in their possession. For the mind will never conceive that one body, a purely passive substance, can in any way whatsoever transmit to another body the power transporting it.

When I open my eyes, it seems clear to me that the sun is brilliant with light, that not only is it visible by itself but that it makes all the bodies surrounding it visible, that it covers the earth with flowers and fruits, gives life to animals, and, penetrating by its heat even to the bowels of the earth, produces stones, marble, and metals. But when I consult Reason, I see nothing of all this; and when I consult it faithfully, I clearly recognize that my senses seduce me, and that it is God who does everything in all things. For since I know that all the changes that occur in bodies have no other principle than the different communications of motion that take place in both visible and invisible bodies, I see that it is God who does everything, since it is His will that causes, and His wisdom that regulates, all these communications.

I assume that locomotion is the principle of generation, corruption, alteration, and generally of all the changes that occur in bodies; this is now an opinion that is

---

[a]See Fonseca, Ruvio, Suarez, and the others already cited.

[b]Bk. 1. of the *Topics*, ch. 1.

[c]I have proved this truth at greater length in the seventh *Dialogue on Metaphysics* and elsewhere. See also the fifth and sixth *Meditations chrétiennes*.

well enough received among the learned. But whatever view is held on this, it makes no difference. For it seems easier to conceive that one body pushes another when it collides with it than it is to understand that fire produces heat and light and that it draws from the potentiality of matter a substance that was not there beforehand. And if God must be recognized as the true cause of the different communications of motion, *a fortiori* we must judge that only He can create and annihilate real qualities and substantial forms. I say *create* and *annihilate*, because it seems to be at least as difficult to draw from matter a substance that was not there, or to introduce it without it being there, as it is to create or annihilate it. But I do not pause over terms; I make use of these only because there are no others I know of that clearly and unequivocally express the changes that philosophers assume are constantly occuring through the power of secondary causes.

I find some difficulty in relating here the other proofs that are ordinarily given of the power and efficacy of natural causes, for they seem so weak to those who resist prejudices and who prefer their reason to their senses, that it does not seem likely they could have persuaded reasonable people. Nevertheless, I relate and answer them because there are many philosophers who use them.

First Proof

If secondary causes did nothing, say Suarez, Fonseca, and some others,[a] we could not distinguish living things from those not living, for neither of them would have an inner principle of their actions.

Reply

I reply that men would still have the same sensible proofs that have convinced them of the distinction they make between living things and those not living. They would still see animals perform certain actions such as eating, growing, crying, running, jumping, and so forth, and they would see nothing similar in stones. And it is this alone that has caused ordinary philosophers to believe that beasts are alive and stones not. For it should not be imagined that they know through a clear and distinct perception of the mind what the life of a dog is; their senses determine their decisions on this question.

If it were necessary, I would prove here that the principle of a dog's life is not very different from that of the motion of a watch. For the life of bodies, whatever they might be, can only consist in the motion of their parts; and it is not difficult to judge that the same subtle matter that produces the fermentation of blood and animal spirits in a dog, and which is the principle of its life, is no more perfect than that which gives motion to the mechanism of watches or which causes heaviness in the weights of clocks, which is the principle of their life, or to speak as do others, of their motion.

It is up to the Peripatetics to give to those whom they term Cartesians a clear idea of what they call *bestial life, corporeal soul, body that perceives, desires,*

---

[a]In *Metaph.* Disp. 18. sec. 1. assert. 12. In *Metaph. Arist.* quest. 7. sec. 2.

sees, senses and wills, and then we shall clearly resolve their difficulties if after this they continue to produce them.

Second Proof

We could recognize neither the differences nor the virtues of the elements. It could happen that fire would cool as water does; nothing would be of a fixed and determinate nature.

Reply

I reply that while nature remains as it is, i.e., while the laws of the communication of motion remain the same, it is a contradiction that fire should not burn or separate the parts of certain bodies. Fire cannot cool like water unless it becomes water, for since fire is only wood whose parts have been agitated with a violent motion by an invisible matter surrounding them, as is easy to demonstrate,[a] it is impossible for these parts not to communicate some of their motion to the bodies with which they collide. Now, since these laws are constant, the nature of fire and its virtues and qualities do not change. But this nature and these virtues are but consequences of the general and efficacious will of God, who does everything in all things. As a result, the study of nature is false and vain in every way when true causes are sought in it other than the volitions of the Almighty, or the general laws according to which He constantly acts.

I grant that recourse to God or the universal cause should not be had when the explanation of particular effects is sought. For we would be ridiculous were we to say, for example, that it is God who dries the roads or who freezes the water of rivers. We should say that the air dries the earth because it stirs and raises with it the water that soaks the earth, and that the air or subtle matter freezes the river because in this season it ceases to communicate enough motion to the parts of which the water is composed to make it fluid. In a word, we must give, if we can, the natural and particular cause of the effects in question. But since the action of these causes consists only in the motor force activating them, and since this motor force is but the will of God, they must not be said to have in themselves any force or power to produce any effects. And when in our reasoning we have come at last to a general effect whose cause is sought, we also philosophize badly if we imagine any other cause of it than the general cause. We must not feign a certain *nature,* a *primum mobile,* a *universal soul,* or any such chimera of which we have no clear and distinct idea; this would be to reason like a pagan philosopher. For example, when we ask how it is that there are bodies in motion, or that agitated air communicates its motion to water, or rather how it is that bodies push one another, then, since motion and its communication is a general effect on which all others depend, it is necessary, I do not say in order to be a Christian but to be a philosopher, to have recourse to God, who is the universal cause, because His will is the motor force of bodies and also produces the communication of their motion. Had He wished not to produce anything new in the world, He

---

[a]See the following Elucidation.

would not have set its parts in motion. And if He wishes some day to make some of the beings He has formed incorruptible, our bodies after the resurrection, for example, He will cease to will certain communications of motion with respect to these beings.

Third Proof

It would be useless to plow,[a] water, and dispose bodies in a certain way in order to prepare them for what we hope will happen to them. For God has no need to prepare the subjects on which He acts.

Reply

I reply that God can absolutely do all He pleases without finding dispositions in the subjects on which He acts. But He cannot do so without a miracle, or by natural ways, i.e., according to the general laws of the communication of motion He has established, and according to which He almost always acts. God does not multiply his volitions without reason; He always acts through the simplest ways, and this is why he uses the collision of bodies to move them, not because their impact is absolutely necessary for their motion, as our senses tell us, but because with impact as the occasion for the communication of motion, very few natural laws are needed to produce all the admirable effects we see.

A plant must be watered in order for it to grow because, according to the laws of the communication of motion, there is almost nothing but the parts of water that, by their motion and due to their shape, can work their way up between the fibres of plants to carry with them certain salts and other small bodies, and by congealing or attaching themselves to each other in different ways take the shape necessary to nourish them. The subtle matter the sun constantly diffuses can raise water in plants by agitating it, but it does not have enough motion to raise coarse parts of earth. Nevertheless, earth and even air are necessary for the growth of plants: earth to keep water at their roots, and air to excite in the same water a moderate fermentation. But since the action of the sun, air, and water consists only in the motion of their parts, properly speaking only God acts. For, as I have just said, only He through the efficacy of His volitions and through the infinite extent of His knowledge can produce and regulate the infinitely infinite communications of motion occurring at each instant and conserving in the universe all the beautiful things we note in it.

Fourth Proof

No one struggles against himself; no one resists himself. Bodies collide, strike, and resist each other. Therefore, God does not act in them, except through His *concourse*. If God alone produced and conserved motion in bodies, He would divert them before their impact, for He knows that they are impenetrable. Why thrust bodies in order to make them rebound, why make them advance in order to make them withdraw, why produce and conserve useless motion? Is it

[a]Suarez, ibid.

not an extravagant thing to say that God struggles against Himself and that He destroys His works when a bull fights with a lion, when a wolf devours a sheep, and when the sheep eats the grass that God makes grow. Therefore, there are secondary causes.

Reply

Therefore, secondary causes do everything and God does nothing. For God does not act against Himself, and to *cooperate* [*concourir*] is to act. To *cooperate* with contrary actions is to give contrary *cooperation*, and consequently to perform contrary actions. To cooperate with the actions of creatures that resist each other is to act against oneself. To cooperate with useless motion is to act uselessly. Now, God does nothing uselessly; He performs no contrary action; He does not struggle against Himself. There'fore, He does not cooperate with the action of creatures, which often destroy each other and perform useless motions or actions. That is where this proof of secondary causes leads. But this is what reason teaches us.

God does everything in all things, and nothing resists Him. He does everything in all things, for His volitions produce and regulate all motion, and nothing resists Him because He does everything He wills. But here is how this must be conceived. Having resolved, as agreeing more with the immutable order of His attributes, to produce through the simplest ways, this infinite variety of creatures we admire, He willed that bodies move in a straight line because that line is the simplest. But since bodies are impenetrable, and since their motion occurs along lines that are contrary or that intersect, they must strike each other and, as a result, cease to move in the same way. God foresaw this, and yet He positively willed the collision or impact of bodies, not because He is pleased to struggle against Himself, but because He intended to make use of this impact of bodies as an occasion to establish the general law of the communication of motion by which He foresaw He must produce an infinity of admirable effects. For I am convinced that these two natural laws, which are the simplest of all—namely, that motion occurs or tends to occur in a straight line, and that the impact of bodies is communicated in proportion to, and along the line of, their pressure— are sufficient, if the first instances of motion are wisely distributed, to produce the world such as we see it, i.e., the sky, the stars, the planets, the comets, earth and water, air and fire, in a word, the elements of all bodies that are not organized or living; for organized bodies depend on the initial construction of those of which they are born, and it is likely that they were formed at the creation of the world, though not as they appear to our eyes, and that with time they receive nothing more than the growth necessary to become visible. Nevertheless, it is certain that they receive this growth only through the general laws of nature according to which all other bodies are formed, with the result that their growth is not always regular and that monsters are bred.

I say, therefore, that God through the first of the natural laws positively wills, and consequently produces, the impact of bodies, and that He then makes use of this impact, which obliges Him to diversify His action due to the impenetrability of bodies, as an occasion to establish the second natural law, which regulates the communication of motion, and that thus actual impact is the natural or *occasional* cause of the actual communication of motion by which God without altering His ways produces an infinity of admirable works.

If you consider this well, you will clearly see that nothing could be better. But on the assumption that God had not ordained it thus, and that He diverted bodies about to strike each other as if there were a void to receive them, then first, bodies would not be subject to that continuous vicissitude which produces the beauty of the universe, for the generation of bodies occurs only through the corruption of certain others; it is the contrariety of their motion that produces their variety. Secondly, God would not act through the simplest ways, because in order for bodies about to strike each other to continue their motion without striking each other, they would have to describe lines curved in an infinity of different ways; and consequently, different volitions would have to be admitted in God in order to determine their motion. Finally, if there were no uniformity in the action of natural bodies, and if their motion did not occur in a straight line, there would be no sure principles for reasoning in physics and, in a number of instances, for conducting ourselves in life.

It is no disorder for lions to eat wolves, wolves sheep, and sheep the grass that God tends so carefully that He has given it all the things necessary for its own preservation and even a seed for the preservation of its species. This no more proves the efficacy of secondary causes than it does the plurality of causes or the contrariety of the principles of good and evil the Manicheans imagined in order to explain these effects. Rather, it is a sure sign[a] of the grandeur, wisdom, and magnificence of God. For God produces only works worthy of an infinite wisdom, and He produces them with a profusion that sufficiently indicates His power and grandeur. Everything that is destroyed is restored by the same law that destroyed it—so great is the wisdom, power, and fecundity of this law. God does not prevent the destruction of beings through a new volition, not only because His first volition suffices to restore them, but especially because His volitions are much more worthy than the restoration of these beings. They are even much more worthy than everything they produce. And if God has produced this visible world, though unworthy in itself of the action by which it is produced, He did so because He had considerations that are not known to philosophers, and because He could honor Himself in Jesus Christ with an honor that creatures cannot give Him.

When a house crushes an honest man to death, there occurs a greater evil than when one beast devours another, or when a body is required to rebound by the impact of the body it strikes; but God does not multiply His volitions in order to remedy the true or apparent disorders that are the necessary consequences of natural laws. God must not correct or change these laws, although they sometimes produce monsters. He must not upset the uniformity of His conduct and the simplicity of His ways. He must ignore insignificant things, i.e., He must not

---

[a]See the *Dialogues on Metaphysics* [9–13] where I explain divine Providence.

have particular volitions to produce effects that do not merit them, or that are unworthy of the action of Him who produces them. God produces miracles only when the order He always follows requires it; I mean the immutable order of justice that He wills to render to His attributes. And this order would have it that He act through the simplest ways, and[a] that there be exceptions to His volitions only when absolutely necessary to his intentions, only when the simplicity and uniformity of His conduct honor His immutability and foreknowledge less than miraculous conduct would honor His wisdom, justice, goodness, or some other of His attributes; in a word, only on certain occasions that are entirely unknown to us. Although we are all joined to the order or wisdom of God, we do not know all its rules. We see in it what we must do, but we do not understand in it, and must not make too much effort to understand, everything that God must will.

We have a great example of what I have just said in the damnation of an infinite number of people whom God has allowed to perish during the centuries of error. God is infinitely good, He loves all His works, He wills that all men be saved and that they arrive at knowledge of the truth, for He made them to possess Him; and yet the greatest number damn themselves, the greatest number live and die in blindness and will remain there for all eternity. Is this not because God acts through the simplest ways[b] and follows order? We have shown that according to order God should not have advised through involuntary pleasures[c] the will of the first man, whose fall caused the disorder of nature. It was fitting that all men come from a single man, not only because this way is simple, but also for reasons that are too theological and too abstract to be deduced here. Finally, we must believe that this agrees with the order God follows and the wisdom He always consults in the formation and execution of his intentions. The sin of the first man produced an infinity of evils, it is true. But certainly order required God to permit it and to place man in a state of being able to sin, as I have proved elsewhere.[d]

In willing to restore His work, God only rarely gives those victorious graces that overcome the malice of the greatest sinners. He often gives graces that are useless for the conversion of those receiving them, although He foresees their uselessness with respect to them. He sometimes distributes a great number of them, which nonetheless produce but very little effect in relation to our salvation. Why all these roundabout or indirect ways? He has only to will positively the sinner's conversion in order to produce it in an invincible and efficacious way. Is it not clearly because He acts through the simplest ways and because order would have it so, although we do not always see it so? For God can act only with order and wisdom, although His order and wisdom are often impenetrable abysses for the human mind. There are certain very simple laws in the order of grace[e]

[a]See the seventh of the *Meditations chrétiennes.*

[b]See the Elucidation on the fourth chapter of the second part on Method. [This was Elucidation 16 in earlier editions; though the Elucidation was withdrawn from later editions, the reference to it stood.]

[c]See the second Elucidation on ch. 5 [5].

[d]See the second Dialogue of the *Conversations chrétiennes* of the Paris edition, 1702, pp. 60 ff.

[e]See the second discourse of the *Treatise on Nature and Grace.*

according to which God ordinarily acts, for this order has its rules as does the order of nature, although we do not know them as we see the rules for the communication of motion. Let us only follow the counsel that He who perfectly knows the laws of grace has given us in the gospel.

I say this to satisfy the unjust complaints of sinners, who despise the counsel of Jesus Christ and blame God for their malice and disorders. They would have God perform miracles in their favor and not follow the ordinary laws of grace. They live in pleasure and seek honors; they constantly reopen the wounds sensible objects have caused in their brain, and they often receive new ones; they would have God heal them through a miracle. They are like the wounded who, in the extremes of their pain, destroy their clothes, reopen their wounds, and then, at the sight of approaching death, complain of the cruelty of those who bandage them. They would have God save them because, they say, God is good, wise, and powerful; it is up to Him only to make us happy; He should not have made us in order to lose us. Let them know that God wills to save them and that, to this end, He has done everything He must according to the order of the justice He owes His attributes. We must not believe that He abandons us, because He has given us His own Son to be our Mediator and our victim. Yes, God wills to save us, and to save us all, but through ways we must study with care and exactly follow. God should not consult our passions in the execution of His intentions. He should consult only His wisdom, He should follow only order—and order would have it that we imitate Jesus Christ and that we follow His counsel in order to sanctify and save ourselves. But if God has not predestined all men to conform to the image of His Son, who is the model and exemplar of the elect, it is because in this God acts through the simplest ways in relation to His intentions, which all favor His glory; it is because God is a universal cause and must not act as do particular causes, which have particular volitions for everything they do; it is because His wisdom, which in this is only an abyss for us, would have it so. Finally, it is because this conduct is more worthy of God than some other that would be more favorable to the damned. For the damned are condemned by an order that is as worthy of our adoration as that by which the elect are sanctified and saved; and only ignorance of order and self-love would make one condemn conduct the angels and saints will eternally admire. Elsewhere[a] I reply more fully to the difficulties that might be raised against divine Providence. But let us return to the proofs of the efficacy of secondary causes.

Fifth Proof

If bodies did not have a certain *nature* or *force* to act, and if God did all things, there would be only the supernatural in even the most ordinary effects. The distinction between the natural and the supernatural, which is so widely accepted and which is established by the universal assent of the learned, would be extravagant and chimerical.

---

[a]See the *Dialogues on Metaphysics,* the *Treatise on Nature and Grace,* and the *Réponses à M. Arnauld,* especially the *Réponse à sa Dissertation sur les Miracles de L'Ancien Testament.*

Reply

I reply that this distinction is extravagant in the mouth of Aristotle, for the *nature* this philosopher has established is a pure chimera. I say that this distinction is not clear in the mouth of the ordinary man, who judges things through the impressions they make on his senses, for he does not know precisely what he means when he asserts that fire burns by its *nature*. I say that this distinction is allowable in the mouth of theologians, if they mean that *natural* effects are those that are the consequences of the general laws that God has established for the production and preservation of all things, and that *supernatural* effects are those that do not depend on these laws. The distinction is genuine in this sense. But the philosophy of Aristotle combined with the impression of the senses renders it dangerous, it seems to me, because this distinction can turn away from God those who have too much respect for the opinions of this miserable and pitiful philosopher, or who consult their senses instead of withdrawing into themselves in order to consult the truth. Therefore, we should not make use of this distinction without explaining it. Having made use of the term *fortuna*, Saint Augustine[a] retracted it, although there are few people who might be deceived with respect to it. Speaking of sacrificial flesh, Saint Paul[b] warns that idols are nothing. If the *nature* of pagan philosophy is a chimera, if this nature is nothing, we must be advised of it, for there are many people who are mistaken with respect to it. There are more than we might think who thoughtlessly attribute to it the works of God, who busy themselves with this idol or fiction of the human mind, and who render to it the honors due only to the Divinity. They would have God be the author of miracles and certain extraordinary effects, which in one sense are little worthy of His grandeur and wisdom, and they attribute to the power of their imaginary *nature* the constant and regulated effects that the wise alone are able to admire. They even pretend that the marvelous disposition that all living bodies have for preserving themselves and begetting their kind is a production of their *nature*, for according to these philosophers, it is the sun and man that beget men.

We can still distinguish the supernatural order from the natural in several ways. For we can say that the supernatural order relates to future goods, that it was established in expectation of the merits of Jesus Christ, that it is the first and principal order in the intentions of God, and other things sufficient to preserve a distinction the elimination of which we perhaps fear without reason.

Sixth Proof

The main proof adduced by philosophers for the efficacy of secondary causes is drawn from man's will and his freedom. Man wills, he determines himself by himself; and to will and determine oneself is to act. Certainly, it is man who commits sin. God is not the author of sin any more than He is of concupiscence and error. Therefore, man acts through his own efficacy.

[a]Bk. 1 of the *Retract*.
[b]1 Cor. 10:19.

Reply

I have sufficiently explained in several passages of the *Search after Truth* what the will is, and what man's freedom is, especially in the first chapter of the first book, and in the first Elucidation on the same chapter; it is useless to repeat it. I grant that man wills and that he determines himself; but this is because God makes him will by constantly leading him toward the good. He determines himself; but this is because God gives him all the ideas and sensations that are the motives by which he determines himself. I also grant that man alone commits sin. But I deny that in this He does something; for sin, error, and even concupiscence are nothing. They are only lacks of something. I have sufficiently explained myself on this topic in the first Elucidation.

Man wills, but his volitions are impotent in themselves; they produce nothing;[a] they do not preclude God's doing everything, because God himself produces our volitions in us through the impression He gives us toward the good in general, for without this impression we would be able to will nothing. From himself man has only error and sin, which are nothing.

There is quite a difference between our minds and the bodies that surround us. Our mind wills, it acts, it determines itself; I have no doubts about this whatsoever. We are convinced of it by the inner sensation we have of ourselves. If we had no freedom, there would be no punishment or future reward, for without freedom there are no good or bad actions. As a result, religion would be an illusion and a phantom. But what we clearly do not see, what seems incomprehensible, and what we deny when we deny the efficacy of secondary causes is that bodies have the power to act.

The mind itself does not act as much as is imagined. I know that I will and that I will freely; I have no reason to doubt it that is stronger than the inner sensation I have of myself. Nor do I deny it. But I deny that my will is the true cause[b] of my arm's movement, of my mind's ideas, and of other things accompanying my volitions, for I see no relation whatever between such different things. I even see clearly that there can be no relation between the volition I have to move my arm and the agitation of the animal spirits, i.e., of certain tiny bodies whose motion and figure I do not know and which choose certain nerve çanals from a million others I do not know in order to cause in me the motion I desire through an infinity of movements I do not desire. I deny that my will produces my ideas in me, for I do not see even how they could produce them, because my will, which is unable to act or will without knowledge, presupposes my ideas and does not produce them. I do not even know precisely what an idea is. I do not know whether they are produced from nothing and whether they return to nothingness as soon as we cease to perceive them. I speak according to the view of some people.

I produce my own ideas, they will say, by the faculty that God has given me for thinking. I move my arm because of the *union* God has established between

---

[a]"Nemo habet de suo nisi mendacium & peccatum." Conc. Araus. 2. Can. 22.

[b]According to the sense explained in the chapter of which this is an Elucidation.

my mind and my body. *Faculty* and *union* are terms from logic; they are vague
and indeterminate words. No particular being or mode of being can be a *faculty*
or a *union*; these terms must be explained. If they say that the union of my mind
with my body consists in the fact that God wills that when I will my arm to move,
animal spirits disperse in the muscles of which it is composed in order to move it
in the way I wish, I clearly understand this explanation and I accept it. But this is
to say exactly what I maintain; for since my will determines the practical will of
God, it is evident that my arm will be moved not by my will, which in itself is
impotent, but by God's, which can never fail to have its effect.

But if they say that the union of my mind with my body consists in the fact that
God has given me the *power*[a] to move my arm, just as He has given to my body
the power to make me feel pleasure and pain in order to apply me to this body and
interest me in its preservation, then surely they suppose what is at issue and go in
a circle. They have no clear idea of this power the soul has over the body, nor of
that the body has over the soul; they do not fully know what they are saying when
they positively assert it. They have arrived at this view through prejudice; they
have believed it to be so since infancy and as long as they have been capable of
sensing; but the mind, reason, and reflection have no role in it. This is sufficiently clear from the things I have said in the *Search after Truth*.

But, they will say, I know through the inner sensation of my action that I truly
have this power; therefore, I am not mistaken in believing it. I reply that when
they move their arm they have an inner sensation of the actual volition by which
they move it; and they are not mistaken in believing that they have this volition.
They also have an inner sensation of a certain effort accompanying this volition,
and they also believe that they make this effort. Finally, I grant[b] that they have an
inner sensation that the arm is moved during this effort; and on this assumption I
also agree to what they say, that the movement of the arm occurs at the instant we
feel this effort, or that they have a *practical* volition to move it. But I deny that
this effort, which is only a modification or sensation of the soul, which is given
to us to make us understand our weakness, and to give us an obscure and
confused sensation of our strength, is by itself able to impart motion to animal
spirits, or to determine them. I deny that there is a relation between our thoughts
and the motion of matter. I deny that the soul has the least knowledge of the
animal spirits of which it makes use to move the body it animates. Finally, even
if the soul had an exact knowledge of the animal spirits, and even if it were
capable of moving them, or of determining their motion, I deny that it could

---

[a]I still mean a true and efficacious power.

[b]It seems to me evident that through inner sensation or consciousness the mind does not even know
the movement of the arm it animates. Through consciousness it knows only its own sensation, for the
soul is conscious only of its thoughts. Through inner sensation or consciousness they know the
sensation they have of the movement of their arm; but it is not through consciousness that they are
informed of the movement of their arm, of the pain they suffer there, any more than they are of the
colors they see on objects. Or if they do not wish to agree with this, I say that inner sensation is not
infallible, for error is almost always found in these sensations when they are compound. I have
sufficiently proved this in the first book of the *Search after Truth*.

thereby select the nerve ducts, of which it has no knowledge, in order to impel the spirits into them and thus move the body with the promptness, exactness, and force observed even in those who least know the structure of their body.

For, even assuming that our volitions were truly the motor force of our bodies (although this seems incomprehensible), how is it conceivable that the soul should move the body? Our arm, for example, is moved only because spirits swell certain of the muscles composing it. Now, in order for the motion that the soul impresses on the spirits in the brain to be communicable to those in the nerves, and thence to others in the muscles of our arm, the soul's volitions must multiply or change proportionately to the almost infinite collisions or impacts that would occur in the particles composing the spirits; for bodies cannot by themselves move those they meet, as I feel I have sufficiently shown. But this is inconceivable, unless we allow in the soul an infinite number of volitions for the least movement of the body, because in order to move it, an infinite number of communications of motion must take place. For, in short, since the soul is a particular cause and cannot know exactly the size and agitation of an infinite number of particles that collide with each other when the spirits are in the muscles, it could neither establish a general law of the communication of motion, nor follow it exactly had it established it. Thus, it is evident that the soul could not move its arm, even if it had the power of determining the motion of the animal spirits in the brain. These things are too clear to pause any longer over them.

The same is true of our faculty of thinking. We know through inner sensation that we will to think about something, that we make an effort to do so, and that at the moment of our desire and effort, the idea of that thing is presented to our mind. But we do not know through inner sensation that our will or effort produces our idea. We do not see through reason that this could happen. It is through prejudice that we believe that our attention or desires are the cause of our ideas; this is due to the fact that a hundred times a day we prove that our ideas follow or accompany them. Since God and His operations contain nothing sensible, and since we sense nothing other than our desires preceding the presence of ideas, we think there can be no cause of these ideas other than our desires. But let us take care. We do not see in us any power to produce them; neither reason nor the inner sensation we have of ourselves tells us anything about this.

I do not think it necessary to relate all the other arguments of which the defenders of the efficacy of secondary causes make use, because these arguments seem to be so weak that it might be imagined that my aim in doing so would be to ridicule them, and I would make myself ridiculous if I were to respond to them seriously. For example, one author says, quite seriously, in favor of his view, "Created beings are true material, formal and final causes; why will they not be efficient or efficacious causes as well?" It seems to me that I would not satisfy many people if to answer this author's question I paused to clarify so gross an equivocation, and to show the difference between an efficacious cause and the cause it pleased philosophers to call *material*. Therefore, I leave such arguments in order to come to those drawn from Sacred Scripture.

Seventh Proof

Those who maintain the efficacy of secondary causes commonly adduce the following passages to support their view: "Germinet terra herbam viventem: Producant aquae reptile animae viventis & volatile: Producat terra animam viventem."[a] Therefore, the earth and the water have received through the word of God the *power* to produce plants and animals. God then commanded the birds and the fishes to multiply: "Crescite & multiplicamini, & replete aquas maris, avesque multiplicentur super terram."[b] Therefore, He gave them the power to beget their kind.

In the fourth chapter of Saint Mark,[c] Jesus Christ says that the seed that falls on good earth yields a hundredfold, and that the earth "produces of itself first the blade, then the ear, then the corn in the ear." Finally, it is also written in the book of Wisdom[d] that fire had, as it were, forgotten in favor of God's people the *power* it has to burn. It is therefore certain from the Old and New Testaments that secondary causes have a true power to act.

Reply

I reply that in Sacred Scripture there are also several passages that attribute to God the alleged efficacy of secondary causes. Here are some of them.

"Ego sum Dominus faciens OMNIA, extendens coelos SOLUS, stabiliens terram, & NULLUS mecum." Isa. 44:24. "Manus tuae fecerunt me & plasmaverunt me TOTUM in circuitu." Job 10:8. "Nescio qualiter in utero me apparuistis. . . . Singulorum membra NON EGO IPSA COMPEGI, sed enim mundi creator qui hominis formavit navitatem," &c. Mach. 1:2, 7:22–23. "Cum ipse Deus det omnibus vitam, inspirationem, & omnia." Acts 17:25. "Producens foenum jumentis, & herbam servituti hominum, ut educas panem de terra." Ps. 103 and 148. There is an infinity of such passages, but these are sufficient.

When an author seems to contradict himself, and natural equity or some stronger reason obliges us to make him agree with himself, it seems to me that we have an infallible rule to discover his real view. For we have only to observe when this author speaks according to his lights, and when he speaks according to common opinion. When a man speaks as do others, that does not always signify that he is of their opinion. But when he positively says the opposite of what is customarily said, though he might say it only once, we have reason to judge that it is his view—provided that we know that he is speaking seriously, and after having given careful thought.

For example, an author speaking about the properties of animals will say in a hundred places that beasts sense, that dogs know their master, that they love and fear him, and in only two or three places will he say that beasts do not sense, that

---

[a]Gen. ch. 1 [vv. 11 and 20–21].

[b]Ibid. [v. 22.].

[c]"Ultro enim terra fructificat primum herbam; deinde spicam, deinde plenum frumentum in spica" [4:28].

[d]"Etiam suae virtutis oblitus est." Ch. 16 [v. 23].

dogs are incapable of knowledge, that they neither fear nor love anything. How shall we make this author agree with himself, for he seems to contradict himself? Shall we group all the passages pro and con, and judge his view by the larger number? If so, I do not think there is a man to whom, for example, we can attribute the view that animals do not have a soul; for even the Cartesians always say that a dog senses when struck, and it rarely happens that they say it does not sense. And although I myself attack an infinity of prejudices in this work, several passages can be drawn from it by which it will be proved, unless the rule I am explaining be received, that I uphold them all, and even that I hold the view concerning the efficacy of secondary causes that I am now refuting; or perhaps it will be concluded that the *Search after Truth* is a book full of gross and obvious contradictions, as some people might conclude who perhaps do not have enough equity and penetration to set themselves up as judges of the works of others.

Sacred Scripture, the Fathers, and most men more often speak of sensible goods, riches, and honors according to the common opinion than according to the true ideas they have of them. Jesus Christ through Abraham says to the evil rich man: "Fili recepisti BONA in vita tua" [Luke 16:25], you have received *goods* during your life, i.e., riches and honors. What through prejudice we call *good*, our good, i.e., our gold and silver, is called in Sacred Scripture in a hundred places, our *support* or our *substance*, and even our *honor*, or what honors us. "Paupertas & honestas a Deo sunt."[a] Do these manners of speaking used by Sacred Scripture and the most virtuous of people make us believe they contradict themselves, or that riches and honors are truly good with regard to us, and that we must love and seek them? Undoubtedly not, because as these manners of speaking agree with prejudice, they signify nothing, and because we see besides that Jesus Christ compared riches to thorns, that He said they must be renounced, that they are deceitful, and that all that is great and glorious in the world is an abomination before God. Passages from Scripture and the Fathers, then, must not be grouped to judge their true opinion by the greatest number of these passages, unless one wishes constantly to attribute to them the most unreasonable prejudices.

With this assumed, we see that Sacred Scripture says positively that it is God who makes everything, right down to the grass of the fields, that it is He who provides the lilies with the adornments that Jesus Christ preferred to those had by Solomon in all his glory.[b] There are, not two or three, but an infinity of passages that attribute to God the alledged efficacy of secondary causes, and that destroy the *nature* of the Peripatetics.

Moreover, we are led by an almost natural prejudice not to think of God with respect to natural effects, and to attribute power and efficacy to natural causes; ordinarily only miracles make us think of God, and sensible impression initiates our view of secondary causes. Philosophers hold this view because, they say, their senses convince them of it; this is their strongest argument. In the end this

---

[a]Eccles. 1:14 [11:14].

[b]Matt. 6:28–30.

view is held by all those who follow the judgment of their senses. Now, language is formed on this prejudice, and we say as commonly that fire has the power to burn as we call gold and silver our good. Therefore, the passages drawn from Scripture or the Fathers for the efficacy of secondary causes prove no more than those an ambitious or avaricious man would choose to justify his conduct. But the same is not true of the passages that can be adduced to prove that God does everything. For as this view is contrary to prejudice, these passages must be understood in a strict sense, for the same reason that we must believe the view of a Cartesian to be that beasts do not sense, although he might have said so only two or three times, and although he might constantly say to the contrary in ordinary discourse that they sense, perceive, and understand.

In the first chapter of Genesis, God commands the earth to produce plants and animals; He also orders the waters to produce fishes. And consequently, say the Peripatetics, the water and the earth have received a *virtue* capable of producing these effects.

I do not see that this conclusion is certain. And even if one were obliged to explain this chapter by itself and without appeal to other passages from Scripture, there would be no necessity to accept this consequence. This way of explaining creation is accommodated to our way of speaking about the production of things. Thus it is not necessary to take it literally. One should not make use of it to support prejudices. Since the animals and plants are on the earth, and since the birds live in the air and fish in the water, God, in order to make us understand that it is through His order that they are in these places, produced them there. From the earth He formed the animals and plants, not because the earth was capable of begetting anything nor because God gave it for this purpose a power or virtue that still subsists now, for there is agreement enough that the earth begets neither horses nor oxen, but because the bodies of these animals were formed from the earth, as is said in the following chapter: "Formatis igitur Dominus Deus de humo cunctis animantibus terrae & universis volatilibus coeli."[a] The animals were formed from the earth, "formatis de humo," and were not produced by the earth. Thus, after Moses related how the animals and fishes were produced by virtue of the command God had made to the earth and water to produce them, he adds that *it is God Himself who made them*, in order not to attribute their production to the earth and water. "CREAVITQUE Deus cete grandia,"; and "omnem animam viventem atque motabilem quam PRODUXERANT AQUAE in species suas, & omne volatile secundum genus suum." And further below, after having spoken of the formation of animals, he adds' "Et FECIT DEUS bestias terrae juxta species suas, & jumenta & omne reptile terrae, in genere suo" [Gen. 1:21, 25].

We might note in passing that where our Vulgate contains "Germinet terra herbam . . . producant aquae reptile animae viventis & volatile super terram" [Gen. 1:11, 20], expressions that might lead one to believe that the earth and the waters have received some true power to produce the animals and plants, the

[a] V.19 [2:19].

words of the original are far from this thought. They signify simply that God said let the earth be covered with plants, let the waters be abundant with fish, and let the birds fly in the air. The verbs and nouns in this passage have the same root, which cannot be translated in other languages. It is as though it had been, let the earth *be verdant with verdure*, let the waters *be fishy with fish*, let the *flying creatures fly*. The Vulgate has also omitted the word *vole*, which has made some people believe that the birds were drawn from the waters, but we find in the Hebrew, *volatile* VOLITET. This last omitted word shows that the birds were not produced by a virtue in the water. Moses' aim here, therefore, was not to prove that the waters had received a real *power* to produce these fishes and birds, but only to indicate the place destined for each thing by God's order, whether to live in it or to be produced in it; *volatile* VOLITET *super terram*. For ordinarily when we say that the earth produces trees and plants, we mean to signify only that it provides the water and salts necessary to the germination and growth of seeds. I do not pause to explain the other passages from Scripture that taken literally favor secondary causes, for one is not obliged, and it is even dangerous to take literally expressions that are based on the ordinary judgments according to which language is formed; since the ordinary man speaks of all things according to the impressions of the senses and the prejudices of youth, the mind of God often accommodates itself to their weakness in order to instruct the simple as well as more enlightened people. "Inclinavit Scripturas Deus usque ad infantium & lactentium capacitatem," says Saint Augustine.[a]

The same reason that obliges us to take literally the passages from Scripture directly opposed to prejudice also permits us to think that the Fathers never had the express intention of maintaining the *efficacy* of secondary causes or the *nature* of Aristotle. For though they often speak in a way that favors the prejudices and judgments of the senses, they sometimes explain themselves in a way that sufficiently discloses the disposition of their mind and heart. Saint Augustine, for example, gives sufficient indication that he believes the will of God to be the *power* or *nature* of each thing when he speaks as follows:[b] "We are wont to say that wonders are contrary to nature; but this is not true. For as the will of the Creator is the nature of each of the creatures, how could what occurs by the will of God be contrary to nature? Miracles or wonders are therefore not contrary to nature, but contrary to what is known to us about nature."

It is true that in several places Saint Augustine speaks according to prejudice. But I maintain that this proves nothing, because only passages contrary to prejudice need be explained literally. I have just related the reasons for this.

If in all his works Saint Augustine had never said anything against the efficacy of secondary causes, and had always favored this view, one perhaps might use his authority in order to establish it. But should it not appear that he seriously

---

[a] In Ps. 8 [8:8].

[b] "Omnia quippe portenta contra naturam dicimus esse, sed non sunt. Quomodo enim est contra naturam quod Dei fit voluntate: cum voluntas tanti utique conditoris conditae rei cujusque natura sit? Portentum ergo fit non contra naturam, sed contra quam est nota natura." St. Aug. *De civitate Dei*, bk. 21. ch.8. See also, ibid., bk.5. ch.11, and his Letter 205 to Consentius, number 17.

examined this question, one would always have the right to think he had no fixed and settled view on this topic, and that perhaps he was carried along, as it were, by the impression of the senses to believe without reflection a thing that appears certain until examined with some care.

It is certain, for example, that Saint Augustine always spoke of animals as if they had souls—I do not say a corporeal soul, for this holy doctor knew too well to distinguish the soul from the body to think that there could be corporeal souls. I say a spiritual soul, for matter is incapable of sensation. Nonetheless, I believe that it is more reasonable to use the authority of Saint Augustine to prove that animals have no soul than to prove that they do; for[a] from the principles he carefully examined and securely established, it manifestly follows that they do not, as Ambrosius Victor shows in his sixth volume of the *Philosophia Christiana*. But since the view that animals have a soul, or that they feel pain when struck, agrees with prejudice (for there is no child who does not believe it), we maintain the right to think that Saint Augustine spoke on this according to common opinion, that he did not seriously examine this question, and that had he begun to doubt it and reflect on it, he would not have said a thing so contrary to his principles.

Should the Fathers have favored the efficacy of secondary causes, therefore, perhaps one would not be obliged to consider their view unless it appeared that they had carefully examined this question and that what they said about it did not result from language formed and based on prejudice. But surely just the opposite is the case, for the Fathers and the holiest and most enlightened people in religion have ordinarily shown in several passages of their works what the disposition of their mind and heart was with respect to the question we are discussing.

The most enlightened, and even the greatest number, of theologians, seeing on the one hand that Sacred Scripture opposed the efficacy of secondary causes and on the other that the impression of the senses, public opinion, and especially the philosophy of Aristotle, which was esteemed by the learned, established it (for Aristotle believes that God does not involve Himself in the detail of what takes place in the sublunary region, that this attention is unworthy of His grandeur, and that the *nature* he supposes in all bodies suffices to produce everything occurring here below)—theologians, I say, in order to accord faith with the philosophy of the pagans and reason with the senses, have been inclined to the view that secondary causes would do nothing unless God lent them His *cooperation*. But because this immediate cooperation by which God acts with secondary causes involves great difficulties, some philosophers have rejected it, claiming that in order for them to act it is enough that God should conserve them with the *virtue*

---

[a]Some of these principles of St. Augustine are: that what has never sinned can suffer no evil; now according to him himself, pain is the greatest of evils, and animals suffer it. That the more noble cannot have as an end the less noble; now according to him the soul of animals is spiritual & more noble than the body, & yet they have no other end than their bodies. That what is spiritual is immortal; & the soul of animals, although spiritual, is subject to death. There are many other such principles in the works of St. Augustine from which we can conclude that animals do not have a spiritual soul such as he admitted in them. See St. Augustine, chs. 22–23 *De anima & ejus origine*.

He gave them in creating them. And as this opinion agrees entirely with prejudice, since God's operation in secondary causes involves nothing sensible, it is ordinarily received by the common man, and by those who have attended more to the physics and medicine of the ancients than to theology and meditation on the truth. Most men imagine that God first created all things, that He gave them all the faculties or qualities necessary for their preservation, that, for example, He gave the first motion to matter and then left it to itself to produce by the communication of its motion this variety of forms we admire. It is ordinarily supposed that bodies can move each other, and this opinion is even attributed to Descartes, contrary to what he expressly says in articles 36 and 37 of the second part of his *Principles of Philosophy*. Since men cannot avoid the realization that creatures depend on God, they reduce this dependence as much as they can, whether through a hidden aversion for God or through stupidity and a dreadful insensitivity toward His operation. But as this view is ordinarily received only by those who have not studied religion, and who follow their senses and the authority of Aristotle rather than their reason and the authority of the holy books, there is no reason to fear their becoming too well established in the mind of those who have any love for truth and religion; for however little we apply ourselves to the examination of this view, we easily discover its falsity. But the opinion of the *immediate cooperation* of God with each action of secondary causes seems to agree with passages from Scripture, which often attribute the same effect to God and to creatures. I shall prove in the last Elucidation (number 43) that God alone can give the soul perceptions of objects, and that no creature, no finite intelligence whatever power it might have, can in this case be prepared to act and to require God's cooperation.

We must consider, then, that there are passages in Scripture where it is said that God alone acts: "Ego sum Dominus," says Isaiah,[a] "faciens OMNIA, extendens coelos SOLUS, stabiliens terram, & NULLUS mecum." A mother moved by the spirit of God tells her children that it was not she who formed them: "Nescio[b] qualiter in utero meo apparuistis, singulorum membra NON EGO IPSA COMPEGI, sed mundi creator," &c.[c] It does not say, as do Aristotle and the school of Peripatetics, that it is to her and the sun that they owe their birth, but to the Creator of the universe. Now, this view that only God acts and forms children in their mother's womb does not agree with common opinion and prejudice.[d] According to the principle I have previously established, these passages must be explained literally. But on the contrary, since the view of the efficacy of secondary causes agrees with common opinion and sensible impression, even if passages should be found that expressly say that secondary causes act alone, they

---

[a] 44:24.

[b] 2 Mach. 7:22–23.

[c] "Sol & homo generant hominem." Arist. *Phys. Ausc.* 1.2 c.2. See St. Thomas on this text.

[d] "Nec qui concumbit, nec qui seminat est aliquid, sed qui format Deus [. . . .] Ipse namque operatione qua nunc usque operatur, facit ut numeros suos explicent semina & a quibusdam latentibus atque invisibilibus involucris in formas visibiles hujus quod aspicimus decoris evolvant." Aug. *De civ. Dei* bk. 22. ch. 24 n.2.

would have no force compared with these. Cooperation, then, is not enough to reconcile the different passages from Sacred Scripture; all force, power, efficacy must be placed on the side of God.

But even if God's immediate *cooperation* with secondary causes could reconcile the different passages of Sacred Scripture, I do not know if withal it should be received. For the holy books were not produced solely for contemporary theologians, but also for the Jewish people. As a result, if the Jews of yore were not enlightened or subtle enough to imagine a *cooperation* such as is admitted in Scholastic theology, or to agree with something the cleverest theologians have difficulty in explaining, it seems to me to follow that the Sacred Scripture that attributes to God, and even to God alone, the production and conservation of all things would plunge them into error, and that the authors of the holy books would have spoken to men a language not only unknown but deceptive. For in telling them that God does all, they would only have claimed that God provides His cooperation for all things; and certainly the Jews did not have this cooperation in mind, those nonphilosophical among them believing that God does everything and not that God cooperates with everything.

But for a surer judgment about cooperation, a careful explanation is required of the different systems the Scholastics have made of it. For besides the impenetrable obscurities common to all opinions that can be explained and supported only by vague and indeterminate terms, there is such a wide variety of views on this matter that we would have no great difficulty in discovering their cause. But I have no wish to involve myself in a discussion that would be too wearisome both for me and for those who will read this. I prefer on the contrary to try to show that my views might agree to some extent with those of the greater number of Scholastic theologians, although I cannot conceal the fact that their language appears to me quite equivocal and confused. I shall explain.

I hold, as I have said elsewhere, that bodies, for example, do not have the force to move themselves and that therefore their *motor force* is but the action of God, or in order not to use a term signifying nothing distinct, their motor force is but the will of God, always necessarily efficacious, which conserves them successively in different places. For I do not believe that God creates certain beings to make them the motor force of bodies—not only because I have no idea of this sort of being, and because I do not see that they could move bodies, but also because these beings would need others to move them, and so on to infinity. For only God is at once both motor and immobile.

This being so, when a body collides with and moves another, I can say that it acts through the cooperation of God, and that this cooperation is not different from its own action. For a body moves the one with which it collides only by its action or its motor force, which ultimately is but God's will, which conserves this body successively in several places—the transport of a body being not its action or its motor force but the effect of its motor force. Almost all theologians speak as follows: that the action of secondary causes is not different from the action by which God cooperates with them. For although they understand it in different ways, they hold that God acts in creatures through the same action as do creatures. And they are obliged to speak this way, it seems to me; for if creatures acted through an action God did not produce in them, their action qua efficacious action would be, it seems to me, independent; now they believe, as they must, that creatures depend immediately on God, not only for their being, but for their operation as well.

Likewise with respect to free causes, I hold that God constantly gives to the mind an impression toward the good in general, and that He even determines this impression toward particular goods by the impression of them He places in us, as I have explained in the first Elucidation; and this is also held by theologians, who assert that God moves and predisposes our wills. Thus, the force that sets our minds in motion is the will of God, which animates us and leads us toward the good; for God does not create beings to make them the motor force of minds for the same reasons He does not create beings to make them the motor force of bodies. Since God's volitions are efficacious by themselves, it is enough that He should will in order to produce, and it is useless to multiply beings without necessity. In addition, everything real in the natural determinations of our impulses also comes solely from God's action in us; for I am not speaking here about our consent to these determinations. So much is clear from the first Elucidation. Now we act and produce nothing except through our volitions, i.e., through the impression of God's will, which is our motor force. For our volitions are efficacious only insofar as they come from God, just as moving bodies impel others only insofar as they have a motor force transporting them. Thus, we act only through God's cooperation,[a] and our action viewed as efficacious and capable of producing some effect is not different from God's; as most theologians say, they are the same action: *Eadem numero actio*.

Now, all the changes occurring in the world have no other natural cause than the motion of bodies and the volitions of minds. For according to the general laws of the communication of motion, the invisible bodies surrounding visible bodies produce by their various motion all the changes whose cause is not apparent to our eyes; and according to the laws concerning the union of soul and body, when the bodies surrounding us act on our own, they produce in our soul an infinity of sensations, ideas, and passions. Likewise, our mind, according to the same laws, excites in itself by its volitions an infinity of different perceptions; for our volitions apply and modify our mind as natural causes, the efficacy of which nonetheless comes from the laws God has established. And when our mind acts on our body, it produces in it several changes, always in virtue of the laws concerning its union with the body; and by means of our body it also produces in those surrounding us a very great number of changes in virtue of the laws of the communication of motion. Consequently, no natural effect has any natural or occasional cause other than the motion of bodies and the volitions of minds. This is something to which one will easily agree however little one attends to it. For I assume that one is not prejudiced by those who speak without knowing what they say, who constantly imagine beings of which they have no clear ideas, and who

---

[a]See Suarez, bk. 1 *De concursu Dei cum voluntate* ch. 4.

claim to explain things they do not understand through things that are absolutely incomprehensible. Thus, since it has been shown that God executes through His cooperation, or rather through His efficacious will, everything the motion of bodies and the volitions of minds do as natural or occasional causes, there is nothing God does not do by the same action as His creature's—not because creatures have any efficacious action by themselves but because God's power is, as it were, communicated to them by the natural laws God has established in their favor.

This is all I can do to reconcile what I think with the view of theologians who maintain (a) the necessity of immediate cooperation and (b) that God does everything in all things through the same action as that of creatures. For as to the other theologians, I believe that their views are untenable in every way, especially Durand's,[a] and that of certain ancients refuted by Saint Augustine,[b] who absolutely denied the necessity of cooperation, and would have had secondary causes do all things through a power God gave them in creating them without further concerning Himself with them. For although this opinion might involve fewer difficulties than that of other theologians, it appears to me so contrary to Scripture, and so consonant with prejudice, to say no more of it, that I do not think it can be maintained.

I grant that the Scholastics who say that God's immediate cooperation is the same action as that of creatures do not understand it exactly as I have explained it, and that with the possible exceptions of Biel and Cardinal d'Ailly,[c] all those I have read think the efficacy that produces effects comes from the secondary cause as well as the primary. But as I am attempting to observe this law, to say only what I conceive clearly and to side with what best agrees with religion, I believe I shall not be found amiss in relinquishing a view that to many people seems the more incomprehensible the more effort is spent to understand it, and in establishing another that perfectly agrees not only with reason but also with the sanctity of religion and Christian morality. This is a truth I have already proved in the chapter being elucidated; but it is appropriate for me to say something additional in order to justify fully what I have already said about the present question.

Reason and religion convince us that God wills to be loved and respected by His creatures—loved as a good, feared and respected as a power; this is a truth that cannot be doubted without impeity and foolishness. To love God as He wills and deserves to be loved, we must, according to the first Commandment of the Law and of the Gospel, and even according to reason, as I have shown elsewhere,[d] love Him with all our strength or according to our capacity for loving. It is not enough to prefer Him to all things; we must also love Him in all things. Otherwise our love is not as perfect as it must be, and we do not render to

---

[a]See Durand, in 2. Dist. 1. Quest. 5. & Dist. 37.

[b]*Lib. imp. de Gen. ad litt.* bk 5. ch. 20.

[c]In 4 Sent. Dist. I. quest. 1. De Aliaco, ibid.

[d]Bk. 4, ch. 1.

God all the love He impresses in us, and impresses in us only for Himself because He acts only for Himself. And to render God all the respect due Him, it is not enough to adore Him as the sovereign power and to fear Him more than His creatures; we must also fear and adore Him in all His creatures, all our reverence must be directed toward Him, for honor and glory are due only Him. This is what God has commanded us with these words: "Diliges[a] Dominum Deum tuum ex toto corde tuo, & ex tota anima tua, & ex tota fortudine tua." And with these: "Dominum Deum tuum timebis, & illi soli servies." Thus, the philosophy that teaches us that the efficacy of secondary causes is a fiction of the mind, that Aristotle's, and certain other philosophers', *nature* is a chimera, that only God is strong and powerful enough not only to act in our soul but also to give the least motion to matter, this philosophy, I say, agrees perfectly with religion, the end of which is to join us to God in the closest way.

We ordinarily love only things capable of doing us some good; this philosophy therefore authorizes only the love of God, and absolutely condemns the love of everything else. We should fear only what can do us some evil; this philosophy therefore sanctions only the fear of God and absolutely condemns all others. Thus, it legitimizes all the soul's impulses that are just and reasonable, and it condemns all those that are contrary to reason and religion. For by this philosophy you will never legitimize love for riches, passion for grandeur, debauched behavior, since the love of the body appears absurd and ridiculous according to the principles established by this philosophy.

It is an incontestable truth, a natural opinion, even a common notion that we should love the cause of our pleasure and should do so in proportion to the felicity it does or can make us enjoy. Not only is it right, it is even necessary, as it were, that the cause of our happiness be the object of our love. Thus, following this philosophy we should love only God, for it teaches us that only He is the cause of our happiness. According to this philosophy, the bodies surrounding us do not act on the one we animate, and *a fortiori*, do not act on our mind. It is not the sun that illumines us and gives us movement and life. It does not cover the earth with fruits and flowers and does not provide us with our food. This philosophy teaches us, as does Scripture, that it is *God who provides the rain and regulates the seasons, who gives to our bodies their food and fills our hearts with joy, that only He can do us good, and that He never ceases to witness thereby what He is, although in ages past He suffered all nations to walk in their own ways.*[b] Following the language of this philosophy, we must not say that *nature* provides us with goods;[c] we must not say that it is God and nature. We must say

---

[a]Deut. ch. 5 [6:5].

[b] "In praeteritis generationibus dimisit omnes gentes ingredi vias suas. Et quidem non sine testimonio semetipsum reliquit benefaciens de coelo, dans pluvias & tempora fractifera, implens cibo & laetitia corda nostra." Acts 14:15–16.

[c] "Ergo nihil agis, ingratissime mortalium, qui te negas Deo debere, sed naturae: quia nec natura sine Deo est, nec Deus sine natura, sed idem: est utrumque, nec distat. Officium si quod a Seneca accepisse, Annaeo te diceres debere, vel Lucio: non creditorem mutares, sed nomen." Seneca *De beneficiis* bk. 4. ch. 8.

that it is God alone and speak in this way without equivocation in order not to deceive the simple. For we must distinctly recognize the sole cause of our happiness if we wish to make it the sole object of our love.

It is also an incontestable truth that we should fear things capable of causing us evil, and fear them in proportion to the evil they can cause us. But this philosophy teaches us that only God can cause us evil—it is He, Isaiah[a] says, "who creates the darkness as well as the light, who makes both good and evil" —and even that no evil occurs that He does not produce, as another prophet says. Thus, we should fear only Him. We should fear neither plague, nor war, nor famine, nor our enemies, nor even devils; we should fear God alone. We should flee a sword with which someone would stab us, we should avoid fire, we should leave a house about to crush us; but we should not fear these things. We can *flee* bodies that are the natural or *occasional* causes of evil; but we should *fear* only God as the *real cause* of all the misfortunes of the wicked, and we should hate only sin, which obliges the cause of all goods to become the cause of all our evils. In a word, *all the mind's impulses* [*mouvemens*] *should be referred only to God, for only God is above the mind, and the motion* [*mouvemens*] *of our body can be referred to those surrounding us.* This is what we are taught by the philosophy that does not admit the efficacy of secondary causes.

But on the assumption of the efficacy of secondary causes, it seems to me that we have some grounds for fearing and loving bodies, and that to regulate our love according to reason, it is enough to prefer God to all things, the first and universal cause to secondary and particular causes. It does not seem necessary to love God with all our strength: "Ex tota mente, ex toto corde, ex tota anima, ex totis viribus," as the Gospel says [Mark 12:30].

Yet when one is content to prefer God to all things and to adore Him with a worship and love by preference, without continually striving to honor and love Him in all things, it often happens that one is deceived, that charity is lost and dissipated, and that one is concerned more with sensible goods than with the sovereign good. For if one were to ask the greatest sinners, and perhaps even idolaters, whether they preferred the universal cause to particular ones, they would perhaps have no fear in reply to us from the midst of their debauches and aberration that they do commit a breach of so essential a duty, and that they fully know what they owe God. I grant that they are mistaken, but without the efficacy of secondary causes they have no likely excuse to justify their behavior; and upon the supposition of this efficacy, the following is what they can say to themselves when their passions blind them and they listen to the reports of their senses.

I am made to be happy; I cannot prevent myself from wishing to be happy. I must therefore occupy my mind with everything that can give me what I invincibly want, and my heart must devote itself to it. Why then should I not love sensible objects, if they are the true causes of the happiness I find in their possession? I recognize the Sovereign Being as alone worthy of sovereign worship; I prefer Him to everything. But since I do not see that He wishes anything

[a]"Ego Dominus, & non est alter, formans lucem & creans tenebras, faciens pacem & creans malum: Ego Dominus faciens omnia haec." Isa. 47:7 [6–7]; Amos 3:6.

of me, I enjoy the goods He gives me by means of the secondary causes to which He has subjected me, and I do not uselessly concern myself with Him. That there is no good He affords me immediately and by Himself, or at least without creatures playing a role in it, is a sign that He does not will that my mind and heart apply themselves immediately to Him, or at least that He wills that the sentiments of my mind and heart be shared between Him and His creatures. Since He has communicated some of His power and glory to the sun, has surrounded it with brilliance and majesty, has made it sovereign over all His works, and since through the influence of this great star we receive all the goods necessary for life, why should we not use part of this life to enjoy ourselves in its light, and to bear it witness of the feeling we have for its grandeur and its benefits? Would it not be the ultimate ingratitude to receive the bounty of all things from this excellent creature and to have for it no feeling of gratefulness? And would it not be dreadful stupidity and blindness not to have any impulse of respect and fear for that the absence of which freezes and kills us, and which approaching us would burn and destroy us? I repeat, we must prefer God to all things and esteem Him infinitely more than His creatures; but we must also fear and love His creatures. This is how we justly honor Him who made them, merit His good graces, and require of God new benefits. It is clear that He approves of the honor we pay His creatures, because He has communicated His power to them, and every power deserves honor. But as the honor must be proportionate to the power, and as the power of the sun and other sensible objects is such that we receive from it all sorts of goods, it is right for us to honor them with all our strength, and to consecrate to them, after God, all that we are.

This is how one naturally reasons when following the prejudice of the efficacy of secondary causes. And this is manifestly how the founders of idolatry reasoned. This is what is thought by the one esteemed most learned among the Jews. He[a] begins a treatise he composed on idolatry as follows: "In the time of Enos men fell into strange errors and the wise men of that age lost their sense and reason. Enos himself was among these deluded people. These were their errors. Because, they said, God created the stars and their heavens to govern the world, placed them in a high place, surrounded them with brilliance and glory, and uses them to carry out his orders, it is right for us to honor them and pay them our homage and respect. It is the will of our God that we honor these things He has raised up and covered with glory, just as a prince wishes his ministers to be honored in his presence because the honor paid them reflects on him. [. . .] After this thought came into their heads, they began to build temples to the stars, make sacrifices to them, speak their encomiums, and even prostrate themselves before them, imagining that they were thereby making themselves pleasing to Him who created them." This is the origin of idolatry.

It is so natural and fitting to have feelings of gratitude in proportion to the goods we receive that almost[b] all people have adored the sun because they have all judged it to be the cause of the goods they enjoyed. And if the Egyptians

[a]R. Moses Maimonides.

[b]See Vossius *De idololatria* bk. 2.

adored not only the sun, the moon, and the river Nile, whose overflow caused the fertility of their country, but also went as far as the vilest animals, it was, according to the report of Cicero,[a] because of some utility they derived from them. Thus, since we cannot and indeed should not banish from the mind of men their natural inclination for the true causes of their happiness, it is clear there is at least some danger in maintaining the efficacy of secondary causes, although there might be joined to it the necessity of *immediate cooperation*, which involves something incomprehensible I know not what, and which comes after the event, as it were, in order to justify our prejudices and the philosophy of Aristotle.

But there is no danger in saying only what we see and attributing power and efficacy only to God, because we see only His volitions to have an absolutely necessary and indispensable connection with natural effects. I grant that men nowadays are sufficiently enlightened not to fall into the gross errors of the pagans and idolaters; but I have no fear in saying that often our mind is turned, or rather that our heart is disposed as was the pagans', and that there will always be a kind of idolatry in the world until the day when Jesus Christ "restores[b] His kingdom to God His father, having destroyed every empire, every dominion, and every power, so that God may be everything in all things." For is it not a kind of idolatry to make a god of one's belly, as Saint Paul[c] says? Is it not to be an idolater of the god of riches to work ceaselessly to acquire goods? Is it to render God the worship due Him and to adore Him in mind and in truth[d] to have a heart full of sensible beauty and a mind dazzled by the brilliance of some imaginary grandeur?

Since men think they will receive from the bodies surrounding them the pleasures they enjoy in using them if they join themselves to these bodies with all the strength of their soul, the source of their disorder is therefore their sensible conviction in the efficacy of secondary causes. Only reason tells them that God alone acts in them. But beside the fact that this reason speaks so low that they almost do not hear it, and that the senses contradicting it cry so loud that their din stuns them, they are further confirmed in their prejudice in ways and by arguments all the more dangerous as they bear the external marks of truth.

Philosophers, and especially Christian philosophers, should constantly battle against the judgments of the senses or prejudices, and especially prejudices as dangerous as that of the efficacy of secondary causes; and yet, for I do not know what reason, people whom I rightfully respect a great deal try to confirm this prejudice, and even to pass off as superstitious and ridiculous a doctrine so holy, pure, and well-founded as that which maintains that only God is a true cause. They do not want us to love and fear God in all things, but, they say, to fear all things in relation to God. We should love creatures, they say, because they are

---

[a]"Ipsi qui irridentur Aegyptii, nullam belluam nisi ob aliquam utilitatem, quam ex ea caperent, consecraverant." *De natura deorum* bk. 1 [ch. 36]. See Sextus Empiricus, bk. 8. ch. 2.

[b]1 Cor. 15:24

[c]"Quorum Deus venter est." Phil. 13:9. [3:19]. "Omnis ornicator, aut immundus, aut avarus, quod est idolorum servitus." Eph. 5:5.

[d]"In spiritu & veritate oportet adorare." John 4:24

good; we must love and respect our father, honor our prince and our superior, because God commands it. I do not deny this, but I deny that we must love creatures as our goods, though they are good or perfect in themselves. I deny that we can serve and respect men as we do our master. Or, to explain myself more clearly, I claim that we must not serve our master, obey our father and our prince with any other intention than to serve and obey God. This is what Saint Paul[a] says, *who became all things to all men and who obliged in all things* for the salvation of those to whom he preached: "Servi, obedite Dominis carnalibus cum timore & tremore in simplicitate cordis vestri SICUT CHRISTO; non ad oculum servientes quasi hominibus placentes, sed ut servi Christi facientes voluntatem Dei ex animo, cum bona voluntate servientes SICUT DOMINO ET NON HOMINIBUS."[b] And in another Epistle:[c] "Non ad oculum servientes quasi hominibus placentes, sed in simplicitate cordis Deum timentes. Quodcumque facitis ex animo operamini SICUT DOMINO ET NON HOMINIBUS." We should therefore obey our father, serve our prince, honor our superiors as UNTO GOD AND NOT UNTO MEN: "Sicut Domino & non hominibus." This is clear and can have no evil consequences. Superiors will always be better honored and better served by it. But I believe I can say that a master who wished to be honored and served, as having in him a power other than God's, would be a demon, and that those serving in this spirit would be idolaters; for I cannot help believing that honor and love unrelated to God are kinds of idolatry. SOLI DEO HONOR ET GLORIA.

[a]1 Cor. 9:22, 10:33.

[b]Eph. 6:6 [5–6].

[c]Col. 3:22 [–23]. "Nos si hominem patrem vocamus, honorem aetati deferimus, non Autorem vitae nostrae ostendimus." Hier. in ch. 23. Matt.

BOOK SIX: PART TWO
Chapter Nine

❧

A last example to show the utility of this work. In this example, we seek the physical cause of hardness or of the union of the parts of bodies.

Bodies are bound together in three ways: *continuity, contiguity,* and in a third manner that has no particular name, but that I shall call by the general term *union.*

By *continuity,* or by the cause of continuity, I mean that unknown something I am trying to discover that makes the parts of a body hold so tightly to each other that effort is needed to separate them, and that causes them to be regarded not as just together, but as a whole.

By *contiguity,* I mean that unknown something that makes me judge that two bodies touch immediately so there is nothing between them, but not that they are closely bound because I can easily separate them.

By this third term, *union,* I mean once more an unknown something that causes two glasses or two slabs of marble, whose surfaces have been used and polished by rubbing them against each other, to be attached in such a way that even though they can be very easily separated by sliding them, we still have some difficulty doing it in any other way.

Now this is not *continuity,* since these two glasses or slabs of marble, being united in this manner, are not conceived merely as making a whole, because there is a way they can be separated with great ease. Neither is it simply *contiguity* although it is very near to it, because these two pieces of glass or marble are quite tightly united, even much more than the parts of soft or liquid bodies, such as those of butter and water.

Our terms being defined, we must now seek the cause that unites bodies and the differences between the *continuity, contiguity,* and *union* of bodies according to the sense I have determined. I will first seek the cause of *continuity,* or what that unknown thing is which makes the parts of a hard body hold so tightly to each other that effort is required to separate them, and which causes them to be regarded not as being together but as a whole. I hope that once this cause is found, there will not be great difficulty in discovering the rest.

It now seems to me that this indefinable something that binds even the tiniest parts of this piece of iron I hold in my hands must be something very strong, since I must make a very great effort to break off a small part. But am I not in error? Is it not possible that this difficulty I have in breaking off the tiniest piece of iron comes from my weakness and not from the resistance of this iron? For I remember that at other times I made more effort than I am making now to break off a piece of iron like the one I am holding; and if I were sick, perhaps I could not succeed even with very great effort. I see clearly that I should not judge so absolutely of the firmness with which the parts of iron are joined together on the basis of the efforts I make to disunite them. I should only judge that they hold very strongly to one another in relation to my small strength; or that they are held more strongly than the parts of my flesh, since the sensations of pain I have when I exert too much effort warn me that I will disunite the parts of my body sooner than those of the iron.

I recognize then that even as I am neither absolutely strong nor absolutely weak, likewise iron or other bodies are neither absolutely hard nor absolutely flexible, but only in relation to the cause acting against them, and that the efforts I make can serve as a rule to measure the magnitude of the force needed to conquer the resistance and hardness of iron. For rules must be invariable, and these efforts vary according to the times, the abundance of animal spirits, and the hardness of flesh, since I cannot always produce the same effects by making the same efforts.

This reflection delivers me from a prejudice I had that made me imagine <that it would take> strong bonds to unite bodies, which bonds perhaps do not exist; and I hope that it will not be useless to me in what follows, for I have an extreme propensity to judge everything in relation to myself and to follow the impressions of my senses, which I will guard against with more care. But let us continue.

After having thought a while and searched with some application for the cause of this tight union without having been able to discover anything, I feel carried by my simplicity and my nature to judge, like several others, that it is the form of bodies that preserves the union between their parts, or the attraction and inclination they have for their fellows, for there is nothing easier than letting oneself be beguiled and thus becoming wise all at once, at little cost.

But since I do not want to believe anything that I do not know, I must not let myself be defeated in this way by my own laziness, nor must I surrender to mere glimmerings [*simples lueurs*]. Therefore, let us leave these forms and inclinations of which we have no distinct and particular ideas but only confused and general ones that we form, it seems to me, only in relation to our nature, and whose very existence several people and perhaps even entire nations doubt.

I seem to see the cause of this tight union of the parts composing hard bodies without admitting in it anything else except what everyone agrees is there, or at least everything everyone distinctly conceives to be capable of being there. For everyone knows distinctly that all bodies are composed, or can be composed, of small parts. Thus, it might happen that some will be crooked and branched, like tiny bonds capable of forcefully binding the others; or that they will completely intertwine themselves in their branches, so that we will not be able to disunite them easily.

I have a strong inclination to give in to this thought, and it is all the stronger when I see that the visible parts of heavy bodies are bound and united to each other in this manner. But I could hardly distrust the preoccupations and impressions of my senses too much. I must therefore once again examine the thing more closely, and I must even seek the explanation of why the tiniest and least solid parts of bodies (in a word, the very parts that make up each of these bonds) are held together. For they cannot be united by other, still smaller bonds, since I assume them to be solid. Or if I say that they are united in this way, I will be asked, and with reason, what will unite these others together, and so on to infinity.

As a result, the knot of the question now is to know how the parts of these tiny bonds or branched parts can be as tightly united together as they are, A, for example, with B, which I assume to be parts of a tiny bond. Or (what is the same thing), since bodies are all the harder as they are the more solid and have fewer pores, the question now is to know how the parts of a column composed of a material that would not have a single pore can be strongly joined together and compose a very hard body, for it cannot be said that the parts of this column are held by tiny bonds, since, being supposedly without pores, they have no particular figures.

$$A \; \backsim \; B$$

I still feel extremely inclined to say that this column is hard by its *nature*, or that the tiny bonds with which hard bodies are composed are atoms whose parts cannot be divided as being the essential and last parts of bodies, and which are *essentially* crooked or branched, or of a confused figure.

But I frankly recognize that this is not to explain the difficulty and that, leaving the preoccupations and illusions of my senses, I would be wrong to resort to an abstract form and to embrace a phantom of logic as the cause I see; I mean that I would be wrong to conceive the vague idea of *nature* or *essence*, which expresses only what is known, as something real and distinct, and thus to take an abstract and universal form as a physical cause of a very real effect. For there are two things I can hardly distrust enough. The first is the impression of my senses, and the other is the facility I have for taking abstract natures and the general ideas of logic for real and particular ones, and I remember having been beguiled several times by these two sources of error.

For, to return to the difficulty, it is not possible for me to conceive how these tiny bonds would be indivisible by their essence and nature, nor how they would consequently be inflexible, since on the contrary I conceive them to be very divisible, and necessarily so, by their essence and nature. For part A is very certainly a substance as well as B, and consequently it is clear that A can exist without B or separated from B, since substances can exist without one another, because otherwise they would not be substances.

To say that A is not a substance—that cannot be; for I can conceive it without thinking of B, and everything that can be conceived of alone is not a mode, since only modes or ways of being cannot be conceived alone or without the beings whose modes they are. Therefore A, not being a mode, is a substance, since every being is necessarily either a substance or a mode of being. For in the end all that is can either be conceived of alone or it cannot; there is no middle in contradictory propositions, and being or substance is called that which can be conceived of and consequently created alone. Part A can therefore exist without part B, and to state it more strongly, it can exist separately from B. So that this bond is divisible in A and B.

Furthermore, if this bond were indivisible or crooked by its nature and essence, the complete opposite of what we see through experience would occur, for one would not be able to break off any body. Let us suppose, as previously, that a piece of iron is composed of an infinity of tiny bonds intertwined with each other, of which A, a, and B, b, are two. I say that we could not disengage them, and consequently we could not break this iron apart; for in order to break it apart, it would be necessary to bend the bonds composing it, which, however, are assumed to be inflexible by essence and nature.

But if one does not suppose them to be inflexible but only indivisible by their nature, the supposition will serve no purpose in resolving the question. For then the difficulty will be to know why it is that these tiny bonds do not obey an effort to bend a bar of iron. Nevertheless, if we do not suppose them to be inflexible, we should not suppose them to be indivisible. For if the parts of these bonds could change situations in relation to one another, it is obvious that they could be separated, since there is no reason why, if one part could be removed from the other at all, it could not be completely removed. Therefore, we cannot resolve the question whether we suppose these tiny bonds to be inflexible or indivisible. For whether we suppose them to be indivisible, or inflexible, it will be impossible to break it, since the tiny bonds composing the iron being entangled in each other, it will be impossible to disengage them. Therefore, let us try to resolve the difficulty through clear and incontestable principles and to find the explanation of why this tiny bond has these two parts, A and B, so strongly attached to each other.

I clearly see that it is necessary for me to divide the subject of my meditation into parts in order to examine it more exactly and with less mental effort since I could not at first, from a simple view and with all the attention of which I am capable, discover what I was seeking. And that is what I was able to do from the beginning, for when the subjects one is considering are somewhat obscure, it is always best to examine them only by parts, and not to tire oneself uselessly with false hopes of luckily encountering the answers.

What I seek is the cause of the tight union found between the tiny parts that compose the tiny bond A, B. Now there are only three things I distinctly conceive that might be the cause I seek, namely: the parts of this tiny bond themselves, or the will of the Author of nature, or finally the invisible bodies that surround these tiny bonds. I might still produce, as a cause for these two things, the form of the bodies, the qualities of hardness or some occult quality, the harmony that would exist between parts of the same type, and so on. But because I have no distinct idea of these lovely things, I neither should nor can apply my reasonings to them. As a result, if I do not find the cause I seek in things of which I have distinct ideas, I will not fruitlessly trouble myself with the contemplation of these vague and general ideas of logic; and I will stop wanting to speak about things I do not understand. But let us examine the first of these things that can be the cause of the strong attachment of the parts of this tiny bond, namely, the parts composing it.

When I consider only the parts of which hard bodies are composed, I feel inclined to believe that: *one cannot imagine any cement uniting the parts of this bond, other than the parts themselves and their own rest; for of what nature could it be? It will not be a thing that subsists in itself; for, all these tiny parts being substances, how would they be united by substances other than themselves? Neither will it be a quality different from rest, because there is no quality more contrary to motion that could separate these parts than the rest that is in them; but aside from substances and their qualities, we do not know that there are other kinds of things.*[a]

It is quite true that the parts of hard bodies remain united to the extent that they are at rest beside each other, and that once they are in a state of rest, they continue by themselves to remain so as much as possible. But this is not what I am seeking; I am not looking for the explanation of why the parts of hard bodies are in rest next to each other; I am trying here to discover why it is that the parts of these bodies have the force to remain in a state of rest alongside each other, and why they resist any effort made to stir or separate them.

I could still tell myself[b] that each body truly has the force to remain in the state it is in, and that this force is equal for motion and rest. But the thing that makes the parts of hard bodies remain at rest alongside each other,[c] and that causes difficulty in separating and agitating them, is that not enough motion is employed to overcome their rest. This is probable, but I seek certitude, if it can be found, and not merely probability. And how can I know with certitude and clarity that each body has this force to remain in the state it is in, and that this force is equal for motion and rest, since matter appears on the contrary to be indifferent to motion and rest, and absolutely without any force? Let us go, then, as did

[a]Descartes, *Principles,* art. 55 of pt. 2.

[b]Descartes, art. 43 of the same part.

[c]Art. 63.

Descartes, to the will of the Creator, which perhaps is the force that bodies appear to have in themselves. That is the second thing we previously said could keep the parts of this tiny bond of which we were speaking so strongly attached to one another.

Certainly it could be that God wills each body to remain in the state it is in, and that His will is the force uniting their parts to one another; just as I also know that it is His will that is the motor force which puts bodies in motion. For, since matter cannot move by itself, it seems to me that I must judge that it is a mind, and even the Author of nature, who preserves and puts it in motion by preserving it successively in several places through His simple will, since an infinitely powerful being does not act with instruments, and because effects necessarily follow from His will.

I realize then that it could be that God wills each thing to remain in the state it is in,[a] whether in rest or in motion, and that this will is the natural power bodies have for remaining in the state in which they were once placed. If that is so, it will be necessary, as Descartes did, to measure this power, to conclude what its effects must be, and thus to provide the laws of force and the communication of motion for the collision of different bodies, in proportion to their relative volumes [*par la proportion de la grandeur qui se trouve entre ces corps*] since we have no other way of knowing this general immutable will of God, which causes the different power of bodies to act upon and resist each other, than their different volumes and speeds.

Nevertheless, I have no certain proof that God wills, through a positive volition, that bodies remain at rest; and it seems to suffice that God wills matter to exist, in order not only that it exist, but also that it exist at rest.

Such is not the case with motion, because the idea of matter in motion certainly includes two powers or efficacies to which it is related, to wit, what created it, and further, what activated it. But the idea of matter at rest includes only the idea of the power that created it, without the necessity of another power to put it at rest, since if we simply conceive of matter without considering any power, we will necessarily conceive of it at rest. This is how I conceive things, I must judge of them according to my ideas; and according to my ideas, rest is merely the privation of motion; I mean that the alleged force which makes rest is merely the privation of that which makes motion; for it is sufficient, it seems to me, that God cease to will that a body be moved, in order that it stop moving, and that it be at rest.

Indeed, reason and thousands upon thousands of experiments teach me that if two bodies of equal volume are moved, the one with one rate of speed, and the other with half that rate, then the force of the first will be double that of the second. If the speed of the second is only a quarter, a hundredth, a millionth that of the first, then the second will only have the fourth, the hundredth, the millionth fraction of the force of the first. From this it is easy to conclude that if the speed of the second is infinitely small, or finally null, as when at rest, then the

---

[a]Descartes, [*Principles*], art. 31, of part 2, art. 45 ff.

force of the second will be infinitely small, or finally null, if it is at rest. Hence, it seems evident to me that the state of rest has no force for resisting the force of motion.

But I remember having heard from several very enlightened persons that it appeared to them that motion was equally the privation of rest as rest the privation of motion. Someone even asserted, for reasons I could not understand, that it was more probable that motion was a privation than rest. I do not distinctly remember the reasons they gave, but they must make me fear that my ideas are false. For even though most men say anything it pleases them to say about things that appear to be of little importance, nevertheless, I believe that the persons of whom I speak took pleasure in relating their conceptions. I must therefore examine my ideas with care once more.

That it is the will of God that moves bodies is a thing that seems indubitable to me, and these gentlemen of whom I speak would agree. Therefore, the force that this ball I see rolling has is the will of God making it roll; what is it necessary for God to do to stop it now? Is it necessary for Him to will with a positive volition for it to be at rest, or is it sufficient that He stop willing it to be active? It is obvious that if God only stops willing this ball to be active, the cessation of this volition of God will cause the cessation of the ball's motion, and consequently it will cause it to be in a state of rest. For the will of God, which was the force moving the ball no longer existing, this force will no longer exist and the ball will therefore no longer be moved. Thus, the cessation of the force of motion causes rest. Therefore, rest has no force that causes it. It is therefore nothing but a pure privation that assumes no positive will in God. Thus, to give bodies some force for remaining at rest would be to admit in God a positive will without reason or necessity.

But let us reverse this argument if possible. Let us suppose for the moment that there is a ball at rest instead of in motion; what must God do to activate it? Does it suffice that He stops willing it to be at rest? If that is so, I have as yet advanced nothing; for motion will as soon be the privation of rest as rest the privation of motion. I therefore assume that God stops willing it to be at rest. But, this assumed, I do not see that the ball is stirred; and, if there are some who conceive that it is moved, I beg them to tell me in which direction, and with what degree of motion it is moved. Certainly, it is impossible that it be moved and that it not have some determination and some degree of motion. And from the single conception that God stops willing it to be at rest it is impossible to conceive that it moves with some particular degree of motion, because <the cases of> motion and rest are not the same. Motions have an infinity of modes; they vary quantitatively; but since rest is nothing, one state of rest cannot differ from another. The same ball that goes twice as fast as another in a given time has twice as much force or motion in that time as the other; but we cannot say that the same ball has twice as much rest in a given time as another.

Therefore, there has to be in God a positive will to put a ball in motion, or to cause a ball to have such a force to be moved, and it is sufficient for it to be at rest that He stops willing it to be moved. Similarly, in order for God to create a world, it is not sufficient that He stop willing it not to exist, but He must positively desire the mode in which it must exist. But to annihilate it, God need not will it not to exist, since God cannot will nothingness through a positive act of will; it suffices only that He stop willing it to exist.

I am not considering motion and rest here according to their relative being; for it is obvious that bodies at rest have relations just as real to those around them as those in motion. I conceive only that bodies in motion have a motor force, and that those at rest have no force for their state of rest, because the relation of moving bodies to those around them is always changing; and therefore there has to be a continuous force producing these continuous changes, for in effect it is these changes which cause everything new that happens in nature. But there need be no force to make nothing happen. When the relation of a body to those around it is always the same, nothing happens; and the preservation of this relation, I mean the action of God's will that preserves this relation, is no different from what preserves the body itself.

If it is true, as I conceive it to be, that rest is merely the privation of motion, then the slightest movement, I mean that of the tiniest activated body, will contain more force and power than the rest of the largest body. Thus, the slightest effort of the tiniest body one can conceive, activated in the void[a] against a very large and vast body, will be capable of moving it slightly, since this large body, being at rest, will have no force to resist that of this tiny body striking against it. Consequently the resistance generated by the parts of hard bodies to hinder their separation necessarily comes from something other than their state of rest.

But what we have just proved by abstract arguments must be demonstrated through sensible experiments to see if our ideas are in agreement with the sensations we receive from objects, for it often happens that such arguments deceive us, or at least that they cannot convince others, especially those prejudiced to the contrary. The authority of Descartes has such a great effect on the reason of some people that this great man must be proved mistaken in every way to disabuse them. What I have just said enters easily into minds that have not filled themselves with the contrary opinion, and I even clearly see that they will be critical of me for stopping too long to prove things that appear incontestable to them. But the Cartesians well deserve the efforts one makes to satisfy them. The others can pass over whatever might annoy them.

Here then are some experiments that sensibly prove that rest has absolutely no power to resist motion, and that consequently show that the will of the Author of nature, which creates the power and force that each body has for continuing in the state it is in, concerns only motion and not rest, since bodies have no power whatsoever in themselves.

Experience teaches that very large vessels, floating in water, can be agitated by very small bodies that knock against them. From this I conclude, in spite of all the evasions of Descartes and the Cartesians, that if these large bodies were in a

---

[a]By a body in a void, I mean a body so separated from others, solid or liquid, that there is nothing that either helps or hinders the communication of motion.

void they could be agitated still more easily. For the reason there is some slight difficulty in moving a vessel in water is that the water resists the force of the motion communicated to it, which would not happen in a void. And what manifestly shows that water resists the motion communicated to the vessel is that the vessel stops being agitated some time after it has been moved; for that would not happen unless the vessel lost its motion by communicating it to the water, or if the water yielded to it without resisting it, or finally if the water gave it its motion. Thus, since an agitated vessel in water gradually stops moving, it is an indubitable sign that the water resists its motion instead of facilitating it as Descartes claims; and consequently it would be infinitely easier to agitate a large body in a void than in water, since there would be no resistance on the part of the surrounding bodies. It is therefore obvious that rest has no force for resisting motion, and that the slightest motion contains more power and force than the greatest body at rest; and that thus we should not compare the force of motion and of rest according to the proportion we find between the size of bodies in motion and those at rest, as did Descartes.

True, there is some reason to believe that a vessel is agitated from the moment it is first in the water because of the continual change occurring in the particles of the water surrounding it, although it appears to us not to change place. And this is what makes Descartes and some others believe that the one pushing it is not the only force making it advance in the water, but that, on the contrary, it has already received a good deal of motion from the tiny particles of the liquid body that surround it and push upon it equally from all sides, and that this motion is only determined by a new motion of the one that pushes it, so that what agitates a body in water could not do so in the void. It is thus that Descartes and those of his opinion defend the rules of motion he gave us.

Let us suppose, for example, that there is a piece of wood, a square foot in size, in a liquid body, and that all the tiny parts of the liquid body act and are moved against the wood; and that because they push it equally in all directions, as much toward A as toward B, it cannot advance in any direction at all. If, therefore, I push another piece of wood from a half-foot away against the first piece in direction A, I see that it advances. And from this I conclude that it could be moved in the void with less force than that with which this piece of wood pushes it, for the reasons I have just stated. But those of whom I speak deny this, and they reply that the reason the large piece of wood advances from the instant it is pushed by the small one is that the small one, which could not move it if it were by itself, being joined with the agitated particles of the liquid body, determines them to push it and to communicate a part of their motion to it. But it is obvious that, according to this reply, the piece of wood, once agitated, should not have diminished its motion, but that on the contrary it should have continuously augmented it. For according to this reply, the piece of wood is pushed by the water more in direction A than in direction B, and therefore it must always advance. And because this impulsion is continuous, its motion must always increase. But, as I have already said, water, far from facilitating its motion, constantly resists it and, since its resistance always diminishes this motion, finally renders it completely imperceptible.

It is now necessary to prove that the piece of wood, which is equally pushed by the tiny particles of the water surrounding it, has no motion or force whatsoever capable of moving it, even though it continually changes its immediate place, or the surface of the water surrounding it is never the same at different times. For if it is the case that a body equally pushed in all directions like this piece of wood has no motion, it will be indubitable that it is only the external force striking against it which gives it motion, since while this external force pushes it, the water resists it and even gradually dissipates the motion communicated to it, for it gradually stops moving.

Now this much appears obvious, for a body equally pushed from all directions can be compressed; but certainly it cannot be transported, since the addition or subtraction of forces has no effect.

Those to whom I speak maintain that there is never more motion at one time than at another in nature, and that bodies at rest are moved only by collision with some agitated bodies that transmit their motion to them. From this I conclude that a body I assume to be created perfectly at rest in water will never receive a single degree of motion nor a single degree of force to move from the particles of water that surround it and that continually strike against it, provided that they push it equally in all directions, because all these particles that strike against it equally from all sides rebound with all their motion and communicate none of it to the body. Consequently, this body must always be considered at rest and without any motor force, although the surface of the body changes continually.

Now, my proof that these particles rebound this way with all their motion is, besides the fact that the thing cannot be conceived otherwise, that the water touching this body would have to be cooled a great deal or even frozen, and become about as hard as wood is on its surface, since the motion of the particles of water must be equally distributed in the tiny parts of the bodies they surround.

But to compromise with those who defend Descartes's view, I am willing to grant that one should not consider a boat in the water as being at rest. I also grant that all particles of the water surrounding it are in harmony with the new motion the boat communicates to the water, although it is only too obvious, from the lessening of the boat's motion, that they resist it more in the direction it is moving than in the direction from which it was pushed. That nevertheless assumed, I say that according to Descartes, of all the particles of water in the river, only those that touch the boat immediately on the side from which it was pushed can aid in its motion. For, according to this philosopher,[a] *water being fluid, all the particles of which it is composed do not act together against the body we want to move. It is only those that, in touching it, press jointly upon it*. Now, those that jointly press against the boat, together with the boatman, are a hundred times smaller than the whole boat. It is therefore obvious, by the explanation[b] Descartes gives in this article on the difficulty we have in breaking a nail between our hands, that a tiny body is capable of activating one much larger than itself. For after all, our hands are not as fluid as water, and when we want to break a

[a]*Principles*, pt. 2, art. 63.
[b]Ibid.

nail, there are more parts joined together that act jointly in our hands than there are in the water pushing a boat.

But here is a more obvious experiment. Take a very solid plank or some other extremely hard surface. Drive a nail halfway into it and incline the plane a bit. I say that, if an iron bar a hundred times thicker than the nail is put on the plane, one or two inches above it, and is allowed to slide, the nail will not break.[a] And yet it must be noted that according to Descartes[b] all the particles of the bar jointly push and act against this nail, for the bar is hard and solid. If therefore there is *no cement other than rest to unite the parts* that compose the nail, the iron bar being a hundred times thicker than the nail, it must, according to Descartes's fifth rule and according to reason, transmit some small amount of its motion to the part of the nail it would strike against, that is to say, [it should] break it and pass beyond, even though this bar slides with a very slow motion. Thus, it is necessary to look for a cause other than the rest of the parts for making bodies hard, or capable of resisting the effort made to break them, since rest has no force to resist motion, and I believe these experiments suffice to show that the abstract proofs we provided are not false.

It is therefore necessary to examine the third thing we previously said might be the cause of the tight union found between the parts of hard bodies, namely, an invisible matter that surrounds them and that, being very agitated, pushes the interior and exterior parts of these bodies with a great deal of violence, and compresses them in such a way that to separate them requires more strength than this extremely agitated invisible matter possesses.

It seems I can conclude that the union of the parts composing hard bodies depends on the subtle matter surrounding and compressing them, since the two other things that could conceivably be the causes of this union are not truly the causes, as we have just seen. For, since I find resistance in breaking off a piece of iron, and since this resistance comes neither from the iron nor from the will of God, as I believe I have proved, it must necessarily come from some invisible matter, which can be none other than the matter that immediately surrounds and compresses it. I shall now explain and prove this opinion.[c]

Let someone take a globe of some metal, hollow inside and cut into two hemispheres, and let him join these two hemispheres by attaching a small strip of wax where they meet, and then, draw the air from them. Experience shows that these two hemispheres are joined to each other in such a way that several horses, harnessed to them with buckles, some on one side and some on the other, cannot separate them, assuming the hemispheres to be large in proportion to the number of horses. Nevertheless, if the air is let back in, a single person can separate them with no trouble whatsoever. It is easy to conclude from this experiment that what united these two hemispheres so strongly to each other was the fact that being pressured on their convex exterior surface by the air surrounding them, they were

---

[a]Art. 63.

[b]Art. 50.

[c]See the *Experiments at Magdeberg* of Otto de Guericke, bk. 3.

not pressured at the same time on their concave interior surface. So that the actions of the horses pulling the two hemispheres from two directions could not overcome the effort of an infinity of particles of air that resisted them by pressing the two hemispheres. But the slightest effort is capable of separating them when the air, being reintroduced into the copper sphere, pressures the concave interior surfaces as much as the air from outside pressures the convex exterior surfaces.

If, on the contrary, we take the bladder of a carp and put it in a vessel from which the air is drawn, then this bladder, being full of air, will burst and break because then there is no air outside the bladder to resist that inside. It is also because of this that two planes of glass or marble, having been rubbed against each other, are joined so that we feel resistance when we try to separate them, because these two parts of marble are pressed and compressed by the outside air that surrounds them, and are not so strongly pushed by that on the inside. I could supply an infinity of other experiments to prove that the heavy air that presses on the bodies it surrounds strongly unites their parts, but what I said suffices to explain my thinking clearly on the present question.

I say, then, that the reason for the very strong union of the parts of hard bodies, and of these tiny bonds of which I previously spoke, is that there are other tiny bodies outside, infinitely more agitated than the gross air we breathe, that push and compress them, and that the reason we have trouble separating them is not their state of rest but the agitation of these tiny bodies that surround and compress them.[a] Consequently, the thing that resists motion is not rest, which is nothing but its privation and has no force in itself, but some contrary motion that must be overcome.

This simple exposition of my opinion might seem reasonable; nevertheless, I can well foresee that several people will have a great deal of difficulty accepting it. Hard bodies make such a great impression on our senses when they strike us or when we make a strong effort to break them that we are led to believe their parts are united much more tightly than they really are. And, on the contrary, the tiny bodies that I said surround them, to which I attributed the strength to cause this union, seem too weak to produce such a noticeable effect because they make no impression on our senses.

But, to destroy this prejudice, which is based only on the impressions of our senses and on the difficulty we have in imagining bodies any tinier and more agitated than those we see every day, it is necessary to notice that the hardness of bodies is not measured in relation to our hands or to the efforts we are capable of making, which are different at various times. For in the final analysis, if the greatest strength of men were not almost nothing in comparison with that of subtle matter, we would be very wrong to believe that diamonds and the hardest rocks cannot have their hardness caused by the compression of the tiny, very agitated bodies that surround them. Now, we will clearly recognize that the strength of men is very insignificant if we consider that their power to move their bodies in so many ways comes only from a very minute fermentation of their

[a]See the sixteenth Elucidation, toward the end, where I calculate the centrifugal force of the vortexes of the subtle matter.

blood, which agitates its tiny parts somewhat, thus producing animal spirits. For it is the agitation of these spirits that constitutes the strength of our bodies and gives us the power to make these efforts we unreasonably regard as something very great and powerful.

But it must be noted carefully that this fermentation of our blood is nothing but a very small communication of the motion of this subtle matter of which we have just spoken; for all fermentations of visible bodies are merely communications of the motion of invisible bodies, since every body receives its agitation from some other one. We must not be surprised therefore if our strength is not as great as that of this same subtle matter from which we receive it. But if our blood were fermented as strongly in our hearts as gunpowder is fermented and agitated when set on fire, i.e., if our blood received a communication of motion from subtle matter as great as the one gunpowder receives, we could do extraordinary things fairly easily, such as breaking iron, turning houses upside down, and so on, provided we assume there was an appropriate proportion between our members and the blood agitated in this way. We should therefore get rid of our prejudice and not imagine, in accordance with the impression of our senses, that the parts of hard bodies are so strongly united to each other just because we have so much trouble breaking them apart.

But if we also consider the effects of fire in mines, on the weight of bodies, and on several other effects of nature that have no cause other than the agitation of these invisible bodies (as Descartes proved in several places), we shall realize clearly that it is not beyond their strength to unite and compress the parts of hard bodies together as powerfully as they do. For in the end, I am not afraid to say that a cannonball, whose motion appears so extraordinary, does not even receive the thousandth part of the motion of the subtle matter surrounding it.

You will not doubt what I am proposing if you consider, first, that gunpowder does not catch fire completely or all at the same instant; and second, that when it catches fire completely and instantaneously, it floats only a very short time in the subtle matter. Now bodies that float for a very short time in others cannot receive very much motion from them, as we can see in boats that are abandoned to currents of water and only receive their motion gradually. In the third and most important place, <this is the case> because each part of the powder can receive only that motion which conforms to the subtle matter; for the water transmits to the boat only the direct motion common to all its parts, and that motion is ordinarily very slight in relation to the others.

I could further prove the magnitude of the motion of subtle matter to those who accept the principles of Descartes by the motion of the earth and the weight of bodies, and I would even thence draw several proofs that would be certain and exact enough, but that is not necessary for my topic. In order to have a sufficient proof for the agitation of subtle matter (which I give as the cause of the hardness of bodies) without having seen the works of Descartes, it suffices, I say, to read with some application what I have already said about it in Book 4, Chapter 2, number 5, or rather what I will say of it in the 16th Elucidation from number 11 to the end.

Therefore, being presently delivered from the prejudices that led us to believe that our efforts are very powerful, and that those of the subtle matter that surrounds and compresses hard bodies are very weak, and being persuaded besides of the violent agitation of this matter in virtue of the things I said about gunpowder, it will not be difficult to see that it is absolutely necessary that this matter must be the cause of the hardness of bodies or of the resistance we feel when we try to break them apart.

Now, as there are always a great many parts of this invisible matter that enter and circulate in the pores <of hard bodies>, they not only make them hard, as we have just explained, but furthermore they are the reason why some spring back and return to their original shape, others remain bent, and <still> others are fluid and liquid;[a] and finally, they are the cause not only of the strength found in the parts of hard bodies for remaining beside each other but also of that found in the parts of fluid bodies for separating from each other; i.e., it is the same force that makes some bodies hard and others fluid; hard, when their parts touch immediately; fluid, when their parts do not touch because the subtle matter slides between them.

Neither shall I pause to resolve a very great number of objections that I foresee might be made against what I have just established; because if those who make these objections have no knowledge of true physics, I will only bore and anger, instead of satisfying, them; but if they are enlightened people and their objections are very strong, I could only respond to them with a great number of figures and lengthly discourse. So that I believe I must entreat those who will find some difficulty in the things I have just said to reread this chapter with more care, and the 16th Elucidation. For I hope that if they read and meditate upon it as is necessary, all their objections will vanish. But in the end, if they find my entreaty troublesome, let them relax, for there is no great danger in being ignorant of the cause of the hardness of bodies.

I do not speak here of *contiguity*, for it is obvious that contiguous things touch each other so slightly that there is always a great deal of subtle matter passing between them, and, in making an effort to continue its motion in a straight line, it hinders their union.

I have explained the *union* found between two slabs of marble that have been polished against each other, and it is easy to see that although subtle matter constantly passes between these two parts, as unified as they are, air cannot pass through; and thus it is the weight of the air that compresses and presses these two pieces of marble upon each other, causing us to have trouble disuniting them unless we slide them along one another.

It is clear from all this that the continuity, contiguity, and union of the two slabs of marble would only be the same thing in the void, because we do not also have separate ideas of them; consequently, to make them differ absolutely and not in relation to the bodies around them is to say what is incomprehensible.

[a]To understand distinctly what I have just said, it is necessary to read what I have said about the nature and effects of subtle matter in the sixteenth Elucidation, number 14 and following.

Here now are some reflections on Descartes's opinion and on the source of his error. I call his opinion an error because I find no way of defending what he says about the rules of motion and the cause of the hardness of bodies toward the end of the second part of his *Principles* in several places, and because he seems to me to have fairly proved the truth of the opposite opinion. I shall give the rules of motion that experience confirms, and the reasons behind these rules.

This great man, conceiving very distinctly that matter cannot move itself and that the natural motor force of all bodies is none other than the general will of the Author of nature, and that hence the communication of the motion of bodies at their collision can come only from this same will, let himself believe that we could provide the rules of the various communication of motions only through the proportion found between the different sizes of the bodies struck, since it is not possible to penetrate the designs and will of God. And because he judged that each thing had the force to remain in the state it was in, whether in rest or motion (because God, whose will makes this force, always acts in the same way), he concluded that rest had as much force as motion. Thus, he measured the effects of the force of rest (like those of the force of motion) by the size of the body at rest, which made him give the rules of the communication of motion in his *Principles*, and the cause of the hardness of bodies I have tried to refute.

It is fairly difficult not to yield to Descartes's opinion when we adopt his viewpoint and when we do not pay attention. But even if God's positive will and efficacy were necessary for rest as well as motion, it does not follow that what would cause rest would be equal to what would produce motion, God having been able to subordinate one to the other and to will that the first always yield to the second.

I am therefore not surprised that Descartes was of this opinion, for it is difficult to think of everything; but I am only surprised that he did not correct it when, having further advanced his knowledge, he recognized the existence and some effects of the subtle matter that surrounds bodies. I am surprised that, in article 132 of the fourth part, he attributes to this subtle matter the force that certain bodies have to rebound, and that in articles 55 and 43 of the second part and elsewhere he does not attribute to it their hardness or the resistance they give when we try to bend and break them, but only to the <state of> rest of their parts. It appears obvious to me that the cause of the elasticity and stiffness of certain bodies is the same as what gives them the force of resistance when we want to break them apart, for in the end the force we use actually to break steel differs only insensibly from that by which it is bent to the point of almost breaking.

I do not want to supply very many reasons here that can be given for proving these things, nor to respond to certain difficulties that might be fashioned about the issue of hard bodies that are not sensibly elastic and that we nevertheless have trouble bending. For it suffices, in order to make these difficulties vanish, to consider that subtle matter cannot easily make new paths for itself in brittle bodies, such as glass and tempered steel, and that it can do so more easily in bodies composed of branched and malleable parts, as with gold and lead; and finally <to consider> that there is no hard body that does not have some elasticity.

It is fairly difficult to be persuaded that Descartes positively believed that the cause of hardness was different from that of elasticity; what appears more probable is that he did not reflect enough upon this matter. When one has meditated on some subject for a long time and is satisfied about the things one wanted to know, one often thinks of it no more. One believes that the thoughts he has are incontestable truths and that it is useless to investigate further. But there are so many things in man that discourage his concentration, and that lead him into overly hasty assent and render him subject to error, that even though the mind remains apparently satisfied, it is not always well informed of the truth. Descartes was a man like us; we have never seen more soundness, accuracy, scope and penetration of mind than appear in his works, I admit, but he was not infallible. Thus, he apparently remained so strongly convinced of his opinion that he did not reflect that he affirmed in consequence of his principles something contrary to them. He had founded it upon quite specious and quite probable reasons, but nevertheless they were not irresistible. He could have further suspended his judgment, and consequently he should have. It did not suffice to examine a hard body to find out what in that body makes it so; he should also have thought about the invisible bodies that can make it hard, as he did at the end of his *Principles of Philosophy*, when he attributes the cause of elasticity to them. He should have made an exact division that encompassed everything that could have contributed to the hardness of bodies. It was not sufficient to look for its cause in general in the will of God, since His volitions, which cause all motion and rest, can be subordinated—that which causes rest to that which produces the motion of bodies. He should have thought further about the subtle matter that surrounds them. For although the existence of this extremely agitated matter was not yet proved in his *Principles* where he speaks of hardness, neither was it rejected. He should therefore have suspended his judgment and carefully recollected that what he had written about the cause of hardness and the rules of motion should have been reviewed all over again, which I believe he did not do with enough care. Or else he did not give enough consideration to the true explanation of a thing that is very easy to recognize, and that nevertheless is of the ultimate importance in physics. Let me explain.

Descartes knew very well that to support his system, the truth of which he perhaps could not doubt, it was absolutely necessary that large bodies always communicate some of their motion to the small ones they encountered, and that the small ones rebound upon colliding with larger ones, with no similar loss of their own. For without this his first element would not have the excess of motion required over the second, nor the second over the third; and his whole system would be absolutely false, as those who have meditated upon it a little know fairly well. But in assuming that rest has force to resist motion and that a large body at rest cannot be stirred by another smaller than it, even though the smaller strikes it with a furious agitation, it is obvious that large bodies must have much less motion than a like volume of smaller ones (since according to this assumption they can always communicate what motion they have) and that they cannot always receive it from smaller ones. Hence, since this assumption is not contrary to everything Descartes had said from the beginning until the establishment of his rules of motion in his *Principles*, and since it adapted very well to the consequences of these same principles, he believed that the rules of motion he thought he had demonstrated through their cause had again been sufficiently confirmed by their effects.

I essentially agree with Descartes that large bodies communicate their motion much more easily than small ones, and that hence his first element is more agitated than the second, and the second than the third. But the cause of this is clear without recourse to his hypothesis. Small bodies and fluid ones, water, air, and such, can communicate to large bodies only that motion uniform and common to all their parts; the water of a river can communicate to a boat only the movement of descent common to all the tiny particles composing the water, and each of these tiny particles, beyond this common movement, has an infinity of other particular ones. Thus, it is obvious from this explanation that a boat, for example, can never have as much motion as an equal volume of water, since the boat can receive from the water only that direct motion common to all the parts composing it. If twenty particles of a fluid body push some other body from one direction, there are as many that push it from the other; it therefore remains immobile, and all the tiny parts of the fluid body in which it floats spring back without losing any of their motion. Thus, heavy bodies whose parts are united with each other can receive only circular and uniform movement from the vortex of subtle matter that surrounds them.

It seems to me that this suffices to explain why gross bodies are not as agitated as small ones, and that it is not necessary for explaining these things to assume that rest has some force to resist motion. Thus, the certitude of the principles of Descartes's philosophy cannot be used as a proof for defending his rules of motion; and there is room to believe that if Descartes himself had once more examined his *Principles* without prejudice and by thinking of explanations similar to those I have stated, he would not have believed that the effects of nature had confirmed his rules, and would not have fallen into contradiction by attributing the hardness of bodies only to the state of rest of their parts, and their elasticity with regard to the effort of subtle matter.

Moreover, I believe I should warn that what damages Descartes's physics most is this false premise that rest has force; for from this he inferred false rules of motion; from this he concluded that the balls of his second element were hard in and of themselves; from which he drew false explanations of the transmission of light and the variety of colors, of the generation of fire, and gave very imperfect explanations of weight. In a word, this false principle that rest has force has influence almost everywhere in his system which aside from that marks a genius superior to the philosophers who preceded him; I hope everyone will agree with all this when they have read and completely understood the sixteenth Elucidation. I admit nevertheless that I owe to Descartes, or to his manner of doing philosophy, the opinions I oppose to his own, and the boldness to criticize him.

DIALOGUES ON METAPHYSICS

❧

FIRST DIALOGUE

✣

The soul and its distinction from the body. The nature of ideas. The world in which our bodies live and which we look at is quite different from the one we see.

THEODORE. Well then, my dear Aristes, since this is what you want, I will have to talk to you about my metaphysical visions. But, to do so, I must leave these enchanted places which beguile our senses and which are too distracting in their variety for a mind such as mine. I am very much afraid of taking some of my prejudices—obscure principles which owe their origin to laws of the union of soul and body—for immediate responses of inner truth; and I cannot in these surroundings, as perhaps you can, silence a certain indistinct noise that introduces confusion and unrest in all my ideas. Let us leave then if you please. Let us go enclose ourselves in your study so that we may enter more easily into ourselves. Let us try to allow nothing to prevent either of us from consulting our common master, universal Reason. For it is inner truth that is to preside at our discussions. Inner truth is to dictate what I shall say to you and what you wish to learn by way of me. In short, to judge and decide our differences is its exclusive prerogative. For today we are thinking only of philosophy; and, although you are perfectly submissive to the authority of the Church, you want me to speak to you at first as if you refused to accept truths of faith as principles of our knowledge. Faith must in fact guide the steps of our minds, but sovereign Reason alone can fill them with understanding.

ARISTES. Let us go wherever you wish, Theodore. I find everything I see in this sensible material world distasteful now that I have heard you speak of another world entirely filled with things of intelligible beauty. Take me away to that happy, enchanted Region. Make me contemplate all those wonderful things which you spoke to me of the other day in a manner so magnificent and with so satisfied an air. Let us go. I am ready to follow you into that land which you believe is inaccessible to those who listen only to their senses.

THEODORE. You are enjoying yourself, Aristes, and I am not angry. You make fun of me in so light and seemly a way that, though I see you want to amuse yourself, I also see you do not want to offend me. I pardon you for this. You follow the hidden promptings of your ever-playful imagination. But permit me to say that you are speaking of something you do not understand. Indeed I shall not take you into a strange land, but perhaps I shall teach you that you are in fact a stranger in your own country. I shall teach you that the world you live in is not such as you believe it to be, since it is not such as you see it or as you feel it. You judge all objects surrounding you on the basis of your senses, and your senses delude you a very great deal more than you can imagine. They are accurate witnesses only with regard to what concerns the good of the body and the preservation of life. As to anything else, there is no accuracy, no truth in their deposition. You will see this, Aristes, without going outside yourself, without my "taking you away to that enchanted Region" which your imagination represents. Imagination is a madwoman who is pleased to play the fool. Its leaps, its unforeseen starts amuse you and me as well. But, if you please, Reason must always be uppermost in our discussions. It must decide and pronounce. Yet it is silent and always eludes us when imagination gets in the way and, instead of imposing silence on the imagination, we listen to its pleasantries and dwell on the various phantoms which it presents to us. Make it respectful therefore in the presence of Reason. Silence it if you wish to hear clearly and distinctly the responses of inner truth.

ARISTES. You are taking very seriously what I said without much reflection, Theodore. I apologize for my little sally. I assure you. . . .

THEODORE. You did not anger me, Aristes; you entertained me. For, once again, you have so quick and pleasing an imagination, and I am so confident of your heart, that you will never offend me and will always entertain me—at any rate so long as you only make fun of me in private—and what I just said to you was simply to make you understand that you have a formidable antagonism to the truth. The quality which makes you brilliant in the eyes of men, which wins hearts for you, which draws esteem to you, which makes all who know you want to possess you, is the most irreconcilable enemy of Reason. I put before you a paradoxical thesis the truth of which I cannot now demonstrate.[1] But you will soon acknowledge it from your own experience, and you will perhaps see the reasons for it in the course of our discussions. There is still a good way to go before that. But, believe me, both the stupid mind and the clever mind are equally closed to the truth. There is only this difference: ordinarily the stupid mind respects it while the clever mind holds it in contempt. Nonetheless, if you are quite resolved to curb your imagination, you will encounter no obstacle entering the place where Reason gives its replies; and, when you have listened to it for some time, you will only have contempt for what has appealed to you up to now, and, if God moves your heart, you will have only disgust.

ARISTES. Then let us go quickly, Theodore. Your promises give me an ardor which I cannot express to you. Certainly I shall do everything you ask of me. Let us double the pace. . . . Praise God, we are here at last at the place destined for our discussions. Let us go in . . . Have a seat. . . . Is there anything here to prevent us from entering into ourselves and consulting Reason? Do you want me

---

[1]*Traité de Morale*, Ch. XII [M XI 135–145].

to close off the sources of light so that darkness will conceal anything in the room that is visible and can strike our senses?

THEODORE. No, my dear fellow. Darkness strikes our senses as well as light. It effaces the brightness of the colors. But, at this time of day, darkness might cause some disquiet or slight alarm in our imaginations. Just draw the curtains. The bright light would disturb us a little and might make certain objects too evident. . . . That is very good. Be seated.

Reject everything which has entered your mind by the senses, Aristes. Silence your imagination. Let everything be in perfect silence in you. Even forget, if you can, that you have a body, and think only of what I am going to say to you. In short, be attentive and do not cavil at my opening remarks. Attention is all I ask of you. Without such endeavor or struggle of the mind against impressions from the body, no conquests are made in the land of truth.

ARISTES. I think that is so, Theodore. Speak, but let me stop you when I cannot follow you.

THEODORE. Fair enough. Listen.

I. Nothing has no properties. I think. Hence I am. But what am I, the I that thinks at the time I am thinking? Am I a body, a mind, a man? As yet I know nothing of all this. I know only that, at the time I think, I am something that thinks. But let us see. Can a body think? Can something extended in length, breadth, and depth reason, desire, sense? Certainly not, for all states (*manières d'être*) of such an extended something consist solely in relations of distance; and it is evident that these relations are not perceptions, reasonings, pleasures, desires, sensations; in a word, thoughts. Since my perceptions, which certainly belong to me, are something entirely different from relations of distance, it follows that this *I* that thinks, my very substance, is not a body.

ARISTES. It seems clear to me that modifications of extension can be nothing other than relations of distance and thus that something extended cannot know, will, or sense. But my body may be something other than an extended something. For it seems to me that it is my finger which feels the pain of a prick, that it is my heart which desires, that it is my brain which reasons. The inner sensation I have of what occurs in me informs me of what I am telling you. Prove to me that my body is merely something extended, and I will admit that my mind—or that in me which thinks, which wills, which reasons—is not material or corporeal.

II. THEODORE. So, Aristes, you believe your body is composed of some substance other than extension? Do you not understand that extension is enough for mind to form brain, heart, arms, hands, all the veins, arteries, nerves, and the rest of which your body is composed? If God destroyed your body's extension, would you still have a brain, arteries, veins, and the rest? Do you suppose that a body can be reduced to a mathematical point? God's ability to form everything in the universe from the extension of a grain of sand, of that I have no doubt. Yet surely, where there is no extension—I say none at all—there is no corporeal substance. Think of this in earnest; and, so that you will be convinced of it, take note of this.

Whatever exists can either be conceived by itself (*seul*) or it cannot. There is no middle ground, for the two propositions are contradictory. Now, whatever can be conceived by itself and without thinking of another thing—whatever I say, can be conceived by itself as existing independently of some other thing or can be conceived without the idea we have of it representing some other thing— that is certainly a being or a substance; and whatever cannot be conceived by itself or without thinking of some other thing, that is a state (*maniere d'être*), or a modification of substance.

Here is an example: we cannot think of roundness without thinking of extension. Roundness, then, is not a being or substance but a state. We can think of extension without thinking of some other thing in particular. Hence, extension is not a state of being: it is itself a being. As the modification of a substance is simply the substance itself in some particular state, it is evident that the idea of a modification includes necessarily the idea of the substance of which it is the modification. And, as a substance is a being which subsists in itself, the idea of a substance does not necessarily include the idea of some other being. We have no way of distinguishing substances or beings from modifications or states of being other than the different manners in which we perceive these things.

Now, enter into yourself, and do you not find that you can think of what is extended without thinking of some other thing? Do you not find that you can perceive what is extended by itself alone? Hence, extension is a substance and in no way a state or manner of being. Hence, extension and matter are but one and the same substance. Now, I can perceive my thought, my desire, my joy, my sadness, without thinking of extension, even when I imagine there is no extension. Hence, all of these are not modifications of extension, but modifications of a substance which thinks, which senses, which desires, and which is quite different from extension.

Modifications of extension consist entirely in relations of distance. Now, it is evident that my pleasure, my desire, and all my thoughts are not relations of distance. For relations of distance can be compared, measured, exactly determined by principles of geometry; and we can neither compare nor measure in this way our perceptions and our sensations. Hence, my soul is not material. It is not the modification of my body. It is a substance which thinks and which has no resemblance to the extended substance of which my body is composed.

ARISTES. That seems to be demonstrated. But what conclusion can you draw from it?

III. THEODORE. I can draw an infinite number of conclusions. The distinction of soul and body is the foundation of the principal tenets of philosophy, including the immortality of our being.[2] For, to speak in passing, if the soul is a substance distinct from the body and is not its modification, it is evident that, even though death were to destroy the substance of which our bodies are composed—which it does not—it would not follow from this that our souls were

---

[2]See *Rech. de la Verité*, Bk. IV, Ch. II [M II 22–26]. In what follows: Third Dialogue, XI and XII. The distinction of soul and body is the foundation of all knowledge relating to man.

destroyed. But it is not as yet time to treat this important question in depth. Before that, there are many other truths I must prove for you. Try to concentrate your attention on what I am about to tell you.

ARISTES. Proceed. I shall follow you with all the attention of which I am capable.

IV. THEODORE. I think of many things: of a number, of a circle, of a house, of certain particular beings, of being. Now all this exists, at least at the time I think of it. Certainly, when I think of a circle, of a number, or being or the infinite, of a certain finite being, I perceive realities. For, if the circle I perceive were nothing, thinking of it I would be thinking of nothing. Thus, at the same time I would be thinking and I would not be thinking. Now, the circle I perceive has properties which no other shape has. Hence, the circle exists at the time I think of it, since nothing has no properties and one nothing cannot differ from some other nothing.

ARISTES. What, Theodore! Everything you think of exists? Does your mind give being to this study, this desk, these chairs, because you think of them?

THEODORE. Not so fast. I say whatever I think of is or, if you will, exists. The study, the desk, the chairs which I see, all of this exists, at least at the time I see it. But you conflate what I am seeing with a piece of furniture which I do not see. There is as much difference between the desk which I do see and the desk which you think you see as there is between your mind and body.

ARISTES. I understand you in part, Theodore, and I am ashamed that I interrupted you. I am convinced that everything we see, or everything we think of, contains some reality. You are not speaking of objects but of their ideas. It is no doubt true that the ideas we have of objects exist at the time they are present in our minds. But I thought you were speaking of the objects themselves.

V. THEODORE. "Of the objects themselves"! Ah, we are not there yet! I am trying to arrange my reflections in order. Many more principles than you think are necessary to demonstrate matters about which no one is in doubt. Is there anyone who doubts he has a body, that he walks on solid ground, that he lives in a material world? But you will soon know what few people understand, namely, that while our bodies walk in a corporeal world, our minds for their part are unceasingly transported into an intelligible world which affects them and which thereby becomes sensible to them.

As men take their ideas of things to be nothing, they give far more reality to the created world than it has. They are not in doubt about the existence of objects, and they attribute to them many qualities which they do not have. Yet they do not even think about the reality of their ideas. This is because they listen to their senses instead of consulting inner truth. For, once again, it is far easier to demonstrate the reality of ideas—or, to use your terms, the reality of "that other world entirely filled with things of intelligible beauty"—than to demonstrate the existence of the material world. Here is the reason.

Ideas have an eternal and necessary existence, whereas a corporeal world exists only because it pleased God to create it. So, in order to see the intelligible world, we need only consult Reason which contains intelligible ideas that are eternal and necessary, the archetype of the visible world; and this can be done by any mind that is rational or united to Reason. But, in order to see the material world—or rather to judge that this world exists, as it is invisible in itself—God must of necessity reveal this to us; for we cannot see His volitions which are contingent (*arbitraires*) in Reason which is necessary.

Now, God reveals the existence of His creatures in two ways, through the authority of Holy Scripture and by means of our senses. Granting the first authority—and we cannot reject it—the existence of bodies can be rigorously demonstrated.[3] By the second, we can be sufficiently assured of the existence of particular bodies. But this second way is not at present infallible. For someone may think he is seeing his enemy before him when the man is far away. Someone may think he has four paws when he has but two legs. Someone may feel pain in his arm when the arm has long since been amputated. Thus, natural revelation, which derives from general laws of the union of soul and body, is at present subject to error—I shall give you reasons for this.[4] But special revelation can never directly lead to error since God cannot will to deceive us. This has been a short digression to give you a glimpse of certain truths which I shall prove to you in what follows, to excite your curiosity about them, and to arouse your attention a bit. I return to the subject. Listen to me.

I think of a number, of a circle, of a study, of your chairs, in short of certain particular beings. I also think of being or the infinite, being that is undetermined (*l'être indéterminé*). All these ideas have some reality at the time I think of them. Since nothing has no properties and these do, you are in no doubt about that. They enlighten the mind, or make themselves known to it; some even strike the mind and make themselves sensible to it, and this comes about in a thousand different ways. In any case it is certain that the properties of certain ones are quite different from those of others. If, then, the reality of our ideas is genuine and, with even greater reason, if it is necessary, eternal, and immutable, it is clear that we are both taken to a world other than the one in which our bodies live. We are "in a world entirely filled with things of intelligible beauty."

Let us suppose, Aristes, that God annihilates all the beings He created with the exception of you and me, your body and mine. (I speak to you as to a man who believes and already knows many things, and I am certain that in this I am not mistaken. I would annoy you if I were to speak to you with an overly scrupulous precision and as if to a man who as yet knows nothing at all.) Let us suppose, moreover, that God impresses all the same traces on our brains, or rather He presents all the same ideas to our minds which we have in our minds today. On that supposition, Aristes, in which world would we spend the day? Would it not be in an intelligible world? Now note that it is in this world that we exist and live, though the body we animate lives and walks in another. It is this intelligible world which we contemplate, which we admire, which we sense. But the world which we look at, or which we consider when we turn our heads on all

---

[3]In the Sixth Dialogue which follows.

[4]Fourth and Sixth Dialogues.

sides, is simply matter, which is invisible in itself and which possesses nothing of all those beauties that we sense and admire when we look at it. Reflect well on this. Nothing has no properties. Hence, if the world were destroyed, it would have no beauty. Now, on the supposition that the world was annihilated and that God nonetheless produced the same traces in our brains or, rather, presented the same ideas to our minds which are produced in the presence of objects, we should see the same beauties. Hence, the beauties we see are not material beauties but intelligible beauties rendered sensible as a consequence of laws of the union of soul and body; for the supposed annihilation of matter does not carry with it the annihilation of the beauties we see when we look at the objects surrounding us.

ARISTES. I am afraid, Theodore, you have supposed something false. For, if God destroyed this room, it would certainly no longer be visible; for nothing has no properties.

VI. THEODORE. You do not follow me, Aristes. Your room is absolutely invisible in itself. You say that if God destroyed it, it would no longer be visible since nothing has no properties. That would be true if the visibility of your room were a property which belonged to it. If it were destroyed, it would no longer be visible. That is true in one sense, and I agree. But what I see when I look at your room, viz. when I turn my eyes on all sides to consider it, will still be visible even should your room have been destroyed and even, I may add, if it had never been built! I maintain that a Chinese who has never been in the room can, in his own country, see everything I see when I look at your room provided—which is by no means impossible—his brain is moved in the same way mine is when I now consider it. Is it not true that people with a high fever and people who sleep see chimeras of all sorts that never were? What they see exists at least at the time they see it. But what they believe they see does not exist. That to which they ascribe what they see is nothing real.

I tell you again, Aristes, your room is not, strictly speaking, visible. It is not really your room which I see when I look at it, since I could very well see what I am now seeing even though God had destroyed it. The dimensions I see are immutable, eternal, necessary. The intelligible dimensions which represent these spaces to me occupy no place. The dimensions of your room are, on the contrary, variable and corruptible: they fill a certain space. But I am afraid that, telling you too many truths, I am now multiplying your difficulties. For you seem to have some trouble distinguishing ideas, which alone are visible in themselves, from the objects which they represent and which are invisible to the mind since they cannot act on it nor be presented to it.

ARISTES. It is true I am a bit stupefied. The reason is I have trouble following you in this land of ideas to which you assign a genuine reality. I get no purchase on anything that is not bodily. And the reality of your ideas, which I cannot keep from believing to be genuine for the reasons you have given me, appears to me to have hardly any solidity. For what, pray tell, becomes of our ideas when we are no longer thinking of them? As for me, it seems to me they return to nothing. And, if that is so, then your intelligible world is destroyed. If I annihilate the intelligible room that I now see when I close my eyes, the reality of that room is certainly very slight and not much of anything (*bien peu de chose*). If opening my eyes suffices to create an intelligible world, this world certainly amounts to less than the one our bodies live in.

VII. THEODORE. The last point is true, Aristes. If you give being to your ideas, if just the wink of an eye is sufficient to annihilate them, there is not much of anything there. But if they are eternal, immutable, necessary, in short, divine—I have in mind the intelligible extension of which they are formed—certainly they will be more considerable than matter, which is inefficacious and is absolutely invisible in itself. Is it really possible for you to believe, Aristes, that when you will to think of a circle, you give being, so to speak, to the substance of which your idea is formed and which, as soon as you cease willing to think of it, is annihilated? Be careful here. If it is you who give being to your ideas, it is by virtue of willing to think of them. Now, I ask you, how can you will to think of a circle if you do not already have some idea of it from which it can be fashioned and formed? Can you will to make something of which you have no knowledge? Can you make something out of nothing? Certainly you cannot will to think of a circle if you do not already have the idea of it—or at least an idea of the extension in which you can consider certain parts without thinking of others. You cannot come to see it close by, see it distinctly, unless you already see it confusedly and as from afar. Your attention takes you to it, it makes it present to you, it even forms it. I agree. But clearly your attention does not produce it from nothing. Your lack of attention takes you away from it, but it does not altogether annihilate it. For, if it were annihilated, how could you form the desire of producing it? What model would you use to make it anew similar to itself? Would that not clearly be impossible?

ARISTES. Clearly? Well not for me, Theodore. You make me consent, but you do not persuade me. This earth is real. I feel it. When my foot strikes it, it resists me. There is some solidity to it. What I cannot be persuaded of, however, is that my ideas have a certain reality independent of my thought, that they exist even when I am not thinking of them.

VIII. THEODORE. That is because you were unable to enter into yourself to question Reason. You tire from the labor of attention and you listen to your imagination and your senses which speak to you without your taking the trouble to consult them. You have not reflected enough on the proofs I gave you that the testimony of the senses is deceptive. Not long ago there was a man, otherwise quite rational, who was of the opinion that there was water up to his waist and who was always afraid it would rise and drown him. He felt that water as you feel your earth. He found it cold, and he always walked very slowly because, he said, the water prevented him from going faster. When people spoke to him contrariwise and he listened attentively, they disabused him of this. But he soon fell back into his error. When a man thinks he is transformed into a cock, a hare, a wolf, or an ox like Nebuchadnezzar, he senses in himself, in place of his legs, the feet of a cock; in place of his arms, the hocks of an ox; in place of his hair, a comb or horns. Why do you not see that the resistance you feel pressing the floor with your foot is only a sensation which strikes the soul? that, absolutely speaking, we can have all our sensations independently of objects? While asleep have you never felt a very heavy body on your chest that kept you from breathing? Or have you never thought you were struck, even wounded, or that you struck others, walked, danced, jumped on solid ground?

You believe this floor exists because you sense it resisting you. Well then, does it follow that air does not have as much reality as your floor because it has less solidity? Does ice have more reality than water because it has greater hardness? But you are twice mistaken: no body can resist a mind. The floor resists your foot. I agree. But it is something entirely different from your floor or your body which resists your mind and gives it the sensation you have of resistance or solidity.

Nonetheless, I will allow that your floor resists you. But do you think your ideas do not resist you? Try then to show me two diameters of a circle which are unequal or three in an ellipse which are equal. Try to find a square root of 8 or the cube root of 9. Try to make it right that we do unto others what we would not have them do unto us; or, to take an example relating to yours, try to make two feet of intelligible extension equal no more than one. Certainly the nature of this extension necessarily will not allow it. It resists your mind. Do not doubt its reality then. Your floor is impenetrable to your foot—that is what your senses teach you in a confused and deceptive way. Intelligible extension is also impenetrable in its fashion—this is what it makes you see clearly by its evidence and its own light.

Listen to me, Aristes. You have the idea of space or extension—of a space, I say, that has no limits. This idea is necessary, eternal, immutable, common to all minds—to men, to Angels, even to God. The idea, you should note, is ineffaceable from your mind, as is that of being or the infinite, of indeterminate being (*l'être indéterminé*). It is always present to the mind. You cannot separate yourself from it or entirely lose sight of it. Now, it is from this vast idea that there are formed in us not only the idea of a circle and any purely intelligible shape, but also the idea of every sensible shape which we see when we look at the created world. All this takes place insofar as intelligible parts of this ideal, immaterial, intelligible extension are variously applied to our minds: if by virtue of our attention, we then know these shapes; if because of traces and movements in our brains, we then imagine or sense them. Right now I cannot explain all of this to you more exactly.[5] Simply consider that this idea of an infinite extension must necessarily have a great deal of reality since you cannot comprehend it and, whatever movement you give your mind, you cannot transverse it. Consider that it cannot possibly be merely a modification of your mind since the infinite cannot actually be the modification of something finite. Say to yourself, my mind cannot comprehend this vast idea. It cannot take its measure. Hence, the idea

[5]See *Conversat. chrétien.*, pp. 123 ff., of the 1702 edition, or *Rép. à M. Regis*, pp. 27 ff., or the following *Entretien sur la Mort*, II, near the end [M IV 74ff.; XVII-1 281 ff.; XII–XIII 407 ff.] [*Entretiens sur la Mort*, which was added in the third edition of *Entretiens sur la métaphysique. . . .*, is not included in this volume.]

goes infinitely beyond my mind. And, since it goes beyond it, it is clearly not its modification. Modifications of beings cannot extend beyond the beings of which they are modifications, since the modifications are simply these beings themselves in some state or other. My mind cannot take the measure of this idea; my mind is finite whereas the idea is infinite. For the finite, however great it may be and however much we seek to apply or repeat it, can never equal the infinite.

ARISTES. How ingenious and quick you are! But not so fast, if you please. I do not grant you that the mind perceives the infinite. I agree that the mind perceives an extension to which it sees no end, but it does not see an infinite extension. A finite mind can see nothing that is infinite.

IX. THEODORE. It is true that the mind does not see an infinite extension, Aristes, in the sense that its thought or its perception is adequate to an infinite extension. If it were, it would comprehend it, and it would itself be infinite. For an infinite thought would be required to take the measure of an infinite idea, to encompass at once everything the infinite comprehends. But the mind actually sees that its immediate object is infinite; it actually sees that intelligible extension is infinite. And this is not, as you think, because it does not see an end to it; for, if that were so, it could hope to find one, or at any rate it could be in doubt whether there is one or not. It is, rather, because the mind sees clearly that there is no end.

Let us imagine a man fallen from the clouds who, on earth, walks continuously in a straight line, I mean, on one of the great circles into which geographers divide it; and let us suppose that nothing keeps him from travelling this way. After several days travel could he conclude that the earth is infinite because he had not found an end? If he were wise and cautious in his judgments, he would believe it to be very large, but he would not judge it to be infinite. And when, as a result of walking, he found himself in the same place from which he had set out, he would realize he had in fact gone round it. But, when the mind thinks of intelligible extension, when it seeks to take the measure of the idea of space, it sees clearly that it is infinite. It cannot doubt that this idea is inexhaustible. Let the mind take enough of it to represent the place of a hundred thousand worlds and again at every instant a hundred thousand more, the idea will never cease to furnish it with all that is required. The mind sees this and cannot doubt it. Yet it is not in this way that it finds out that the idea is infinite. It is, on the contrary, because it sees it as actually infinite and knows that it will never exhaust it.

Geometers are the most exact of those engaged in reasoning. Now, everyone agrees that there is no fraction which, simply multiplied by itself, gives the product eight, although this number can be approached without limit by increasing the terms of the fractions. Everyone agrees that a hyperbola and its asymptotes, as well as several other similar lines continued to infinity, will approach one another indefinitely without ever meeting. Do you think they discover these truths by trying, and form a judgment about what they do not see on the basis of some small part which they have seen? No, Aristes. This is the way imagination and the senses, or those who follow their testimony, judge.

True philosophers form judgments only about what precisely they see. Yet, without ever having tested it, they are not afraid of affirming that no part of the diagonal of a square, were it a million times smaller than the smallest particle of dust, can be used to measure exactly and without remainder the diagonal of the square and one of its sides. So true is it that the mind sees the infinite in the small as well as in the large—not by division or reiterated multiplication of its finite ideas, which could never attain the infinite, but by the very infinity which it discovers in its ideas and which belongs to them—that it learns at once that, on the one hand, there is no unity and, on the other hand, there are no limits in infinite intelligible extension.

ARISTES. I give up, Theodore. Ideas have more reality than I thought; and their reality is immutable, necessary, eternal, common to all intellects, and does not consist in modifications of the intellect's own being, which, being finite, cannot receive modifications that are actually infinite. The perception I have of intelligible extension belongs to me: it is a modification of my mind. It is I who perceives this extension. But the extension I perceive is not a modification of my mind. I am aware it is not myself I see when I think of infinite spaces, of a circle, of a square, or of a cube, when I look at this room, when I turn my eyes towards the heavens. The perception of extension is my own. But, as for the extension along with all the shapes I discover in it, I should like to know in what way all that is not my own. The perception I have of extension cannot exist without me. It is thus a modification of my mind. But the extension I see does subsist without me. You can contemplate it without my thinking of it, you and any other man.

X. THEODORE. You need not be afraid to add, "And God Himself." For all our clear ideas are in God in their intelligible reality. It is only in Him that we see them. Do not imagine that what I say here is new. It is the opinion of St. Augustine.[6] If our ideas are eternal, immutable, necessary, you plainly see they can only exist in a nature which is immutable. It is true, Aristes, that God sees intelligible extension in Himself, *i.e.* the archetype of the matter of which the world is formed and in which our bodies live; and, I repeat, it is only in Him that we see it. For our minds live entirely in universal Reason, in that intelligible substance which contains the ideas of all the truths we discover, whether as a consequence of general laws of the union of our minds with this same Reason[7] or in consequence of general laws of the union of our souls with our bodies, the occasional or natural cause of the latter being nothing other than traces imprinted in the brain by the action of objects or the flow of animal spirits.

Order does not permit me to explain all this in detail at present, but, to satisfy in part your desire to know how the mind can discover all sorts of shapes and see the sensible world in intelligible extension, think of your perceiving, say, a circle in three ways. You conceive it, you imagine it, you sense or see it. When you

---

[6]See *Réponse au Livre des vrayes & des fausses Idées*, Ch. VII and Ch. XXI [M VI–VII 63–69, 143–150]

[7]Twelfth Dialogue, which follows.

conceive a circle, intelligible extension is applied to your mind with indeterminate limits as to size but with all points equidistant from some given point and all in the same plane. You thus conceive a circle in general. When you imagine one, a determinate part of this extension, the limits of which are equidistant from a point, affects your mind lightly. And, when you sense or see a circle, a determinate part of this extension sensibly affects your soul and modifies it with the sensation of a certain color. For intelligible extension becomes visible and represents some body in particular only through color, since it is only from the diversity of colors that we judge the difference of objects we see. All the intelligible parts of intelligible extension are of the same nature in their capacity as idea, as the parts of local or material extension are of the same nature viewed as substance. But, sensations of color being essentially different, it is by them that we form judgments of the variety of bodies. When I distinguish your hand from your coat and both from the air surrounding them, it is because my sensations of them differ in light and color. That is evident. If I had the same sensation of color of everything in your room, I would not by my sense of sight see a diversity of objects. You judge rightly then that intelligible extension diversely applied to our minds can give us our ideas of mathematical figures as well as ideas of objects we admire in the universe and also of everything our imagination represents to us.[8] For, just as we can form all sorts of figures from a block of marble by use of a chisel, God can represent all material beings to us by diverse applications of intelligible extension to our minds. But how this is done, and why God does it this way, are matters we shall have occasion to examine later.

This suffices for an initial discussion, Aristes. Try to become accustomed to metaphysical ideas and rise above your senses. You are thus transported, if I am not mistaken, into an intelligible world. Contemplate its beauties. Go over in your mind everything I have told you. Nourish yourself on the substance of truth and prepare yourself to proceed farther into this unknown land where you have as yet made only an entrance. Tomorrow I shall try to take you to the Throne of the sovereign Majesty to whom belongs from all eternity this happy and unchanging place wherein our minds live.

ARISTES. I am still utterly astonished and shaken. My body weighs down my mind, and I have trouble keeping a firm hold on the truths you have opened up to me. Yet you intend to lift me even higher. My head will spin, Theodore; and, if I feel tomorrow as I do today, I will not have the confidence to follow you.

THEODORE. Meditate on what I have told you today, Aristes, and tomorrow I promise you you will be ready for anything. Meditation will strengthen your mind and give you the ardor and the wings to rise above creatures to the presence of the Creator. Goodbye, my dear fellow. Be of good courage.

ARISTES. Goodbye, Theodore. I shall do as you say.

---

[8]See *Rech. de la Verité*, Bk. III, Part Two, and *Eclaircissement* [X] on this matter [M I 413–492, III 127–161]. See also my *Rép. au Liv. des vrayes & des fausses Idées de M. Arnaud* [M VI–VII 11–189] and my first *Lett. touchant sa Défense* [M VI–VII 193–274]. Or my *Rép. a la III. Lett. posthume de Monsieur Arnaud* [M VIII–IX 901–989].

SECOND DIALOGUE

✤

The existence of God. We can see all things in Him, and nothing finite can represent Him. Consequently, thinking of Him is sufficient to know that He exists.[a]

THEODORE. Well there, Aristes, what do you think of the intelligible world to which I took you yesterday? Is your imagination no longer frightened by it? Does your mind walk with a firm and sure step in that land of meditators, in that Region inaccessible to those who listen only to their senses?

ARISTES. What a beautiful spectacle that Archetype of the Universe is, Theodore! I have contemplated it with extreme gratification. What a pleasing surprise it is when, without suffering death, the soul is transported into the land of truth and finds there an abundance of that which is required to nourish it. I am not, it is true, as yet quite accustomed to that celestial manna, to that entirely spiritual food. At certain times it seems to me quite hollow and light. But, when I taste it attentively, I find so much savor and solidity in it that I can no longer bring myself to come feed with the brutes on a material earth.

THEODORE. Oh, my dear Aristes, what are you saying to me? Are you speaking seriously?

ARISTES. Most seriously. No, I no longer wish to listen to my senses. I want to enter for all times the innermost part of myself and live on the abundancy I find there. My senses are meet for leading my body to its usual pasture, and I acquiesce in its following them. But that I myself follow them! That I will no more do. I want to follow Reason exclusively and, by attending to it, march into the land of truth and find there the delicious food which can alone nourish intellects.

THEODORE. That is because for the time being, you have forgotten you have a body. But you will not be long not thinking of it, or rather not thinking in its terms. The body which you at present neglect will soon oblige you to drive it to

---

[a]In the fourth edition (as in the second and third), we find—*sçavoir ce qu'il est*. For reasons that will be apparent, I have followed Professor Robinet's emendation in the standard edition and translate the expression used in the first edition and in the Table of Chapter Headings in all four editions, i.e.—*sçavoir qu'il est*.

pasture yourself and busy yourself with its needs. The mind is not now so easily disengaged from matter. But, while you remain pure spirit, tell me please: What have you discovered in the land of ideas? Do you now know what Reason is—that of which, in this terrestrial and material world, we speak so much yet know so little? Yesterday I promised you I would raise you above all creatures and take you to the very presence of the Creator. Were you not inclined to fly there by yourself and without thinking of Theodore?

I. ARISTES. I confess I did think—without lacking in the respect I owe you—that I could go along the path you showed me alone. I followed it, and I had, it seems to me, clear knowledge of what you told me yesterday, namely, that universal Reason is an immutable nature and exists in God alone. Here, in a few words, are the steps I took. Judge them and tell me whether I have gone astray. After you left me, I remained for some time unsteady and taken aback. But, urged on by an inner ardor, it seemed to me I said to myself—I know not how—"Since Reason is common to me and to Theodore, why can I not then consult it and follow it without him?" I consulted it, and I followed it. And it took me, if I am not mistaken, to the One who possesses it as His own and by the necessity of His being. Indeed, it seems to me to lead there as a matter of course. This, then, is quite simply and straightforwardly the line of reasoning I followed.

Infinite intelligible extension is not a modification of my mind. It is immutable, eternal, necessary. I cannot doubt its reality and its immensity. But anything immutable, eternal, necessary, and especially infinite is not a creature and cannot belong to a creature. Hence, it belongs to the Creator and cannot exist except in God. Hence, there is a God and Reason. There is a God in whom there exists the archetype which I contemplate of the created world I live in. There is a God in whom there exists the Reason which enlightens me by purely intelligible ideas supplied abundantly to my mind and to the minds of all men. I am certain that all men are united to the same Reason as I am; for I am certain that they see, or can see, what I see when I enter into myself and discover the truths or necessary relations contained in the intelligible substance of universal Reason which lives in me—or, rather, in which all intellects live.

II. THEODORE. You have not gone astray, my dear Aristes. You have followed Reason, and it has led you to the One who engenders it from His own substance and who possesses it eternally. But do not imagine that it disclosed to you the nature of the supreme Being to whom it led you. When you contemplate intelligible extension, you see simply the archetype of the material world we live in, and the archetype of an infinity of other possible worlds. As a matter of fact, you also see the divine substance, for it alone is visible and can enlighten the mind. But you do not see it in itself or in its own nature. You see it only in its relation to material creatures and only in so far as it can be participated in by them or is representative of them. Consequently, it is not, properly speaking, God whom you see but rather the matter which He can produce.

Certainly, by way of infinite intelligible extension, you see that God is. Since nothing finite can contain an infinite reality, He alone can contain what you see. But you do not see what God is. The Deity has no limits in His perfections, and what you see when you think of immense spaces is devoid of an infinity of perfections. I say "what you see" and not the substance which represents to you what you see; for that substance, which you do not see in itself, has infinite perfections.

To be sure, the substance which contains intelligible extension is all-powerful. It is infinitely wise. It contains an infinity of perfections and realities. It contains, for example, an infinity of intelligible numbers. Yet intelligible extension has nothing in common with all these things. There is no wisdom, no power, no unity in the extension that you contemplate. You know that all numbers are mutually commensurable since they have unity as a common base. If the parts of extension as it is divided and subdivided by the mind could be reduced to unity, they would then be mutually commensurable by virtue of that unity. But you know that that is certainly false. Thus, the divine substance in its simplicity, which is beyond our reach, contains an infinity of intelligible perfections that are quite different; and by them God enlightens us, showing Himself to us not as He is or in His particular and absolute reality, but in His reality as it is general and relative to what He can produce. Try, however, to follow me. I shall take you as near as possible to the Deity.

III. Infinite intelligible extension is the archetype simply of an infinity of possible worlds like our own. By means of it, I see only particular beings, only material beings. When I think of this extension, I see the divine substance only in so far as it is representative of bodies and can be participated in by them. But note that when I think of being and not of certain particular beings, and when I think of the infinite and not of a certain particular infinite, it is certain, first, that I do not see so vast a reality in the modifications of my mind. For, if I cannot find in them enough reality to represent the infinite in extension, there is all the more reason that I shall not find in them enough to represent the infinite in every kind. Thus, it is only God, only the infinite, indefinite being or the infinitely infinite infinite that can contain the infinitely infinite reality I see when I think of being and not of certain particular beings or certain particular infinites.

IV. In the second place, it is certain that the idea of being, of reality, of indeterminate perfection, or of the infinite in every kind, is not the divine substance in so far as it is representative of a certain creature or can be participated in by a certain creature. For every creature is necessarily a being of a certain sort. It is a contradiction that God should make or engender a being in general or infinite in every kind, for such a being would be God Himself or identical with its own principle. The Son and the Holy Ghost do not participate in the divine Being: they receive it in its entirety. Or, to speak of things more proportionate to our minds, it is evident that the idea of a circle in general is not intelligible extension in so far as it is representative of a certain circle or can be participated in by a certain circle. The idea of a circle in general, or the essence of a circle, represents or pertains to an infinite number of circles. To think of a circle in general is to perceive as a single circle an infinite number of circles, and so that idea [of a circle in general] contains the idea of the infinite. I do not know whether you grasp what I want you to understand. Here it is in a few words. The idea of being without restriction, of the infinite, of generality, is not the idea of creatures, or the essence that pertains to them: it is the idea which represents the Deity, or the essence that pertains to it. All particular beings participate in being, but no particular being is identical with it. Being contains all things; but all beings both created and possible, in their multiplicity, cannot fill the vast extension of being.

ARISTES. It seems to me I do see your meaning. You define God as He defined Himself in speaking to Moses, "I am that I am."[1] Intelligible extension is the idea or archetype of bodies. But being without restriction, or in a word "Being," is the idea of God: it is what represents Him to our minds as we see Him in this life.

V. THEODORE. Very good. But note especially that God or the infinite is not visible by an idea which represents it. The infinite is its own idea. It has no archetype. It can be known, but it cannot be formed. What is formed are creatures, or certain particular beings, which are visible by way of ideas that represent them even before they are made. We can see a circle, a house, a sun, without there being such a thing. All finite things can be seen in the infinite, which contains intelligible ideas of them. But the infinite can be seen only in itself. For nothing finite can represent the infinite. If we think of God, He must exist. A being of a certain sort, though known, may not exist. We can see its essence without its existence, its idea without it. But we cannot see the essence of the infinite without its existence, the idea of being without being. For being has no idea that represents it. It has no archetype that contains all its intelligible reality. It is its own archetype, and it contains in itself the archetype of all beings.

Thus, you see that the proposition "There is a God" is intrinsically the clearest of all propositions affirming the existence of some thing and that it is even as certain as "I think, therefore I am." Since God and being or the infinite are but one and the same thing, you see besides what God is.

VI. But, once again, make no mistake about this. You see only confusedly and as from afar what God is. Though you see the infinite or being without restriction, you see it only in a very imperfect way, and so you do not see God as He is Himself. You do not see the infinite as a simple being. You see the multiplicity of creatures in the infinity of uncreated being, but you do not see distinctly its unity. This is because you do not see it in its absolute reality but rather in its nature in relation to possible creatures, the number of which it can increase to infinity without their ever equalling the reality that represents them. This is because you see it as universal Reason enlightening intellects in proportion to the light that is necessary at present for them to lead their lives and to discover the perfections of God in so far as these can be participated in by limited beings. But you do not discover the property which is essential to the infinite: being at once one and also all things—or being composed, as it were, of an infinity of different perfections yet so simple that, in it, each perfection contains all the others without there being any real distinction.[2]

God does not impart His substance to creatures. He imparts only His perfections, not as they are in His substance, but as His substance represents them and as the limitation of creatures can bear. Intelligible extension, for example, represents bodies: it is their archetype or their idea. But, though this extension occupies no place, bodies are extended in a place, and they cannot but be extended in a place because of the limitation essential to creatures and because no finite substance can have that property incomprehensible to the human mind of being at the same time one and also all things, perfectly simple yet possessing every sort of perfection.[b]

Thus, intelligible extension represents infinite spaces, but it fills none of them; and, though it, so to speak, fills all minds and discloses itself to them, it in no way follows that our minds are spacious (*spacieux*). They would have had to be infinitely so to see infinite spaces if they saw them by local union with spaces which are extended in a place.[3]

The divine substance is everywhere without being extended in a place. It has no limits. It is not contained in the Universe. But it is not this substance as spread out everywhere that we see when we think of spaces.[4] If that were so, since our minds are finite, we could never think of infinite spaces. The intelligible extension we see in the divine substance containing it is just that substance itself in so far as it is representative of material beings and can be participated in by them. That is all I can tell you. But note that being without restriction, or the infinite in every way that we perceive, is not simply the divine substance in so far as it is representative of all possible beings. For, though we do not have particular ideas of all these beings, we are assured that they cannot equal the intelligible reality of the infinite. In a sense, then, it is God's substance itself that we see. Yet in this life we see it only in a way so confused and far removed that we see rather that it is than what it is; we see that it is the source and exemplar of all beings rather than seeing its own nature or its perfections in themselves.

ARISTES. Is there not a contradiction in what you are telling me? If, as appears evident to me, nothing finite can have enough reality to represent the infinite, must we not of necessity see God's substance in itself?

VII. THEODORE. I do not deny that we see God's substance in itself. We see it in itself in the sense that we do not see it by means of something finite that represents it. But we do not see it in itself in the sense of attaining its simplicity while distinguishing perfections in it.

Since you agree that nothing finite can represent infinite reality, it is clear that, if you see the infinite, you see it only in itself. But it is certain that you do see it.

---

[2]See the first *Lettre touchant la Défense de Mr. Arnauld,* 18 [M VI 249–253].

[b]The topic under discussion in this paragraph and the two that follow is admittedly less than entirely clear. I run the risk of implanting an interpretation in the translation.

[3]See the same *Lettre,* 2, 11 *ff* [M VI 210–213].

[4]*Ibid.,* and the Eighth Dialogue that follows.

Otherwise, when you ask me whether God or an infinite being exists, you would be raising a ridiculous question involving a proposition the terms of which you would not understand. It is as if you were to ask me whether a "Blictri" exists,[5] that is, a something you know not what.

Surely all men have the idea of God, or think of the infinite, when they ask whether there is such a thing. But, since they do not reflect on the fact that nothing finite can represent it, they believe they can think of it without its existing. As they can think of many things that do not exist (since creatures can be seen without their existing, because we do not see them in themselves but in the ideas that represent them), they imagine that it is the same with the infinite and that they can think of it without its existing. That is why they look for and do not recognize that which they encounter at every moment and which they would recognize soon enough if they entered into themselves and reflected on their ideas.

ARISTES. You convince me, Theodore, but I still have a lingering doubt. It seems to me that the idea I have of being in general, or of the infinite, is an idea of my own workmanship. It seems to me that the mind can make general ideas for itself out of a number of particular ideas. When we have seen a number of trees, an apple tree, a pear tree, a plum tree, etc., we get from them a general idea of a tree. Also, when we have seen a number of beings, we form from them the general idea of being. Thus, this general idea of being may be only a confused assemblage of all the others. That is what I have been taught and how I have always understood the matter.

VIII. THEODORE. Your mind is a wonderful workman, Aristes. It can derive the infinite from the finite, the idea of being without restriction from ideas of certain particular beings. Perhaps it finds in its own resources enough reality to give finite ideas what is missing in order for them to be infinite. I do not know whether that is what you have been taught, but I think I know you have never understood the matter.

ARISTES. If our ideas were infinite, they would assuredly not be our workmanship nor modifications of our minds. That cannot be contested. But perhaps, although we can perceive the infinite by means of them, they are finite. Or it may be that the infinite we [seem to] see is not fundamentally such. It may be, as I have just said, only a confused assemblage of a number of finite things. The general idea of being may be only a confused accumulation of ideas of particular beings. I have trouble ridding my mind of this thought.

IX. THEODORE. Yes, Aristes, our ideas are finite if by "our ideas" you mean our perceptions or the modifications of our minds. But, if by "idea of the infinite" you mean what the mind sees when it thinks of it, or what is then the immediate object of the mind, certainly that is infinite, for we see it as such. Note, I say to you, that we see it as such. The impression that the infinite makes on the mind is finite. There is indeed more perception in the mind, more impression of an idea, in short, more thought, when we clearly and distinctly

[5]A term which awakens no idea.

know a small object than when we confusedly think of a large one, or indeed of the infinite. Yet, although the mind is almost always more affected, more permeated, more modified by a finite idea than by an infinite one, nonetheless there is more reality in the infinite idea than in the finite, in being without restriction than in certain particular beings.

You could not get it out of your mind that general ideas are only a confused assemblage of particular ideas, or at any rate that you have the power of forming them from that assemblage. Let us see what is true and what is false in this thought by which you are so strongly prepossessed. You think, Aristes, of a circle one foot in diameter, then of one two feet, one three, one four, etc., and then you do not determine the size of the diameter and you think of a circle in general. You then say, "The idea of a circle in general is only the confused assemblage of the circles I have thought of." But that conclusion is certainly false; for the idea of a circle in general represents an infinite number of circles and pertains to all of them, while you have only thought of a finite number of circles.

Or is it rather that you have found the secret of forming the idea of a circle in general from the five or six you have seen. This is true in one sense and false in another. It is false in the sense that there is enough reality in the idea of five or six circles to derive the idea of a circle in general. But it is true in the sense that, after recognizing that the size of circles does not change their properties, you may have stopped considering them one after another with a determinate size and thence come to consider them in general with an indeterminate size. Thus, you have, so to speak, formed the idea of a circle in general by spreading (*répandant*) the idea of generality over the confused ideas of the circles you have imagined. But I maintain that you could form a general idea only because you find enough reality in the idea of the infinite to give generality to your ideas. You can think of an indeterminate diameter only because you see the infinite in extension and can augment or diminish the diameter infinitely. I maintain that, if the idea of the infinite, which is inseparable from your mind, were not joined quite naturally to the particular ideas you perceive, you could never think of those abstract forms of genera and species. You could think of a certain circle but never of the circle. You could perceive a certain equality of radii but never a general equality of indeterminate radii. The reason is that no finite and determinate idea can ever represent anything infinite and indeterminate. Yet, unreflectingly, the mind joins the idea of generality it finds in the infinite to its finite ideas. Just as the mind spreads the idea of indivisible unity over the idea of a certain extension which is in fact infinitely divisible, so it also spreads the general idea of perfect equality over particular ideas; and this is what throws it into an infinity of errors. For all the falsity in our ideas comes from the fact that we confound them with one another and furthermore mingle them with our own modifications. But that is a matter we will talk about another time.

ARISTES. That is all very well, Theodore. But are you not considering our ideas as distinct from our perceptions? It seems to me that the idea of a circle in general is only a confused perception of a number of circles of different sizes, that is, an accumulation of different modifications of my mind which are almost effaced yet each of which is the idea or perception of a certain circle.

X. THEODORE. No doubt I do accept the difference between our ideas and our perceptions, between ourselves who perceive and what we perceive.[6] It is because I know that the finite cannot find in itself what is required to represent the infinite. It is because I know, Aristes, that I contain no intelligible reality in myself and, far indeed from finding the ideas of all things in my substance, I do not even find there the idea of my own being.[7] I am entirely unintelligible to myself, and I shall never see what I am unless it please God to disclose to me the idea or archetype of minds which universal Reason contains. But that is a topic we shall discuss another time.

Surely, Aristes, if your ideas were only modifications of your mind, the confused assemblage of thousands and thousands of ideas would never be anything but a confused composite incapable of any generality. Take twenty different colors and mix them together to excite in yourself a color in general—produce several different sensations in yourself at the same time to derive a sensation in general. You will soon see that this is not possible. By mixing diverse colors, say green, gray, and blue, you will always get some particular color. Dizziness is produced by a great number of different movements of the brain fibers and animal spirits, but that is nonetheless only a particular sensation. This is so because any modification of a particular being, such as our minds, can only be particular. It can never rise to the generality which exists in ideas. It is true you can think of pain in general, but you could never be modified by anything but a particular pain. And, if you can think of pain in general, that is because you can attach generality to anything. But, once again, you could not draw this idea of generality from your own resources. It has too much reality; it must be supplied to you by the infinite in its abundance.

ARISTES. I have nothing to say to you in reply. Everything you are telling me appears evident to me. But I am surprised that these general ideas, which have infinitely more reality than particular ideas, make less of an impression on me than particular ideas do and appear to me to have much less solidity.

XI. THEODORE. The reason is that they make themselves less felt or, rather, that they do not make themselves felt at all. Do not judge the reality of ideas, Aristes, as children judge the reality of bodies. Children believe that all the spaces between heaven and earth are nothing real since they do not make themselves felt. And there are but few people who know that there is as much matter in a cubic foot of air as in a cubic foot of lead, since lead is harder, heavier, in short, more sensible than air. Do not imitate them. Judge the reality of ideas not by the sensation you have of them, which confusedly indicates their action to you, but by the intelligible light which discloses their nature to you. Otherwise,

---

[6]See *Réponse au Livre des vrayes & des fausses idées* [M VI 1–189] or my *Réponse à la 3. Lettre de M. Arn.* [M IX 901–989].

[7]See *Rech. de la verité,* Book III, Part 2, Ch. 7, No. 4 [M I 451–453], and the *Eclaircissement* [XI] corresponding to this chapter [M III 163–171].

you will think that sensible ideas which make an impression on you, such as the idea you have of the floor you press with your foot, have more reality than purely intelligible ideas, though there is fundamentally no difference between them.

ARISTES. "No difference," Theodore! The idea of the extension I think of not different from the idea of the extension which I see, which I press with my foot, and which resists me!

XII. THEODORE. No, Aristes, there are not two kinds of extension, nor two kinds of ideas representing them. If the extension you think of affected you or modified your soul by some sensation, it would appear to you, intelligible though it is, to be sensible. It would appear to you to be hard, cold, colored, and perhaps painful, for you might attribute to it all the sensations you have. Once again, we should not judge things by the sensation we have of them. We should not think ice has more reality than water because it resists us more.

If you thought that fire has more force or efficacy than earth, your error would have some foundation. For there is some reason to judge the magnitude of powers by that of their effects. But to believe that the idea of extension which affects you with a sensation is of another nature, or has more reality, than that which you think of when you get no sensible impression is to mistake the absolute for the relative, i.e. to judge what things are in themselves by the relation they have to you. This is the way to giving more reality to the point of a thorn than to all the rest of the Universe, and more even than to infinite being. But, when you become accustomed to distinguishing your sensations from your ideas, you will recognize that the same idea of extension can be known, can be imagined, and can be sensed, as the divine substance which contains it applies it in diverse ways to our minds.[8] Do not believe then that the infinite or being in general has less reality than the idea of a certain object which at present affects you in a very lively and sensible way. Judge things by the ideas which represent them, and do not attribute to them anything like the sensations impressed upon you. You will in due time understand more distinctly what I am presently hinting at.

ARISTES. Everything you have said to me, Theodore, is terribly abstract, and I have great difficulty keeping it before me. My mind is working queerly—a little rest, please. I must think at leisure of all these grand and sublime truths. I shall try to become familiar with them by strenuous efforts of attention which are entirely pure. But at present I am not capable of that. I must rest in order to regain my strength.

THEODORE. I knew you would not be pure spirit for long, Aristes. Go, lead your body to pasture. Divert your imagination with the variety of objects which can hearten it and give it pleasure. But try nonetheless to retain some taste for the truth; and, as soon as you feel yourself capable of nourishing yourself with it and meditating on it, leave everything for it. Forget even what you are so far as that is possible. It is a necessity that you think of the needs of the body, but it is a great disorder to be preoccupied with its pleasure.

---

[8]See *Entretien sur la mort*, II [M XIII 385–415].

THIRD DIALOGUE

✤

The difference between our sensations and our ideas. We must judge things only by the ideas which represent them and not at all by the sensations by which we are affected in their presence, or on their occasion.

THEODORE. Hallo, Aristes! What a dreamer you are! What are you thinking of so intently?

ARISTES. Who is it? Ah, Theodore, you surprised me. I am returning from that other world to which you transported me these last days. Now I go there all alone without fearing the phantoms which block the way. But, when I am there, I find so many obscure places that I am afraid I shall lose my way and get lost.

I. THEODORE. It is a lot, Aristes, to be able to leave our bodies when we wish and rise in spirit to the land of intellects. But it is not enough. We must have some knowledge of the map of the land, of what places are inaccessible to poor mortals, and of where they can go freely without fear of illusions. It seems to me it is through not taking sufficient heed of what I am going to point out to you that most travellers in these dangerous regions have been led astray. Certain seductive specters draw them into precipices from which return is morally impossible. Listen to me very carefully. Today I shall tell you what you are never to forget.

Never, Aristes, mistake your own sensations for our ideas, the modifications which affect your soul for the ideas which enlighten all minds. This is the foremost of the precepts for avoiding error. You will never contemplate ideas without discovering something true; but, whatever attention you give to your own modifications, you will never be enlightened by them. You cannot quite understand what I am saying to you—I shall have to explain myself some more.

II. You know, Aristes, that the divine Word, insofar as it is universal Reason, contains in its substance the primordial ideas of all beings created and possible. You know that all intellects, which are united with sovereign Reason, discover in it some of these ideas, as it pleases God to manifest the ideas to them. This occurs as a consequence of general laws which He established to make us rational and to form among ourselves and with Him a kind of society. Someday I shall elaborate on the whole mystery. You do not doubt that intelligible exten-

168

sion, for instance, which is the primordial idea or archetype of bodies, is contained in universal Reason, which enlightens every mind including the One with whom Reason is consubstantial. But you may not have reflected sufficiently on the difference between the intelligible ideas it contains and our own sensations or modifications of our souls, and perhaps believe it pointless to mark the difference exactly.

III. What a difference there is, my dear Aristes, between the light of our ideas and the obscurity of our sensations, between knowing and sensing, and how necessary it is to get used to distinguishing them readily. If someone has not reflected sufficiently on the difference and all the time believes he knows very clearly what he senses most vividly, he cannot but go astray in the darkness of his own modifications. So get a good grasp of this important truth. Man is not a light unto himself. His substance, far from enlightening him, is itself unintelligible to him. He knows nothing except by the light of universal Reason which enlightens all minds, by the intelligible ideas which it discloses to them in its entirely luminous substance.

IV. Created reason, our soul, the human mind, the purest and most sublime intellects can indeed see the light; but they cannot produce it or draw it from their own resources, nor can they engender it from their substance. They can discover eternal, immutable, necessary truths in the divine Word, in eternal, immutable, necessary Wisdom; but in themselves they find only sensations which are often very lively yet always obscure and confused, i.e. modalities full of darkness. In short, they cannot discover the truth while contemplating themselves. They cannot be nourished by their own substance. Only in the universal Reason which enlivens all minds and which enlightens and guides all men can they find the life of the intellect. For it is Reason which is the internal solace of those who follow it, it is Reason which recalls those who leave it, and it is Reason which, by its terrible reproaches and threats, fills those who are determined to abandon it with confusion, anxiety, and despair.

ARISTES. By the reflections I have made on what you told me these last days, I am indeed persuaded, Theodore. It is the divine Word uniquely which enlightens us by the intelligible ideas it contains. For there are not two or more Wisdoms, two or more universal Reasons. Truth is immutable, necessary, eternal; the same in time and in eternity; the same for foreigners and for us; the same in heaven and in hell. The eternal Word speaks the same language to all nations—to the Chinese and Tartar as to Frenchman and Spaniard. If they are not equally enlightened, it is because they are not equally attentive, and they mingle—some more, some less—their modalities with ideas, particular promptings of their self-esteem with the general responses of internal truth. Two times two equals four among all peoples. We all hear the voice of truth which enjoins us not to do unto others what we would not have them do unto us. And those who do not obey this voice feel the internal reproaches which threaten them and punish them for their disobedience if only they enter into themselves and listen to Reason. I am now quite convinced of these principles. But I do not yet understand too well the difference between knowing and sensing which you judge to be so necessary for avoiding error. Please make me attend to it.

V. THEODORE. If you had indeed meditated on the principles of which you say you are convinced, you would clearly see what you are asking for. But, without taking you on too painful a way, answer me. Do you think that God feels the pain which we suffer?

ARISTES. Certainly not, for the feeling of pain involves unhappiness.

THEODORE. Very well. But do you believe He knows it?

ARISTES. Yes, I believe He does. For He knows everything that happens to His creatures. God's knowledge has no limits, and for Him to know my pain is not to be either unhappy or imperfect. On the contrary. . . .

THEODORE. Well, Aristes! God knows pain, pleasure, heat, and the rest, yet He does not feel these things! He knows pain since He knows what that modification of the soul is in which pain consists. He knows it since He alone causes it in us, as I shall prove to you in what follows, and He knows what He does. In short, He knows it since His knowledge has no limits. But He does not feel it, for He would be unhappy. To know pain is not then to feel it.

ARISTES. That is true. But is not feeling pain knowing it?

VI. THEODORE. Certainly not, since God in no way feels it yet He knows it perfectly. But—not to get stopped by an equivocation of terms—if you will have it that feeling pain is knowing it, at least agree that it is not knowing it clearly, not knowing it by light and evidence, in short not knowing its nature and so, strictly speaking, not knowing it. To feel pain, for example, is to be unhappy without knowing what it is we are nor what that modality of our being is which renders us unhappy. But to know is to have a clear idea of the nature of the object and to discover certain of its relations by light and evidence.

I know the parts of extension clearly because I can see their relations evidently. I see clearly that similar triangles have proportional sides, that there is no plane triangle the three angles of which are not equal to two right angles. I see these truths or relations clearly in the idea or archetype of extension. For that idea is so luminous that contemplating it is what makes Geometers and good Physicists, and it is so fertile in truths that all minds together will never exhaust it.

VII. It is not the same with my being. I have no idea of it: I do not see its archetype. I cannot discover relations (*rapports*) among the modifications affecting my mind. Turning to myself, I cannot discover any of my faculties or my capacities. The internal sensation which I have of myself teaches me that I am, that I think, that I will, that I sense, that I suffer, etc.; but it does not reveal to me what I am, the nature of my thought, of my will, of my sensations, of my passions, of my pain, nor the relations which all these things have to one another. This is because once again, having no idea of my soul and not seeing its archetype in the divine Word, I cannot discover by contemplation what the soul is, nor what modalities it is capable of, nor finally the relations among its modalities—relations which I sense keenly without knowing them but which God knows clearly without sensing them. All this follows, my dear Aristes, because—as I have already said to you—I am not a light unto myself, because my substance and my modalities are total darkness, and because for many reasons God has not found it fitting to disclose to me the idea or archetype which represents the nature of spiritual beings. If my substance were intelligible of itself or in itself, if it were luminous, if it could enlighten me, it would certainly be the case (as I am not distinct from myself) that, contemplating myself, I would be able to see that I am capable of being affected by certain particular sensations which I have never experienced and which I may never have any knowledge of. I would not have needed a concert to know what the sweetness of harmony is; and, although I had never tasted a certain fruit, I would have been able, I do not say, to sense, but to know by evidence the nature of the sensation which it excites in me. But, as we can only know the nature of beings in that Reason which contains them in an intelligible manner, and though I can sense what is in myself, it is only in Reason that I can discover what I am and the modalities to which my nature is susceptible. There is all the more reason for thinking that it is only in Reason that I can discover the principles of the sciences and all the truths which are capable of enlightening the mind.

ARISTES. Let us move on a bit, Theodore. I believe there are essential differences between knowing and sensing, between the ideas which enlighten the mind and the sensations which affect it; and I agree that, though I sense simply in myself, I cannot know what I am except in that Reason which contains the archetype of my being and intelligible ideas of all things.

VIII. THEODORE. Very well, Aristes. You are now ready to make thousands and thousands of discoveries in the land of truth. Distinguish ideas from your sensations, but distinguish them well. Once again, distinguish them well, and all those cajoling phantoms of which I have spoken to you will not lead you into error. Always rise above yourself. Your modalities are total darkness, remember. Go higher to Reason, and you will see light. Silence your senses, your imagination, and your passions; and you will hear the pure voice of internal truth, the clear and evident responses of our common Master. Do not confuse evidence, which derives from the comparison of ideas, with the vivacity of the sensations which affect and move us. The more lively our sensations are, the more darkness they spread. The more striking or agreeable are our phantoms, the more body and reality they appear to have, the more dangerous they are and apt to seduce us. Dissipate them, or distrust them. In a few words, flee from whatever affects you and go attach yourself to whatever enlightens you. Reason must be followed despite the cajolings, the threats, the insults of the bodies with which we are united, despite the action of the objects that surround us. Do you conceive all this quite distinctly? Are you quite convinced of it by the reasons I have given you and by your own reflections?

ARISTES. Your exhortation seems very lively for a discussion of Metaphysics, Theodore. It seems to me that you excite sensations in me rather than giving birth to clear ideas. I use your language. In all good faith, I do not understand too well what you are telling me. I see it, and a moment later I do not see it. This is because I still only catch sight of it. It seems to me that you are right, but I do not understand you too well.

IX. THEODORE. Ah, my dear Aristes, your reply is more proof of what we were just saying. There is nothing wrong in your thinking about the matter. I tell you what I see, yet you do not see it. This is proof that man does not instruct man. This is because I am not your Master or your Doctor. It is because I am only a monitor, vehement perhaps, but hardly exact and little understood. I speak to your ears. Apparently I produce just a lot of noise in them. Our unique Master does not yet speak clearly enough to your mind—or, rather, Reason speaks quite clearly to it at all times yet, through lack of attention, you do not hear sufficiently well what it tells you. From the things you have said to me and from those I have been telling you, I thought, however, that you did have a sufficient understanding of my principle and the consequences which must be drawn from it. But I see it is not enough to give you general counsel based on abstract and metaphysical ideas. I must also give you some particular proofs of the necessity of this counsel.

I exhorted you to become accustomed to readily recognizing the difference between knowing and feeling, between our clear ideas and our invariably obscure and confused sensations. And I maintain that this by itself suffices to discover an infinite number of truths. I make this claim, I say, on the ground that it is Reason alone which enlightens us, that we are not a light unto ourselves nor an intellect to anyone else. You will clearly see whether this foundation is solid when you cease listening to me and when, in your study, you attentively consult internal Truth. Yet, to facilitate your understanding my principle and give you a better knowledge of its necessity and consequences, answer me, please. You know music, for I often see you playing instruments in so knowledgeable and assured a way.

ARISTES. I know enough to charm away my chagrin and chase away my melancholy.

X. THEODORE. Very well. Give me some account of the nature of the various sounds you combine in so exact and pleasing a manner. What is an octave, a fifth, a fourth? Why is it that, when two strings are in unison, we cannot touch one of them without moving the other? You have a very fine and delicate ear. Consult it so that it will answer you regarding what I wish to learn from you.

ARISTES. I think you are making fun of me. It is Reason and not the senses we must consult.

THEODORE. That is true. We should consult the senses only about facts. Their power is very limited, but Reason applies to everything. Consult it then. And be wary of confounding its replies with the testimony of your senses. Well then, what does it reply?

ARISTES. You hurry me too much. Still, it seems to me that sound is a quality spread out in the air which can affect only the sense of hearing, for each sense has its proper object.

THEODORE. Do you call that consulting Reason?

ARISTES. What do you want me to say to you? Come, here is an octave—Do—do. Here is a fifth—Do—so. Here is a fourth—Do—fa.

THEODORE. You sing well. But how badly you reason! I believe it is because you want to amuse yourself.

ARISTES. To be sure, Theodore. But, as for your other question, I reply it is by sympathy that strings of the same pitch move each other. Have I not hit the nail on the head?

THEODORE. Let us speak seriously, Aristes. If you want to please me now, try to instruct me.

ARISTES. I shall do nothing of the sort, if you please. You take your part, and let me take mine. Mine is to listen.

THEODORE. How nice and pleasing your manners! Come, then, let me have the monochord and attend to what I shall do and what I shall say to you. Plucking or drawing this string toward me, I move it from the state in which the binding holds it; and, when I let go, you see—without my having to prove it to you—that it moves for some time this way and that and thus it makes a great number of vibrations and as a consequence many other small commotions which are imperceptible to our senses. For, a straight line being shorter than a curve, a string cannot vibrate, or become alternately straight and curved, unless the parts which compose it lengthen and contract very quickly. Now I ask you, is a body in motion not capable of moving one that it encounters? This string can therefore move the air which surrounds it (and even the subtle matter filling its pores), and this in turn moves something else, and so on to your ear and mine.

ARISTES. That is true. But what I hear is a sound, a sound spread out in the air, a quality which is quite different from vibrations of a string or commotions of air in motion.

THEODORE. Slowly, Aristes. Do not consult your senses, and do not judge on their testimony. It is true that sound is entirely different from air that is moved. But it is precisely for this reason that you have no ground for saying that sound is spread out in the air. For note this: touching this string, I simply make it move, and a string which is moved simply agitates the air that surrounds it.

ARISTES. "A string which is moved simply agitates the air that surrounds it"! Why, do you not hear it produce a sound in the air?

THEODORE. Clearly I hear what you hear. But, when I want to be apprised of some truth, I do not consult my ears—yet you consult yours, notwithstanding all the good resolutions you made. Enter into yourself then, and consult the clear ideas which Reason contains. Can you conceive that air—or small bodies of whatever shape you please which are agitated in some way or other—is capable of containing the sound which you hear and that a string can produce this sound? Once again, do not consult your ears; and, just to be safe, imagine you are deaf. Consider attentively the clear idea of extension: it is the archetype of bodies; it represents their nature and properties. Is it not evident that the only possible properties of extension are relations of distance? Think seriously about this.

ARISTES. It is evident. The properties of extension can consist only in its different states (*manieres d'être*). These are just relations of distance.

THEODORE. Then the properties or possible modalities of extension are simply shapes—relations of distance which are stable and fixed—and motions—

relations of distance which are successive and always changing. Then, Aristes, the sound which you admit is something other than motion is not spread out in the air, and a string cannot produce it in the air. Rather, it is simply a sensation or a modality of the soul.

ARISTES. I see I must give in or deny the principle that the idea of extension represents the nature of bodies. Perhaps it represents only one of its properties. Indeed, who informed you that bodies are nothing but extension? The essence of matter may consist in something else, and this something else may be capable of containing sounds and even producing them. Give me proof of the contrary.

THEODORE. But *you* prove to me that this other thing which you take the essence of matter to consist in will not be capable of thinking, of willing, of reasoning. I claim that the strings of your lute think as much as you do, or at any rate they complain of your disturbing their rest. Give me proof to the contrary of that, and I will convince you that the strings spread no sound.

ARISTES. It is true that, if the nature of body consists in something other than extension, I, having no idea of that thing, cannot prove to you that it does not think. But please prove to me that matter is nothing other than extension and so is incapable of thinking. For it seems to me that this is necessary to silence freethinkers, who conflate soul with body and maintain that the one, like the other, is mortal because, on their view, all our thoughts are only modalities of that unknown thing we call body and all modalities can cease to be.

XI. THEODORE. I have already answered the question you put to me,[1] but it is so important that, although it is out of place, I am very glad to call your attention to the fact that the resolution of this question, along with all other truths, depends on that grand principle that universal Reason contains the ideas which enlighten us and, as God's works have been formed on the basis of these ideas, we can do no better than contemplate them in order to discover the nature and properties of created beings. Take note of this then. We can think of extension without thinking of anything else. Hence, it is a being or a substance and not a state of being (*maniere d'être*). For we cannot think of a state without thinking of the being which it modifies since states of being simply are the being itself in some condition or other (*de telle & telle facon*). We cannot think of shapes and motions without thinking of extension because shapes and motions simply are states of extension. This is clear, if I am not mistaken. And, if it does not appear so to you, I maintain you have no way at all of distinguishing modalities of substances from the substances themselves. If it does not appear evident to you, let us stop philosophizing. For. . . .

ARISTES. Let us go on philosophizing, please.

THEODORE. We shall go on then. The idea or archetype of extension is eternal and necessary. We see this idea, as I have already proved to you; and God sees it also, since there is nothing in Him that He does not discern. We see it, I say, clearly and distinctly without thinking of anything else. We can perceive it by itself, or rather we cannot perceive it as the state of some other thing, since it

---

[1]First Dialogue, II.

contains no necessary relation to other ideas. Now, God can bring about what He sees and what He makes us see clearly and distinctly in His light. He can bring about everything that contains no contradiction, for He is all-powerful. Hence, He can bring about extension entirely by itself. It follows this extension will be a being or a substance, and the idea we have of it will represent its nature to us. If, then, God created this extension, there will certainly be matter. For what genus of being would that extension be? Now I believe you see that this matter is incapable of thinking, of sensing, or reasoning.

ARISTES. I admit that, as our ideas are necessary and eternal and the very ideas that God consults, He will if He acts make what these ideas represent; and we will not be mistaken if we attribute to matter only what we see in its archetype. But perhaps we do not see this archetype in its entirety. Since modalities of extension can only be relations of distance, extension is incapable of thinking. I accept this. But the subject of extension—that other thing which may be contained in the archetype of matter yet which is unknown to us—will be capable of thinking.

XII. THEODORE. It will be capable of doing much more. For it will be able to do whatever you wish, and no one can contest it. It can have thousands and thousands of faculties, virtues, wonderful properties. It can act on your soul, enlighten it, make it happy and unhappy. In short, there will be as many powers and, if you press the matter, as many Deities as there are different bodies. For do I really know that this other thing, which you take to be the essence of matter, does not have all the qualities it is your pleasure to attribute to it since I have no knowledge of it at all? From this you may see that, to know God's works, we must consult the ideas He gives us of them, those which are clear, those on the basis of which He framed His works; and we run very great risks if we follow another way. For, if we consult our senses and yield blindly to their testimony, they will persuade us that there are at least certain bodies the power and intelligence of which are marvelous.

Our senses tell us that fire spreads heat and light. They persuade us that plants and animals work for the conservation of their being and their species with much skill and a kind of intelligence. We see then that these faculties are something other than shapes and motions. And so, on the obscure and confused testimony of our senses, we judge that there must be something in bodies other than extension, since the modalities of extension can be nothing other than motions and shapes. But let us consult Reason attentively. Let us consider the clear idea we have of bodies. Let us not confound bodies with our own being, and we shall then discover perhaps that we are attributing to them qualities and properties which they do not have and which belong uniquely to us.

It may be the case, you say, that we do not see the archetype or idea of matter in its entirety. If that were indeed the case, we ought to attribute to it only what the idea represents to us of it; for we must not form a judgment about what we do not know. If, to be sure, freethinkers believe they are allowed to reason on the basis of chimeras of which they have no idea, they must allow us to reason about things by means of the ideas which we do have of them. But, to obviate any reason for their mistake and for confidence in their strange errors, note once again that we can think of extension without thinking of anything else. That is our principle. Accordingly, God can create extension without creating anything else. And this extension will subsist without that unknown thing which they attribute to matter. Extension will then be a substance and not a modality of substance. And, for a number of reasons, this is what I believe should be called body or matter. For one thing, we cannot think of the modalities of beings without thinking of the beings of which they are the modalities, and there is no other way of distinguishing beings from their modalities than to see if the former can be thought of without the latter. Moreover, extension by itself with the properties everyone attributes to it is sufficient to explain all natural effects; that is to say, we observe no effect of matter the natural cause of which cannot be discovered in the idea of extension, provided the effect is clearly known.

ARISTES. What you are now saying appears to me convincing. I understand more clearly than ever that, to know God's works, we must consult attentively the ideas which He contains in His wisdom, and we must silence our senses and especially our imaginings. But this way of discovering the truth is so rough and difficult that almost no one follows it. To see that the sun is brilliant with light, we need only open our eyes. To judge if sound is in the air, it suffices to make some noise. Nothing is easier. But the mind works prodigiously in the attention it gives to the ideas which do not strike the senses. We tire very soon, I know by experience. How fortunate you are to be able to meditate on metaphysical matters!

THEODORE. I am made like others, my dear Aristes. Judge me by yourself, and you will do me honor—any mistake you make will do me credit. What do you want? The difficulty we all find in uniting ourselves to Reason is a penalty and proof of sin, and its principle is the rebellion of the body. We are condemned to earn our livelihood by the sweat of our brows. In its present state, the mind must work to be nourished by truth. This all men have in common. But believe me, this food of the mind is so delicious—and it gives the soul that has tasted it so much ardor—that, although we tire looking for it, we never tire of desiring it and of renewing our search; for this is what we are made for. Yet, if I have overly tired you, give me that instrument so that I may relieve your attention and make sensible, so far as possible, the truths which I want to get you to understand.

ARISTES. What do you want to do? I understand clearly that sound is not spread out in the air and that a string cannot produce it. The reasons you gave me appear to be convincing. Since all modalities of bodies consist only in relations of distance, it follows that neither sound nor the power of producing it is contained in the idea of matter. That is enough for me. Still, here is another proof which occurs to me and which is convincing. During a fever I had some time ago, I heard the incessant howling of an animal which was certainly not howling as it was dead. I think also in sleep it happens to you as it does to me that I hear a concert, or at any rate the sound of a trumpet or a drum, even when everything is in total silence. While sick then I heard cries and howls. Even today I remember their giving me a great deal of anxiety. Now these disagreeable sounds were not in the air, although I heard them there as plainly as the sound this instrument makes. Thus, though we hear sounds as if spread out in the air, it does not follow that they are. They are actually only in the soul, for they are just sensations which affect it, modalities which belong to it. I could press the matter even further. Everything you told me up to now leads me to think that there is nothing in objects of our senses similar to the sensations we have of them. These objects correspond (*ont rapport avec*) to their ideas, but it seems to me they have no affinity with our sensations. Bodies are merely extension capable of motion and various shapes. This is evident when we consult the idea which represents them.

THEODORE. Bodies, you say, have no resemblance to the sensations we have; and, to know their properties, we must consult not the senses but the clear idea of extension which represents their nature. Keep this important truth well in mind.

ARISTES. It is evident, and I shall never forget it.

XIII. THEODORE. Never! Well then, please tell me what an octave is and what is a fifth, or rather instruct me as to what must be done to hear these consonances.

ARISTES. That is very easy. Touch the whole string, and then put your finger there and touch one or the other part of the string, and you will hear an octave.

THEODORE. Why my finger there and not here?

ARISTES. That is because what you would get is a fifth and not an octave. Look, look at that. There, all the notes are marked. . . . You laugh.

THEODORE. I am now very knowledgeable, Aristes. I can make you hear any note I wish. But, if we had broken our instrument, all our knowledge would be in bits.

ARISTES. Not at all. I would make another. It is only a string on a board. Anyone can do that.

THEODORE. Yes. But that is not enough. The consonances must be marked exactly on the board. How would you divide it then to mark where we should put our fingers to hear an octave, a fifth, and other consonances?

ARISTES. I would strike the whole string and, sliding my finger along it, I would locate the sound I wished to mark. For I know music well enough to tune instruments.

THEODORE. Your method is hardly exact since it is only by trial that you find what you are looking for. If you became deaf, or rather if the small nerve which tenses your eardrum and tunes it to your instrument were to loosen, what would become of your knowledge? Would you no longer be able to mark exactly the different notes? Can we not become deaf without forgetting music? If not, your science is not founded on clear ideas. Reason has no part in it, for Reason is immutable and necessary.

ARISTES. Ah, Theodore! I had already forgotten what I just told you I would never forget. What am I thinking of? I gave you ridiculous answers, you had reason to laugh. That is because I naturally listen more to my senses than to my

Reason. I am so accustomed to consulting my ears that I was not in fact thinking of what you asked me. Here is another answer with which you will be more content. To mark an octave on this instrument, we must divide the space along the string in two equal parts. For then, if we touch the whole string and then touch one or the other of its parts, we will get an octave. If we touch the whole string and then two-thirds, we will get a fifth. And finally, if we touch the whole string and then three-quarters, we get a fourth; and the two last consonances will come to an octave.

XIV. THEODORE. That answer instructs me. I understand it distinctly. I see from it that an octave, or rather the natural cause which produces it, is as 2 to 1, the fifth as 3 to 2, and the fourth as 4 to 3. These relations of numbers are clear. And, since you tell me that a string divided and moved in accordance with the magnitude expressed by these numbers makes these consonances, I would be able to mark them on the monochord even if I should become deaf. That is reasoning on the basis of clear ideas and is solid instruction. But why are a fifth and a fourth equivalent to an octave?

ARISTES. That is because sound is to sound as string is to string. Thus, since an octave is sounded when we move a string and then half of it, an octave is as 2 to 1 or equally as 4 to 2. Now the relation of 4 to 2 is composed of the relation of 4 to 3, which is the fourth, and of 3 to 2, which is the fifth. For you know that the relation of one number to another is composed of all the relations which hold between all the numbers that the two numbers contain. The relation of 3 to 6, for example, which is the relation of 1 to 2, is composed of the relations of 3 to 4, of 4 to 5, and of 5 to 6. From this you see that the major third and the minor third are equivalent to the fifth. For the ratio or relation of 4 to 6, which equals that of 2 to 3, is composed of the relations of 4 to 5, which gives the major third, and of 5 to 6, which is the minor third.

THEODORE. I conceive all this clearly provided that sound is to sound as string to string. But I do not understand this principle. Do you think it is based on clear ideas?

ARISTES. Yes, I think so. For the string or its different vibrations are the cause of different sounds. Now, the whole cause is to its half as 2 to 1, and effects correspond exactly to their causes. So the effect of the whole cause is double the effect of half of it. And the sound of the whole string is to the sound of half of it as 2 to 1.

THEODORE. Do you conceive distinctly what you are telling me? As for me, I find some obscurity in it, and, so far as I am able, I submit only to the evidence accompanying clear ideas.

ARISTES. What do you take exception to in my reasoning?

XV. THEODORE. It is ingenious enough. For you are not lacking on that account. But the underlying principle is obscure. It is not based on clear ideas. Pay attention to this. You think you know what you do in sensing, and for a principle you take a prejudice the falsity of which you acknowledged before. But, to make you aware of the fallacy in your proof, let me subject you to a little experiment. Give me your hand, I will not do you any great harm. I am now rubbing the hollow of your hand with the cuff of my sleeve, do you not feel anything?

ARISTES. I feel a little heat, or a kind of tickling that is rather pleasant.

THEODORE. And now.

ARISTES. Oh, Theodore, you are hurting me! You are rubbing too hard. I feel a pain that distresses me.

THEODORE. You are mistaken, Aristes. Let me go on. You feel a pleasure two or three times greater than the one you felt just before. I am going to prove it to you by your own reasoning. Listen. "My rubbing your hand is the cause of what you feel. Now the whole cause is to half of it as 2 to 1, and effects correspond exactly to the action of their causes. Hence, the effect of the whole cause or the entire action of the cause is double the effect of half of it." Hence, rubbing twice as hard or fast, the doubled motion should produce twice as much pleasure. Hence, I have not given you pain, unless you maintain that pain is to pleasure as 2 to 1.

ARISTES. I am indeed punished for having reasoned on an obscure principle. You have done me harm, and your excuse is you prove to me you have given me a double pleasure. That is not pleasant at all.

THEODORE. You got off easily; if we had been near the fire, I might have done something much worse.

ARISTES. What would you have done?

THEODORE. I might have taken a burning coal—I would first have put it somewhere near your hand; and, if you said that gave you pleasure, I would have put it—to give you more pleasure—up against your hand; and then I would have proved to you by your own reasoning that you were wrong to complain.

ARISTES. Truly I have had a narrow escape! Is that how you instruct people?

THEODORE. What do you want me to do? When I give you metaphysical proofs, you forget them immediately. I have to make them sensible so that you will have no difficulty understanding them and will always remember them. Why did you forget so quickly that our reasoning must be based only on clear ideas, that a string in motion can at most only agitate the air surrounding it, and that it cannot produce the different sounds you hear?

ARISTES. It is because, as soon as I move the string, I hear the sound.

THEODORE. I realize that. But you do not conceive clearly that the vibrations of a string can spread or produce sound. You agreed to that. Sound is not contained in the idea of matter any more than the power of acting on the soul and making it hear sound. From the fact that vibrations of a string or of the air are followed by one sound or another, infer that, things being as they are, this is necessary for you to hear the sound. But do not imagine that there is a necessary relation between these things. It appears that I do not hear the same sounds as you, though I may hear the same tones or consonances. For, if my eardrum differs in thickness from yours by a certain amount and so resonates more easily at a different pitch—and this is quite likely—, I will surely hear (other things being equal) a louder sound than you when the string is plucked. Last, I see no quantitative relation between consonances. It is not clear that the difference of the sounds composing them is greater or less, as in the strings producing them. This appears evident to me.

ARISTES. It seems so to me. But, since the vibrations of a string are not the cause of sound, how does it come about that I hear the sound when the string is touched?

THEODORE. This is not the time to resolve that question, Aristes. When we have treated the efficacy of causes, or laws of the union of soul and body, it will be easily resolved. I am thinking now only of getting you to observe the difference between knowing clearly and sensing confusedly. My sole intent is to convince you of this important truth: to know God's works, we must attend, not to the sensations which we have of them, but to the ideas which represent them. For I cannot reiterate too often that we must consult not the senses and their respective modalities, which are sheer darkness, but Reason which enlightens us by its divine ideas, by ideas that are immutable, necessary, eternal.

ARISTES. I agree. I am fully convinced. Let us move on, for I get tired of hearing you say the same old things over again.

XVI. THEODORE. We shall move on to what pleases you. But, believe me, it does not suffice to see a principle—we must see it well. For, between seeing and seeing, there are a great many differences; and the principle I am inculcating in you is so necessary and of such great use that it must be present to the mind at all times and must not be forgotten, as you do. Let us see if you are quite convinced of it and if you do indeed know how to use it. Tell me why, when two strings are in unison, we cannot strike one of them without moving the other.

ARISTES. That question appears to me to be very difficult. In different authors I have read many explanations which hardly satisfy me. I am afraid that my answer may again bring forth some little pleasantry, or that you may perform some experiment at my expense.

THEODORE. No, no, Aristes, fear nothing. But do not forget the principle of clear ideas. I should not admonish you so often. But I am afraid that "sympathy," or some other chimera, will keep you from following it.

ARISTES. Let us just see. When I touch a string, it moves the air by its vibrations. Now the air, which is agitated, can communicate motion to other strings it encounters.

THEODORE. Very well. But dissonant strings, as well as those making the same sound, will be moved.

ARISTES. That is what I thought. A little sympathy would go a long way here, but you will have none of it.

THEODORE. I accept the word willingly for what it is worth. There is "sympathy" between strings of the same pitch. This is certain since they act one on the other, and that is what the word signifies. But what produces this sympathy? That is where the problem lies.

ARISTES. It is not because of their length or their thicknesses. For there is sympathy between strings that are unequal, and there is no sympathy between strings that are equal when they do not make the same sound. Everything must depend then on the sound. But, as for this, the sound is not a modality of the string and the string cannot produce it. What, then, explains the sympathy? Here I am indeed at a loss.

THEODORE. You are easily at a loss. There is sympathy between strings when there is the same sound. That is the fact you want to explain. Then see what makes two strings produce the same sound, and you will have everything you need to discover what you are looking for.

ARISTES. If two strings are equal in length and in thickness, it is equality of tension that will make them produce the same sound; and, if they are unequal in length only—if, for example, one is double the length of the other—, tension of fourfold strength is required.

THEODORE. What then does greater or less tension in equal strings produce?

ARISTES. It makes them capable of sound that is more or less high pitched.

THEODORE. Yes, but that is not what we want. We have here only a difference in sound, and no sound can move that string. Sound is the effect rather than the cause of motion. Tell me then how tension makes the sound become higher.

ARISTES. Apparently it is because it makes the string vibrate more quickly.

THEODORE. Good, that is just what we want. The vibration, and not the sound of my string, will make yours vibrate. Two strings equal in length and thickness and equally taut make the same sound because their vibrations are equally quick; and, if one rises higher than the other, this indicates that it is more taut and each of its vibrations is made more quickly. Now one string moves another only by means of its vibrations. For a body is moved by another only by means of that other body's motion. This being so, tell me now why strings of the same sound communicate their vibration, and why dissonant strings do not—so far at any rate, as the senses can tell.

XVII. ARISTES. I see the reason for this clearly. Here are two strings with the same sound. Here is yours, and here is mine. When I release my string, it pushes the air towards you, and the air which is pushed moves your string a little bit. Mine again makes in a very short time a number of similar vibrations, each of which moves the air and pushes your string as the first jolt did. This is what makes it vibrate. For several small jolts rightly given will produce a sensible movement. But, when these small jolts come intermittently, they interfere with one another. Thus, when two strings are dissonant—i.e. when they cannot vibrate in equal or multiple times or at any rate in times that are commensurable because they are unequally tensed or are of unequal and incommensurable length or thickness—, they cannot move one another. For, if the first moves and pushes the air and second string towards you at the time the second is returning towards me, then it will diminish the motion instead of augmenting it. The vibrations of the strings must then be made in equal or multiple times if there is to be a transfer of motion great enough to be sensible; and their motion will be the more sensible the more the consonance they produce approaches unison. That is why in an octave they move more than in a fifth, and in a fifth more than in a fourth: the two strings begin their vibrations more often at the same instant. Are you happy with this reason?

THEODORE. Quite, Aristes. You have followed the principle of clear ideas. I understand quite well that strings having the same sound move each other, not by "sympathy" of their sound since sound cannot be the cause of motion, but by agreement in their vibrations that move or shake the air in which they are strung. So long as you reason about the properties of bodies on the basis of ideas of shapes and motions, I shall be happy with you. You have such a good mind that it is difficult for you to engage in bad reasoning while you follow a principle that is clear. In fact, our falling into error so very often derives from the falsity or obscurity of our ideas rather than from weakness of our minds. Geometers make mistakes rarely and Physicists almost always. Why so? It is because the latter generally reason with confused ideas and the former with ideas which are the clearest we have.

ARISTES. I see the necessity of your principle better than ever. You did well to reiterate it often and make it sensible to me. I will try to remember it. We should not judge sensible objects on the basis of sensations they strike us with, but in accordance with ideas which represent them. Our sensations are confused. They are just modalities of our soul which cannot enlighten us. But ideas which Reason discloses to us are luminous: evidence attends them. Considering them attentively suffices to discover relations among them and to be solidly informed of the truth. Is this not what you want me to keep well in mind, Theodore?

THEODORE. Yes, Aristes; and, if you do, you will travel without fear in the land of intellects. You will prudently avoid places that are inaccessible or too dangerous, and you will no longer fear those seductive phantoms which get new travellers in these countries imperceptibly into error. But do not suppose you know full well what I just told you and what you repeated yourself. You will know it exactly only when you have meditated on it often. For we never fully apprehend what we hear from men unless internal truth repeats it to us in the silence of all creatures. Goodbye now, Aristes. I leave you alone with Reason. Consult it in earnest and forget everything else.

FOURTH DIALOGUE

✤

The nature and properties of the senses in general. The wisdom of the laws of the union of soul and body. This union changed to dependence by the sin of the first man.

ARISTES. Where have you been, Theodore? I was impatient not meeting you.

I. THEODORE. Well then! Does Reason not suffice for you? Can you not spend your time contentedly with Reason if Theodore is not of the company? Reason suffices for eternity for intellects that are blessed. Yet, though I left you with it for only a few hours, impatience sets in when you do not see me. What are you thinking of? Do you expect me to let you have a blind and disordered attachment to me? Love reason, consult it, follow it. For I declare to you I renounce the friendship of those who neglect it and refuse to submit to its laws.

ARISTES. Just a minute, Theodore. Listen to me.

II. THEODORE. There can be no lasting and sincere friendship which is not based on Reason, on an immutable good—on a good which can be possessed by everyone without being divided. Friendships founded on goods which are parceled out and dissipated by use always have troublesome consequences and last only a short time. Are they not false and dangerous friendships?

ARISTES. Right. That is all true and there is nothing more certain. But Theodore!

THEODORE. What do you wish to say?

III. ARISTES. What a difference there is between seeing and seeing, between knowing what men tell us at the time they are telling it to us and knowing what Reason tells us when it replies to us! What a difference there is between knowing and sensing, between ideas which enlighten us and confused sensations which excite and trouble us! How fertile this principle is in spreading light! What errors, what prejudices it dispels! I meditated on the principle, Theodore. I followed its consequences, and I was anxious to see you to thank you for teaching it to me. Allow me to say to you what the Faithful of Samaria said to the woman of Samaria after they, as well as she, had listened to our common Master: "Now we believe, not because of thy saying," they said to the woman, "for we have heard him ourselves and know."[a] Yes, now I am convinced, not by the force of your words, but by the evident replies of internal truth. I understand what you told me, but how many other matters have I understood of which you did not speak to me! I understood them clearly, and what persists the more deeply engraved in my memory is that I have lived all my life in an illusion— forever seduced by the testimony of my senses, always corrupted by their inducements. How unworthy sensible goods are! How powerless bodies appear to me to be! No, this sun, brilliant as it appears to my eyes, does not possess nor spread the light which enlightens me. The colors which beguile me in their variety and vivacity, the beauties which charm me when I turn my eyes on what surrounds me, all of this belongs to me. All of it comes not from bodies nor is it in bodies. For none of it is contained in the idea of matter. And I am persuaded we must not judge God's works by the various sensations which we have of them, but by immutable, necessary, eternal ideas which represent them—by the archetype on the basis of which they have all been formed.

THEODORE. What pleasure I feel hearing you! I see you have consulted Reason in the silence of creatures, for you are still quite enlightened by it, quite animated, quite penetrated. And what good friends we will be with Reason ever our common good and the bond of our society! We shall both enjoy the same pleasures, we shall possess the same riches. For truth is given in its entirety to everyone and in its entirety to each of us. All minds are nourished by it without any of its abundance being diminished. What joy I have once again seeing you so imbued with the truths which you are telling me!

IV. ARISTES. I am also quite imbued with gratitude for what I owe you. That was the reason for my impatience. Yes, you taught me about that tree of the terrestrial Paradise which gives life and immortality to minds. You have shown me the celestial manna on which I am to be nourished in the desert of this present life. You have taken me imperceptibly to the inner Master who alone enlightens all intellects. Just a little serious attention to the clear and luminous ideas which are thus presented to the mind taught me more truths, and delivered me from more prejudices, than everything I had read in the books of the Philosophers, than everything I had heard from my Masters and indeed from you, Theodore. For, however exact your expressions are when you speak to me and when I consult Reason, there is the confused sound of two replies which are simultaneous yet different, one sensible and the other intelligible. The least of the trouble that comes of this is that the reply which strikes my ear shares the capacity of my mind and lessens its liveliness and penetration. It takes you time to pronounce your words, but the replies of Reason are eternal and immutable. These replies have always been made, or rather they are made at all times without succession of time; and, though we require some time to hear them, it takes no time to make them since they are not actually made. They are eternal, immutable, necessary. Allow me the pleasure of declaring to you a part of what

[a]*John* 4:42.

I believe I have learned from our common Master whom you had the goodness of introducing me to.

V. As soon as you left me, Theodore, I entered into myself to consult Reason, and I perceived everything in a different way from when you spoke to me and I deferred to your proofs—proofs that the ideas of creatures are eternal, that God formed bodies on the basis of the idea of extension, that this idea must then represent their nature, and that I should thus consider it attentively to discover their properties. I understood clearly that consulting my senses and looking for truth in my own modalities was to prefer darkness to light and to renounce Reason. At first my senses opposed my conclusions as if they were jealous of these ideas, of seeing themselves excluded by these ideas from a prerogative which they had long possessed in my mind. But I found so many falsities and contradictions in the opposition they formed that I condemned them as deceivers and false witnesses. Indeed, I saw no evidence in their testimony, and I observed on the other side a wonderful clarity in the ideas which they tried to obscure. Thus, although they again spoke to me with assurance, with arrogance, with an extreme importunity, I obliged them to be silent, and I recalled the ideas which had left me because they could not stand the confused noise and tumult of the rebellious senses.

I must admit, Theodore, that the sensible proofs you had given me against the authority of the senses have been marvelously useful to me. By them I silenced these importunate ones. I convicted them of falsity by their own testimony. At every moment they betrayed themselves. Besides saying nothing that was not incomprehensible and quite unbelievable, they gave me the same reports of quite different things and contrary reports of the same things depending on the interest they took in them. I silenced them then, fully resolved not to judge God's works on their testimony but rather by the ideas which represent these works and on the basis of which they were formed.

Following this principle, I came to understand that light was neither in the sun nor in the air where we see it, nor colors on the surface of bodies; that the sun might be able to move the subtle parts of the air and these in turn impress the same motion on the optic nerve which transmits it to the part of the brain where the soul resides; and that these small bodies, the motion of which would be altered when they encounter solid objects, could be reflected in different ways depending on the diversity of the surfaces which reflected them. Thus we would get the light and variety of colors supposed to be in bodies.

VI. I also understood that the heat I feel was certainly not in the fire, nor cold in ice, nor even—I say—pain in my own body where I have often felt something so sharply and so cruelly, nor sweetness in sugar, nor bitterness in aloes, nor acidity in sour grapes, nor sourness in vinegar, nor in wine that sweetness and strength that takes in and besots so many drinkers. All this is for the same reason that sound is not in the air and that there is an infinite difference between vibrations of strings and sound they make, between the proportions of these vibrations and the variety of consonances.

It would take too long, Theodore, if I were to enter into the detail of the proofs which convinced me that bodies have no other qualities than those which result from their shapes and no other action than their different motions.[1] But I cannot conceal from you a difficulty I have not been able to overcome, whatever effort of mind I made to free myself from it. I have no difficulty following the action of the sun, as through all the spaces between it and me. For, on the supposition that everything is a plenum, I can conceive how the impression it makes where it is is transmitted to the place where I am—to my eyes and, by means of my eyes, to my brain. But, from the clear idea of this motion, I have not been able to understand the origin of the sensation of light. I saw that the motion of the optic nerve by itself made me sense light. For, when I pressed my finger against the corner of my eye at the place where I know this nerve ends, I saw intense light in a dark place on the side opposite the one where my eye was pressed. But this change of motion into light appeared to me to be, and still appears to me to be, altogether incomprehensible. What a strange meta-morphosis from a movement or pressure in my eye to a flash of light! This flash, moreover, I do not see in my soul, of which it is a modality; nor in my brain, where the movement terminates; nor in my eye, where the pressure is exerted; nor on the side where I press my eye; but in the air—in the air, I say, which is incapable of such a modality and on the other side from the side of the eye that I press. What a wonderful thing this is!

VII. I thought at first that my soul, being informed of the movement taking place in my body, was the cause of the sensation which it had of the things surrounding it. But a little reflection disabused me of that thought. For it is not true, it seems to me, that the soul is informed of the sun moving the fibers of the brain. I saw light before I knew anything about this movement. Children, who do not even know they have a brain, are affected by a flash of light as well as Philosophers. Moreover, what relation is there between the movements of a body and the various sensations which follow? How can I see light in bodies when it is a modality of my mind? and how can I see it in the bodies surrounding me when the movement is only in my own body? I press the corner of my eye on the right side. Why do I then see light on the left side, despite the certain knowledge I have it is not on that side that the eye is pressed?

I realized from all this, and from a number of other things it would take me too long to tell you, that sensations were in me involuntarily; that I was then in no way their cause; and that, if bodies were capable of acting on me and making themselves sensed in the way I sensed them they would have to be constituted by a nature more excellent than mine, endowed with a terrible power and some of them even with wonderful wisdom, always uniform in their behavior, always efficacious in their action, always incomprehensible in the surprising effects of their power. That thought seemed monstrous and horrible to me, although my senses supported this madness and were entirely consistent with it. But please, Theodore, explain the matter to me.

---

[1] See *Recherche de la Verité,* Book I, Ch. 6, and the chapters following [M I 79–189].

THEODORE. It is not time to resolve your difficulties, Aristes, unless you want to leave the general truths of Metaphysics for explanation of the principles of Physics and laws of the union of soul and body.

ARISTES. A few words on the subject, please. I want very much to meditate on the matter. My mind now is all ready for it.

VIII. THEODORE. Listen then, but remember to meditate on what I am going to tell you. When we look for the reason for certain effects and, ascending from effects to causes, we come finally to a general cause or a cause that we see bears no relation between itself and the effect which it produces or rather which it seems to produce, what we must then do, instead of imagining chimeras, is to have recourse to the author of the laws of nature. For example, if you asked me for the cause of the pain we feel when we are pricked, I would be wrong to answer you straight off that it is one of the laws of the author of nature that a prick is followed by pain. I would tell you rather that a prick cannot separate the fibers of my flesh without moving the nerves leading to the brain and without moving the brain itself. But if you wanted to know why, when a part of my brain is moved in a certain way, I feel the pain of a prick—since this question concerns a general effect and, ascending from it, we can no longer find a particular or natural cause—what we must do is to have recourse to the general cause. For it is as if you were asking what is the author of the general laws of union of body and soul. Since you see clearly that there can be no necessary relation or connection between movements in the brain and certain sensations in the soul, it is evident that we must have recourse to a power which is not to be found in these two beings. It does not suffice to say that, because the pricking wounds the body, the soul must be informed of this by pain so that it will attend to the preservation of the body. This would be to give the final cause rather than the efficient cause, and the difficulty would remain; for that consists in knowing the cause that brings it about that, when the body is wounded, the soul suffers and that it suffers a certain pain given a wound of a certain sort.

IX. Some philosophers say that the soul is the cause of its pain because pain is simply the sadness the soul conceives as a result of a disorder which occurs in the body it loves and of which it is informed by the difficulty it experiences in the exercise of its functions. But this surely is a failure to attend to what takes place in ourselves. For instance, each of us senses when he is bled or is burnt that he is not the cause of his pain. He feels it against his will, and he cannot doubt its origin in an extraneous cause. Moreover, the soul does not wait to feel pain, and feel a certain pain, until it has learned of there being some movement, and a movement of a certain kind, in the brain. Nothing is more certain. Finally, pain and sadness are quite different. Pain precedes knowledge of an ill, while sadness follows it. There is nothing pleasant about pain, yet sadness pleases us so much that those who wish to drive it from our minds without at the same time freeing us of the evil which causes it make themselves as irritating and disagreeable as if they disturbed our joy. This is because sadness is the state of the soul which is most suitable to us at the time we are suffering some ill or are deprived of some good, and the sensation accompanying this passion is the sweetest that we can enjoy in the state we are in. Pain is therefore quite different from sadness. And I maintain furthermore that the cause of sadness is not the soul and that the thought we have of the loss of some good produces this passion only as a consequence of the natural and necessary movement toward the good which God Himself impresses on us incessantly. But let us return to the difficulties you have regarding the action and qualities of light.

X. 1. There is no metamorphosis. Motion in the brain cannot be changed into light or color. Since modalities of bodies are simply the bodies themselves in some particular condition (*de telle & telle facon*), they cannot be transformed into modalities of minds. This is evident.

2. You press the corner of your eye, and you have a certain sensation. This is because the One who alone can act on minds has established certain laws through the efficacy of which soul and body act and suffer reciprocally.[2]

3. When you press your eye, you see light, even though there is no luminous body. This is because it is by pressure, similar to the pressure your finger makes on your eye and thence in your brain, that the bodies we call luminous act on the bodies surrounding them and thereby on our eyes and our brains. All of this is the result of natural laws. For one of the laws of the union of soul and body— one of the laws according to which God acts invariably on the two substances—is that a pressure or movement of this kind is followed by a certain sensation.

4. You see the light, which is a modality of your mind and which consequently can only exist in it since it is a contradiction that a modality of a being should exist where the being itself does not—you see it, I say, in great spaces which your mind does not fill, since your mind occupies no place. This is because the great spaces which you see are simply intelligible spaces that fill no place.[3] The spaces you see are quite different from the material spaces which you look at. We must not conflate ideas of things with the things themselves. Remember, we do not see bodies in themselves, and it is only by way of their ideas that they are visible. Often we see something when there is nothing there, which is certain proof that what we see is intelligible and is quite different from what we look at.

5. Finally, you see the light not on the side on which you press your eye but on the opposite side because, as the [optic] nerve was constructed and disposed for receiving the impression of luminous bodies through the pupil and not other-wise, the pressure of your finger on the left has the same effect on your eye as a luminous body on your right would have if the rays from it pass through the pupil and transparent parts of the eye. When you press the eye on the outside, you press the optic nerve within against what is called the "vitreous" humor, which offers some resistance. Thus God makes you sense the light on the side where you see it since He invariably follows the laws which He has established thereby maintaining a perfect uniformity in His conduct. God never performs miracles, He never acts by special volitions contrary to His own laws which Order does not require or permit. His conduct always manifests the character of

---

[2]See the Twelfth Dialogue.

[3]First *Lettre touchant la Défense de Monsieur Arnauld* [M VI 193–274].

His attributes. He remains always the same, unless what is due His immutability is of lesser consideration than what is due another of His perfections, as I shall prove to you in what follows. Here, I believe, we have the unravelling of your difficulties. To dispel them, I have recourse to God and His attributes. But this is not to say, Aristes, that God remains with arms crossed, as some philosophers have it. Certainly, if God still acts at present, when can we say he is the cause of certain effects if we are not permitted to have recourse to Him in the case of those effects which are general, in the case of those which we see clearly have no necessary and essential relation to their natural causes? What I have just told you, my dear Aristes—preserve it tenderly in your memory, place it with your most precious possessions. Although you understand it, allow me to summarize the essence of the matter so that you may easily pick it up when you are able to meditate on it.

XI. There is no necessary relation between the two substances of which we are composed. Modalities of our bodies cannot through their own efficacy change those of our minds. Nonetheless, modalities of a certain part of the brain, which I shall not characterize here, are always followed by modalities or sensations of our souls; and this happens entirely as a result of laws, invariably efficacious, of the union of these two substances, that is, to speak more clearly, as a result of the uniform and invariably efficacious volitions of the Author of our being. There is no relation of causality between body and mind. What am I saying? No more is there such a relation between mind and body. I say furthermore that there is no such relation between body and body, nor between one mind and another mind. No created being can in short act on any other by an efficacy which it has of itself. This is what I shall prove to you shortly.[4] But is it not at least evident that a body, extension, merely passive substance cannot act of its own efficacy on a mind, on a being which is of another nature and infinitely more excellent than it is? Thus it is clear that, in the union of body and soul, there is no linkage other than the efficacy of divine decrees, decrees which are immutable and efficacious and never without their effects. God has so willed, and He wills unceasingly, that various movements in the brain are uniformly followed by various thoughts in the mind which is united to it. And it is this constant and efficacious will of the Creator that properly constitutes the union of the two substances. For there is no other nature, that is, no natural laws other than the efficacious volitions of the Almighty.

XII. Do not ask why God wills to unite minds to bodies, Aristes. That is an established fact the ultimate reasons for which have so far been unknown to Philosophy. Here, nonetheless, is one which it is well for me to propose to you. Apparently God willed to give to us, as to His Son, a sacrifice which we can offer to Him. Apparently He willed that, by a kind of sacrifice and annihilation of ourselves, we make ourselves worthy of the possession of eternal goods. To be sure, this appears right and in conformity with Order. We are now on trial in our bodies. It is through them as the occasional cause that we receive from God

---

[4]Seventh Dialogue.

thousands and thousands of different sensations which are material for our merit through the grace of Jesus Christ. As I shall prove to you shortly, occasional causes were actually necessary for a general cause, so that the general cause, always acting in a uniform and constant manner, could produce in its work an infinity of different effects by the simplest means and by general laws that are always the same. We must not think, however, that God could not find occasional causes other than bodies to give His conduct the simplicity and uniformity that governs it. There are actually others to be found in the angelic nature. These blessed spirits, by various movements of their wills, may be the occasional causes—among one another and in themselves—of the action of God who enlightens them and governs them. But let us not speak of what is beyond us. Here is what I am not afraid of affirming, it is absolutely necessary to illuminate the topic of our discussion, and I ask you to retain it in order to meditate on it at leisure.

XIII. God loves Order inviolably and through the necessity of His being. He loves, esteems, all things in proportion as they are estimable and lovable. He necessarily hates disorder. This is perhaps clearer and more unassailable than the proof I shall some day give you and which I am passing over.[5] Now it is manifestly a disorder that a mind, which is capable of knowing and loving God and hence is made for this purpose, should be obliged to concern itself with the needs of the body. Hence, since the soul is in fact united to the body and must take an interest in its preservation, it had to be informed by proofs which are instinctive, by proofs which are short yet convincing, of the relation which bodies surrounding us have with the one which we animate.

XIV. God alone is our light and the cause of our happiness. He possesses the perfections of all beings. He has all their ideas. So He contains in his wisdom all truths, speculative and practical: for these truths are simply relations of magnitude and perfection obtaining among ideas, as I shall prove to you shortly.[6] God alone then should be the object of our minds' attention, as it is He alone who is capable of enlightening them and of governing all their movements, as it is He alone who stands above us. Certainly a mind concerned with creatures, turned toward creatures however excellent they may be, is not in the Order in which God requires it nor in the state in which God has placed it. Now, if we had to examine every relation that the bodies surrounding us have with the present disposition of our own bodies in order to judge whether, how, or to what extent we should have commerce with them, it would occupy, it would—I should say—entirely fill the capacity of our minds. And certainly our bodies would not be the better for it. They would soon be destroyed by some involuntary distraction. For our needs change so often and sometimes so quickly that, if we are not to be taken unawares by some untoward accident, we should have to exercise a vigilance of which we are not capable. When should we eat, for example, what would we eat? when would we stop? What a fine occupation for a mind walking

---

[5] In the Eighth Dialogue.

[6] Eighth Dialogue.

and exercising its body to know at each step it has the body take that the body exists in air which is a fluid incapable of injuring or hurting it by cold or heat, wind or rain, or some evil and poisonous vapor; that, at each place where it is going to put its foot, there is not some hard and sharp body capable of injuring it; that it must quickly lower the head to avoid a stone yet keep equilibrium for fear of falling. A man constantly occupied with what is happening in all the parts comprising his body and in the great number of objects surrounding it could not think of the true goods—or at least think of them in the way in which the true goods require and in which consequently we ought to think of them, since our minds are made, and can only be made, to be concerned with the goods which can enlighten them and make them happy.

XV. Thus it is evident that, when God willed to unite minds to bodies, the occasional cause that He had to establish of our confused knowledge of the presence of objects and their properties in relation to us was not our attention, which would require clear and distinct knowledge of these bodies, but the various movements of the bodies themselves. He had to give us instinctive proofs, not of the nature and properties of the bodies surrounding us, but of their relations to our own bodies, so that we could succeed in the work of preserving our lives without being unceasingly attentive to our needs. He had, as it were, to undertake to reveal to us by prevenient sensations at the proper time and place what concerns the body's good so that we could be left totally absorbed in the search for the true goods. He had to give us proofs which were short and would convince us quickly of what relates to our bodies, proofs which were forceful and would be efficacious in determining us, proofs which were certain and which no one would think of denying so that we could the more surely preserve ourselves. Yet note that the proofs were confused and were certain, not with regard to relations objects have among themselves, i.e. in which the evidence of truth consists, but with regard to the relations they have with our bodies—relations which depend on the state of our bodies at the time. I say, "depend on the state of our bodies at the time." For we find, for instance, tepid water hot if the hand feeling it is cold, and this is appropriately so; and we find it cold if it is felt with a hand that is warm. We find it pleasant when we are moved by thirst, and appropriately so; but, as soon as our thirst is quenched, we find it flat and distasteful. Let us then admire the wisdom of the laws of the union of soul and body, Aristes. Although all our senses tell us that sensible qualities are spread out over objects, let us attribute to bodies only what we see clearly belongs to them after we have assiduously consulted the idea which represents them. Since the senses speak to us about the same things differently according to the interest which they take in them and since they inevitably contradict themselves when the good of the body demands it, let us regard them as false witnesses with regard to truth but as faithful advisers in relation to the preservation and conveniences of life.

XVI. ARISTES. How moved I am by what you are telling me, Theodore! and how vexed I am at having all my life been the dupe of these false witnesses! They speak with so much assurance and force that they, as it were, spread conviction

and certainty in our minds. They command with so much arrogance and importunity that we yield without examination. How are we to enter into ourselves
when they call us and pull us without? and can we listen to the replies of internal
truth during the noise and the tumult they raise? You made me understand that
light cannot be a modality of bodies. But, as soon as I open my eyes, I begin to
doubt it. When the sun strikes me, it dazzles me and blurs all my ideas. I now
understand that, if I pressed the point of this pin against my hand, it could only
make a quite small hole in the hand. Yet, if I actually pressed it, a very great
pain would seem to be produced in it. I should certainly not doubt this the
moment I was stuck. How much power our senses have, and how much force
they have for casting us into error! What disorder, Theodore! And yet, even in
the disorder, the wisdom of the Creator shines forth wonderfully. Light and
colors had to appear spread out on objects so that we could readily distinguish
them. Fruit had to seem filled with taste for us to eat it with pleasure. Pain had
to be attached to the finger which was pricked in order that the vivacity of the
sensation would make us draw back. In the Order which has been established by
God, there is infinite wisdom. I accept it, I cannot doubt it. But, at the same
time, I find there a very great disorder which appears to me to be unworthy of
the wisdom and goodness of our God. For in fact this Order is for us unfortunate
creatures an abundant source of errors and the inevitable cause of the greatest
evils which attend life. The end of my finger is pricked, and I suffer: I am
unhappy, I am incapable of thinking of the true goods, my soul can only attend
(*s'appliquer*) to my injured finger, and it is altogether filled with pain. What a
strange affliction! A mind is dependent on a body and, because of it, loses sight
of the truth. It is occupied—rather, it is more occupied by its finger than by its
true good. What disorder, Theodore! There is surely some mystery here. Please
unravel it for me.

XVII. THEODORE. Yes, there is undoubtedly some mystery here. How indebted Philosophers are to Religion, my dear Aristes! For only Religion can get
them out of the difficulty they are in. Everything appears to be in opposition in
God's conduct yet nothing is more uniform. Good and evil—I am speaking of
physical evil—do not have two principles that differ. It is one God who does
everything in accordance with the same laws. But sin brings it about that God,
without changing anything in His laws, becomes the righteous avenger of the
crimes of sinners. I cannot tell you now everything which would be necessary to
enlighten you thoroughly on the matter. But here in a few words is the resolution
of your difficulty.

God is wise. He judges all things rightly. He esteems all things to the extent
that they are estimable. He loves them to the extent that they are lovable. In
short, God loves order invincibly. He follows it inviolably. He cannot belie
Himself. He cannot sin. Now, minds are more estimable than bodies. Note then
that, though God can unite minds to bodies, he cannot subject them to bodies.
The pricking of my finger informs and warns me—that is right and in conformity
with Order. Yet it also hurts me and makes me unhappy, it engages me in spite
of myself, it blurs my ideas, it keeps me from thinking of the true goods—that is

certainly a disorder. It is unworthy of the wisdom and goodness of the Creator. That is what Reason makes me see by evidence. Experience convinces me, however, that my mind depends on my body. I suffer, I am unhappy, I am incapable of thinking when I am pricked. It is impossible for me to doubt this. There is, then, a manifest contradiction between the certainty of experience and the evidence of Reason. But here is the resolution of the difficulty. Before God, the mind of man has lost its dignity and its excellence. We are no longer such as God made us, and the union of our minds with our bodies has changed to dependence. Man having disobeyed God, it was right that his body ceased to be under his control. We are born corrupt and sinners, worthy of divine anger, and quite unworthy of thinking of God, of loving Him, of worshipping Him, of taking our pleasure in Him. He no longer wills to be our good or cause of our happiness; and, if He remains the cause of our being and does not annihilate us, that is because His mercy prepares for us a Redeemer through whom we shall have access to Him, association with Him, communion of the true goods with Him, according to the eternal decree by which He resolved to re-unite all things in our divine Head, God-in-Man, who was predestined from time eternal to be the foundation, the architect, the sacrifice, and the sovereign priest of the spiritual Temple where divine Majesty will live eternally. Thus Reason dispels the terrible contradiction which has so strongly moved you. It makes us clearly understand the most sublime truths. But this is because faith leads us to understanding and, by its authority, changes our doubts and uncertain and disturbing distrust into conviction and certainty.

XVIII. So remain steadfast in the thought to which Reason gives birth in you, Aristes, that infinitely perfect Being invariably follows immutable Order as its law and thus can unite the more noble with the less noble, mind with body, but that it cannot subject the one to the other—that infinitely perfect being cannot deprive the mind of liberty and the exercise of its most excellent functions to be pre-occupied in spite of itself and by the most cruel of penalties, losing sight of its sovereign good for the vilest of creatures. And conclude from what has been said that, prior to sin, exceptions were made in man's favor to the laws of the union of soul and body. Or, rather, conclude from this that initially there was a law, since abolished, by which man's will was the occasional cause of the disposition of his brain whereby his soul was sheltered from the action of objects, though his body was affected by them, and thus his soul was never interrupted involuntarily in its meditations and its ecstasy. When you are deep in thought and the light of truth fills and delights you, do you not feel in yourself a remnant of this power? It seems then that noise, colors, odors, and other less intrusive and lively sensations hardly interrupt you at all. But you are not superior to pain; you find it disruptive despite every effort of your mind. I judge you from my own case, Aristes. But, to speak accurately of innocent man made in God's image, we must consult divine ideas of immutable Order. It is there we find the model of a perfect man, such as was our Father before his sin. Our senses blur our ideas and tire our attention. But, in the case of Adam, his senses informed him respectfully. They were silenced by the least sign from him. They even ceased to inform him of the approach of certain objects when this was his wish. He could eat without pleasure, look without seeing, sleep without dreaming of all those vain phantoms which distress our minds and disturb our rest. Do not consider this paradoxical. About the state of the first man in whom everything was in conformity with the immutable Order God inviolably follows, consult Reason, and do not judge on the basis of what you sense in a body that is disordered. We are sinners, and I am speaking of man who is innocent. Order does not permit the mind to be deprived of the liberty of its thoughts while the body is repairing its forces during sleep. At that time and at all times, righteous man thought of what he willed. But man become sinner is no longer worthy of there being exceptions to the laws of nature on his account. He deserves to be stripped of his power over an inferior nature since, by his rebellion, he has made himself the most despicable of creatures—worthy not only of being reduced to nothingness but of being reduced to a state which is worse for him even than nothingness.

XIX. Do not then cease to admire the wisdom and wonderful order of the laws of the union of soul and body, through which we have so many different sensations of objects surrounding us. These laws are altogether wise. Viewed as they were instituted, they were indeed beneficial to us in every sense, and it is quite right that they subsist after sin, though they have distressing consequences. For the uniformity of God's conduct ought not to be dependent on an irregularity in ours. But it is not right after man's rebellion that his body should be perfectly submissive to him. It ought to be so only so far as that is necessary for the sinner to preserve for awhile his wretched life and perpetuate the human species until the accomplishment of the work which his posterity is to enter into through the righteousness and power of the Redeemer-to-come. For all the generations following one another, all the lands peopled by idolators, the whole natural order of the Universe that is preserved, is only to furnish Jesus Christ an abundance of materials necessary for the construction of the eternal Temple. A day will come when descendants of the most barbarous peoples will be enlightened by the light of the Gospel and they will enter in great numbers into the Church of the elect. Our Fathers died in idolatry, and we recognize the true God and our adorable Savior. The arm of the Lord is not shortened. His power will extend to the most distant nations; and it may be that our descendants will fall back into darkness when light lights up the new world. But let us assemble in a few words the principal things I have just told you, Aristes, so that you may readily retain them and make them the subject of your meditations.

XX. Man is composed of two substances, mind and body. Thus, he has two quite different sorts of goods to distinguish and look for—goods of the mind and goods of the body. God has also given him two quite sure means of discerning the different goods: reason for the mind's good and the senses for the body's good, evidence and light for the true goods and confused instinct for the false goods. I call goods of the body false or deceptive goods because they are not such as they appear to our senses to be and because, although they are good in relation to the preservation of life, they do not have the efficacy of their goodness in themselves but have it only in consequence of divine volitions or the natural laws for which they are occasional causes. I cannot explain this point more clearly at present. Now it was appropriate that the mind sense as in bodies qualities which the bodies do not have. Thus it could will, not to love or fear them, but to unite or separate itself to or from them according to the pressing needs of the machine the delicate springs of which require a vigilant and prompt guardian. It was necessary for the mind to receive a kind of compensation for the service rendered the body which God orders it to preserve, so that the mind would take an interest in its preservation. This is the cause now of our errors and our prejudices. This is the reason why, not being content to join certain bodies and detach ourselves from others, we are stupid enough to love them and fear them. In short, this is the cause of the corruption of our hearts, of which every movement should tend toward God, and of the blindness of our minds, the judgments of which should rest with light alone. Note this, and we shall see an explanation. We do not make use of the two means I have spoken of for the purpose which God has given them us; and, instead of consulting Reason to discover the truth, instead of yielding only to the evidence attending clear ideas, we submit to confused and deceptive instinct, which speaks rightly only in terms of bodily goods. Now, this is what the first man did not do before his sin. For there is no doubt he did not confound modalities the mind is capable of with those of extension. His ideas were not then confused; and his senses, which were perfectly submissive, did not prevent him from consulting Reason.

XXI. The mind now is as much punished as rewarded in its relation to the body. If we are pricked, we suffer from the prick, whatever effort we make not to think of it. That is a fact. But, as I told you, the reason is that it is not right for exceptions to be made to laws of nature in favor of a rebel, or rather that we should have a power over our bodies which we do not deserve. It is enough for us that, by the grace of Jesus Christ, the miseries to which we are subjected today will be the basis of our triumph and our glory tomorrow. We are not aware of true goods. Meditation bores us. We are not naturally affected by some prepossessing pleasure in what leads to the perfection of our minds. This is because the true good deserves to be loved by reason uniquely. The true good should be loved with a love of our own choosing, with a love which is enlightened, and not by the blind love that instinct inspires. It merits our application and our efforts. The true good does not need, as bodies do, borrowed qualities to make itself lovable to those who know it perfectly. In our present state, for us to love it, we must be prompted by the thought of spiritual pleasure. But this is because we are feeble and corrupt; it is because desire puts us out of order and, to conquer it, God must inspire us with a different desire which is entirely holy; it is because, for us to acquire the equilibrium of perfect freedom, we must have a counterweight—since we have a weight pulling us to the ground—which raises us to heaven.

XXII. Let us enter into ourselves unceasingly then, my dear Aristes, and try to silence not only our senses but also our imagination and our passions. I have spoken to you only of the senses because it is from them that imagination and the passions derive what force and malignancy they possess. In general, everything which comes to the mind from the body solely in consequence of natural laws concerns only the body. Do not then consider it. Follow the light of Reason which should direct our minds' judgments and regulate our hearts' movements. We should distinguish soul and body and the quite different modalities of which these two substances are capable; and we should frequently reflect on the wonderful order and wisdom of the general laws of their union. It is by such reflections that we acquire knowledge of ourselves and get rid of a vast number of prejudices. It is thus that we learn to know man—and we have to live among men and with ourselves. It is by these reflections that the entire Universe appears to our minds such as it is—that it appears, I submit, stripped of a thousand beauties which belong only to us, yet possessing the springs and movements which make us admire the wisdom of its author. Finally, it is thus, as you have just seen, that we recognize sensibly not only the corruption of nature and the necessity of a Mediator—two great principles of our faith—but also a vast number of other truths essential to Religion and Morality. Continue to meditate as you have begun, Aristes, and you will see the truth in what I am saying to you. You will see that the job of Meditator ought to be the job of every person who is rational.

ARISTES. What confusion the word "Meditator" still produces now that I understand in part what you just said and am quite imbued with the matter! Because of the blind contempt which I had of Reason, I believed you to be suffering a kind of illusion, Theodore. I must confess this. I treated you and some of your friends as a "Meditator." I looked on this stupid joke as witty and clever; and I think you are well aware of what is intended by it. I protest that even so I did not want to believe it of you, and I opposed the bad effect of this term of pleasantry with sincere praise which I always believed was quite justified.

THEODORE. I am convinced of that, Aristes. You had a bit of fun at my expense. I am glad of that. But I think you will not be sorry today to learn that it cost you more than it did me. You should know that, in the group, there was one of those "Meditators" who, as soon as you had left, thought himself obliged to defend, not me, but the honor of universal Reason against which you had offended in turning minds away from consulting it. When at first the Meditator spoke, everyone rose in your favor. But, after he had put up with some jokes and the contemptuous airs inspired by an imagination in revolt against Reason, he pleaded his cause so well that imagination succumbed. You were not made fun of, Aristes. The Meditator appeared to be sorrowed by your blindness. As for the others, they were moved by a certain indignation. Hence, if you were still of the same mind—and you are very far from it—, I should not advise you to visit Philander to retail commonplaces and jokes against Reason with the object of making taciturn Meditators objects of contempt.

ARISTES. Would you believe it, Theodore? I experience inner joy from what you tell me. The evil I was afraid I had done was soon enough remedied. But to whom am I obliged for this? Is it not Theotimus?

THEODORE. You will know that when I am quite convinced your love for the truth is great enough to be extended to those to whom you owe this rather ambiguous obligation.

ARISTES. The obligation is not ambiguous. I protest that, if it is Theotimus, I shall love him for it and esteem him the more for it. As I continue to meditate, I sense an increase of the inclination I have toward those who search for the truth, toward those whom I called "Meditators" when I was mad enough to deem visionaries those who render to Reason the attentions which are due it. Oblige me then by telling me who the excellent man is who wished to spare me the embarrassment which I deserved and who maintained the honor of Reason so well without making me ridiculous. I wish to have him for a friend. I want to merit his good graces; and, if I cannot succeed in that, I want him to know at any rate that I am no longer what I was.

THEODORE. Well then, Aristes, he will know this. And, if you wish to be among the number of the Meditators, I promise you he will in turn be among the number of your good friends. Meditate and all will be well. You will soon win him over when he sees you with an ardor for the truth, with a submission to the faith, and with a deep respect for our common Master.

FIFTH DIALOGUE

✤

The use of the senses in the sciences. In our sensations there is a clear idea and a confused sensation. The idea does not belong to the sensation. It is the idea which enlightens the mind, whereas the sensation moves (applique) the mind and makes it attentive. The sensation is the means by which the intelligible idea becomes sensible.

ARISTES. I have made good progress since you left me, Theodore. I have gone way ahead. I made a general survey of all the objects of my senses, guided, it seems to me, solely by Reason. Though I had already become somewhat used to these new discoveries, I was never more surprised. Good God, what poverty I discerned in what just a while ago appeared to me to be absolute magnificence! and what wisdom, what greatness, what wonders there are in everything the world holds in contempt! The man who sees only with his eyes is indeed a stranger in his own land. He admires everything and knows nothing. He is only too happy if what overtakes him does not bring about his death. On the part of sensible objects, there are endless illusions. Everything deceives us, everything corrupts us, everything speaks to the soul solely for the sake of the body. Only Reason disguises nothing. How happy I am with it, and how happy I am with you who taught me to consult it, who raised me above my senses and above myself in order to contemplate its light! I have recognized very clearly, it seems to me, the truth of what you told me. Yes, Theodore, let me have the pleasure of telling it to you—man's mind is simply darkness; its own modalities do not enlighten it; its substance, entirely spiritual as it is, has nothing intelligible about it; his senses, his imagination, his passions lead him astray at every moment. Today I believe I can assure you I am fully convinced of this. I speak to you with confidence given me by the vision of the truth. Test me and see if I am not a little too bold in thinking this.

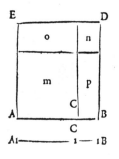

198

I. THEODORE. I believe what you are telling me, Aristes. I am persuaded that an hour's studious meditation can take a mind such as yours a very long way. Nevertheless, in order that I may be further assured of the progress you have made, answer me. You see the line *AB*. Let it be divided in two parts at some point, say, *C*. I shall now prove to you that the square on the whole line is equal to the squares on each of the parts plus the two parallelograms formed on these two parts.

ARISTES. What are you attempting to do? Everyone knows that that is the same as reproducing a whole or all the parts comprising the whole.

THEODORE. You know it. But let us suppose you do not know it. I mean to demonstrate it to your eyes and prove to you thereby that your senses clearly disclose the truth to you.

ARISTES. Let us see.

THEODORE. Look intently—that is all I ask of you. Without entering into yourself to consult Reason, you will discover an evident truth. *ABDE* is the square of *AB*. Now, the square is equal to all that it contains. It is equal to itself. Hence, it is equal to the two squares on the two parts, *m* and *n*, plus the two parallelograms, *o* and *p*, formed on the parts, *AC* and *CB*.

ARISTES. That is apparent to the eye.

THEODORE. Very well. But it is, in addition, evident. Hence, there are evident truths which are apparent to the eye. Thus, our senses evidently teach us truths.

ARISTES. That is a fine truth and quite difficult to discover! Is that all you have to say in defending the honor of the senses?

THEODORE. You are not replying, Aristes. It is not Reason that prompts you to this subterfuge. For is it not, I ask you, an evident truth which your senses just taught you?

ARISTES. There is nothing easier.

THEODORE. That is because our senses are excellent masters. They have easy ways of teaching us the truth. But Reason with its clear ideas leaves us in darkness. This is what people will tell you, Aristes. They will say to you: prove to someone who does not know it, for example, that the square of 10 equals the sum of the squares of 4 and 6 plus twice the product of 4 and 6. These ideas of numbers are clear; and the truth to be proved in intelligible numbers is the same as if it were a question of a line exhibited to your eyes which would be, say, ten inches long and divided into 4 and 6. Nonetheless, you will see there is some

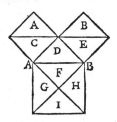

difficulty in making the truth understood because the principle—i.e. that to multiply a number by itself is the same as to multiply each of its parts by itself and together—is not so evident as the truth that a square equals all the figures which it contains. And that is what your eyes teach you, as you have just seen.

II. But, if you find the Theorem which your eyes taught you too easy, here is another which is more difficult. I shall prove to you that the square on the diagonal of a square is double the square on its sides. Open your eyes—that is all I ask of you.

Look at the figure I am drawing on this piece of paper. Do your eyes not tell you, Aristes, that all the triangles which I imagine and which you see—*A, B, C, D, E, F, G, H,* and *I,* each having a right angle and two equal sides—are equal to one another? Now, you see that the square constructed on the diagonal *AB* contains four of these triangles and that each of the squares on the sides contains two of them. Hence, the large square is double the others.

ARISTES. Yes, Theodore. But you are reasoning.

THEODORE. I am reasoning! I look, and I see what I am telling you. I am reasoning, if you will; but it is on the faithful testimony of my senses. Just open your eyes and look at what I show you. Triangle *D* is equal to *E,* and *E* equals *B;* and, on the other side, *D* is equal to *F,* and *F* equals *G.* Hence, the small square is equal to half the large one. The same is true of the other side. That is apparent to the eye, as you say. To discover this truth, it is enough to look intently at the figure and, by a movement of the eyes, compare the parts which compose it. Hence, our senses can teach us the truth.

ARISTES. I reject that conclusion, Theodore. It is not our senses but Reason joined (*jointe*) to our senses that enlightens us and discloses the truth to us. Do you not perceive that, in the sensible view we have of this figure, there is at once the clear idea of extension joined to the confused sensation of color that affects us? Now it is in the clear idea of extension, not in the white and black which make it sensible, that we discover the relations in which the truth consists; it is, I say, in the clear idea of extension that Reason contains, not in the white and black that are mere sensations, confused modalities of our senses whose relations it is not possible to discover. There is always a clear idea and a confused sensation in the view we have of sensible objects, the idea representing their essence, the sensation informing us of their existence. The idea makes known to us their nature, their properties, the relations they have, or can have, to one another, in short, the truth; the sensation, on the other hand, makes us sense the difference among them and the relation they have to the convenience and preservation of life.

III. THEODORE. By your answer, I see you have reconnoitered the land since yesterday. I am pleased with you, Aristes. But, I ask you, is not the color that is here on the paper itself extended? Certainly I see it as such. Now, if it is, I shall be able to discover clearly the relations of the parts without thinking of the extension which Reason contains. The extension of the color will suffice for me to learn Physics and Geometry.

ARISTES. I deny that the color is extended, Theodore. We see it as extended, but our eyes deceive us. For the mind will never comprehend that extension belongs to color. We see this whiteness as extended: but the reason is that we refer (*rapportons*) it to extension because it is by this sensation in the soul that we see the paper or, rather, intelligible extension affects the soul, modifies it in a certain fashion, and thereby becomes sensible to it. I say, Theodore, do you want to say that pain is extended because, when we have gout or rheumatism, we feel it as extended? Do you want to say that sound is extended because we hear it filling the air? Do you want to say that light is spread out in vast spaces because we see them filled with light? Since it is a matter only of modalities or sensations in the soul and since the soul never derives the idea which it has of extension from its own resources, all these qualities are referred (*se rapportent*) to extension and make it sensed by the soul, but they are in no way extended.

IV. THEODORE. I grant you that color, like pain, is not locally extended, Aristes. Since experience teaches that we feel pain in an arm that we no longer possess and that, while asleep at night, we see colors as spread out on imaginary objects, it is evident that this is only a matter of sensations or modalities of the soul; and certainly the soul does not fill the many places it sees since it fills none of them and modalities of a substance cannot be where that substance is not. This is incontestable. Pain cannot be locally extended in my arm, nor colors on the surfaces of bodies. But why not suppose that they are, as it were, sensibly extended, in the same way as the idea of bodies, intelligible extension, is intelligibly extended? Why not suppose that the light which I see when I press the corner of my eye, or the like, brings with it the sensible space it occupies? Why do you suppose that the light is referred (*se rapporte*) to intelligible extension? In short, why do you suppose that it is the idea or archetype of bodies which affects the soul when it sees or senses sensible qualities as spread out on bodies?

ARISTES. It is because only the archetype of bodies can represent their nature to me and only universal Reason can enlighten me through the display of its ideas. The substance of the soul has nothing in common with matter. The mind does not contain the perfections of all the beings which it can know. But there is nothing that does not participate in the divine Being. Thus, God sees all things in Himself. But the soul cannot see them in itself. It can find them only in universal and divine Reason. Hence, the extension which I see or feel does not belong to me. Otherwise, I would be able to know the works of God through contemplating myself. Considering attentively my own modalities, I would be able to learn Physics and several other sciences which are comprised by knowledge of the relations of extension, as you indeed know. In short, I should be a light unto myself—something I cannot think of without a certain kind of horror. But please explain the difficulty you put to me, Theodore.

V. THEODORE. It is impossible to explain it directly. For that, the idea or archetype of the soul would have to be disclosed to us. We should then see clearly that color, pain, taste, and the other sensations of the soul have nothing in common with the extension that we sense joined with (*jointe avec*) them. We should see intuitively that there is as much difference between the extension we see and the color making it visible to us as there is between numbers, for example, the infinite or whatever other intelligible idea you please, and the perception we have of them; and we should see at the same time that our ideas are quite different from our perceptions and from our sensations. This is a truth which we can discover only by serious reflections, by long and difficult reasonings.

But I can prove to you indirectly that our sensations or modalities do not contain the idea of extension to which they are referred—referred necessarily because it is that idea which produces them in our souls and it is the nature of the soul to perceive what affects it. Let us suppose that you are looking at the color of your hand and at the same time feel pain in it. You would then see the color of the hand as extended, and you would at the same time feel the pain as extended. Do you not agree with this?

ARISTES. Yes, Theodore. Moreover, if I touched it, I would also feel it as extended; and, if I plunged it into hot or cold water, I would feel the heat and cold as extended.

THEODORE. Note this then. Pain is not color, color is not heat, nor heat cold. Now, the extension of the color—or joined to the color—which you see when you look at your hand is the same as the extension of the pain, the extension of the heat, the extension of the cold which you are also able to sense. Hence, the extension belongs neither to the color, nor to the pain, nor to any of your other sensations. For you would sense as many different hands as you have different sensations on the supposition that our sensations are extended in themselves, as they appear to us to be, or that the colored extension we see is but a sensation in the soul as are the color, the pain, or the taste—a supposition accepted by some of the Cartesians who are aware of the fact that we do not see objects in themselves. There is, then, one and only one idea of a hand, Aristes, an idea which affects us in different ways, which acts on our souls and which modifies the soul with color, heat, pain, etc.; for it is not the bodies we look at which affect us with our various sensations, as we often see bodies that do not in fact exist. It is also evident that bodies cannot act on the mind, modify it, enlighten it, make it happy and unhappy through pleasurable or disagreeable sensations. Nor is it indeed the soul which acts on itself and which modifies itself with pain, color, etc. This does not need to be proved after what has already been said. It is, then, the idea or archetype of bodies which affects us in different ways. That is to say, it is the intelligible substance of Reason which acts on our minds through all powerful efficacy and which affects and modifies the mind with color, taste, pain, by what there is in it [the intelligible substance of Reason] which represents bodies.

Therefore you must not be surprised, my dear Aristes, that you can learn certain evident truths by the testimony of the senses. Although the substance of the soul is not intelligible to the soul itself and though its modalities cannot enlighten it, these same modalities, when they are joined to the intelligible extension which is the archetype of bodies and they make this extension sensible, can show us the inter-relations in which the truths of Geometry and Physics consist. But still it is true to say that the soul is not a light unto itself: that its modalities are only darkness, and that it discovers exact truths only in ideas contained in Reason.

VI. ARISTES. I think I understand what you are telling me. But, as this is abstract, I shall meditate on it at leisure. It is not pain or color in itself that teaches me the relations bodies have among themselves. I can discover these relations only in the idea of extension which represents them; and that idea, though joined to color or pain, i.e. the sensations making it sensible, is not a modality of the soul.[1] The idea becomes sensible, or is made sensible, precisely because the intelligible substance of Reason acts on the soul and impresses on it a certain modality or sensation, thereby as it were revealing, though in a confused manner, that a certain body exists. When ideas of bodies become sensible, they make us judge that there are bodies acting on us; whereas, when these ideas are simply intelligible, we do not naturally believe that there is anything outside us which is acting on us. It seems to me the reason for this is that thinking of extension depends on us while sensing it does not depend on us. For, sensing extension in spite of ourselves, there does in fact have to be something other than us which impresses the sensation on us. Now, we believe that this other thing is simply what we are in fact sensing. We thereupon come to judge that the bodies surrounding us cause in us the sensations we have of them. In this we are always mistaken. Moreover, we do not doubt that these bodies exist, and in this we are often mistaken. But, as we think of bodies and as we imagine them when we will, we judge that it is our volitions which are the true cause of the ideas we then have of them, or of the images we form of them. And the internal sensation we have of the effort of our attention at the time confirms us in this false thought. Although only God can act on us and enlighten us, yet, as His operation is not sensible, we attribute to objects what He effects in us without our willing, and we attribute to our own power what He effects in us depending on our volitions. What do you think of this reflection, Theodore?

VII. THEODORE. It is very judicious, Aristes, and the work of a Meditator. You might also add that, when the idea of body affects the soul with a very engaging sensation, such as pain, the idea makes us judge not only that body exists but in addition that it belongs to us, as happens even to those whose arms have been amputated. But let us return to the sensible demonstration I gave you of the equality of the square on the diagonal of a square and the two squares on the sides. Observe that the demonstration derives its evidence and generality only from the clear and general idea of extension, rightness and equality of lines, angles, triangles, and in no way from the white and the black, which make all these things sensible and particular while not making them clearer or more intelligible in themselves. Observe that, from my demonstration, it is evident as a general truth that the square on the diagonal of any square is equal to the squares on the two sides, but that it is by no means certain that the particular square you see with your eyes is equal to the two others. For you are not even certain that what you see is a square, that a certain line is straight, that a certain angle is right. The relations which your mind conceives between magnitudes are not the same as those of these figures. Observe finally that, although our senses do not enlighten the mind by themselves, yet, as they make the ideas we have of bodies sensible, they awaken our attention, and they thereby lead us indirectly to an understanding of the truth. Thus, we should make use of our senses in studying any science which has for its object relations of extension; and we

---

[1]In this work, I call *sentimens* what in other places I recall having called *sensations*. [*Sentiment* is usually translated "sensation" here.]

should not be afraid that they will get us into error provided we strictly observe the precept—judge things only by the ideas which represent them and never by the sensations which we have of them—, a precept of the utmost importance which we should never forget.

VIII. ARISTES. All of this is exactly true, Theodore; and it is just how I have understood the matter since I thought seriously about it. Nothing is more certain than that our modalities are simply darkness, that of themselves they do not enlighten the mind, that we do not know clearly whatever we sense most keenly.[2] The square here is not such as I see it. It is not the size I see it. Certainly you see it as larger or smaller than I do. The color which I see it as having does not belong to it. Perhaps you see it with another color than I do. It is not strictly the square which I see. I judge it to be drawn on this paper; and it is not impossible that there is here neither square nor paper, just as it is certain that there is here no color. But, though my eyes provide me with so many doubtful or false reports concerning the figures drawn on the paper, this is nothing by comparison with the illusions of my other senses. The testimony of my eyes often approaches the truth. This sense can help the mind discover it. It does not wholly disguise its object. Making me attentive, it leads me to understanding. But the other senses are so false that we are always under an illusion when we allow ourselves to be guided by them. Still, it is not the case that our eyes are given to us for discovering exact truths in Geometry and Physics. They are given to us simply to keep watch on movements of our bodies in relation to the bodies surrounding us and for the convenience and preservation of life; also, as a necessity for preserving our lives, we must have a kind of knowledge of sensible objects which somewhat approaches the truth. For this reason, we have, for instance, a certain consciousness (*sentiment*) of the size of a given body at a certain distance. If the body were too far from us to be capable of harming us or, if being closer, it were too small, we should without fail lose sight of it. It would be annihilated for our eyes (though it continues to subsist before our minds and, in this respect, can never be destroyed by division), because the relation of a large body when quite distant or a body near us but too small to harm us—the relation, I say, of such bodies to our own—is as nothing and ought not to be perceptible to the senses which speak, and are bound to speak, only with regard to the preservation of life. All this appears evident to me and conforms to what took place in my mind at the time I meditated.

THEODORE. I see you have been very far into the land of truth, Aristes; and, by the communication you have had with Reason, you acquired riches far more precious and rare than what is brought us from the new world. You have come upon the fountainhead. You have drawn from it. And you are now richer for all time provided you do not quit it. You no longer need me nor anyone else, having found the faithful master who enlightens and enriches anyone who devotes himself to Him.

---

[2]See *Rech. de la Verité,* Book I [M I 39–189], and *Réponse au Livre des vrayes & des fausses Idées* [M VI 1–189].

ARISTES. But Theodore! do you want to break off our discussions now? I know it is with Reason we must philosophize. But I do not know the way it should be done. Reason itself will teach me. That is not impossible. But I have no occasion to hope for it if I do not have a vigilant and faithful monitor to lead me and inspire me. Goodbye to Philosophy if you leave me; for, by myself, I should fear going astray. I should soon take replies I made to myself for those of our common Master.

IX. THEODORE. I have no intention of leaving you, my dear Aristes. For, now that you meditate on everything that is said to you, I hope you will keep me from the misfortune you fear will befall you. Each of us needs the other, though we receive nothing from any other person. You have taken quite literally a word that slipped out in honor paid to Reason. Yes, it is from it alone that we receive light. But Reason uses those who are in touch with it to recall its stray children to it and lead them by way of their senses to understanding. Do you not know, Aristes, that Reason has itself become incarnate in order to be within reach of every man, to strike the eyes and ears of those who can neither see nor understand save by way of their senses? Men have seen with their eyes eternal Wisdom, the invisible God who lives within them. Their hands have handled, as the well-beloved Disciple says, the Word that gives life.[3] Internal truth has appeared outside us, coarse and stupid as we are, in order to teach us in a sensible and palpable way the eternal commands of divine Law, commands which it gives us internally at all times, yet which we do not hear, being outwardly disposed as we are. Do you not know that the grand truths which Faith teaches us are lodged in the Church and we can learn them simply by an authority emanated from Wisdom incarnate? It is internal Truth that invariably instructs us, to be sure. But it uses every possible means to recall us to it and fill us with understanding. So do not be afraid I will leave you. For I hope internal Truth will use you to keep me from abandoning it and from taking my imaginings and reveries for its divine oracles.

ARISTES. You do me much honor. But I see I must accept it since it redounds to our common Master, Reason.

THEODORE. I do you the honor of believing you to be rational. The honor is great. For, by virtue of Reason, each man, when he consults and follows it, becomes the superior among all creatures. By it he judges and passes sentence without appeal—or, rather, Reason decides and passes judgement through him. But do not think I am deferring to you. I defer only to Reason, which can speak to me through you, as it can speak to you by way of me; and I thus rise above the brutes, above those who renounce the most essential of their qualities. Yet, my dear Aristes, though we are both rational, let us not forget that we are extremely prone to error. This is because we can both of us come to a decision without waiting for the infallible judgment of the true Judge, without waiting for evidence that, as it were, tears our assent from us. If we always did honor to Reason by letting it deliver its decisions for us, it would make us infallible. But,

[3]I John 1:1.

instead of waiting for its replies and following its light step by step, we go ahead of it and go astray. Restive as we are, impatience sets in at having to remain attentive and unmoving. Our indigence is urgent, and the ardor we have for the true goods often precipitates us into the greatest evils. This is because it is up to us to follow the light of Reason or to walk in the dark with the false and deceptive glimmer of our modalities. Nothing is pleasanter than blindly following the impulses of instinct, while nothing is more difficult than holding fast to the delicate and sublime ideas of truth despite the body's weighing the mind down. Let us try, however, to support each other without trusting each other too much, my dear Aristes. Perhaps both of us will not lose our footing at the same time provided we walk quite slowly and are as careful as possible not to look for support to bad ground!

ARISTES. Let us move on a little, Theodore. What are you afraid of? Reason is an excellent support. There is nothing moving in clear ideas. They do not give way to time. They do not adapt themselves to special interests. They do not change their words as our modalities do, speaking pro or con according to the body's urging. I am fully convinced that we must follow only ideas which spread light and that all our sensations and other modalities can never lead to the truth. Let us please go on to some other matter, as I agree with you entirely on this one.

X. THEODORE. Let us not go so fast, my dear fellow. I am afraid you are granting me more than I ask, or you do not yet understand distinctly enough what I am telling you. Our senses deceive us, it is true; but that is principally because we refer (*rapportons*) sensations we have of sensible objects to those objects. Now there are in us several sensations (*sentimens*) which we do not refer to objects. For example we have feelings (*sentiment*) of joy, sadness, hate, in short, all the feelings attending movements of the soul (*sentimens qui accompagnent les mouvemens de l'ame*). Color is not in the object, pain is not in my body, heat is neither in the fire nor in my body where these sensations are referred. Our external senses are false witnesses. Agreed. But the feelings attending (*sentimens qui accompagnent*) love and hate, joy and sorrow, are not referred to the objects of these passions. We feel them in the soul, and that is where they are. Hence, they are good witnesses, for they speak the truth.

ARISTES. Yes, Theodore, they speak the truth, and the other sensations do so as well. For, when I feel pain, it is true that I feel it; it is also true in a sense that I suffer it through the action of the very object which affects me. Great truths, these! Well then, are not feelings of love, hate, and the other passions referred (*se rapportent*) to the objects which are the occasions of them? Do they not spread their malignity on objects and represent them to us as altogether other than what they in fact are? In my case, when I have an aversion to someone, I am aware of a disposition to interpret everything he does as malign. His innocent actions appear to me to be criminal. I want to have good reasons for hating and scorning him. All my passions seek justification at the cost of the object on which they depend. If my eyes spread colors on the surface of bodies, so too my heart spreads its internal dispositions, or certain false colors, so far as possible on the objects of its passions. I do not know whether passions in you, Theodore, have the effect they have in me; but I can assure you I am even more afraid of listening to and following them than I am of giving in to the often innocent and benign illusions of my senses.

XI. THEODORE. I am not saying we should give in to the inner promptings of our passions, Aristes; and I am glad to see you are aware of their power and malignity. But you must agree that they teach us certain truths. For it is after all a truth that I now feel much joy hearing you. It is quite true that the pleasure I am now feeling is greater than the pleasure I had in our previous discussions. Hence I know the difference between the two pleasures. And I do not know this in any other way than by the sensation I have of them, in any way other than by the modalities with which my soul is affected—modalities which are not, then, so dark that they do not teach me an objective truth.

ARISTES. Say that you sense the difference in your modalities and pleasures, Theodore. But please do not say you know it. God knows it yet does not sense it. But, in your case, you sense it without knowing it. If you had a clear idea of your soul, if you saw its archetype, then you would know what you only sense: you would then be able to have exact knowledge of the difference in the different sensations of joy that your goodness to me excites in your heart. But you certainly do not know this. Compare the feeling of joy with which you are now affected with the feeling of the other day, Theodore, and tell me precisely what their proportion (*rapport*) is: then will I believe that your modalities are known to you. We know things only when we know the proportion (*rapport*) they have one to another (*entr'elles*). You know that one pleasure is greater than another. But by how much is it greater? We know that a square inscribed in a circle is smaller than the circle. Yet we do not know how to square the circle since we do not know the proportion of circle to square. We can approach it to infinity and can see evidently that the difference between a circle and some other figure is smaller than any given amount. But note that this is because we have a clear idea of extension. The difficulty of discovering the proportions (*rapport*) of circle to square is due simply to the limitations of our minds; whereas it is the obscurity of our sensations and the darkness of our modalities that make it impossible to discover relations among them. It seems evident to me that, were we geniuses as great as the most sublime intellects, we would still not be able to discover relations among our modalities unless God were to show us their archetype on the basis of which He formed them. For you have convinced me that we can know beings and their properties only by way of the eternal, immutable, and necessary ideas which represent them.

XII. THEODORE. Very well, Aristes. Our senses and our passions cannot enlighten us. But what do you say about our imagination? In Geometry the imagination forms such clear and distinct images of shapes that you cannot deny that it is by means of them that we learn this science.

ARISTES. Do you think I have already forgotten what you just told me, Theodore? or that I did not understand it? The evidence attending the Geometer's reasoning, the clarity of lines and shapes formed by the imagination, comes solely from our ideas and not at all from our modalities, not at all from the confused traces left behind by the course of animal spirits. When I imagine a figure, when I construct a building in my mind, I work on property that does not belong to me. It is from the clear idea of extension, it is from the archetype of bodies, that I derive all the intelligible materials which represent my plan to me, all the space which provides me my terrain. It is from this idea, which is furnished me by Reason, that I frame in my mind the body of my work and it is on the basis of ideas of equality and proportions that I work and fashion it, relating everything to an arbitrary unit which will be the common measure of all the parts composing it, or at least all the parts which can be envisaged from the same point and at the same time. It is certainly by intelligible ideas that we direct the course of [animal] spirits which trace these images or figures in our imaginations. And everything luminous and evident about these figures proceeds, not from the confused sensations which belong to us, but from the intelligible reality which belongs to Reason. All this comes not from particular modalities peculiar to us. It is a ray from the luminous substance of our common Master.

I cannot imagine, say, a square, Theodore, without at the same time conceiving it. And it appears evident to me that the image of the square I imagine is precise and regular only so far as it corresponds exactly to the intelligible idea I have of a square, that is, of a space enclosed by four entirely straight and absolutely equal lines which, joined together at their endpoints, make four perfectly right angles. Now, it is about such a square that I am sure that the square on the diagonal is double the square on one of its sides. It is of such a square that I am sure that there is no common measure between diagonal and sides. In short, it is of such a square that properties can be discovered and demonstrated to others. On the other hand, we can know nothing with respect to the confused and irregular image which is traced in the brain by the course of [animal] spirits. The same can be said of all other figures. Hence, Geometers do not derive their knowledge from confused images in their imaginations but derive it solely from clear ideas of Reason. Those rough images can indeed hold their attention by giving, so to speak, body to their ideas, but it is the ideas which they get hold of that enlighten Geometers and convince them of the truth of their science.

XIII. Do you want me to spend more time, Theodore, picturing the illusions and phantoms of an imagination which has revolted against Reason and is supported and enlivened by the passions—those beguiling phantoms which lead us astray, those terrible phantoms which make us afraid, those monsters of all varieties which are born of our disorders and which grow and multiply in an instant? They are mere chimeras in fact, but chimeras on which our minds feast and with which they busy themselves with the utmost alacrity. For our imaginations find much more reality in the specters to which they give birth than in the necessary and immutable ideas of eternal Truth. That is because these dangerous specters strike the imagination, whereas ideas do not affect it. Of what use can so disordered a faculty be—a mad person taking pleasure in playing the fool, someone fickle whom we have so much trouble restraining, an insolent person who is not afraid of interrupting us in our most serious exchanges with Reason? I grant you, all the same, that our imaginations can make our minds attentive. The imagination has such charms and empire over the mind that the mind is made willingly to think of what is affecting the imagination. Yet, other than its capacity to be in contact with ideas representing bodies, it is so subject to illusion and so hot-headed that, if it is not curbed unceasingly, if its moves and starts are not controlled, it transports you instantly into the land of chimeras.

THEODORE. There is only too much of that, Aristes. From everything you have told me, which fills me with surprise and joy, I see you have grasped the principle and probed very far into the consequences it contains. I see you have a sufficient understanding that it is Reason alone that enlightens us by intelligible ideas contained in its entirely luminous substance, and I see you have a perfect knowledge of how to distinguish its clear ideas from our dark and obscure modalities. But be sure to note that abstract principles, pure ideas, escape the mind as soon as we forget to contemplate them and dwell on what is sensible. So I admonish you to meditate often on this matter so that your possession of it will be so perfect, and the principles and consequences will have been rendered so familiar, that you will never inadvertently take the vivacity of your sensations for the evidence of truth. It is not enough to have understood that the general principle behind our prejudices is our not distinguishing *knowing* and *sensing* and that, instead of judging things by *ideas* which represent them, we judge them by *sensations* which we have of them. We must strengthen our belief in this fundamental truth by following out its consequences. Principles of practice are perfectly understood only through the use we make of them. Hence, by repeated and serious reflection, try to acquire a firm and felicitous habit of being on guard against the springs and inner promptings of your false and deceptive modalities. No endeavor is more worthy of a Philosopher. If we distinguish the replies of inner Truth from what we say to ourselves on our own, if we distinguish what comes immediately from Reason from what comes to us by way of the body or on occasion of the body, if we distinguish what is immutable, eternal, necessary from what changes at every moment, in short, if we distinguish the evidence of light from the vivacity of instinct, it is almost impossible for us to fall into error.

ARISTES. I understand everything you are telling me. And I have found so much satisfaction in the reflections I have already made on the matter that you should not be apprehensive that I will not think of it any more. Let us go on to something else if you think it a good idea.

THEODORE. It is quite late now, Aristes, for us to start out on a path that is a little long. But, as for tomorrow, what direction do you want us to take? Please think of this and tell me.

ARISTES. It is up to you to lead me.

THEODORE. Not at all: it is your choice. You should not be indifferent to the way I take you. Might I not deceive you? Might I not take you where you should not go? Most imprudently plunge into useless studies, my dear Aristes. Such a person, simply hearing praise for Chemistry, Astronomy, or some other science that is empty and of little use, throws himself bodily into it. Such a person will not know whether his soul is immortal; he may well be at a loss to prove to you that there is a God; yet he will solve equations in Algebra with amazing facility. Another will know all the subtle nuances of language, all the rules of the Grammarians; yet he will never have meditated on the order of his duties. What an inversion of mind! With an impassioned air, a dominant imagination praises knowledge of medallions, Poetry of the Italians, language of Arabs and Persians, before a young man full of ardor for the sciences. As a result, he plunges blindly into studies of these sorts, and he then disregards knowledge of man and rules of morality and may even forget what children are taught in their Catechism. Such a man is a machine that goes whichever way it is impelled. It is much more chance than Reason that directs it. All such live by opinion. They act in imitation. They even take pride in following those who go before without knowing where. Reflect on the various occupations of your friends, or rather go over in your mind the course you have adopted in your studies; and decide whether you were right to do as others did. I ask you to decide this, not on the plaudits you have received, but by the authoritative replies of inner Truth. Decide on the basis of eternal law, immutable Order, without regard to foolish thoughts of mankind. Now, Aristes, because everyone throws himself into a bagatelle, each in his way and according to his taste, do you have to follow course so as not to appear the Philosopher in the minds of fools? Do we indeed have to follow Philosophers everywhere in their abstractions and their chimeras for fear of their regarding us as ignorant or as innovators? Everything must be put in its place. Preference should be given to knowledge that has merit. We should learn what we ought to know and not let our heads be filled with useless furniture, striking as it may appear to be, when we lack the necessities. Think of this, Aristes; and tell me tomorrow what the topic of our discussion is to be. This is enough for today.

ARISTES. It is much better for you to tell me, Theodore.

THEODORE. It is infinitely better for Reason to tell both of us. Consult it seriously, and I shall think of the matter as well.

SIXTH DIALOGUE

✤

Proofs of the existence of bodies derived from revelation. Two sorts of revelation. How it comes about that natural revelations in sensation provide us with an occasion for error.

ARISTES. What a difficult question you gave me to settle, Theodore! I was quite right to say that it was up to you—you who know the strong and the weak among the sciences, and the utility and fertility of their principles—to guide my steps in the intelligible world to which you transported me. For I admit I do not know which way to turn. What you taught me can indeed be of use to keep me from going astray in this unknown land. To this end, I need but follow the light step by step and yield only to the evidence which attends clear ideas. But it is not enough to go ahead, I also need to know where I am going. It is not enough to keep on discovering new truths; I need to know how to locate those fertile principles that give the mind all the perfection of which it is now capable, those truths that are to order the judgments to be made of God and His wonderful works and to order movements of the heart and give us the taste, or at least the foretaste, of the sovereign good which we desire.

If we were to insist on evidence without weighing utility in our choice among the sciences, Arithmetic would be preferable to all others. Truths about numbers are the clearest of all since any other relation is clearly known only in so far as it can be expressed by these common measures of all the exact relations which are based on unity. This science is also so fertile and so deep that, if I spent thousands of centuries plumbing its depths, I would continue to find an inexhaustible supply of clear and luminous truths. Still, I do not think you were intent on our turning in that direction, charmed as we are by the evidence that shines forth there in every way. For what indeed would be the use of penetrating the most hidden mysteries of Arithmetic and Algebra? It is not enough to dash through a lot of country, to penetrate far into sterile lands, to discover places where no one has ever been; we must go straight to those fortunate countries where fruit is to be found in abundance, solid foods that are capable of nourishing us.

When I thence compared the sciences with one another according to my lights and their different advantages with respect to their evidence versus their utility, I found myself in a strange predicament. Sometimes the fear of falling into error gave preference to the exact sciences, such as Arithmetic and Geometry, the demonstrations of which satisfy admirably our vain curiosity. At other times, the desire of knowing not relations of ideas among themselves but relations to us and among themselves and the works of God with which we live urged me on to Physics, Morality, and the other sciences which frequently depend on experiences and phenomena that are rather uncertain. It is a strange thing, Theodore, that the most useful sciences are filled with impenetrable obscurities and that we find a sure way, quite easy and smooth, in the sciences which are not so necessary! Now, I ask you, what way is there to make a true appraisal of the relation between the ease of some and the utility of others and thus give preference to the science that deserves it? How, also, can we make sure whether just those that appear the most useful are actually so, and whether those that appear to be merely evident do not possess great utilities which do not come to mind? I confess that, after having thought a lot about the matter, I still do not know which way to go, Theodore.

I. THEODORE. You did not waste your time in the reflections you made, my dear Aristes. Though you do not know precisely what you should devote yourself to, still I am quite sure you will not give in to numerous false studies in which more than half the world are furiously engaged. I am quite certain that, if I were to make a mistake in the choice of what to do in the course of our discussions, you are capable of disabusing me. When men raise their heads and look in every direction, they do not always follow those who go in front. They follow only when the leaders go the right way and where they themselves want to go. Moreover, when the leader of the group imprudently takes dangerous routes which end nowhere, the others make him turn back. So continue with your reflections on your steps and on mine. Do not trust too much in me. Watch carefully to see if I am taking you where we should both be going.

Take not of this then, Aristes. There are sciences of two sorts. Some consider relations of ideas; others relations among things by means of their ideas. The first are evident in every respect; the second can be only on the assumption that things are similar to the ideas which we have of them and which we use in reasoning about them. The latter are very useful, but they are surrounded by great obscurities because they assume certain facts the truth of which is very difficult to know exactly. If we could find some means of making sure our assumptions are correct, we could avoid error and at the same time discover truths which concern us very much. For again, truths or relations of ideas with one another concern us only when they represent relations among things having some connection with us.

Thus it seems to me to be evident that the best use we can make of our minds is to examine which are the things that have some connection with us, the different ways in which these things are connected, the cause of the connections and their effects—all of this in conformity with clear ideas and unquestionable observations, the former assuring us of the nature and properties of things and the latter assuring us of the relation and connection that things have with us. Yet, to avoid falling into the trivial and useless, the whole of our inquiry should be directed to what can make us happy and perfect. Thus, to reduce all of this to a few words, it appears to me to be evident that the best use we can make of our minds is to try to acquire an understanding of the truths which we believe on faith and of everything which serves to corroborate them. For no comparison can be drawn between the utility of these truths and the advantage to be derived from knowledge of others. We do indeed believe these great truths, it is true. Yet faith does not exempt those who are able from filling their minds with these truths and becoming assured of them in every possible way. On the contrary, faith is given us as a basis for regulating every step of our minds as well as every movement of our hearts. It is given us to lead us to an understanding of the very truths which it teaches us. There are so many people who scandalize the faithful with far-fetched Metaphysics and insultingly ask for proofs of what they ought to believe on the infallible authority of the Church that, although the solidity of your faith makes you unshakeable by their attacks, your charity should lead you to remedy the disorder and confusion which they introduce everywhere. Do you then approve the plan I am proposing for what we are to discuss, Aristes?

ARISTES. Yes certainly, I approve it. But I did not think you would be willing to leave Metaphysics. If I had thought that, I think I would easily have resolved the question of preference regarding the sciences. For it is clear that no discovery is comparable to understanding the truths of Faith. I thought that you thought only of making me something of a Philosopher and a good Metaphysician.

II. THEODORE. I am still thinking only of that, and I do not intend to leave Metaphysics, although I may allow myself the liberty in what follows of exceeding somewhat its usual limits. This general science has precedence over all others. It can draw examples from them and a little detail that is necessary to make its general principles perceptible. For, by "Metaphysics," I do not understand those abstract considerations about certain imaginary properties the principal use of which is to furnish those who want to dispute material for endless disputation; I mean by this science the general truths which can serve as principles for the particular sciences.

I am convinced, Aristes, that, to gain understanding of the truths of Faith, we must be good Philosophers and, the stronger we are with respect to the true principles of Metaphysics, the firmer we shall be in the truths of Religion. I am just supposing, you may well think, what is necessary to make this proposition acceptable. But no, I shall never believe that true Philosophy is opposed to Faith and that good Philosophers can have different opinions from true Christians. For, whether Jesus Christ in His Divinity speaks to Philosophers in their innermost selves or instructs Christians through the visible authority of the Church, He cannot possibly contradict Himself, though it is quite possible to imagine contradictions in His utterances or take our own conclusions for utterances of His. Truth speaks to us in different ways, but it certainly always says the same thing. It follows that Philosophy is not to be opposed to Religion unless it is the false Philosophy of the Pagans, Philosophy based on human authority, in short, opinions which are not revealed and do not bear the mark of truth, i.e. the invincible evidence that compels attentive minds to assent. From Metaphysical truths we discovered in our previous discussions, you can judge whether true Philosophy contradicts Religion. As for me, I am convinced that it does not. If I have advanced propositions contrary to the truths which Jesus Christ teaches us through the visible authority of His Church, these propositions, having their basis in me alone and not having the mark of invincible evidence, do not belong at all to true and solid Philosophy. But I do not know why I am pausing to tell you truths that are indubitable, however little attention we give them.

ARISTES. Permit me to tell you, Theodore, that I was charmed to see the wonderful relation between what you taught me—or, rather, what reason taught me by your mediation—and the great and necessary truths which the Church's authority makes simple and ignorant men believe, men whom God wishes to save along with Philosophers. You have convinced me, for instance, of the corruption of my nature and the necessity of a Redeemer. I know that all intellects have but a single unique Master, the Divine Word, and that only Reason incarnate and made sensible can deliver carnal man from the blindness in which we are all born. With extreme satisfaction I grant that the fundamental truths of our faith, and several others it would take me too long to relate to you, are necessary consequences of the principles you demonstrated to me. Please continue. I shall try to follow you anywhere you lead me.

THEODORE. Ah, my dear Aristes, once again watch out that I do not go astray. I am apprehensive that you may be too easy-minded and your approbation induce negligence in me and make me fall into error. Fear for me, and do not believe everything that a man who is subject to illusion may tell you. Also, you will learn nothing if it is not your own reflections which put you in possession of the truths that I shall attempt to demonstrate.

III. There are only three sorts of Beings of which we have any knowledge and with which we can have some connection: God or infinitely perfect Being, is the principle or cause of all things; minds, which are known only through internal consciousness (*sentiment*) which we have of our nature; and bodies, of the existence of which we are assured by the revelation we have of them. Now, what we call a man is simply a composite. . . .

ARISTES. Not so fast, Theodore. I know there is a God or infinitely perfect Being.[1] For, if I think of such a being, which I certainly do, that being must exist, since nothing finite can represent the infinite. I also know that minds exist, on the assumption that there are beings resembling me.[2] For I cannot doubt that I think, and I know that what thinks is something other than extension or matter. You have proved these truths to me. But what do you mean by our being assured of the existence of bodies "by the revelation we have of them"? What! Do we not see them? Do we not feel them? We do not need "revelation" to teach us that we have a body when we are pricked: we very truly sense it.

[1]Second Dialogue.
[2]First Dialogue.

THEODORE. Yes, no doubt we sense it. But the sensation of pain we have is a kind of "revelation." That expression makes an impression on you. But it is expressly for this reason that I use it. You still forget that it is God Himself who produces in our souls all the different sensations affecting them on the occasion of changes happening to our bodies and in consequence of general laws for the union of the two substances composing man, laws which are simply the uniform efficacious volitions of the Creator, as I shall explain subsequently. The point which pricks the hand does not pour pain into the hole which it makes in the body; no more does the soul produce this unpleasant sensation in itself, since it suffers pain in spite of itself. It must be a superior power. It is then God Himself who, by sensations with which He affects us, reveals to us what is happening outside us; I mean, in our bodies and in the bodies surrounding us. Remember, if you please, what I have told you so many times before.

IV. ARISTES. I was wrong, Theodore. But what you are saying brings to mind a very strange thought. I almost do not dare propose it to you, for I am afraid you will regard me as a visionary. It is that I am beginning to doubt the existence of bodies. The reason is that the revelation which God gives us of their existence is not sure. It is after all certain that we sometimes see what does not exist, for instance, when we are asleep or when fever causes a disturbance in our brains. If God can, as you say, sometimes give us deceptive sensations in consequence of His general laws, if through our senses He can reveal to us things that are false, why can He not always do this, and how then will we be able to distinguish truth from falsity in the obscure and confused testimony of our senses? It seems to me that prudence dictates that I suspend judgment with regard to the existence of bodies. Please give me an exact demonstration of their existence.

THEODORE. "An exact demonstration"! That is a bit much, Aristes. I admit I do not have one. On the contrary, it seems to me that I have an "exact demonstration" of the impossibility of such a demonstration. But do not be disturbed. I do not lack proofs that are certain and are capable of dispelling your doubt. And I am glad such a doubt entered your mind. For indeed, if we doubt there are bodies for reasons which make it impossible for us to doubt that there is a God and that the soul is not corporeal, this is a certain mark that we have risen above prejudices and that, in place of subjecting reason to the senses as most men do, we acknowledge its right to make sovereign judgments in us. Here is, if I am not mistaken, a demonstrative proof that it is impossible to give an exact demonstration of the existence of bodies.

V. The notion of infinitely perfect Being does not contain a necessary relation to any creature. God is entirely self-sufficient. Matter is not then a necessary emanation from the Deity. Or, at least—and this is enough for now—, it is not evident that matter is a necessary emanation from the Deity. Now, we cannot give an "exact demonstration" of a truth if we cannot show a necessary connection between it and its principle, if we cannot show that there is a relation necessarily contained in the ideas we are comparing. It follows that it is not possible to give a rigorous demonstration of the existence of bodies.

The existence of bodies is indeed contingent (*arbitraire*). If bodies exist, it is because God willed to create them. Now, what is true of the volitions to punish crimes or reward good works, to require love or fear from us, and the like is not true of the volition to create bodies. These other volitions of God's, and a thousand like them, are contained necessarily in divine Reason, in the substantial Law which is the inviolable rule of the volitions of the infinitely perfect Being and in general of any intellect. But the will to create bodies is not contained necessarily in the notion of infinitely perfect Being, of Being that is entirely self-sufficient. Very far from it, this notion seems to exclude such a volition from God. Hence, there is no way other than revelation which can assure us that God has willed to create bodies, given what admittedly you no longer doubt, namely, that bodies are not visible in themselves, that they cannot act on our minds nor make themselves represented in them, and that our minds can know them only by ideas which represent them and can sense them only by modalities or sensations which they can cause solely in consequence of contingent laws of the union of soul and body.

VI. ARISTES. I understand, Theodore, that we cannot deduce demonstratively the existence of bodies from the notion of Being infinitely perfect and self-sufficient. God's volitions relating to the world are not contained in the notion we have of Him. Now, since only these volitions can give being to creatures, clearly we cannot demonstrate the existence of bodies. For we can only demonstrate truths having a necessary connection with their principle. Thus, since we cannot be assured of the existence of bodies through the evidence of a demonstration, there can be no other way than the authority of revelation. But that does not appear to me to be sure. For, though I clearly discover in the notion of an infinitely perfect Being that He cannot will to deceive me, experience teaches me that His revelations are deceptive, and I cannot reconcile these two truths. After all, we often have sensations that reveal falsities to us. Someone feels pain in an arm he no longer has. Those people we call mad see objects before them that do not exist. And there is perhaps no one has not in sleep often been altogether shaken and terrified by mere phantoms. God is not a deceiver. He can will to deceive no person, neither fool nor wise. And yet we are all misled by sensations with which He affects us and by which He reveals to us the existence of bodies. It is, therefore, quite certain that we are often deceived. But it does not appear to me to be certain that we are not always deceived. Let us see then on what foundation you rest the certainty you claim to have about the existence of bodies.

VII. THEODORE. There are, in general, revelations of two sorts. Some are natural, others supernatural. I mean that some take place in consequence of certain general laws which are known to us, in accordance with which the Author of nature acts on our minds on the occasion of happenings in our bodies, and that others occur by means of general laws which are unknown to us or by means of particular volitions added to general laws in order to remedy the disturbing results these laws have on account of sin, which puts everything in disorder. Now, both kinds of revelation, natural and supernatural, are true in themselves. But the former are at present an occasion of error for us, not because they are false in themselves, but because we do not make the use of them for which they are given us and because sin has corrupted nature and put a kind of contradiction in the relation that general laws have to us. Certainly the general laws of union of soul and body, in consequence of which God reveals to us that we have a body and are surrounded by many other bodies, are very wisely instituted. Remember our previous discussions. These laws are not deceptive in themselves, in their institution viewed prior to sin and in the plan of their Author. For it should be known that, prior to sin, before the blindness and confusion which rebellion of the body produces in the mind, man had clear knowledge by the light of Reason:

1. That God alone could act on him, make him happy or unhappy by pleasure or pain, or, in short, modify or affect him.

2. He knew by experience that God affected him always in the same way in the same circumstances.

3. Hence, he realized by experience, as well as by Reason, that God's conduct was, and had to be, uniform.

4. Thus, he was led to believe in the existence of beings that were the occasional causes for the general laws in accordance with which he sensed that God acted on him. For, once again, he knew that God alone acted on him.

5. Whenever he willed, he could keep himself from sensing the action of sensible objects.

6. The internal sensation which he had of his own volitions and of the submissive and deferential behavior of sensible objects taught him that they were his inferiors, as they were subordinated to him. For, at that time, everything was perfectly in Order.

7. Thus, consulting the clear idea joined to (*jointe au*) the sensation with which he was affected on the occasion of these objects, he saw clearly that this was entirely a matter of bodies, since the idea represents bodies only.

8. He concluded from this that the various sensations with which God affected him were simply the revelations by which God taught him that he had a body and was surrounded by many other bodies.

9. But, knowing by Reason that God's conduct must be uniform and by experience that laws of the union of soul and body were at all times the same, realizing that these laws were established simply to inform him of what he must do for the preservation of his life, he readily found out that he should not judge the nature of bodies by the sensations he had of them, nor should he let himself be persuaded of their existence by these sensations when his brain was not moved by an external cause but simply by a movement of [animal] spirits excited by an internal cause. Now, he could recognize when an external cause was producing the present traces in his brain since the course of the animal spirits was perfectly submissive to his volitions. Thus, he was not like the mad or the feverish, nor like us while asleep, that is, liable to mistake phantoms for realities; for he could tell whether the traces in his brain were produced by the internal involuntary course of spirits or by the action of objects, the course of the spirits being subject to his will and depending on his free desires (*desirs pratiques*). Everything about this appears to be evident and to be a necessary conse-

quence of two incontrovertible truths: first, that, prior to sin, man had very clear ideas, and his mind was free of prejudices; second, that his body, or at any rate the principal part of this brain, was perfectly submissive to him.

Granting this, Aristes, you can see that the general laws in consequence of which God gives us the sensations or natural revelations that assure us of the existence of bodies and their relation to us are very wisely instituted: you see that these revelations are not at all deceptive in themselves. It could not have been better arranged, for the reasons I gave you before. How does it come about then that these laws now throw us into an infinity of errors? It is, to be sure, because our minds are dimmed, because we are filled with prejudices from our child-hood, because we are unable to make the use of our senses for which they were given us. And all of this, take note, is precisely because man, by his own fault, lost the power he was to have over the principal part of his brain, over the part of the brain in which every change is invariably followed by some new thought. For our union with universal Reason is greatly weakened by our dependence on our bodies. And, finally, our minds are so situated between God who enlightens us and bodies which blind us that, the more they are united to one, necessarily the less they are united to the other.

As God follows exactly, and is bound to follow exactly, the laws He has established for the union of the two substances of which we are composed, and as we have lost the power of keeping the rebellious [animal] spirits from making traces in our brains, we take phantoms for realities. But the cause of our error does not derive precisely from falsity in our natural revelations but from impru-dence and temerity in our judgments, from our state of ignorance with respect to the line of conduct that God is bound to follow, in brief, from the disorder that sin has caused in all our faculties and the confusion that it has introduced in our ideas, not by changing the laws of the union of soul and body but by inciting our bodies which, rebelling, deprive us of the exercise of an ability to put these laws to the use for which they were established. You will understand all this more clearly in the course of our discussions or when you have meditated on it. Still, Aristes, notwithstanding what I have just said, I do not see that there can be any good reason here for doubting the existence of bodies in general. For, although I can be mistaken with regard to the existence of a certain body, I see that this is because God follows exactly laws of the union of soul and body; I see that it is this uniformity in God's conduct that cannot be disturbed by an irregularity in ours and that the loss, through our own fault, of the power we had over our bodies should not have changed anything in the laws of their union with our souls. This reason suffices to keep me from being mistaken about the existence of a particular body. I am not led invincibly to believe that the body exists. But I do not have this reason, and I do not see how there can possibly be another, to keep me from believing in the existence of bodies in general in the face of the many different sensations I have of them, sensations which are so coherent, so connected, so well-ordered that it appears to me to be a certainty that God would will to deceive us if there were nothing in all of what we see.

VIII. Yet, in order that you may be entirely free of your speculative doubt, faith furnishes us with a demonstration which it is impossible to resist. Now, whether bodies do or do not exist, it is certain that we [seem to] see them and that it is only God who can give us these sensations. Hence, it is God who presents to my mind appearances of men with whom I live, of books I consult, of preachers whom I hear. Now, I read in the appearance of the New Testament about the miracles of a Man-God, His Resurrection, His ascending to Heaven, the preaching of the Apostles, and the happy outcome, the establishment of the Church. I compare all this with what I know from History, with the Law of the Jews, with the Prophecies of the Old Testament. We are still only considering appearances. Yet, once again, I am certain that it is God alone who gives me these appearances and that He is not a deceiver. I then compare afresh all the appearances I just mentioned with the idea of God, the beauty of Religion, the holiness of Morality, the necessity of a creed; and I find myself led in the end to believe what Faith teaches us. In a word, I believe this without the need of an absolutely rigorous demonstrative proof. For nothing appears to me to be more irrational than lack of faith, nothing appears to me to be more imprudent than not accepting the greatest authority we can have in matters which we cannot examine with Geometrical precision because time is lacking or for a thousand other reasons. Men are in need of an authority to teach them truths that are necessary, that serve to lead them to their end; and it is a subversion of Providence to reject the authority of the Church. This appears evident to me, and I shall prove it to you subsequently.[3] Now, Faith teaches me that God created heaven and earth. It teaches me that Scripture is a divine book. And this book, or the appearance of it, tells me clearly and positively that there exist thousands and thousands of creatures. Hence, we have here all my appearances changed into realities. Bodies exist: this is absolutely demonstrated when faith is assumed. Thus, I am assured that bodies exist, not just by the natural revelation of sensations which God gives me of them, but far more still by the supernatural revelation of faith. There, my dear Aristes, are the grand arguments against a doubt that hardly arises naturally in the mind. Few people have enough of the philosopher in them to propose it. And, though difficulties that appear insurmountable, principally to persons who do not know that God must act on us through general laws, can be raised against the existence of bodies, still I do not believe anyone can ever seriously doubt their existence. Thus, it was not really necessary to spend our time allaying a doubt that is of so little danger. For I am quite certain that you were not in need of all that I said in order to be sure that you are here with Theodore.

ARISTES. I am not so sure of that. I am certain you are here. But that is because you say things to me that another would not say to me and that I would never say to myself. Moreover, the affection I have for Theodore is such that I [seem to] encounter him everywhere. How do I know whether this affection will not increase and, though it seems hardly possible, I will not always be able to tell the true from the false Theodore?

---

[3]Thirteenth Dialogue.

THEODORE. You are being foolish, my dear Aristes. Will you never give up these ingratiating ways? It is unworthy of a Philosopher.

ARISTES. How severe you are! I was not expecting that answer.

THEODORE. Nor was I yours. I thought you were following my reasoning. But your answer gives me cause for fearing that your have made me speak to you on the subject of your doubt to little avail. Most men propose problems without thinking; and, instead of attending seriously to the answers that they get, they think only of some retort that will make us admire the nicety of their imaginations. Far indeed from mutual instruction, such men think only of flattering one another. They are mutually corrupted by the inner promptings of the most criminal of passions; and, instead of stifling the various feelings that are excited in them by the lust of pride, instead of communicating to one another the true goods of which Reason apprises them, they bestow flattery on one another which intoxicates and befuddles them.

ARISTES. How keenly I feel what you are saying, Theodore! But now! are you reading my heart?

THEODORE. No, Aristes. It is in my heart that I read what I am telling you. It is in mine that I find the source of the lust and vanity which makes me malign the human species. I know nothing of what happens in your heart except in relation to what I feel in my own. I fear for you what I am afraid of for myself. But I am not sufficiently rash to judge what your dispositions are. My manners surprise you. They are harsh and irritating, you might say boorish. But what! do you think that sincere friendship founded on Reason looks for evasion and dissemblance? You do not know the privileges of "Meditators." They have the right to speak to their friends without ceremony about what they have occasion to find fault with in their friends' conduct. I should like to observe in your answers, my dear Aristes, somewhat more simplicity and far more attentiveness. I should like Reason always to have been the superior in you and imagination to have been silenced. But, if your imagination is too fatigued now by its silence, let us leave Metaphysics. We shall take it up another time. Do you know that the Meditator of whom I spoke awhile ago wants to come here?

ARISTES. Who? Theotimus?

THEODORE. Indeed yes, Theotimus himself.

ARISTES. Ah, that excellent man! What a joy this is! What an honor!

THEODORE. He learned in some way or other that I was here and that we were doing philosophy together. For, where Aristes is, that is soon known. Everyone wants him. That is what it is to be a fine wit and have so many brilliant qualities. Such a person must be everywhere if he is not to disappoint anyone. He is no longer his own master.

ARISTES. What bondage!

THEODORE. Do you want to be free of it? Become meditative, and soon everyone will leave you at it. The great secret of being free of the importunity of many people is to speak reason to them. This is a language they do not understand, it dismisses them forever, and they have no cause for complaint.

ARISTES. That is true. But when will Theotimus be with us?

IX. THEODORE. When you please.

ARISTES. Well, please let him know without delay that we expect him and assure him on the matter that I no longer am what I formerly was. But please do not let this break off our discussion. I give up my doubt. But I am not sorry I raised it. From the things you told me, I catch a glimpse of the resolution of a number of apparent contradictions which I could not reconcile with our notion of the Deity. When we sleep, God makes us see a thousand objects which do not exist. The reason for this is that He follows, and is bound to follow, general laws for the union of soul and body. It is not that He wills to deceive us. If He acted on us by particular volitions, we would not see all these phantoms during sleep. I am no longer surprised at seeing monsters and the manifold irregularities in nature. I see the cause of them in the simplicity of God's ways. Innocence oppressed no longer surprises me; and, if the stronger ordinarily get their way, it is because God governs the world by general laws and He puts off avenging crimes to another time. God is just—the good fortune of the impious notwith-standing and notwithstanding the prosperity of the forces of the most unjust Conquerors. He is wise, though the Universe is filled with works in which we find a thousand defects. He is immutable, although He seems to contradict Himself all the time, although he ravages the land with hail which, through an abundancy of rain, He covered with fruit. All the effects that are contradictory mark neither contradiction nor change in the Cause that produces them. On the contrary, God inviolably follows the same laws and His conduct is not dependent on ours (*n'a nul rapport a la notre*). If someone suffers pain in an arm he no longer has, it is not because God purposefully deceives him; it is simply that God does not change His plans and obeys His own laws strictly; it is because He approves them and will never condemn them; it is because nothing can disturb the uniformity of His conduct, nothing can oblige Him to depart from what He has done. It seems to me, Theodore, I get some idea of this principle of general laws having an infinite number of consequences of very great utility.

THEODORE. That is good, my dear Aristes. You give me much joy. I thought you had not been sufficiently attentive to grasp the principles on which the answers I gave you depend. That is very good. But we shall have to examine these principles in depth so that you will know more clearly their solidity and their wonderful fertility. For do not imagine that it is enough to get some idea of them, or even to have understood them, if you are to be able to apply them to the problems depending on them. Use is necessary to make us master of them and acquire the ability of relating everything they can clarify to them. But I am of a mind to put off the examination of these great principles until Theotimus has arrived. Try to discover for yourself, however, what the things are that have some connection with us, what the causes of these connections are, and what are their effects. For it is a good thing for your mind to be prepared regarding the topic of our future discussions. Thereby you will be able more easily to right me if I go astray or to follow me if I lead you directly where we ought to head with all our might.

SEVENTH DIALOGUE

✤

The inefficacy of natural causes and the lack of power in creatures. We are immediately and directly united to God alone.

After many compliments back and forth between Aristes and Theotimus, Aristes observed that Theodore was not altogether pleased that this was not over and, wishing to yield the honor to the newcomer in this skirmish of wit, fell silent. Theodore, entering the conversation, thought he should speak to Theotimus on Aristes' behalf.

THEODORE. Really, Theotimus, I did not think you were so mannered a man. You have obliged Aristes to give way, someone who never gives way to anyone. That is a victory which would do you much honor if you had brought it off at Philander's place. But no doubt it would have cost you more dearly. For do not be deceived. Aristes gives way because he wishes to do the honors in his own house. He yields to you here through complaisance and a kind of duty.

THEOTIMUS. I do not doubt that, Theodore. I see very well that he wishes to spare me.

ARISTES. Oh! do stop egging me on, both of you; or at least, Theodore, allow me the liberty of defending myself.

THEODORE. No, Aristes. There is only too much useless talk. We desist, Theotimus and I. Let us talk about something better. Tell us please what has entered your mind on the topic that I proposed to you in our last discussion. What are the things with which we have some connection? What are the causes of these connections, and what are their effects? For we prefer to hear you philosophize than to see ourselves overwhelmed by a profusion of favors and civilities.

ARISTES. I think, Theodore, you suppose I stayed up all night in order to treat Theotimus to a prepared speech.

THEODORE. Let us drop all this, Aristes, and speak naturally.

I. ARISTES. It seems to me, Theodore, that there is nothing to which I am more closely united than to my own body. For it cannot be touched without my being affected. As soon as it is wounded, I feel that I am injured and discomfited. There is nothing smaller than the proboscises of our importunate friends who affront us on our walks in the evening; and yet, no matter how slightly they sink the imperceptible points of their venomous proboscises into my skin, I feel a drilling in my soul. The mere noise they make in my ears sounds an alarm in me, and this is a certain mark that I am more closely united to my body than to anything else. Yes, Theodore, this is true to such a degree that only through our bodies are we united to all the objects which surround us. If the sun did not affect my eyes, it would be invisible to me; and, if I had the misfortune of becoming deaf, I would no longer find so much pleasure in the society I have with my friends. It is by way of the body also that I adhere to my Religion. For it is through my eyes and through my ears that faith entered my mind and my heart. In short, it is by way of my body that I am related to everything. Hence, I am more closely united to my body than to anything else.

THEODORE. Did you meditate a long time, my dear Aristes, to make this great discovery?

THEOTIMUS. All that may very well be said, Theodore.

THEODORE. Yes, Theotimus, by people who consult their senses only. Whom do you take Aristes for to sanction in his mouth something even a peasant might say? I no longer recognize Aristes in this reply.

ARISTES. I see I have gotten off to a very bad start.

THEODORE. Very bad indeed. I did not expect this beginning. I did not think you would have forgotten today what you knew yesterday. But prejudices always return in force and drive us from our conquests unless, by vigilance and entrenchment, we are able to maintain our positions. Oh well, I submit that we are in no way united to our bodies, let alone more closely united to them than to anything else. I exaggerate my way of speaking a bit so that it will impress you and you will not again forget what I tell you. No, Aristes, speaking exactly and strictly, your mind is not, and cannot be, united to your body. It can only be united to what can act on it. Now, do you think your body can act on your mind? Do you think that it is your body that makes you rational, happy or unhappy, and the like? Does your body unite you to God, to Reason which enlightens us? Or is it not rather God who unites you to your body and, by way of your body, to everything surrounding you?

ARISTES. To be sure, Theodore, it is God who has united my mind to my body. But could it not be said. . . .

THEODORE. What! that it is your mind which now acts on your body and your body on your mind? I understand you. God made this union of mind and body. And then it is your body and, by means of it, all objects are capable of acting on your mind. The union once established, your mind is also capable of acting on your body and, by way of it, on the bodies around you. Could that not be said?

ARISTES. There is something about it that I do not completely understand. How does it all take place? I speak to you as if I had forgotten the better part of what you told me for lack of thinking about it.

THEODORE. I doubt that. You want me to prove more exactly and in greater detail the principles of which I have spoken to you thus far. I must try to satisfy you. But please be attentive and answer me; and you, Theotimus, can observe both of us.

II. Do you think, Aristes, that matter, which you judge perhaps not to be capable of moving itself or giving itself any modality, can ever modify a mind, make it happy or unhappy, represent ideas to it, give it different sensations? Think of this and answer me.

ARISTES. That does not appear to me to be possible.

THEODORE. Once again, think about it. Consult the idea of extension and judge by that idea, which represents bodies if anything does, whether they can have some property other than the passive faculty of receiving various shapes and various motions. Is it not evident to the last degree that properties of extension can consist only in relations of distance?

ARISTES. That is clear, and I have already agreed to it.

THEODORE. It follows that bodies cannot possibly act on minds.

ARISTES. Not of themselves, not by their own force, so it will be said. But why can they not do so by a power resulting from their union with minds?

THEODORE. What are you saying, "by a power resulting from their union"? I understand nothing by these general terms. Remember the principle of clear ideas, Aristes. If you abandon it, then you are in darkness. At the first step you will fall into the precipice. I understand how bodies, in consequence of certain natural laws, can act on our minds in the sense that their modalities bring about the efficacy of divine volitions or general laws of the union of soul and body—a matter I shall explain shortly. But what I do not understand is how bodies can acquire in themselves a certain power by the efficacy of which they can act on our minds. What would that power be? Would it be a substance or a modality? If a substance, then it is not bodies that act but that substance which is in bodies. If the power is a modality, then there will be a modality in bodies which is neither motion nor shape. Extension will be able to have modalities other than relations of distance. But what am I arguing for? It is up to you, Aristes, to give me some idea of that power which you conceive to be the effect of the union of soul and body.

ARISTES. We do not know, it will be said, what that power is. But what can you conclude from an avowal of ignorance on our part?

THEODORE. That it is better to say nothing than not to know what one is saying.

ARISTES. Agreed. But we say only what we know when we propose that bodies act on minds. Nothing is more certain. Experience does not allow us to doubt it.

THEODORE. Yet I doubt it very much, or rather I do not believe any of it. Experience teaches me that I feel pain when, for example, a thorn pricks me. That is a certainty. But let us stop there. Experience by no means teaches us that the thorn acts on our minds nor that it has some power. We are not to believe any of that, I admonish you.

III. ARISTES. I do not believe that a thorn can act on my mind, Theodore. But it might be said that it can act on my body and, by way of my body, on my mind in consequence of their union. I admit that matter cannot act immediately on a mind. But note the word "immediately."

THEODORE. Yet your body, is it not matter?

ARISTES. Yes, undoubtedly.

THEODORE. Your body cannot then act "immediately" on your mind. Thus, though your finger was stuck by a thorn, though your brain was moved by its action, neither finger nor brain could act on your soul and make it feel pain. Your brain and your finger are nothing but matter, and so neither can act immediately on your mind.

ARISTES. But it is not my soul either that produces in itself the sensation of pain that afflicts it, for it feels the pain in spite of itself. I feel that the pain comes to me from an external cause. Thus, your reasoning proves too much. I see you are going to tell me that it is God who causes my pain in me; and I agree. But He causes it simply in consequence of the general laws of union of soul and body.

THEODORE. What do you mean, Aristes? All that is true. Explain your thought more distinctly.

ARISTES. I think, Theodore, that God has united my mind to my body and that, by virtue of that union, my mind and my body mutually act on each other in consequence of natural laws that God always follows quite exactly. That is everything I have to say to you on the matter.

THEODORE. You do not explain yourself, Aristes. That is a rather good indication that you do not understand what you are saying. "Union," "general laws"—what sort of reality do you understand by these terms?

THEOTIMUS. Apparently Aristes thinks the terms clear and unequivocal because usage has made them so common. When we read something obscure and false many times and do not stop to examine it, we can hardly believe it is not true. The word "union" is one of the most equivocal of terms. Yet it is so common and easy that it passes everywhere without being questioned, without anyone considering whether it arouses a distinct idea in the mind. For what is familiar does not excite that attention without which nothing can possibly be understood; and whatever affects the imagination agreeably appears very clear to the mind, which distrusts nothing when it is paid in currency.

ARISTES. What, Theotimus! would you be entirely of Theodore's mind? Can we doubt that soul and body are united in the closest manner in the world? I would be tempted to think that the two of you are in league to send me out of my mind and amuse yourselves at my expense were I not persuaded that you are persons too estimable for so uncharitable a design.

THEOTIMUS. You are a little too opinionated, Aristes. Theodore upholds the side of truth, and, if he overdoes things a bit, it is to set us right. He sees that the weight of our prejudices carries us along and the force he uses on us is simply to hold us back. Let us listen to him if you please.

IV. THEODORE. You would have it, Aristes, that your soul is united to your body more closely than to anything else. Well, I will go along with that for the time being but only on condition that you will also agree with me for a day or two not to explain certain effects by a principle of which neither you nor I have any knowledge. Is that not quite reasonable?

ARISTES. Only too reasonable. But what do you mean?

THEODORE. Here we go. "Between your mind and your body there is the closest union in the world." How can we doubt that! But you were unable to say what precisely this union is. Let us not then take this as a principle explaining effects whose cause we are looking for.

ARISTES. But if the effects depend necessarily on it?

THEODORE. If they do depend on it, we shall indeed be obliged to return to it. But let us not take it for granted. If I asked you, Aristes, how it comes about that, when the arm of this chair is moved, the rest of the chair follows, would you think you had given me a sufficient explanation if you replied that this happens because the arm of the chair is united with the other parts of which it is composed? Certainly Theotimus would not be satisfied with such a reply. Children are permitted to give answers like that but not Philosophers, except in so far as they are not claiming to philosophize. To satisfy the mind of Theotimus on this question, we should have to go back to the physical cause of the union of the parts of which hard bodies are composed,[1] and we should have to prove to him that the hardness of bodies can only derive from compression by an invisible matter surrounding them. Hence, the word "union" explains nothing. It is itself in need of explanation. So, Aristes, you may if you like take vague and general words for reasons. But do not try to pay us in that currency. Although many people accept it and are satisfied by it, we are a bit difficult because of the fear we have of being deceived.

ARISTES. What do you want me to do? I pay you in currency that I have accepted in good faith. I have no better. As it has currency in the world, you might well be satisfied with it. But let us have some idea how you go about paying people. Give me good reasons to prove that body and mind act mutually on each other without having recourse to their union.

THEODORE. Do not assume that they act mutually on each other, Aristes, but only that their modalities are reciprocal. Accept only precisely what experience teaches you, and try to be attentive to what I am going to say. Do you think that a body can act on matter and move it?

ARISTES. Who can deny it?

V. THEODORE. Theotimus and I, and perhaps Aristes soon. For it is a contradiction—a "contradiction," I say—that bodies can act on bodies. I shall prove this paradox, which appears so contrary to experience, so opposed to the tradition of the Philosophers, so incredible to the learned and to the ignorant. Answer me: can a body on its own move itself? I ask you to consult the idea you have of body; for always remember that we must judge things by the ideas which represent them and not at all by the sensations which we have of them.[2]

ARISTES. No, I do not see that bodies are able to move by themselves. But no more do I see that they cannot. I am in doubt of this.

THEODORE. You do well to doubt and stop short when you lack clear vision. But try to see clearly and dispel your doubt. Courage. Let us get on.

---

[1] See *Recherche de la Verité*, Book VI, last chapter [M II 420–449].

[2] Third, Fourth and Fifth Dialogues.

ARISTES. I am afraid of taking a false step for want of light. Enlighten me a little.

THEODORE. Consult clear ideas attentively, my dear Aristes. To attentive minds, they spread the light which you lack. Contemplate the archetype of bodies, intelligible extension. This represents them since it is in accordance with it that they have all been made. The idea is entirely luminous. Consult it, then. Do you not see clearly that bodies can be moved but that they cannot move themselves? You hesitate. Well then, let us suppose that this chair can move itself: Which way will it go? With what velocity? At what time will it take it into its head to move? You would have to give the chair an intellect and a will capable of determining itself. You would in short have to make a man out of your armchair. Otherwise, a power of moving itself would be of no use at all to it.

ARISTES. A man of my armchair! What a strange thought!

THEOTIMUS. Only too common and in fact the case, as Theodore realizes. Everyone who judges things from his own case or by sensations which he has of them rather than by the ideas which represent them makes of each object something resembling himself. Such a person makes God act like a man. He attributes to beasts what he senses in himself. To fire and the other elements, he assigns inclinations of which he has no other idea than the sensation he has of them. Thus, he humanizes all things. But do not stop at this point. Follow Theodore and answer him.

ARISTES. I do not think this chair can move by itself. But how do I know there is not some other body to which God has given the power of moving? Remember, Theodore, you have to prove that it is a contradiction that bodies act on one another.

VI. THEODORE. Well then, Aristes, I shall prove it to you. It is a contradiction for a body to be neither in motion nor at rest. For even God, all-powerful though He is, cannot create a body which is nowhere or does not have certain relations of distance with other bodies. A body is at rest when it has the same relation of distance to others, and it is in motion when this relation keeps changing. Now, it is evident that every body either changes or does not change its relation of distance. There is no middle ground. The two propositions, "It changes" and "It does not change," are contradictions. Hence, it is a contradiction that a body be neither in motion nor at rest.

ARISTES. That did not need proving.

THEODORE. Now it is the will of God that gives existence to bodies and to all creatures, the existence of which is certainly not necessary. As the same will that created them always subsists, they always exist; and were this will to cease (I speak to you of God according to our manner of conceiving), it is a necessity that bodies cease to exist. It is hence this same will that places bodies in motion or at rest since it is this will that gives them being and they cannot exist without being in motion or at rest. Note that God cannot do what is impossible or what contains a manifest contradiction. He cannot will what cannot be conceived. Hence, He cannot will that this chair exist without willing at the same time that it exist in some place or other and without His will putting it there, since you are unable to conceive that this chair exists and that it does not exist in some place, there or elsewhere.

ARISTES. Still, I seem to be able to think of a body without conceiving of it as in motion or at rest.

THEODORE. That is not what I am saying. You are able to think of a body in general and make what abstractions you will. I agree. That is what often deceives you. But, once again, I say to you that you are unable to conceive that a body exists and that it is not at the same time somewhere and that the relation it has with other bodies neither changes nor does not change and consequently that it is not either in motion or at rest. Hence, it is a contradiction that God make a body without making it in motion or at rest.

ARISTES. Oh well, Theodore, I grant you that. When God creates a body, He must at first place it in motion or at rest. But, once the instant of creation is past, this is no longer so: bodies are disposed by chance, or according to the law of the stronger.

VII. THEODORE. "The instant of creation past"! But, if that instant does not pass, then you are up against the wall, and you will have to give in. Now observe. God wills that there be a world. His will is all-powerful, and so the world is made. Let God no longer will that there be a world, and it is thereby annihilated. For the world certainly depends on the volitions of the Creator. If the world subsists, it is because God continues to will that the world exist. On the part of God, the conservation of creatures is simply their continued creation. I say, on the part of God who acts. For, on the part of creatures, there appears to be a difference since, in creation, they pass from nothing to being whereas, in conservation, they continue to be. But, in reality, creation does not pass away because, in God, conservation and creation are one and the same volition which consequently is necessarily followed by the same effects.

ARISTES. I understand your reasons, Theodore, but I am not convinced by them. The proposition "Let God no longer will that there be a world, and it is thereby annihilated" appears to me to be false. It seems to me not to be sufficient for the annihilation of the world that God no longer will that it exist, He would have to will positively that it no longer exist. There is no necessity of a volition when nothing is to be done. Thus, now that the world is made, let God leave it so, and it will always be.

VIII. THEODORE. You are not thinking, Aristes. You are making creatures independent. You judge God and His works by the works of men, men who are provided nature and do not make it. Your house subsists although your architect is dead. This is because its foundations are solid and it has no connection with the life of the person who built it. It depends on him in no way. But the ground of our being depends essentially on the Creator. Though the arrangement of certain stones depends in a sense on man's will in consequence of the action of natural causes, the product is not so dependent. But, as the universe is derived from nothing, it depends to such an extent on the universal Cause that, if God ceased to conserve it, it would necessarily revert to nothing. For God does not will, and indeed He cannot make, a creature independent of His volitions.

ARISTES. I admit that, between creatures and Creator, there is a relation, a connection, an essential dependence, Theodore. But could we not say that, to maintain the dependence of created beings, it is sufficient that God can annihilate them when He pleases?

THEODORE. Certainly not, my dear Aristes. What greater mark of independence than to subsist by itself and without support? Strictly speaking, your house does not depend on you. Why is that? Because it subsists without you. You can set fire to it whenever you will, but you do not sustain it. That is why, between you and it, there is no essential dependence. Thus, even if God is able to destroy creatures whenever He pleases, still, if they are able to subsist without the continual influence of the Creator, they are not essentially dependent on Him.

For you to be fully convinced of what I am saying, imagine for a moment that God is no more. The Universe, on your view, will not stop subsisting. For a cause which has no influence (*n'influe point*) is no more necessary for the production of an effect than a cause which is no more. That is evident. Now, on the supposition [that the universe subsists and God does not], you are unable to conceive that the world is essentially dependent on the Creator since the Creator is conceived as no longer existing. The supposition involves an impossibility, it is true. Yet the mind can join or separate things as it pleases to discover their relations. Hence, if bodies are essentially dependent on the Creator, for their subsistence they need to be sustained by His continual influence, by the efficacy of the same will which created them. If God merely ceases to will that they exist, it will follow necessarily—and precisely for this reason alone—that they will no longer exist. If they continued to exist though God no longer continued to will their existence, they would be independent and also, it should be noted, independent to such an extent that it would be impossible for God to destroy them. This is what I shall now prove to you.

IX. An infinitely wise God can will nothing which is not, so to speak, worthy of being willed: He can love nothing which is not lovable. Now there is nothing lovable about nothingness. Hence, it cannot be the object of divine volitions. Certainly nothingness does not have enough reality, as indeed it has none at all, to have some relation with the action of a God, with an action of infinite worth. Hence, God cannot will positively the annihilation of the Universe. Only creatures, through lack of power or error, can make nothingness the object of their volitions. The reason is that a certain object can be an obstacle to the realization of their desires, or so they suppose. But, when you have thought about it, you will see that there is nothing more evident than that an infinitely wise and all-powerful God cannot without contradiction deploy His power to do nothing! To do nothing! why that is to destroy His own work, not to correct disorders in it that He did not put there, but to annihilate natures which He has made. Thus, Aristes, on the supposition that, to annihilate the world, it is not sufficient for God to cease willing its existence—on the supposition that God must also will positively that it no longer exist: I hold the world is necessary and independent. For God could not destroy it without renouncing His attributes, and it is a contradiction that He should renounce them.

Do not, therefore, lessen the dependence of creatures lest you fall into the impiety of ruining it altogether. God can annihilate them whenever He pleases, as you say. But this is because He can cease willing what He freely willed. As He is entirely self-sufficient, He invincibly loves only His own substance. Though eternal and immutable, the will to create the world, as well as immanent operations, contain nothing of necessity. As God was able to form the decree to create the world in time, He was able, and is still able, to cease willing that the world exist, not because the enactment of His decree can be or not be, but because this immutable and eternal act is perfectly free and involves the eternal duration of created beings only *ex hypothesi* (*par supposition*). From all eternity God has willed, and to all eternity He will continue to will—or, to speak more accurately, God wills unceasingly though without variation, without succession, without necessity—everything He will do in the course of time. The enactment of His eternal decree, though simple and immutable, is necessary only because it is. It cannot not be only because it is. But it is only because God wills it. A man at the time of moving his arm is free not to move it although, on the supposition that he does move it, it is contradictory that he not move it. Analogously, as God wills at all times, yet without succession, what He wills, although His decrees are immutable, they do not cease to be perfectly free since they are necessary only, you will note, *ex hypothesi* (*par la force de la supposition*), only because God is immutable in His plans. But I am afraid I am digressing. Let us return to our subject. Are you now convinced that creatures are essentially dependent on the Creator, dependent to such an extent that they cannot subsist without His influence, that they cannot continue to exist unless God continues to will that they exist?

ARISTES. I have done everything I could to combat your reasons. But I give in. I have no answer to give you. The dependence of creatures is altogether different from what I thought.

X. THEODORE. Let us then recapitulate what has been said and draw some consequences from it. But take care that I do not draw consequences which are not clearly contained in the principle.

Creation does not pass: the conservation of creatures is on the part of God simply a continued creation, simply the same volition which subsists and operates unceasingly. Now, God cannot conceive, nor consequently will, that a body be nowhere or that it not have certain relations of distance with other bodies. Hence, God cannot will that this chair exist and, by this volition, create or conserve it without His placing it here or there or elsewhere. Hence, it is a contradiction that one body be able to move another. I say further: it is a contradiction that you should be able to move your chair. Even that is not enough. It is a contradiction that all the Angels and Demons joined together should be able to move a wisp of straw. The demonstration of this is clear. No power, however great we imagine it, can surpass or even equal the power of God. Now, it is a contradiction that God should will the existence of the chair yet not will that it exist somewhere and, by the efficacy of His volition, not put it there, not conserve it there, not create it there. Hence, no power can transport it where

God does not transport it, nor fix or stop it where God does not stop it, unless it is because God accommodates the efficacy of His action to the inefficacious action of his creatures. This is what needs to be explained in order to make reason agree with experience and provide the intellect with the greatest, the most fruitful, and the most necessary of principles; namely, that God communicates (*communique*) His power to creatures and unites them among themselves solely by virtue of the fact that He makes their modalities occasional causes of effects which He produces Himself—occasional causes, I say, which determine the efficacy of His volitions in consequence of general laws that He has prescribed for Himself to make His conduct bear the character of His attributes and spread throughout His work the uniformity of action necessary to bind together all the parts that compose it and to extricate it from the confusion and irregularity of a kind of chaos in which minds could never understand anything. I tell you this, my dear Aristes, to give you ardor and arouse your attention. Since what I have said about motion and rest in matter could well appear to you to be of little consequence, you might perhaps think that principles so minor and so simple could not lead you to the great and important truths of which you have already caught a glimpse and on which rests almost everything I have said to you up to now.

ARISTES. Do not be afraid that I will lose sight of you, Theodore. It seems to me I am following you quite closely, and you charm me so that I seem to be carried away. Courage, then. I shall be able to stop you if you pass too lightly over some places that are too difficult and too dangerous for me.

XI. THEODORE. Let us suppose then, Aristes, that God wills that there is a certain body on the floor, say, a ball. No sooner said than done. Nothing is more mobile than a sphere on a plane, yet all the powers imaginable cannot move it if God does not intervene. For once again, in so far as God wills to create or conserve the ball at point A or at whatever other point you please—and it is a necessity that he put it somewhere—no force will be able to make it leave that place. Do not forget this. It is our principle.

ARISTES. I believe it, this principle. It is only the Creator who can be the mover; only the one who gives being to bodies can put them in the places they occupy.

THEODORE. Very well. The moving force of a body is, then, simply the efficacy of the volition of God who conserves it successively in different places. Granting this, let us imagine that the ball is moved and that, in the line of its motion, it encounters another ball at rest: experience teaches us that the second ball will be moved without fail and in accordance with certain proportions that are always exactly observed. Now, it is not the first ball that moves the second. That is clear from the principle. One body could not move another without communicating to it some of its moving force (*lui communique de sa force mouvante*). Now, the moving force of a body in motion is simply the volition of the Creator who conserves it successively in different places. It is not a quality which belongs to the body. Nothing belongs to it other than its modalities; and modalities are inseparable from substances. Hence, bodies cannot move one

another, and their encounter or impact is only an occasional cause of the distribution of their motion. Since bodies are impenetrable, it is a kind of necessity
that God, who I suppose acts at all times with the same efficacy or quantity of
moving force, distributes, as it were, the moving force from the striking body to
the body struck and that He does so in proportion to the magnitude of the impact
yet in accordance with the law that, when two bodies collide, the stronger, or the
one that is transported with a greater moving force, must overcome the weaker
and make it rebound without receiving anything from it, that is, without receiving anything from the weaker. For a body that is perfectly hard, as I am now
supposing, cannot receive two impressions or two contrary motions in parts of
which it is composed. This can happen only in bodies that are soft or that are
elastic. But it is pointless at present to enter into detail about the laws of
motion.[3] It is sufficient for you to know that bodies cannot move themselves or
other bodies that they encounter, as Reason has shown us, and that there are
certain laws in accordance with which God moves them without fail, as we learn
from experience.

ARISTES. That seems to me to be incontestable. But what do you think,
Theotimus? You never contradict Theodore.

XII. THEOTIMUS. I have been convinced of these truths for a long time. Yet, as
you wish me to oppose Theodore's opinions, please resolve a little difficulty I
have. Here it is. I understand that a body cannot move itself. But, supposing that
it is in motion, I claim that it can move another body as true cause, as cause
between which and its effect there is a necessary connection. For, if we suppose
that God has not yet established laws for communication of motion, there will
certainly not yet be occasional causes. This being so, let body A be in motion
and, in its line of motion, let there be body B, which I suppose to be concave
and like a mold to body A: what will happen? Choose.

ARISTES. What will happen? Nothing. For, where there is no cause, there can
be no effect.

THEOTIMUS. What, nothing? Surely something new must happen. For either
body B will be moved on impact, or it will not.

ARISTES. It will not be moved.

THEOTIMUS. So far, so good. But what will become of body A on encountering B, Aristes? Either it will rebound, or it will not rebound. If it rebounds, we
shall have a new effect of which B is the cause. If it does not rebound, this will
be even worse; for then we shall have a force which is destroyed or at any rate
ineffectual (*sans action*). Hence, the impact of bodies is not an occasional cause
but a very real and very true cause, since there is a necessary connection
between the impact and whatever effect you choose. Thus . . . .

ARISTES. Just a minute, Theotimus. What are you proving? Given that bodies
are impenetrable, it is a necessity that, at the instant of impact, God make up

[3]See "Loix des communications des mouvemens" at the end of *Rech. de la Verité,* Vol. III, 1700
edition [M I 57–143]. [In earlier editions, Malebranche did enter into some detail, detail which he
came to think contained a mistake and chose to delete rather than to correct.]

His mind to choose between the alternatives you have proposed. That is all. I did not take that into consideration. You by no means prove that a body in motion is able, by means of something which belongs to it, to move a body it encounters. If God has not as yet established laws for the communication of motions, the nature of bodies, their impenetrability, will oblige Him to make laws which He judges appropriate; and He will opt for those which are simplest provided they suffice for the execution of the works which He wills to form from matter. But it is clear that impenetrability has no efficacy in itself and that it serves only to provide God, who treats things in accordance with their nature, with an occasion for diversifying His action without changing anything in His conduct.

Nevertheless, I am willing to say that a body in motion is the true cause of motion of the bodies it encounters, for there is no need to dispute over a word. But what is a body in motion? It is a body transported by divine action. The action which transports it can also transport the body it meets if this action is applied to it. Who doubts that? But this action, this moving force, does not belong to bodies at all. It is the efficacy of the will of the One who creates them and conserves them successively in different places. Matter is essentially movable. By its nature, it has a passive capacity of motion. But it does not have an active capacity, and it is in fact moved only by the continual action of the Creator. Thus, one body cannot move another by an efficacy which belongs to its nature. If bodies had in themselves the force of moving, the stronger would overpower those they encounter as efficient causes. But, as bodies are moved only by something other than themselves, their encounter is but an occasional cause which, because of their impenetrability, obliges the Mover or Creator to distribute His action. And, because God is bound to act in a simple and uniform way, He had to set Himself laws which are general, and the simplest possible, so that, when change was necessary, He changed as little as was possible and yet, by this behavior, He produced an infinity of different effects. That is how I understand matters, Theotimus.

Theotimus. You understand them very well.

XIII. Theodore. Perfectly well. We agree on the principle. Let us follow it a little further. It follows, Aristes, that by yourself you cannot move your arm, change place, situation, posture, do unto others either good or evil, make the least change in the universe. Here you are in the world without any power, as incapable of motion as a rock, dumb as a log, as it were. Your soul can be united to your body as closely as you please and be attached through it to all the bodies surrounding you, yet what advantage will you derive from this imaginary union? What will you do to move merely the end of your finger, to utter merely a one-syllable word? If, alas, God does not come to your aid, you will only make efforts in vain; you will only form desires that are without power. For, on a little reflection, do you really know just what you need do to pronounce the name of your best friend, to bend or straighten the finger you use most? Let us suppose that you do know what everyone does not know—what even certain learned men do not agree on—namely, that our arms can be moved only by means of animal spirits flowing through the nerves to the muscles, contracting the muscles, and drawing to them the bones to which they are attached. Let us suppose you know anatomy and the working of your machine as exactly as a clockmaker knows his own work. But remember in any event the principle that it is only the Creator of bodies who can be their mover. This principle is sufficient to stop—why do I say "stop"?—to annihilate all your alleged faculties. For animal spirits are after all bodies, however small they may be: they are just the subtlest part of the blood and the humors. Hence, God alone can move these small bodies. He alone knows how, and is able, to make them flow from the brain into the nerves, from the nerves to the muscles, and from one muscle to its antagonist—all of which is necessary for the movement of your members. Hence, notwithstanding a union of soul and body such as you choose to imagine, you are still motionless and dead unless God wills to attune His volitions to yours, His volitions, which are always efficacious, to your desires, which are always powerless. There is the unravelling of the mystery, my dear Aristes. Creatures are united by an immediate union to God alone. They depend essentially and directly only on Him. As they are all equally powerless, they do not mutually depend on one another. It can be said that they are united among themselves and even that they do depend on one another. I admit this, provided it is not understood according to vulgar ideas, provided we agree that it comes about only in consequence of the immutable and invariably efficacious volitions of the Creator, only in consequence of general laws which God has established and by which He regulates the ordinary course of His Providence. God willed that my arm move at the instant I will it. (I take for granted the necessary conditions.) His will is efficacious, it is immutable. It is the origin of my power and my faculties. He willed that I have certain sensations, certain emotions, when there are certain traces in my brain, certain movements of [animal] spirits. In short, He willed, and He wills unceasingly, that modalities of mind and body be reciprocal. This constitutes the union and natural dependence of the two parts of which we are composed. It consists exclusively in the mutual reciprocity of our modalities based on the unshakeable foundation of divine decrees, decrees which, by their efficacy, communicate to me the power that I have over my body and through it over others, decrees which, by their immutability, unite me to my body and through it to my friends, to my belongings, to everything surrounding me. I get nothing from my nature, nothing from that imaginary nature of the Philosophers; everything is from God and His decrees. God has joined all His works together, though He has not produced connecting entities in them. He has subordinated them among themselves without investing them with efficacious qualities. Those are vain pretentions of human pride, chimerical productions of the ignorance of Philosophers! They arise because, when men have been sensibly moved in the presence of bodies and when they have been internally affected by the sensation of their own efforts, they have not recognized the invisible operation of the Creator, the uniformity of His conduct, the fertility of His laws, the everpresent efficacy of His volitions, the infinite wisdom of His ordinary providence. Please no longer say, my dear Aristes, that your soul is united to your body more closely than to anything else. It is united immediately only to God alone, and His divine decrees are the indissoluble links among the parts of the Universe and the wonderful chain of subordination of all causes.

XIV. ARISTES. Ah, Theodore! How clear your principles are, how sound they are, how Christian! Yet how attractive and moving! I am entirely filled with them. So! God is Himself present in our midst, not as a simple spectator and observer of our good or bad actions, but as the principle of our society, the link of our friendship, the soul, so to speak, of the relations and discussions we have together. I am able to speak to you only through the efficacy of His power, I can affect or move you only through the motion which he communicates to me. I do not even know what dispositions of my vocal organs are required to utter what I unhesitatingly say. The working of these organs is beyond me. The variety of words, tones, cadences yields seemingly infinite detail. God knows this detail: He alone ordains the motion at the very instant of my desires. Yes, it is He who exhales the air which He also made me breathe. It is He who, through my organs, produces the air's shocks and vibrations. It is He who propagates it externally and who forms the words by which I get to your mind and pour into your heart what cannot be contained in mine. In fact, it is not I who breathe; I breathe in spite of myself. It is not I who speaks to you: I simply will to speak to you. But let my breathing depend on me, let me have exact knowledge of what I must do to explain myself, let me form the words and let me utter them. How would they get to you, how would they strike your ears, how move your brain, how affect your heart without the efficacy of the divine power which joins together the parts of the universe? Yes, Theodore, all of this is a necessary consequence of laws of the union of soul and body and laws of the communication of motion. All of this depends on the two principles of which I am convinced: that only the Creator of bodies can be their mover and that God communicates His power to us only through the establishment of certain general laws the efficacy of which we determine by our various modalities. Well, Theodore! Well, Theotimus! God alone is the bond of our society. Since He is its principle, let Him be its end. Let us not impose upon His power. Unfortunate are those who make it serve their criminal passions. Nothing is more sacred than power. Nothing is more divine. It is a kind of sacrilege to put it to profane uses. I now understand, this would be to make the just avenger of crimes serve iniquity. By ourselves we can do nothing. Hence, by ourselves we should not will anything. We can act only through the efficacy of divine power. Hence, we should will nothing other than what agrees with divine law. Nothing is more evident than these truths.

THEODORE. They are excellent consequences.

XV. THEOTIMUS. They are marvelous principles for Morality. But let us return to Metaphysics. Our souls are not united to our bodies in the way the Vulgar imagine. They are united immediately and directly to God alone. Only through the efficacy of His action are all three of us here face-to-face. "Face-to-face"! Rather, the three of us are united here in belief, are filled with the same truth, are animated—it seems to me—by a single spirit (*esprit*), inflamed as it were by the same ardor. As a consequence of laws of the communication of motion, God unites us together by way of our bodies. As a consequence of laws for the union of soul and body, He affects us with the same sensations. But how are we united to such a degree in mind, Aristes? Theodore utters certain words in your ears. This is just air struck by the vocal chords. God, as it were, transforms the air into words, into various sounds. He makes you hear the various sounds by way of modalities by which He affects you. But where do you get the sense of these words? What reveals to you and me the same truths which Theodore contemplates? If the air he moves in speaking does not contain the sounds which you hear, certainly it will not contain the truths which you understand.

ARISTES. I understand you, Theotimus. It is because we are each united to universal Reason which enlightens all intellects. I am more knowledgeable than you think. Theodore has already transported me to where you wish to take me. He persuaded me that there is nothing visible, nothing which can act on the mind and be revealed to it, other than the substance—intelligible as well as efficacious—of Reason. Yes, nothing created can be the immediate object of our knowledge. We see nothing in the material world inhabited by our bodies unless our minds, by attention, walk in another world and contemplate the beauties of an archetypal and intelligible world contained in Reason. As our bodies live on the earth and feed on the different fruits which it produces, our minds are nourished by the same truths which are contained in the intelligible and immutable substance of the divine Word. It follows in consequence of laws of the union of soul and body that the words Theodore utters in my ears tell me to be attentive to truths which he discovers in sovereign Reason. This turns my mind in the same direction as his. I see what he sees because I look where he looks. And, by words uttered in response to his, though his utterances and mine are both devoid of sense, I converse with him and with him enjoy a good which is common to us all. For we are all essentially united to Reason, united in such a way that, without it, we cannot enter into society with anyone.

THEOTIMUS. Your reply surprises me extremely, Aristes. How is it that, knowing all you have just told me now, you could reply to Theodore that we are united to our bodies more closely than to anything else?

ARISTES. This is because we say just what memory brings to mind, and abstract truths do not come to mind so naturally as what we have been told all our lives. When I have meditated as much as Theotimus, I shall no longer speak in this mechanical way, and I shall base my words on the replies of inner truth. I understand then today, and I shall not forget throughout my life, that we are united immediately and directly only to God. By the light of His wisdom, He makes us see the magnificence of His works, the model on which He forms them, the immutable artifice which controls their springs and motions; and, by the efficacy of His volitions, He unites us to our bodies and, through our bodies, to the bodies surrounding us.

XVI. THEODORE. You could add that, by the love which He has for Himself, He communicates to us the invincible ardor which we have for the good. But that is a matter we shall talk about another time. It is sufficient now for you to be convinced, fully convinced, that the mind can be united immediately and directly to God alone; that we can have relations with creatures only through the power of the Creator which is communicated to us solely in consequence of His laws; and that we can be joined together in society with Him only by means of Reason, which is consubstantial with Him. Once this is accepted, you see that it is of the utmost consequence for us to try to acquire some knowledge of the attributes of this Sovereign Being on whom we are dependent to so great an extent. Finally He acts in us necessarily in accordance with His nature (*selon ce qu'il est*). His way of acting should bear the character of His attributes. Not only should our duties be related to His perfections, but our conduct should be directed by His in order that we may take the right measures for executing our plans and find a combination of causes which furthers them. On this matter, faith and experience teach us many truths by the short method of authority and by proofs from sensation that are very pleasing and helpful. But all this does not now give us understanding: that must be the fruit and reward of our industry and application. Besides, since we are made to know and love God, it is clear that there is no occupation preferable to meditation on the divine perfections, meditation which should inspire us with love and order every duty of a rational creature.

ARISTES. I understand, Theodore, that the worship which God requires of minds is a spiritual worship. It is for Him to be known and to be loved, and it is for us to form judgments of Him worthy of His attributes and to direct every movement of our hearts by His volitions. For God is mind [esprit], and He wants to be worshipped in mind and in truth. But I must confess I am terribly afraid of forming judgments of the divine perfections that dishonor them. Is it not better to honor them by silence and admiration and to engage solely in the search for truths which are less sublime, and more in proportion to the capacity of our minds?

THEODORE. What do you mean, Aristes? You are not thinking. We are made to know and love God, and yet you do not want us to think of Him, to speak of Him, and—I might also say—for us to worship Him! You say we ought to honor Him by silence and admiration. Indeed we should, by respectful silence which contemplation of His greatness imposes on us; by religious silence to which the splendor of His majesty reduces us; by, as it were, forced silence which derives from our powerlessness and which does not have as its principle the criminal negligence of a disordered curiosity to know, instead of Him, objects far less worthy of our attention. What will you admire in the Deity if you know nothing of Him? How will you love Him if you do not contemplate Him? How will we inform one another in love if we banish from our discussions Him whom you have acknowledged as the soul of our association, as the bond of our small society? Surely, Aristes, the more you know the Sovereign Being, the more you will admire His infinite perfections. So do not be afraid of thinking too much of Him or of speaking in a way that is unworthy of Him provided that faith guides you. Do not be afraid of false judgments about Him provided your judgments are always in conformity with the notion of infinitely perfect Being. You will not dishonor the divine perfections by judgments unworthy of them provided you never judge them from your own case, provided you do not give the Creator the imperfections and limitations of creatures. Think of them then, Aristes. I shall think of them for my part, and I hope Theotimus will do the same. This is necessary for the development of the principles which I think we should discuss. Until tomorrow, then, at the usual time; for it is time now for me to leave.

ARISTES. Goodbye, Theodore. If you please, Theotimus, the three of us will meet at the appointed hour.

THEOTIMUS. I am going with Theodore. But I shall return with him as you wish. . . . Well, Theodore, how altered Aristes is! He is attentive, he no longer jokes, he is not so preoccupied with manners, in short, he listens to reason and is sincerely submissive to it.

THEODORE. True. But his prejudices return to get in his way and introduce some confusion in his ideas. Reason and prejudices speak turn about from his mouth. At times truth makes him speak, and at times memory takes its turn. But his imagination no longer dares to rebel. That indicates a good foundation and gives me every hope.

THEOTIMUS. You want prejudices to go away like old clothes we never think of, Theodore! It seems to me we have been like Aristes. We are not born Philosophers, we become Philosophers. We shall have to go over the great principles incessantly so that, by thinking of them so often, Aristes' mind will take possession of them and, when needed, they will take over as a matter of course.

THEODORE. That is what I have been trying to do up to now. But it is an effort for him, for he loves detail and variety of thoughts. Please always stress the necessity of fully understanding principles, so as to arrest the vivacity of his mind; and please do not forget to meditate on the topic of our discussion.

From
EIGHTH DIALOGUE

✤

God and His attributes

THEODORE. Well then, Aristes, how do you feel? We must know what state you are in so that we can accommodate what we have to say to you to your state.

ARISTES. I have gone over in my mind what you said to me thus far, and I confess I have not been able to resist the evidence of the proofs on which your principles are supported. Yet, wishing to meditate on the topic of the divine attributes which you proposed for us, I found so many difficulties in it that I was put off. I was going to tell you that the matter is too sublime, or too abstract, for me. I could not get to it, and I could get no hold on it.

THEODORE. What! you do not want to say anything to us?

ARISTES. It is because I haven't anything good to say, nothing that satisfies me. I shall listen to the two of you if you please.

THEODORE. That does not please us at all. But, since you do not wish to tell us what you thought, at least follow me and tell me your opinion of what has come to my mind.

ARISTES. Willingly. But Theotimus?

THEODORE. Theotimus will be the judge of the little differences which may well arise from the diversity of our ideas.

THEOTIMUS. "The judge!" What do you mean? It is for Reason to preside among us and decide absolutely.

THEODORE. I mean, Theotimus, you will be subaltern judge dependent on Reason and you may decide only according to the laws which it prescribes to you as to us. Let us lose no time, please. Just compare what we shall say to each other with the replies of internal Truth in order to warn, and set right, the one who goes astray. Come, Aristes. Follow me and stop me only when I pass over difficult places too lightly.

I. By "Deity" we all understand the Infinite, Being without restriction, infinitely perfect Being. Now nothing finite can represent the infinite. Hence, to think of God is sufficient to know that He exists. Do not be surprised if Aristes allows me this, Theotimus. For he already agreed to it before you were here.[1]

ARISTES. Yes, Theotimus, I am convinced that nothing finite can have enough reality to represent the infinite—that, when we see the finite, we cannot discover in it an infinite which it does not contain. Yet I am certain I see the infinite. Hence, the infinite exists since I see it and I can see it only in itself. As my mind is finite, the knowledge I have of the infinite is finite. I do not understand it, I do not encompass (*mesure*) it; I am also quite certain I shall never be able to encompass it. Not only do I find no end in it, I see in addition that it has none. In short, the perception I have of the infinite is limited; but the objective reality in which my mind, so to speak, gets lost has no limits. It is now a matter impossible for me to doubt.

THEOTIMUS. I do not doubt it either.

THEODORE. Granting this, it is clear that, as the word "God" is only a shortened expression for infinitely perfect Being, it is a contradiction that we might be mistaken when we attribute to God only what we see clearly pertains to infinitely perfect Being. For let us admit we are never mistaken when we judge God's works solely in accordance with what we see clearly and distinctly in their ideas since, God having modelled them on these ideas which are their archetype, it cannot be that the ideas do not naturally represent their nature. There is all the more reason, then, that we shall never be mistaken provided we attribute to God only what we see clearly and distinctly belongs to infinitely perfect Being, what we discover, not in an idea which is distinguished from God, but in His substance itself. Let us then attribute to God or infinitely perfect Being all perfections, however incomprehensible they may seem to us, provided we are certain of their being realities or true perfections—realities and perfections, I say, which do not resemble nothingness, which are not limited by imperfections or limitations similar to those of creatures. Take note of this.

II. God is infinitely perfect Being. Hence, God is independent. Think of this, Aristes, and stop me only when I say something you do not see clearly to be a perfection and belong to infinitely perfect Being. God is independent. Hence, He is immutable.

ARISTES. "God is independent. Hence, He is immutable"! Why immutable?

THEODORE. Because there cannot be an effect or change without a cause. Now God is independent of the efficacy of causes. Hence, if a change occurred in God, it would be He who is the cause of it. Now, though God is the cause or principle of His volitions and decrees, He did not at any time produce a change in Himself. For His decrees, though perfectly free, are themselves eternal and immutable, as I have already told you.[2] God made these decrees, or rather He fashions them unceasingly on eternal Wisdom, which is the inviolable rule of His volitions. And, although the effects of these decrees are infinite and produce thousands upon thousands of changes in the universe, the decrees are at all times

[1]Second Dialogue.

[2]Preceding [Seventh] Dialogue [Section IX].

the same. This is because the efficacy of these immutable decrees is determined to action only by the circumstances of the causes which are called natural and which I believe we ought to call "occasional," for fear of encouraging the dangerous prejudice of a "nature" or efficacy which is distinguished from the will of God and His omnipotence.

ARISTES. I do not understand all this too well. God is free and indifferent, for instance, with respect to the movement of a certain body or whatever effect you please. If He is indifferent, He can produce that effect or not produce it. The effect is indeed a consequence of His decrees, I agree. But it is certain that God can *not* produce it. Hence, He can *not* will to produce it. Hence, God is not immutable since He can change His will and not will tomorrow what He wills today.

THEODORE. You do not remember what I told you in our last discussion, Aristes.[3] God is free and indeed indifferent with regard to thousands upon thousands of effects. He can change His will in the sense that He is indifferent to willing or not willing a certain effect. But note: now that you are seated, can you be standing? You can absolutely; but *ex hypothesi* (*par la supposition*) you cannot. For you cannot be standing and seated at the same time. You must understand that, in God, there is no succession of thoughts and volitions—that, by an eternal and immutable act, He knows everything and wills everything that He wills. God wills, with a perfect freedom and a total indifference, to create the world. He wills to make decrees and establish simple and general laws in order to govern it in a way that bears the character of His attributes. But, these decrees posited, they cannot be changed—not that they are necessary absolutely but are so *ex hypothesi*. Take note: it is simply that they are posited and that, when God made them, He knew so well what He was doing that they cannot be revoked. For, though some of them He made [only] for a time, it is not that He changed His mind and will when the time comes; but rather one and the same act of His will refers to differences in time which are contained in His eternity. So God does not change, and cannot change His thoughts, His designs, His volitions. He is immutable: this is one of the perfections of His nature. And nonetheless He is perfectly free in everything He does outside (Himself). He cannot change because what He wills He wills without succession by a simple and invariable act. But He can *not* will it because He wills freely what He does in fact will.

ARISTES. I shall think about what you are telling me, Theodore. Let us go on. I believe that God is immutable. It appears evident to me that it is a perfection not to be subject to change. That is enough for me. Even if I should not be able to reconcile God's immutability with His freedom, I believe Him to possess these two attributes since He is infinitely perfect.

III. THEOTIMUS. Permit me to propose a small problem for you, Theodore. You just said that the efficacy of God's immutable decrees is determined to action only by circumstances of causes which are called natural and which we

---

[3]Section IX [Seventh Dialogue].

call occasional. Those are your words. But tell me, what will happen to miracles? The impact of bodies, for example, is the occasional cause of the communication of motion from striking body to body struck. But will God not be able to suspend the effect of the general law of the communication of motion in a particular case? and has He not often suspended it?

THEODORE. Once for all, my dear Aristes. . . . For do I not see it is because of you that Theotimus wants further explanation from me?—he is afraid you did not get my thought. Once for all, Aristes, when I say that God always follows the general laws which He has prescribed, I speak only of His ordinary and general providence. I do not exclude miracles or effects which do not follow His general laws. But besides—and now it is to you I am speaking, Theotimus—when God performs a miracle and does not act in accordance with the general laws that are known to us, I claim that either He acts in accordance with other general laws which are unknown to us, or what He does then is determined at that time by certain circumstances which He had in view from all eternity when He enacts that simple, eternal, invariable act which contains both the general laws of His ordinary providence and also exceptions to these very laws. But these circumstances should not be called occasional causes in the same sense that, for example, impact of bodies is the occasional cause of the communication of motion, since God did not make general laws to regulate the efficacy of His volitions uniformly on the occurrence of these circumstances. In the exceptions to the general laws, God acts sometimes one way and sometimes another although invariably in accordance with what is required of Him by that one of His attributes which is, so to speak, most valuable to him at the time. That is to say, if what He owes then to His justice is of greater consideration than what He owes to His wisdom or to all His other attributes, He will follow the direction of His justice in the exception. For God never acts except according to His nature, to honor His divine attributes, to satisfy what He owes to Himself. For He is to Himself principle and end of all His volitions, whether He punishes us or is merciful to us or rewards in us His own gifts, the merits which we have acquired through His grace.

From
NINTH DIALOGUE

why God created the world the way he did

✤

IX. THEODORE. We must try to understand the principles that are most general, Aristes. For then everything else follows of itself, everything unfolds to the mind with order and with a wonderful clarity. Let us then observe again in the notion of infinitely perfect Being what God's plans can be. I do not claim that we can discover the detail of His plans; but perhaps we shall discern what there is of a more general nature, and you will see subsequently that the little we have discovered of them will be of great use to us. Do you think then that God wishes to make the most beautiful and most perfect work possible?

ARISTES. Yes, without doubt. For the more perfect His work is, the more it will express the qualities and perfections in which God prides Himself. This is evident from everything you have just told us.

THEODORE. The Universe then is the most perfect that God can make? But really! So many monsters, so many disorders, the great number of impious men—does all this contribute to the perfection of the Universe?

ARISTES. You perplex me, Theodore. God wishes to make a work that is the most perfect possible. For, the more perfect it is, the more it will honor Him. This appears evident to me. Yet I understand that the work would be more accomplished if it were free of thousands upon thousands of defects which disfigure it. Here is a contradiction that stops me quite short. It seems that God did not accomplish His plan, or that He did not adopt the plan most worthy of His attributes.

THEODORE. This results from your not having yet fully understood the principles. You have not meditated sufficiently on the notion of infinitely perfect Being that contains them. You do not know how to make God act according to His nature.

THEOTIMUS. But, Aristes, may it not be that the disorders of nature, the monsters, also the impious men, are the shadows in a picture which give force to the work and relief to the figures?

ARISTES. That thought has an indescribable something which pleases the imagination, but the mind is not satisfied with it. For I understand well enough that the Universe would be more perfect if there were nothing disordered in any of the parts composing it, yet there is almost none in which there is not some defect.

THEOTIMUS. Then it is because God does not will that His work be perfect.

ARISTES. It is definitely not that either. For God cannot will positively and directly irregularities which disfigure His work and express none of the perfections which He possesses and on which He prides Himself. That seems to me evident. God permits disorder, but He does not make it, He does not will it.

THEOTIMUS. "God *permits.*" I really do not understand that expression. Whom does God permit to freeze the vines and destroy the harvest that He made grow? Why does he permit the occurrence in His work of monsters which He does not make and does not will? What then! Is it that the Universe is not such as God willed it?

ARISTES. No, for the Universe is not such as God made it.

THEOTIMUS. That may be true with regard to disorders that have slipped in through the bad use of freedom. For God did not make impious men: He permitted men to become so. I understand this, though I do not know the reasons for it. But certainly it is only God who makes the monsters.

ARISTES. They are strange creatures, these monsters, if they do not do honor to Him who gives them being. Do you know why, Theotimus, God covers the whole countryside with flowers and fruit today and will ravage it with frost or hail tomorrow?

THEOTIMUS. Because the countryside will be more beautiful in its sterility than in its fecundity, though that does not suit us. We often judge the beauty of God's works by the utility we receive from them, and we make mistakes.

ARISTES. Still it is better to judge their beauty by their utility than by their disutility. What a beautiful thing, a country desolated by tempest!

THEOTIMUS. Quite beautiful. A country inhabited by sinners ought to be in desolation.

ARISTES. If the storm spared the lands of good men, you would perhaps be right. It would be even more fitting to deny rain to the field of a brute than to make his wheat germinate and grow in order to destroy it by hail. That would surely be the shorter way. But it is often however the less guilty who are the more maltreated. What apparent contradictions in God's behavior! Theodore has already given me the principles to dispel these contradictions. But I have understood them so badly that I no longer remember them. If, Theotimus, you do not wish to put me on the right track (for I see that you are amused by the predicament in which I find myself), let Theodore speak.

THEOTIMUS. That is fair.

X. THEODORE. You see, Aristes, that it is not enough to have caught a glimpse of the principles. They have to be well understood so that they will be present to the mind when needed. Listen then, since Theotimus is unwilling to tell you what he perfectly well knows.

You are not mistaken in thinking that, the more perfect a work is, the more it expresses the perfections of the workman, that it does him all the more honor as the perfections which it expresses are the more pleasing to the person who possesses them, and that God thus wants to make His work the most perfect that is possible. But you grasp only half of the principle, and this is what leaves you in a predicament. God wants His work to honor Him: you understand that. But note: God does not want His ways to dishonor Him. This is the other half of the principle. God wants His action, as well as His work, to bear the character of His attributes. Not satisfied that the Universe honor Him by its excellence and its beauty, He wants His ways to glorify Him by their simplicity, their fecundity, their universality, their uniformity, by all the characteristics expressing qualities which He glories in possessing.

So do not suppose that God willed absolutely to make the work which is the most perfect that is possible; rather, He willed to make the one which is most perfect in relation to the ways which are most worthy of Him. For what God in His plans wills simply, directly, absolutely is always to act in the most divine manner possible; and that is to make His action, as well as His work, bear the character of His attributes: it is to act exactly according to His nature and according to His whole nature. From all eternity, God has seen all possible works and all possible ways of producing each of them; and, as He acts only for His glory, only according to His nature, He determined to will the work that could be produced and preserved in ways which, in conjunction with that work, would do Him more honor than any other work produced in any other way. He formed the plan which had more of the character of His attributes, which expressed more exactly the qualities that He possesses and prides Himself in possessing. Latch onto this principle, my dear Aristes, for fear it escapes you. For, of all principles, it is perhaps the most fruitful.

Once again, do not suppose that God ever forms a plan blindly, that is, without relating it to the ways necessary for its execution. That is the way men act, who often regret their decisions because of difficulties which they find are involved in them. Nothing is difficult for God. But bear in mind that all things are not equally worthy of Him. His ways must bear the character of His attributes, as well as His work. God must therefore take into consideration ways as well as works. It is not enough that His work honor Him by its excellence; it is necessary in addition that His ways glorify Him by their Divinity. Suppose that a world more perfect than ours could be created and conserved but only by ways which are reciprocally less perfect, with the result that, as it were, the expression of the divine qualities by this new world and these new ways would be less than that of ours. I have no fear of saying that God is too wise, He loves His glory too much, He acts too exactly in accordance with His nature, for Him to be able to prefer this new world to the Universe that He created. For God is indifferent in His plans only when they are equally wise, equally divine, of equal glory to Him, equally worthy of His attributes, only when the proportion of beauty of the work and simplicity of ways is exactly equal. When the proportion is not equal, although God can not act at all because he is sufficient unto Himself, He cannot choose and take the lesser course. He can not act: but He cannot act except in due course (*inutilement*) nor multiply His ways unless He increases proportionally the beauty of His work. His wisdom prevents Him from following, among all possible plans, any but the wisest. [The love which He bears for Himself does not allow Him to choose one which does not honor Him the most.]

XI. ARISTES. I get your principle, Theodore. God acts only according to His nature, only in a manner which bears the character of His attributes, only for the glory which He finds simply in the relation of His work and His ways taken conjointly to the perfections which He possesses and glories in possessing. It is the magnitude of this relation that God considers in the formation of His plans. For there we have the principle. God can act only according to His nature, can will absolutely and directly only His glory. If the defects of the Universe we inhabit diminish this relation, then the simplicity, the fruitfulness, the wisdom of the ways or laws God follows add more to it. A more perfect world but one produced in ways which are less simple and less fruitful would not bear the character of the divine attributes as much as ours. This is why the world is filled with the impious, with monsters, with disorders of every variety. God could convert all men, prevent all disorders. But He must not on that account disturb the simplicity and uniformity of His conduct. For He is bound to honor Himself by the wisdom of His ways, as well as by the perfection of His creatures. He does not permit monsters; it is He who makes them. But He makes them only in order to avoid changing anything in His conduct, only out of respect for the generality of His ways, only to follow exactly the natural laws which He has established, laws which He has established however not because of the monstrous effects they would produce but for effects which are more worthy of His wisdom and His goodness. This is why it can be said that He "permits" them, though it is in fact He who produces them. For He wills them only indirectly, only because they are a natural consequence of His laws.

THEODORE. How readily you draw your consequences!

ARISTES. That is because the principle is clear; it is because it is fruitful.

THEODORE. This principle seems at first, Aristes, to have no solidity because of its generality. But, when we follow it closely, it so moves us, and moves us so readily by the number of astonishing truths which it reveals, that we are captivated by it. You can learn from this that the most general principles are the most fruitful. They appear at first as mere chimeras. It is their generality that is the cause of this, for the mind counts as nothing what does not affect it. But hold fast to these principles if you can and follow them: they will give you a good view of the country in a short time.

ARISTES. I get a feeling of that when I meditate a little on what you are telling me, Theodore; and even now, without any effort of mind, I seem to see all at once in your principle the explanation of a number of difficulties which I have always had about God's conduct. I understand that all the effects which contradict one another, the works which war with and destroy one another, the disorders which disfigure the Universe, that all this indicates no contradiction in the cause that governs it, no defect of understanding, no lack of power, but a prodigious fruitfulness and a perfect uniformity in the laws of nature.

THEODORE. Not so fast, Aristes; for we shall explain all this more exactly later on.

XII. ARISTES. I even see how the reason for men's predestination is necessarily contained in your principle. I used to believe that God had chosen certain individuals from all eternity because He so willed it, with no reason for His choice either on His part or on ours, and that afterward He consulted His wisdom for means for sanctifying them and leading them surely to Heaven. But I now understand that I was mistaken. God does not form His plans blindly without relating them to means. He is wise in the formation of His decrees, as well as in their execution. There are in Him reasons for the predestination of the elect. He does so because the future Church, formed in the ways God employs for it, does Him more honor than any other Church formed in any other way. For God can act only for His glory, only in a manner that best conveys the character of His attributes. God did not predestinate either us nor even our divine Head because of our natural merits, but for reasons furnished Him by His inviolable Law, by immutable Order, by the necessary relation of perfections which are contained in His substance. He willed to unite His Word to a certain nature, and to predestinate in His Son certain individuals, because His wisdom indicated to Him such treatment of them for His own glory. Am I in fact following your grand principle, Theodore?

THEODORE. Quite well. But are you not afraid of going too far into Theology? You are already in the thick of the greatest mysteries.

ARISTES. Let us return. For it is not for me to penetrate these mysteries.

THEOTIMUS. You do well to return quickly, Aristes. For St. Augustine, the great Doctor of grace, does not want us to look for reasons for the choice God makes among men. Predestination is completely free, and the reason why God takes certain ones and leaves others is that He is merciful to whom He pleases to be merciful.

ARISTES. What, Theodore! Does St. Augustine claim that God does not consult His wisdom in the formation of His plans but only in their execution?

THEODORE. No, Aristes. But apparently Theotimus explains St. Augustine along lines that certain men have taken in their thinking. The sacred Doctor, writing against the heretics of his time, was rejecting a bad reason which the heretics gave for God's choice and the distribution of His grace. But he was always ready to consider reasons which are in the Analogy of Faith and do not destroy the freedom of grace. Here in short is the reasoning of these heretics. It is good you know it and be able to answer it. God wills that all men be saved and arrive at knowledge of the truth. Hence, they can all be saved by their own efforts (*forces naturelles*). But, if this is not possible without the help of internal grace, as the more moderate held, we must then see whom God will give it to. God makes a choice of some rather than others. That is all very well, but at least His choice must be rational. Now, it is a common notion that he who chooses the worse chooses badly. Hence, if God does not bestow His grace equally on all, if He makes a choice, He must choose the better, or the less wicked over the more wicked. For there can be no doubt that the choice He makes of some rather than others is wise and rational. There is in Him no partiality toward any person. It is absolutely necessary therefore that the reason for His choice in the distribution of His grace is to be found in the good use that we can still make of our own efforts (*forces naturelles*). It is up to us to will, to desire our cure, to believe in the Mediator, to implore His mercy, in short to make a start, and God will come to our aid. Through good use of our free will, we will merit God's bestowing His grace on us.

ARISTES. These people reason well.

THEODORE. Perfectly well, but from false ideas. They did not consult the notion of infinitely perfect Being. They made God act as men do. For, mark you, why do you think God makes it rain?

ARISTES. To make the lands we cultivate fertile.

THEODORE. We need only sow or plant a field then in order for it to rain there. For, as God does not make it rain equally on all lands, as He makes a choice, He must choose rationally and make it rain on lands which have been sown rather than on others, rather than on sand and on sea. By means of this analogy, find the fallacy in the reasoning of these enemies of grace. But do not nitpick if you please.

ARISTES. I understand, Theodore. Whether we cultivate lands or let them lie fallow, it rains on them neither more nor less. This is because it rains ordinarily only in consequence of the general laws of nature according to which God conserves the Universe. In like manner, the reason for the distribution of grace does not derive from our own merits (*merites naturels*). God bestows primary grace (*premiere graces*) only in consequence of certain general laws.[14] For God does not act as particular causes or limited intellects do. The reason for His choice comes from the wisdom of His laws, and the wisdom of His laws from the relation they have with His attributes, from their simplicity, from their fecundity, in short from their Divinity. The choice which God makes of men in the distribution of His grace is therefore rational and perfectly worthy of God's wisdom, though it is not based either on a difference of natures nor on an inequality of merits.

THEODORE. You have done it, Aristes. In a few words you have overthrown the firmest support of Pelagianism. A man who waters the sands or carries water needed for his field to the sea would not be wise. Yet this is just what God does in consequence of His laws, and, so doing, He acts most wisely, divinely. This is sufficient to silence those proud heretics who want to teach God to make a wise and rational choice among men.

Well now, Theotimus, will you go on being afraid of Aristes falling into the precipice which St. Augustine fears—and with reason—for those who look to their own merits for the cause of their election? Aristes wants the distribution of grace to be entirely gratuitous. Let us not be concerned on his account. Rather, let us pity certain others you know of who claim that God chooses His elect out of sheer goodness toward them, without wisdom and reason on His part. For it is a horrible sacrilege to believe that God is not wise in the formation of His plans

---

[14]See Twelfth Dialogue, XVI ff. *Traité de la Nature & de la Grace*, Discourse II [M V 65–116]. *Réponse à la Dissert. de M. Arn.*, Ch. 7, 8, 9, 10, 11, etc. [M VII 512 ff.].

as well as in their execution. Predestination to grace is gratuitous on our side (*de notre part*). Grace is not distributed according to our merits, as St. Augustine maintains, following St. Paul and all the Church; but it is directed by a law to which God makes no exceptions. For God made a plan containing the predestination of certain individuals rather than a number of others, because there is no plan wiser than this, none more worthy of His attributes. This is what your friends were unable to understand.

XIII. THEOTIMUS. What Theodore! that we of course strike the reef of judging God from our own case? We all like independence; it is a kind of servitude for us to submit to Reason, a kind of lack of power not to be able to do what it forbids. Thus, we are afraid of making God impotent by dint of making Him wise. But God is His own wisdom. Sovereign Reason is co-eternal and consubstantial with Him. He necessarily loves it; and, though He is obliged to follow it, He remains independent. [Everything God wills is wise and rational, not because God is above reason, not because what He wills is just simply and solely because He wills it, but because He cannot belie Himself, cannot will anything that does not conform to His law, to the immutable and necessary Order of the divine perfections.]

THEODORE. To be sure, Theotimus, we overturn everything if we claim that God is above reason and that He has no other rule in His plans than simply His will. That false principle casts darkness so thick that it confounds the good with the bad, the true with the false, and makes everything a chaos in which the mind no longer knows anything. St. Augustine proved original sin invincibly by the disorders we experience in ourselves. Man suffers, hence, he is not innocent. Mind depends on body; hence man is corrupt, he is not such as God made him. God cannot subject the more noble to the less noble, for Order does not allow it. What conclusions these are for those who are not afraid to say that God's will is the sole rule of His actions! They have only to say that God so willed it; that it is our self-love which makes us find the pain we suffer unjust; that it is our pride which takes offence at the mind being subject to the body; that, since God willed these alleged disorders, it is sacrilege to appeal to Reason regarding them, as God's will does not recognize Reason as the rule of its conduct. According to this principle, the Universe is perfect because God willed it. Monsters are works as accomplished as other things, according to God's plans. It is good to have eyes so situated in our heads, but they would just as wisely have been placed anywhere else had God put them there. Thus we turn the world upside down, we make a chaos of it, and it will still be equally admirable, since all its beauty consists in conformity with the divine will, which is not bound to conform to Order. But that will is unknown to us! Hence, it follows that all the beauty of the Universe disappears in light of this great principle, this principle that God is superior to the Reason which enlightens all minds, and that God's mere will of itself is the unique rule of His actions.

ARISTES. My, Theodore, how all your principles hang together! I also understand from what you are telling me that it is in God and an immutable Order that we see beauty, truth, justice, since we have no fear of criticizing His work, of noting defects in it, and of even concluding from this that it is corrupt. It is necessary then that the immutable Order which we see in part is the very law of God, inscribed in His substance in characters eternal and divine, since we have no fear of judging His conduct by the knowledge we have of this law. ⸢We are unhesitatingly certain that man is not such as God made him, that his nature is corrupt, that, in creating him, God could not subject mind to body. Are we impious or foolhardy to judge in this way what God must or must not do? Not at all. Rather, we would be either impious or blind if we were to suspend our judgment on these matters. That is because, Theodore, we do not judge God by our authority, but by the sovereign authority of the divine law.⸥

THEODORE. There we have a reflection worthy of you, my dear Aristes. Do not forget then to study this Law, since it is in this sacred Code of immutable Order that judgments of such importance are to be found.

From
TWELFTH DIALOGUE

❖

XI. ARISTES. It seems to me, Theodore, that you consider the Wisdom of Providence solely in the establishment of general laws and in the linkage of causes with their effects, letting all creatures act according to their own nature, the free freely and the necessary in accordance with the power which they have in consequence of the general laws. You want me to admire and adore the impenetrable profundity of God's foreknowledge in the infinitely infinite combinations which He necessarily made in order to choose from among an infinity of ways of producing the Universe that one which He had to follow in order to act in the most divine way possible. Certainly, Theodore, this is the most beautiful part of Providence, but it is not the most acceptable. This infinite foreknowledge is the foundation of the generality and uniformity of action that conveys the character of Wisdom and the immutability of God; but this does not convey, it seems to me, the character of His goodness toward men nor the severity of His justice against the wicked. It is not possible that, by general Providence, God avenges us of those who do some injustice nor that He provides for all our needs. And how are we to be satisfied when we are lacking something? Thus, Theodore, I admire your Providence, but I am not very satisfied with it. It is excellent for God but not too good for us, for I want a God who provides for all His creatures.

THEODORE. He does provide for them Aristes, very abundantly. Do you want me to display the good deeds of the Creator?

ARISTES. I know that every day God does thousands of things for us. It seems that the whole Universe exists only for us.

THEODORE. What more do you want?

ARISTES. That we lack nothing. God made all creatures for us; yet a certain person does not have bread. A Providence which would provide an equal supply to all natures that are equal or would distribute good and evil exactly according to merits would be a true Providence. What good is an infinite number of stars? What does it matter to us that the motions of the Heavens are so well ordered? God should leave all that and think a little more about us. The earth is devastated by the injustice and malignity of its inhabitants. God should make Himself feared; it seems He does not interfere in the particularity (*détail*) of our affairs. The simplicity and generality of His ways brings this thought to my mind.

THEODORE. I understand, Aristes; you are assuming the part of those who do not want Providence and who think that here below it is chance that makes and rules everything. And I understand how, for this reason, you want to dispute the generality and uniformity of God's action in the governance of the world because this conduct is not fitted to our needs or our inclinations. But please note that I am reasoning from established facts and from the idea of infinitely perfect Being. For after all the sun rises indifferently on the good and on the wicked. Often it scorches the lands of good men, while it makes those of the impious fertile. [In short, men are not miserable in proportion to their guilt. And this is what must be reconciled with a Providence worthy of infinitely perfect Being.]

Hail ravages the crops of a good man, Aristes. Either this unfortunate effect is a natural result of general laws or God produces it by special Providence. If God produces this effect by special Providence, so far is He from providing for all that He positively wills and also brings it about that the best man in the country lacks bread. It is therefore far better to maintain that this sad effect is a natural result of general laws. And this is also what we commonly mean when we say that God permitted a certain misfortune. But in addition you agree that to govern the world by general laws is action that is fine and great, worthy of the divine attributes. You maintain only that it does not sufficiently convey the character of God's paternal goodness toward the good and of the severity of His justice toward the wicked. This is because you do not take heed of the misery of good men and the prosperity of the impious. For, things being as we see they are, I submit to you that a special Providence on the part of God would in no way convey the character of His goodness and His justice, since very often the righteous are overwhelmed by ills and the wicked are laden with goods. But, on the supposition that God's conduct must convey the character of His wisdom as well as His goodness and His justice, although goods and evils are not now proportioned to the merits of men, I find no harshness in His general Providence. For I submit to you first that, from an infinity of possible combinations of causes with their effects, God has chosen the one which most happily reconciled the physical with the moral and that that hailstorm, which it was foreseen was to fall on the land of a certain good man, was not from God's vantage point one of the motives for making His choice, but rather that the hail which He foresaw should fall on the land of a wicked man. I say one of his "motives". Note the signification of this term. [For, if God afflicts the just, it is because he wishes to try them and make them deserve their reward. There truly is His motive.] I reply to you in the second place that, all men being sinners, none merits God's abandoning the simplicity and generality of His ways in order at present to proportion goods and evils to their merits and their demerits, that sooner or later God will render to each according to his deeds, at least on the day when He will come to judge the living and the dead and enact general laws of punishment which will last eternally.

XII. Yet, Aristes, do not suppose I am claiming that God never acts by special volitions and that all he does now is follow the natural laws which He established at first. I am claiming only that God never abandons the simplicity of His ways or the uniformity of His conduct without weighty reasons. For, the more general Providence is, the more it conveys the character of the divine attributes.

ARISTES. But when does He have these great reasons? Perhaps he never has them.

THEODORE. God has these great reasons when the glory which he can derive from the perfection of His work counterbalances that which He would receive from the uniformity of His conduct. He has these great reasons when what He owes His immutability is equal to, or is of lesser consideration than, what He owes some other one of His attributes. In short, He has these reasons when He acts as much or more according to His nature by abandoning than by following the general laws that He has prescribed. For God acts always according to His nature. He inviolably follows the immutable Order of His own perfections because it is in His own substance that He finds His law and He cannot but do justice to Himself or act for His glory, in the sense which I explained to you these last days.[4] If you ask me when it happens that God acts as much or more according to His nature by abandoning rather than following His general laws, I reply to you that I know nothing of that. But I do know that it sometimes happens. I know it, I say, because faith teaches me this. For Reason, which makes me know that it is possible, does not assure me that it does happen.

ARISTES. I understand your thought, Theodore, and I see nothing more in conformity with Reason and also with experience. For actually we do see in all the effects that are known to us that they have natural causes and that thus God governs the world according to general laws which He established for that purpose.

[4]Ninth Dialogue.

TREATISE ON NATURE AND GRACE

✤

DISCOURSE I

On the Necessity of the General Laws of Nature and of Grace

✤

Part I

On the Necessity of the General Laws of Nature

I

Since God can act only for His own glory and can find this only in Himself, He could have had no other design in the creation of the world than the establishment of His church.

II

Jesus Christ, who is the head of it, is the beginning of the ways of the lord. He is the first born of creatures and, though born among men, in the fullness of time was their exemplar in the eternal designs of His Father. All men were formed in His image, both those who preceded His temporal birth as well as ourselves. In a word, it is in Him that all subsists, since He alone can make the work of God perfectly worthy of its author.

III

There must be some proportion between the world and the action that produced it. But the action that drew the world out of nothing is that of God, who is of an infinite worth, while the world, however perfect it may be, is not infinitely desirable; nor can it render to its Author an honor worthy of Him. Thus separate Jesus Christ from the rest of creatures, and see if He who acts only for His own glory and whose wisdom has no bounds can plan the production of any external work. But by joining Jesus Christ to His church, and the church to the rest of the world, from which it is drawn, you raise to the glory of God a temple so majestic, magnificent, and holy, that you will perhaps be surprised He laid the foundations of it so late.

IV

Yet if you observe that the glory that redounds to God from His work is not essential to Him; if you agree that the world cannot be a necessary emanation of the deity, you will evidently see that it must not have been eternal, though it ought never to end. Eternity is the mark of independence. The world, therefore, must have a beginning. Annihilation of substances is a sign of inconstancy in Him that produced them; therefore they will have no end.

V

If it is true, then, that the world had to have a beginning and that the incarnation of Jesus Christ could not have been as ancient as the eternal generation of His divine person, an eternity must necessarily have preceded time. Do not think, therefore, that God delayed the production of His work. He has too great a love for the glory He receives from it in Jesus Christ. In one sense it may be most truly affirmed that He made it as soon as He was able to make it, for though from our point of view He might have created it ten thousand years before the beginning of the ages, yet, ten thousand years having no proportion to eternity, He could have done it neither sooner nor later, since an eternity must have preceded it.

VI

It is clear that 'soon' and 'late' are properties of time. And even if we suppose that God had created the world before He did by as many millions of years as there are grains of sand on the seashore, could not one still ask why God, who so loves the glory He receives in the establishment of His church, had not begun it many ages before? Thus, it suffices to say that an eternity had to precede the incarnation of the Word, to make it understood why this great mystery was accomplished neither too soon nor too late. God, then, must have created the universe for the church, and the church for Jesus Christ, and Jesus Christ so that He might find in Him a sacrifice and high priest worthy of the divine majesty. No one will doubt this order of the designs of God if it is observed that He can have no end for His actions other than Himself. And if one realizes that eternity is not appropriate for creatures, one will acknowledge that they were produced when it was required they should be. Now, having supposed these truths, let us try to discover something in the method God takes for the execution of His grand design.

VII

Were I not persuaded that all men are reasonable only because they are enlightened by Eternal Wisdom, it would, no doubt, be great temerity to speak of the designs of God and to want to discover any of His ways in the production of His works. But since it is certain that the Eternal Word is the universal Reason of minds and that, by the light which he continually sheds on us, we may have some communication with God, I ought not to be blamed for consulting that light, which, though consubstantial with God Himself, does not fail to answer those who know how to interrogate it with serious attention.

VIII

However, I confess that faith teaches a great many truths not discoverable by the natural union of the mind with Reason. Eternal Truth does not answer all our questions, since we sometimes ask for more than we can receive. But this must not serve as a pretence to justify our laziness and inapplication.

IX

Vulgar heads are soon wearied with the natural prayer that the mind, by its attention, ought to make to inner truth in order to receive light and understanding from it. And thus fatigued by that painful exercise, they talk about it in a contemptuous manner. They discourage one another and cover their weakness and ignorance under the delusive appearances of a false humility.

X

But their example must not inspire in us that agreeable virtue which nourishes carelessness and negligence in the mind and comforts it in its ignorance of the truths which are most necessary for it. We must pray constantly to Him who enlightens all men, that He will bestow His light upon us, recompense our faith with the gift of understanding, and especially prevent us from mistaking probability and confused sensations, which precipitate proud minds into darkness and error, for the evidence which accompanies His responses.

XI

When we intend to speak of God with any exactness, we must not consult ourselves or speak like the common run of men, but elevate our thoughts above all creatures and, with great reverence and attention, consult the vast and immense idea of a perfectly infinite Being, and since this idea represents the true God in a manner very different from how the vulgar fancy Him to themselves, we are not to speak of Him in popular language. Everybody is allowed to say, with Scripture, that God repented for having created man, that He was angry with His people, that He delivered Israel from captivity by the strength of His arm. But these or similar expressions are not permitted to theologians when they must speak accurately and justly. Therefore, it is no wonder if, in the following discourse, my expressions should seem uncommon. It ought rather to be carefully observed whether they are clear and perfectly adapted to the idea which all men have of an infinitely perfect Being.

XII

This idea of an infinitely perfect Being includes two attributes absolutely necessary to the creation of the world: an unlimited wisdom and an irresistible power. The wisdom of God affords infinite ideas of different works, and all possible ways for the execution of His designs, and His power renders Him so absolutely master of all things and so independent of all assistances whatsoever that it suffices for Him to will in order for His volitions to be executed. For we must note above all that God needs no instruments to work with, that His volitions are necessarily efficacious, in a word, that as His wisdom is His own understanding, His power is nothing other than His will. Among these innumerable ways by which God might have executed His design, let us see which was preferable to all others, and let us begin with the creation of this visible world, from which and in which He forms the invisible, which is the eternal object of His love.

XIII

An excellent craftsman must proportion his action to his work. He does not accomplish by complex means that which may be performed by more simple ones. He does not act without an end and never makes insignificant efforts. From this we must conclude that God, discovering in the infinite treasures of His wisdom an infinity of possible worlds, as necessary consequences of the laws of motion which He could establish, was determined to the creation of the one which might be produced and preserved by the simplest laws or which must be the most perfect possible, considering the simplicity of the ways necessary for its production or preservation.

XIV

God, no doubt, could have made a world more perfect than the one we inhabit. He could, for instance, have made it such that rain, which makes the earth fertile, falls more regularly on plowed lands than in the sea, where it is not as necessary. But in order to make this more perfect world, He would have had to change the simplicity of His ways and multiply the laws of the communication of motion, by which our world subsists, and so there would not have been that proportion between the action of God and His work, which is necessary to determine an infinitely wise Being to act, or, at least, there would not have been the same proportion between the action of God and this so perfect world as there is between the laws of nature and the world we inhabit. For our world, however imperfect one imagines it to be, is founded on laws of motion so simple and natural that it is perfectly worthy of the infinite wisdom of its Author.

XV

And indeed I am of the opinion that the laws of motion, necessary to the production and preservation of the earth and all the stars in the heavens, reduce to these two: First, that moving bodies tend to continue their motion in a straight line; second, that when two bodies meet, their motion is distributed to each, in proportion to their magnitude, such that they must afterwards move at an equal speed. These two laws are the cause of all those motions which produce that variety of forms which we admire in nature.

XVI

I grant, nonetheless, that it does not seem that the second law is ever observed in the experiences that can be had on the subject. But that is because we see only what happens in visible bodies and do not think about the invisible ones which surround them which, by the efficacy of the same law, give visible bodies their elasticity and oblige those same visible bodies to rebound and hinder them from observing that same law between themselves. But I ought not to explain this any further.

XVII

Now, these two laws are so simple, so natural, and at the same time so fruitful, that, even if we had no other reason for judging that it is they that are observed in nature, we would be justified in believing that they were established by Him who works always by the simplest ways, in whose action there is nothing but what is so justly uniform and wisely proportioned to His work, that He performs infinite wonders by a very small number of volitions.

XVIII

It does not fare with the general cause as with particular causes, with infinite wisdom as with limited understandings. God, foreseeing before the establishment of natural laws all that must follow from them, ought not to have established them if He had to annul them. The laws of nature are constant and immutable and are general for all times and places. If two bodies of such and such degrees of magnitude and speed collide, they rebound now as they always have. If the rain falls upon certain lands, and the sun scorches others, if a seasonable time for harvest is followed by a destructive hail, if an infant comes into the world with a monstrous and useless head growing from his breast that makes him wretched, it is not because God has willed these things by particular volitions, but rather because He has established the laws of the communication of motions, of which these effects are necessary consequences; laws at once so simple and so fruitful that they serve to produce everything beautiful that we see in the world and even to repair in a little time the most general barrenness and mortality.

XIX

He who, having built a house, throws one wing of it down in order to rebuild it, betrays his ignorance, and he who, having planted a vine, plucks it up as soon as it has taken root, manifests his levity, because he who wills and unwills lacks either knowledge or resolution of mind. But it cannot be said that God acts either by caprice or by ignorance when a child comes into the world with superfluous members that prevent him from living, or when a hailstone breaks off a half-ripened fruit. The reason for this is that if God causes a fruit to fall through hail before it is ripe, it is not that He wills and unwills, for God does not act like particular causes, by particular volitions. Nor has He established the laws of the communication of motions with a design to produce monsters or to make fruit fall before maturity. He willed these laws because of their fecundity, not their sterility. Therefore, what He once willed He still wills, and the world in general, for which these laws were constituted, will eternally subsist.

XX

It ought here to be observed that the essential rule of the will of God is the immutable order of justice and that, if man, for example, had not sinned (a supposition which would have quite changed the plans), then, order not allowing him to be punished, the natural laws of the communication of motions would never have been capable of making him unhappy. For the law of order, which requires that a righteous person should suffer nothing against his will, being essential to God, the arbitrary law of the communication of motions must necessarily be subservient to it.

XXI

There are still some rare occasions when these general laws of motion must cease to produce their effect. Not that God changes His laws or corrects Himself, but some miracles must happen on particular occasions, by the order of Grace, which must supersede the order of nature. Besides, it is fitting that men should know that God is so much the master of nature that if He submits to His established laws, it is rather because He so desires than by an absolute necessity.

XXII

If, then, it is true that the general cause must not produce His work by particular volitions and that God had to establish certain constant and invariable laws of the communication of motions, by whose efficacy He foresaw the world could subsist such as we find it, then in one sense it may be most truly said that God desires that all His creatures should be perfect, that He does not will that children perish in the womb of their mothers, that He does not love monstrous productions, nor that He has made the laws of nature with the design of causing them, and that if it were possible by equally simple ways to make and preserve a more perfect world, He would never have established those laws, from which so many monsters necessarily result, but that it would have been unworthy of His wisdom to multiply His volitions to prevent some particular disorders, which by their diversity make a kind of beauty in the universe.

XXIII

God has given to every seed a germ, which contains in miniature the plant and fruit, another germ depending upon the former, which contains the root of the plant, which root contains still another root, whose imperceptible branches expand themselves into the two lobes or meal of the seed. Does not this show that in a very real sense He wants all seeds to produce their like? For why would He have given to those grains of corn He designed to be barren all the parts requisite to render them fecund? However, since rain is necessary to make them thrive, and it falls on the earth by general laws, which do not distribute it precisely on well-manured grounds and in the fittest seasons, not all of these grains profit, or, if they do, hail or some other mischievous accident, which is a necessary consequence of these same natural laws, prevents their earing. Now, since God established these laws, we might say that He willed the fecundity of some seeds rather than others, if we did not otherwise know that, since a general cause must not act by particular volitions nor an infinitely wise being by complicated ways, God must not take any measures other than those He has taken for regulating the rains according to the seasons and place or according to the desires of laborers. This suffices for the order of nature. . . .

*   *   *

From the First Elucidation (appended to the second edition [1681]):

WHAT IS MEANT BY ACTING BY GENERAL AND PARTICULAR VOLITIONS

I

I say that God acts by general volitions when He acts in consequence of the general laws which He has established. For example, I say that God acts in me by general volitions when He gives me a sensation of pain when I am pricked, since in consequence of the general and efficacious laws of the union of my soul and body which He has established, He makes me suffer pain when my body is ill-disposed.

In the same way, when a ball strikes another, I say God moves the second ball by a general volition, because He moves it in consequence of the general and efficacious laws of the communication of motions, God having generally ordained that at the instant of collision of two bodies the motion should be distributed between them according to certain proportions; and it is by the efficacy of that general volition that bodies have the force of moving one another.

II

I say, on the contrary, that God acts by particular volitions when the efficacy of His will is not determined by some general law to produce some effect. Thus, supposing that God should make me feel the pain of pricking without there occurring any change in my body or in any creature whatsoever, which determines Him to act in me by some general law, I say that then God acts by particular volitions.

Similarly, supposing that a body begins to move without being struck by another or without any alteration happening in the will of spirits or in any other creature which determines the efficacy of some general laws, I say that God would be moving that body by a particular volition.

III

According to these definitions, it is clear that, so far from denying providence, I suppose on the contrary that God works in all things, that the nature of the heathen philosophers is a chimera, and that, to speak properly, nature is nothing but the general laws which God has established for the construction or preservation of His work by the simplest ways, by an action that is always uniform, constant, and perfectly worthy of an infinite wisdom and a universal cause. But that which I here suppose, though certain, for the reasons I have given in *The Search after Truth,* is not absolutely necessary for what I plan to prove. For if it is supposed that God had communicated His power to creatures in such a manner that the bodies surrounding us had a real and true force by which they might act on our soul and make it happy and miserable by pleasure and pain and that bodies in motion had in themselves a certain entity, called an *impressed quality,* that they can communicate to those about them and with that promptness and uniformity we observe, it would still be equally easy to prove what I intend. For then the efficacy of the concurrent action of the general cause would be necessarily determined by the action of the particular cause. God, for instance, would be obliged by these principles to lend His concourse to a body at the instant it collides with others, in order that this body might communicate its motion to them, which is still to act in virtue of a general law. Yet I do not base my reasoning upon that supposition, since I believe it to be utterly false. . . .

MARKS BY WHICH WE MAY JUDGE WHETHER AN EFFECT IS PRODUCED BY A GENERAL OR PARTICULAR VOLITION

IV

When we see an effect immediately produced after the action of an occasional cause, we ought to judge that it is produced by the efficacy of a general volition. A body moves immediately after a collision; the collision of bodies is the action of an occasional cause; therefore, this body moves by a general volition. A stone falls on the head of a man and kills him, and this stone falls like all others, that is, continues its motion almost in arithmetical proportion (1, 3, 5, 7, 9, etc.). That being supposed, I say it moves by the efficacy of a general volition, or by the laws of the communication of motions, as is easy to demonstrate.

V

When we see an effect produced without the mediation of the known occasional cause, we have reason to think that it is produced by a particular volition, supposing that this effect is not obviously unworthy of its cause, as I shall say in what follows.

For example, when a body is moved without being struck by another body, there is a great probability that it was moved by a particular volition, but yet we cannot be certain of it. For on the supposition that there is a general law that bodies are moved according to the diverse volitions of angels or the like, it is clear this body could be put in motion without being struck, the particular volition of some angel being able in this case to determine the will of the general cause to move it. Thus we may often be certain that God acts by general volitions, but we cannot have the same certainty that He acts by particular volitions, even in the most well-attested miracles.

VI

Since we do not have sufficient knowledge of the various combinations of occasional causes to discover whether such and such effects come about in consequence of their action and are not sufficiently intelligent to discover, for instance, whether a certain rain is natural or miraculous—produced by a necessary consequence of the communication of motions or by a particular volition—we must judge that an effect is produced by a general volition when it is clear that the cause did not propose for Himself a particular end. For the volitions of intelligences necessarily have an end: general volitions a general end and particular volitions a particular design. Nothing can be more plain and evident.

For example, though I cannot discover whether the rain which falls on a meadow falls in consequence of general laws or by a particular volition of God, I have reason to think that it falls by a general volition if I see it fall as well on neighboring lands, or on the river which bounds the meadow, no less than on the meadow itself. For if God caused it to rain on this meadow by a particular good volition for its owner, this rain would not fall on the river, where it is useless, since it could not fall there without a cause or volition in God which has necessarily some end.

VII

But we have still more reason to think that an effect is produced by a general volition when this effect is contrary or even useless to the design which we are taught, by faith or reason, the cause has set Himself.

For instance, the end which God sets Himself in the various sensations He affords the soul in our tasting different fruits is that we should eat those which are fit for nourishment and reject the rest; I am supposing thus. Therefore, when God gives us an agreeable sensation at the moment we eat poison or poisonous fruits, He does not act in us by particular volitions. Or so we ought to conclude, since that agreeable sensation is the cause of our death, while God's purpose in giving us our various sensations is to preserve our life by convenient nourishment; once more I suppose thus. For I speak only with reference to the grace which God gives us, no doubt to convert us, so that it is clear that God does not distribute it to men by particular volitions, since it frequently renders them more culpable and criminal. God cannot have so fatal a design. God therefore does not give us agreeable sensations by particular volitions when we eat poisonous fruits. But because a poisonous fruit excites in our brain motions like those produced by wholesome fruits, God give us the same sensations, by reason of the general laws which unite the soul to the body, in order that it might be wakeful for the latter's preservation.

So likewise God does not give to those who have lost an arm sensations of pain relating to it except by a general volition. For it is useless to the body of this man that his soul should suffer pain relating to an arm that is lost. It is the same with motions produced in the body of a man who is committing a crime.

Finally, supposing that we are obliged to think that God distributes rain upon the earth with the intent to make it fruitful, we cannot believe that He distributes it by particular volitions, since it falls upon the sands and in the sea, as well as on plowed lands, and is often so excessive on seeded ground that it uproots shoots and frustrates the labors of men.

Thus, it is certain that rains which are useless or noxious to the fruits of the earth are necessary consequences of the general laws of the communication of motions, which God has established for the production of better effects in the world, supposing (which I again repeat) that God cannot will, by a particular volition, that rain should cause the barrenness of the earth.

VIII

Lastly, when an effect happens which has something quite singular about it, it is reasonable to believe that it is not produced by a general volition.

Nevertheless, it is impossible to be sure of it. If, for example, in the procession of the holy sacrament it rains on those who are present, with the exception of the priests and those who carry it, we have reason to think this proceeds from a particular volition of the universal cause. Yet we cannot be certain of it, because an intelligent occasional cause may have this particular plan and so determine the efficacy of the general law to execute it.

IX

When the preceding marks are not sufficient for us to judge whether a certain effect is or is not produced by a general volition, we are to believe that it is, if it is certain that there is an occasional cause established for such effects.

For example, we see that it rains quite appropriately in a field. We do not examine whether or not this rain falls in the great roads; we do not know whether it is noxious to the bordering grounds; we suppose that it does only good and that all the attending circumstances are perfectly accommodated to the design for which we ought to believe God would have it rain. Nevertheless, I say that we ought to judge that this rain is produced by a general volition, if we know that God has settled an occasional cause for such effects. For we must not have recourse to miracles without necessity. We ought to suppose that God acts in this by the simplest ways. And though the owner of the field should thank God for the bounty, he must not think that it was caused in a miraculous manner by a particular volition.

The owner of the field should thank God for the good he has received, since God saw and willed the good effect of the rain when He established the general laws of which it is a necessary consequence, and it is for such effects that He has established these laws. On the other hand, if the rains are sometimes harmful to our lands, since it was not to render them unfruitful that God established the laws which make it rain, since drought suffices to make them barren, it is clear that we should thank God and adore the wisdom of His providence, even when we do not feel the effects of the laws He has established in our favor.

X

But, to conclude, when we cannot be assured by the circumstances which accompany certain effects that there is an occasional cause established to produce them, it is sufficient to know that they are very common and relate to the principal design of the general cause, in order to judge that they are produced by a general volition.

For example, the springs which water the surface of the earth are subservient to the principal design of God, which is that men should not lack things necessary to life; I suppose so. Besides, these fountains are very common. Therefore, we ought to conclude that they are formed by some general laws. For as there is much more wisdom in executing His designs by simple and general means than by complicated and particular ways, as I think I have sufficiently proved elsewhere, we owe to God the honor of believing that His way of acting is general, uniform, constant, and proportionate to the idea we have of an infinite wisdom. These are the marks by which we are to judge whether an effect is produced by a general volition. . . .

*   *   *

DISCOURSE III

On Grace

On the Manner in Which It Acts in Us

❦

PART I

ON LIBERTY

I

There is nothing more unformed than the substance of minds, if we separate it from God. For what is a mind without understanding and reason, without motion and love? Yet it is the word and wisdom of God which are the universal reason of minds, and it is the love by which God loves Himself that gives the soul the motion it has towards good. If the mind knows truth, it is by its natural and necessary union with truth itself. It can be reasonable only through reason. Lastly, it can be, in one sense, mind or intelligence only because its substance is enlightened, penetrated, and perfected by the light of God Himself. These truths I have explained elsewhere. Similarly, the substance of the soul is not capable of loving good except through its natural and necessary union with the eternal and substantial love of the sovereign good. It does not advance towards good except insofar as it is conveyed by God; it wills only from the motion that it continually receives from Him; it lives only through charity and desires only through the love of good in which God makes it participate, though it abuses it. For, in short, since God makes and preserves minds only for Himself, He inclines them towards Him as long as He preserves their being, and communicates the love of good to them while they are capable of receiving it. Now, that natural and continual motion of the soul towards good in general, towards indefinite good, towards God, is what I here call *will*, since it is that motion which enables the substance of the soul to love different goods.

II

This natural motion of the soul towards good in general is invincible, for it does not depend upon us to will to be happy. We necessarily love what we clearly know and vividly feel to be the true good. All minds love God by the necessity of their nature, and if they love anything else by a free choice of their will, it is not because they do not seek God or the cause of their felicity, but because they are deceived. It is because, feeling in a confused manner that the bodies that surround them make them happy, they consider them as goods and, as an ordinary and natural consequence, love them and join themselves to them.

III

But the love of all these particular goods is not naturally invincible. Man considered such as God made him can refrain from loving those goods that do not fill his whole capacity for loving. Since there is only one good which includes all others, he can sacrifice every other love to the love of this good. For God, having made minds only for Himself, cannot carry them invincibly to love anything besides Himself and without relation to Him. Lastly, our own inner consciousness informs us that we can reject a fruit, though we are inclined to take it. Now, that power of loving or not loving particular goods, the noninvincibility which is found in the motion which carries minds to love what does not seem to them in every way inclusive of all goods, this power or noninvincibility is what I call *liberty*. Thus, putting the definition in the place of the thing defined, that expression 'our will is free' signifies that the natural motion of the soul towards good in general is not invincible with respect to good in particular. To the word *free* is commonly annexed the idea of "voluntary"; but in the rest of this discourse I shall take the word in the sense I have indicated, since it is the most natural and ordinary.

IV

The word *good* is equivocal and may signify either pleasure which makes one formally happy or the true or apparent cause of pleasure. In this discourse I shall always take the word *good* in the second sense, because indeed pleasure is imprinted on the soul in order that it may love the cause that makes it happy, in order that it may advance towards it by the motion of its love and may directly unite itself to it, to be perpetually happy. When the soul loves nothing but its own pleasure, it in effect loves nothing distinct from itself. For pleasure is only a condition or modification of the soul, which renders it actually happy. But since the soul cannot be the cause of its own pleasure, it is unjust, ungrateful, and blind if it loves its pleasure without rendering the love and respect which is due to the true cause that produces it in the soul. Since only God can act immediately and by Himself on the soul and make it feel pleasure by the actual efficacy of His omnipotent will, He alone is truly good. However, I call 'good' the creatures which are the apparent causes of the pleasures we feel occasionally from them. For I am unwilling to deviate from the customary way of speaking any farther than is necessary to explain myself clearly. All creatures, though good in themselves or perfect in relation to the designs of God, are not good in relation to us. They are not our good nor the true cause of our pleasure or happiness.

V

The natural motion which God constantly imprints on the soul to carry it to love Him, or (to make use of a term which is the abridgement of several ideas and which should no longer be equivocal or confused after the definition I have given of it) the *will,* is determined towards particular goods either by a clear and evident knowledge or by a confused sensation which points these goods out to us. If the mind does not perceive or taste any particular good, the motion of the soul remains as it were undetermined; it tends towards good in general. But this motion receives a particular determination as soon as the mind has the idea or sensation of some particular good. For the soul, being continually pushed towards indeterminate good, ought to move when the good appears.

VI

But when the good, which is present to the mind and senses, does not fill these two faculties, when it is discovered under the idea of a particular good, of a good that does not comprehend all goods, and when it is tasted by a sensation that does not take up the whole capacity of the soul, the soul may still desire the perception and enjoyment of some other good. It may suspend the judgment of its love. It may refuse to acquiesce in the actual enjoyment and by its desires seek out some novel object. And as its desires are the occasional causes of its enlightenment, it may, by the natural and necessary union of all minds with Him who includes the ideas of all goods, discover the true good, and in the true, many other particular goods different from the one it perceived and enjoyed before.

Therefore, having some knowledge of the emptiness and vanity of sensible goods, and attending to the secret reproaches of reason, to the remorses of conscience, and to the complaints and threats of the true good, which does not want to be sacrificed to apparent and imaginary goods, the soul may, by the motion which God continually imprints on it for good in general, sovereign good, that is, for Himself, check itself in its course towards any particular good. The soul may resist sensible allurements, seek and find out other objects, compare them together and with the indelible idea of the supreme good, and love none of them with a determinate love. And if this sovereign good comes to be somewhat relished, the soul may prefer it to all particular goods, though the sweetness they seem to infuse into the soul be extremely great and very agreeable. But these truths require a longer explication.

VII

The soul is constantly driven towards good in general. It desires the possession of all goods and will never limit its love, there being no good that appears such that the soul refuses to love it. Therefore, when it actually enjoys a particular good, it has a tendency to proceed farther. It still desires something more by the natural and invincible impression which God gives it, and to change or divide its love, it suffices to present to it another good besides that of its present enjoyment and to give it a taste of the pleasure it affords. Now, the soul may ordinarily seek and discover new goods. It may likewise approach and enjoy them. For, in short, its desires are the natural or occasional causes of its knowledge, and objects appear to it and draw towards it in proportion to its earnestness to know them. A man of ambition, who considers the luster of some dignity, may likewise ponder the slavery, constraint, and the true evils that accompany human grandeur; he may sum up the account, weigh and compare all together, if his passion does not blind him. For I confess that there are moments when passion takes away all liberty from the mind and that it always lessens it. Thus, since a dignity, however great it appears, cannot be taken by a perfectly free and rational man for the universal and infinite good and since the will extends to all goods, every perfectly free and perfectly rational man may seek after and find out others, inasmuch as he can desire them, it being his desires which discover and present them to him. He may then examine them and compare them with that which he enjoys. But since he can find only particular goods on earth, he may and ought, while he lives here below, to examine them and perpetually seek and never acquiesce. Or, rather, in order that he not undertake change at every moment, he ought in general to neglect all transitory goods and desire only such as are immutable and eternal.

VIII

But since we do not love to seek but to enjoy and since the labor of examination is at present very painful, and repose and enjoyment always very agreeable, the soul commonly rests when it has found any good. It stops at it to enjoy it. It deceives itself, because in deceiving itself and in judging that it has found what it is looking for, its desire is changed into pleasure, and pleasure makes it happier than desire. But its happiness cannot last long. Its pleasure, being ill-grounded, unjust, and deceitful, immediately troubles and disquiets it, because it desires to be solidly and truly happy. Thus, the natural love of good quickens the soul and produces in it new desires. These confused desires represent new objects. The love of pleasure puts it on the pursuit of those which afford or seem to afford it, and the love of repose fastens it upon them. The soul does not immediately examine the defects of the present good when possessed with its sweetness, but rather contemplates it on its best side, devotes itself to that which charms it, and thinks only of enjoying it. But the more it enjoys it, the more it loves it, and the closer it approaches, the more curiously it considers it. But the more it considers it, the more imperfections it discovers in it. And since it desires to be truly happy, it cannot deceive itself forever. When it is thirsty and hungry and weary with seeking, it becomes intoxicated and fills itself with the first good it finds. But it is soon disgusted with a nourishment for which man was not made. Thus, the love of the true good excites in it new desires for new goods, and while it constantly changes its pursuit, all its life and its whole happiness on earth consists only in a continual circulation of thoughts, desires, and pleasures. Such is a soul which makes no use of its liberty but lets itself be led aimlessly by the motion which transports it and by the fortuitous encounter with the objects that determine it. But this is the state of a man whose understanding is so weak that he constantly mistakes false goods for true goods and whose heart is so corrupt that he betrays and sells himself to everything that touches him, to the good which makes him actually feel the most sweet and agreeable pleasures.

IX

But a man who is perfectly free, such as we conceive Adam to be immediately after his creation, knows clearly that only God is his good, or the true cause of the pleasures he enjoys. Though he feels satisfaction upon the approach of surrounding bodies, he does not love them; he loves only God, and if God forbids him to become attached to bodies, he is ready to forsake them, whatever pleasure he finds in them. He resolves to rest only in the enjoyment of the supreme good and to sacrifice all others to it, and however desirous of happiness or the enjoyment of pleasures he may be, no pleasure is stronger than his light. Not that pleasures cannot blind him, disturb his reason, and fill up his thinking capacity, for the mind being finite, every pleasure is capable of dividing and distracting it. But since pleasures are subjected to his volitions, he does not let himself be intoxicated by them, if he uses his liberty as he ought. For the sole invincible pleasure is that of the blessed, or that which the first man would have found in God, if God had prevented and hindered his fall, not only because this pleasure fills all the faculties of the soul, without disturbing reason or carrying it to the love of a false good, but also because nothing withstands the enjoyment of this pleasure, neither the desire of perfection nor that of happiness. For when we love God, we are perfect; when we enjoy him, we are happy; and when we love him with pleasure, we are happy and perfect all at once. Thus, the most perfect liberty is that of minds which can at all times overcome the greatest pleasures, of minds to which no motion towards particular goods is ever irresistible. It is that of a man before sin, before concupiscience has troubled his mind and corrupted his heart. And the most imperfect liberty is that of those to whom every motion towards a particular good, though never so little, is invincible in all sorts of circumstances.

X

Now, between these two sorts of liberty, there are others more or less perfect in infinitely many degrees, which is a thing not sufficiently noted. It is commonly imagined that liberty is equal in all men and that it is an essential faculty of the mind, the nature of which remains constantly the same, though its action varies according to the diversity of objects. For we assume, without reflection, a perfect equality in all things in which no sensible inequality appears. We indulge the mind and free it from all effort by giving all things an abstract form, whose essence consists in a sort of indivisibility. But this is an error, liberty not being a faculty such as it is imagined to be. There are no two persons equally free with respect to the same objects. Children have less liberty than men who have the complete exercise of their reason. Nor are there two men whose reason is equally clear, constant, and certain in regard to the same objects. Those whose passions are unruly and who are not accustomed to resisting them are less free than others who have courageously fought them and who are naturally moderate, and there are no two men equally moderate, equally sensible to the same objects, and who have equally fought for the preservation of their liberty. There are even some persons so sold to sin that they resist it less and think less of resisting it when awake than pious men do when they are asleep, since we are taught by the word of truth that he who sins becomes a slave to it.

XI

It is true that by the institution of nature all men are equally free, for God does not invincibly determine men to love any particular good. But concupiscence corrupts the heart and reason, and since man has lost the power of obliterating the marks of sensible pleasures and of stopping the motions of concupiscence, that liberty which would have been equal in all men, if they had not sinned, has become unequal, according to their different degrees of enlightenment and as concupiscence acts variously in them. For concupiscence itself, which is equal in all men, inasmuch as they have all lost the power they had over their bodies, is unequal in a thousand ways because of the diversity that is found in the structure of the body, in the multiplicity and motion of the spirits, and in the almost infinite alliances and relations that obtain through the commerce of the world.

XII

In order to understand even more distinctly the inequality which is found in the liberty of different persons, we must observe that every man who is perfectly reasonable and perfectly free and who desires to be truly happy can and ought, upon the presence of any object which makes him feel pleasure, suspend his love and carefully examine whether this object is the true good or whether the motion which carries him towards it comports exactly with that which leads him to the true good. Otherwise, he would love by instinct and not by reason, and if he could not suspend the judgement of his love before he had examined it, he would not be perfectly free. But if he clearly discovers that this object, which gives him pleasure, is truly good with respect to him and if the evidence in conjunction with the sensation is such as will not permit him to suspend his judgment, then, though perfectly free, he is no longer free in respect to that good, but he invincibly loves it, because pleasure agrees with evidence. But since God alone can act in us, or is our good, and since the motion which inclines us towards creatures is repugnant to that which carries us towards God, every man who is perfectly reasonable and entirely free can and must refrain from judging that sensible objects are his goods. He can and ought to suspend the judgment which regulates or should regulate his love. For he can never see with evidence that sensible goods are true goods, since that which is not can never be evidently seen.

XIII

This power of suspending judgment, which actually governs love, this power, which is the principle of our liberty and by which pleasures are not always invincible, is very much diminished since original sin, though not quite destroyed. And in order that we may actually have this power, when we are tempted by an object, it is necessary to have, besides the love of order, a thoughtful mind and to be sensible to the regrets of conscience, for a child or a man asleep does not actually have this power. But all men are not equally enlightened. The mind of sinners is full of darkness. Consciences are not equally tender; the heart of sinners is hardened. The love of order and actual graces are unequal in all men. Therefore, they are not equally free, nor do they have an equal power of suspending their judgment. Pleasure determines them and moves some rather than others. One man can suspend his judgment or halt his consent; another is of so narrow a mind and corrupt a heart that the least pleasure is irresistible and the least pain insupportable. Since he is not accustomed to fighting against sensible allurements, he becomes so disposed that he does not even think of resisting them. Thus, he does not have a true power of deferring his consent, since he lacks even the power of reflecting upon it. And in regard to that object, he is like a man who is asleep or out of his wits.

XIV

The weaker reason is, the more sensible the soul grows and the more readily and falsely it judges of sensible goods and evils. If a leaf pricks or even tickles a man when he is asleep, he wakes up in a start, frightened, as if bitten by a serpent. He perceives this little evil and judges of it as if it were the greatest of misfortunes, so intolerable does it appear to him. His reason weakened by slumber, he cannot suspend his judgment. To him, the least goods as well as the least evils are almost always insuperable. For it is the senses which act in him, and these are hasty judges, which must be so for several reasons. When reason is less disabled, little pleasures are not invincible, nor little evils intolerable, and one does not always go where the greatest pleasure lies. For some pleasures are so meager that they are despicable to reason, which is never quite destitute of the love of order. Nor is the presence of little evils very frightful. A man, for example, resolves to be bled and suffers it. He does not judge so hastily, but rather suspends and examines, and the stronger reason is, the longer it can suspend its judgment against sensible invitations and discouragements. Now, there is nothing more certain than that all men who partake of the same reason do not partake of it equally, that all are not equally sensible, at least to the same objects, that they are not all equally well born, equally well bred, equally assisted by the grace of Jesus Christ, and therefore not equally free, or capable of suspending the judgment of their love with respect to the same objects.

XV

But we must note that the chief duty of minds is to preserve and increase their liberty, since it is by the good use that they can make of it that they might merit their happiness, if succored by the grace of Jesus Christ, or at least lessen their misery, if left to themselves. That which weakens our liberty, or makes most pleasures irresistible to us, is the eclipse of our reason and the loss of the power we ought to have over our body. Reason, therefore, must be instructed by continual meditations; we must consider our duties so that we may perform them, and our infirmities so that we may have recourse to Him who is our strength. And since we have lost the power of stopping the impressions made on the body by the presence of objects, which then corrupt the mind and heart, we ought to avoid these objects and make use of the power that remains to us. We ought to watch constantly over the purity of our imagination and labor with all our powers to efface the marks imprinted there by false goods, since these marks kindle desires in us which divide our mind and weaken our liberty. By this means the man whose liberty is just expiring, who cannot conquer the least of pleasures, may obtain such a strength and such a freedom that he will yield nothing to the greatest souls, their succors being supposed equal. For, at least, during the time that these pleasures do not solicit him to do evil, he can seek to avoid them. He can fortify himself by some reason that may, through future pleasures, counterbalance those he does not actually enjoy. For as everyone has some love of order, there is no man who cannot vanquish a feeble and light pleasure by a strong and solid reason, by a reasonable fear of some evil or by the hope of some great good. Lastly, there is no one who cannot, by the ordinary aids of grace, vanquish some pleasures and avoid others. Now, these pleasures, formerly invincible or sought after, being vanquished or avoided, one can prepare oneself for assaulting others, at least before they tempt us. For the satisfaction we find in the victory provokes us again to battle, and the joy of a good conscience and the grace of Jesus Christ administer courage. Even the fear of defeat is not useless, since it makes us fly to Him who can do all things and makes us wisely avoid perilous occasions. Thus we always gain in this sort of exercise, for if we succumb, we become more humble, wise, circumspect, and sometimes more eager for the combat, and more capable of conquering or resisting.

XVI

As in the study of the sciences, those who do not submit to the false glimmers of probabilities and who are accustomed to suspending their judgment until the light of truth appears rarely fall into error, whereas the common run of men are constantly deceived by their precipitate judgments; so in the governance of morals, those who are used to sacrificing their pleasures to the love of order and who continually mortify their senses and passions, especially in things which seem of little consequence, which everyone may do, will in important things obtain a great facility for suspending the judgment which regulates their love. Pleasure does not surprise them, like other men, or at least it does not drag them along unawares. It seems, on the contrary, that while it sensibly affects them it cautions them to take care of themselves and to consult reason, or the rules of the gospel. Their conscience is more tender and more delicate than that of others, who, in the scriptural phrase, "drink sin like water." They are sensible to the secret reproaches of reason and the wholesome precautions of inward truth. In this way the acquired habit of resisting feeble and light pleasures makes way for the conquering of the more violent, or at least for the suffering of some regret and shame when a man is conquered, which immediately creates dislike and abhorrence. Liberty thus insensibly increasing and perfecting itself by exercise and the assistance of grace, we may at last put ourselves in a condition for performing the most difficult commandments, inasmuch as, by the ordinary graces which are constantly afforded Christians, we may overcome common temptations and for the most part avoid the greatest, and by the assistance of the grace of Jesus Christ, there is none that cannot be vanquished.

XVII

It is true that a sinner who is so disposed as to not even be able to think of resisting a surprising pleasure cannot actually accomplish the commandment that orders him not to enjoy it. For the pleasure is invincible to him in that condition. And if we suppose this person to be in this state of impotence through a natural necessity, his sin, not being free, would not make him more culpable, that is to say, more worthy of the punishment of pain, than if he were disordered in his sleep. Indeed, if this impotency were a necessary consequence of the free disorders which had preceded his conversion, it would not be imputed to him, by reason of his charity. But since he was both able and obliged to accustom himself to resisting pleasure and fighting for the preservation and augmentation of his liberty, this sin, though actually committed by a kind of necessity, renders him guilty and punishable, if not by reason of his sin at least because of his negligence, which is the principle of it. The commandment of God is not absolutely impossible, and the sinner can and ought, for the foregoing reasons, to put himself into a condition for observing it, since men are obliged, as well as able, to labor constantly to augment and perfect their liberty, not only by the aid of the grace of Jesus Christ but also by their natural forces, or ordinary graces. For, in brief, nature may be made subservient to grace in a thousand instances.

INDEX